K·I·S·S

The Only Guides You'll Ever Need!

THIS SERIES IS YOUR TRUSTED GUIDE through all of life's stages and situations. Want to learn how to surf the Internet or care for your new dog? Or maybe you'd like to become a wine connoisseur or an expert gardener? The solution is simple: Just pick up a K.I.S.S. Guide and turn to the first page.

Expert authors will walk you through the subject from start to finish, using simple blocks of knowledge to build your skills one step at a time. Build upon these learning blocks and by the end of the book, you'll be an expert yourself! Or, if you are familiar with the topic but want to learn more, it's easy to dive in and pick up where you left off.

The K.I.S.S. Guides deliver what they promise: simple access to all the information you'll need on one subject. Other titles you might want to check out include: Living with a Dog, the Internet, Microsoft Windows, Managing Your Career, and Astrology.

GUIDE TO

Wine

ROBERT JOSEPH & MARGARET RAND

Foreword by Robert G. Mondavi

A Dorling Kindersley Book

Dorling Kindersley

LONDON, NEW YORK, SYDNEY, DELHI, PARIS,
MUNICH AND JOHANNESBURG

Dorling Kindersley Publishing, Inc.
Editorial Director LaVonne Carlson
Series Editor Beth Adelman
Editor Matthew Kiernan
Copy Editor Cheryl Smith

Dorling Kindersley Limited
Managing Editor Maxine Lewis
Editorial Director Valerie Buckingham

Jacket Designer Neal Cobourne

Created and produced for Dorling Kindersley by
THE FOUNDRY, part of The Foundry Creative Media Company Ltd,
Crabtree Hall, Crabtree Lane, Fulham, London SW6 6TY

The Foundry project team
Frances Banfield, Lucy Bradbury, Josephine Cutts, Sue Evans, Douglas Hall, Sasha Heseltine,
Dave Jones, Ian Powling, Graham Stride, Bridget Tily and Nick Wells.
Special thanks to Polly Willis, Jennifer Kenna, and Karen Fitzpatrick.

Published in the United States by
Dorling Kindersley Publishing, Inc.
95 Madison Avenue
New York, New York 10016

Library of Congress Cataloging-in-Publication Data

Joseph, Robert.
    KISS guide to wine / Robert Joseph & Margaret Rand ; foreword by
Robert Mondavi.
        p. cm. -- (Keep it simple series)
            Includes index.
            0-7894-5981-7 (alk. paper)
    1. Wine and wine making. I. Rand, Margaret. II. Title. III. Series.
TP548 .J723 2000
    641.2'2--dc21
                                                    00-057062
                                                        CIP
Dorling Kindersley Publishing, Inc. offers special discounts for bulk purchases for sales promotions or premiums.
    Specific, large-quantity needs can be met with special editions, including personalized covers,
    excerpts of existing guides, and corporate imprints. For more information, contact Special Markets Department,
    Dorling Kindersley Publishing, Inc., 95 Madison Avenue, New York, NY 10016 Fax: 800-600-9098.

Color reproduction by Modern Age and The Foundry
Printed and bound by Printer Industria Grafica, S.A., Barcelona, Spain

For our complete catalog visit

www.dk.com

Contents at a Glance

CONTENTS

PART ONE Why Wine?   22

CHAPTER 1 Wine Culture   24

PART FOUR What Makes Wine Taste the Way it Does? 162

Foreword

I MET ROBERT JOSEPH *midway through my wine career.*
For a California vintner, even from Napa Valley, the route had to
take you to London, where so many of the world's wine experts
resided. So there I was, presenting our wines and trusting the experts
to understand what we were doing. Fortunately, Robert did.

This guide, written by Robert and the award-winning wine writer
Margaret Rand, can help both the beginner and the wine enthusiast.
I'm especially pleased that the writers start with a view of wine in
culture, because this is where it belongs. And there's some very good
information on wine and health – it seems as though every day
independent researchers are finding new aspects of the positive wine
and health story.

Now, with over 60 years in the wine business, and with the
international travel that I still do, I find that people everywhere
are still asking the old questions about winemaking, about wine and
food, but also about new things – what new research is showing us
about developments in the vineyards and in the wineries. This book
has the answers to many of these questions.

I know that in this millennium we will bring even greater quality to
grapes which will be grown more naturally, with better clonal
selection, and with a larger number of grape varieties from all over
the world.

The wines will be made more gently and more naturally, using gravity flow operations, and a total lack of filtration for fine wines. These new approaches will make great differences in the appreciation of wine.

So, wine enjoyment, which has been with us for over 7,000 years, will continue to grow, and the K.I.S.S. Guide to Wine *will make a fine contribution.*

ROBERT G. MONDAVI
Napa Valley, California

Introduction

WINE USED TO BE the simplest drink in the world. Farmers simply took grapes, crushed them, and allowed the juice to ferment into a tasty alcoholic beverage. Most of it was drunk by those who made it for their family, friends, and neighbors. It generally wouldn't have had a name, any more than milk would have had a brand back in the days when it was sold from the farm.

But human beings like to complicate things. It wasn't long before people noticed that wines from some vineyards, villages, and regions tasted better than others and that the quality varied from year to year depending on the climate. Because wine can only be produced every 12 months – after the annual grape harvest – it also had to be stored. Some years wines deteriorated over time. But others improved, even when the storage vessels were amphorae whose surfaces were covered in olive oil. So, even a millennium ago, when they were planning their orgies and bacchanalian feasts, Roman emperors could select between wines from different places and years – or, as we'd now call them, vintages.

Fortunately for the ancient drinkers, however, the range of wines available was fairly limited. Today, there are tens of thousands of different labels and bottles to choose from. All over the world, all sorts of winemakers are busily using all sorts of grapes and methods to produce all sorts of wines. Some so-called white wines are the color of liquid gold, while others are pale enough almost to be mistaken for water; red wines likewise range in hue from violet-red to almost black. There are strong wines and weak ones; still wines and fizzy ones; sweet wines and dry ones; wines that taste of litches and wines that smell of freshly ground pepper.

All these wines have names and origins. Look at a map of France or Italy, and it could seem as though almost every village is producing a wine bearing its name. And, as if that weren't enough, barely a day passes without yet another ambitious winemaker in California, Australia, or South Africa launching yet another brand-new wine onto the market. The world of wine is like a jungle where people are still eagerly planting trees.

Though we have many years of experience tasting and drinking and talking to the men and women who make, sell, and pour it for a living, we can't promise to turn this complicated subject into a simple one. To do so, after all, would be to strip it of some of its appeal. Part of the magic of wine lies in the unexpected pleasures it can deliver. What we will be doing over the next 400 pages, though, is removing the unnecessarily tricky stuff.

The journey we'll take follows wine from its earliest history to the present day and beyond into the future. We'll visit vineyards and producers across the globe, and along the way, we'll share the secrets of why wines taste the way they do and how to enjoy them at their best. We'll discover the tricks of the taster's trade – how the professionals tell good wines from less good, and how they manage to identify where and when a glass of red or white was made without ever seeing the label.

We won't be using jargon (or if we really find we have to, we'll explain precisely what it means), and we won't be cloaking the subject in poetry. Most importantly, we'll never forget that, however smart the label and illustrious the name, a glass of wine is essentially a drink that has to taste good. We've both had tremendous fun writing this book – we hope you'll get just as much pleasure from reading it.

ROBERT JOSEPH & MARGARET RAND
London

What's Inside?

THE INFORMATION IN *the* K.I.S.S. Guide to Wine *is arranged from the simple to the more advanced, making it most effective if you start from the beginning and slowly work your way to the more involved chapters.*

PART ONE

In Part One, we ask, "Why Wine?" Why indeed. What is it about this particular drink that has made it the most enduring in the history of human civilization? By looking at the role that wine has played, and continues to play, in society, we will try and get to the bottom of the question. Maybe it's simply because wine tastes so good.

PART TWO

Hint of blackcurrant? Bouquet of melon? Contrary to popular belief, to be able to taste wine is not on a par with rocket science. Part Two will give you a well-rounded guide to the ins and outs of testing and tasting, and show you what to look for in a wine, so that you will soon be able to tell the difference between a vintage and a *vin de table*.

PART THREE

Now that you can tell one wine from another, we will look at more practical matters. From store to cellar, via the table, Part Three will steer you in the right direction by taking a look at some simple decisions to make before you buy. Whether you want to stock your cellar, or choose the perfect partner to salmon, all the right advice is here.

PART FOUR

And what of the winemaking process? How does a grape become that fine Merlot that you enjoyed last night? In Part Four we will start off by sampling the basic ingredients – the grapes, adding a dash of information about the vineyard, and finally blending it all together by trying out the particular flavors that the producers bring to the wine.

PART FIVE

Having learned about the history, the taste, and the process, it is time to look at where wine actually comes from. From Austria to Australia, Chile to China, and just about everywhere else in between, the winemaking industry is thriving. In Part Five, we try to identify what it is that distinguishes a wine from one region or country from another.

The Extras

THROUGHOUT THE BOOK, *you will notice a number of boxes and symbols. They are there to emphasize certain points we want you to pay special attention to, because they will help you enjoy your wine. You'll find:*

Very Important Point

This symbol points out a topic we believe deserve careful attention. You really need to know this information before continuing.

Complete No-No

This is a warning, something we want to advise you not to do or to be aware of.

Getting Technical

When the information is about to get a bit technical, we'll let you know so that you can read carefully.

Inside Scoop

These are special suggestions and pieces of information that come with the wisdom of our experience.

You'll also find some little boxes that include information we think is important, useful, or just plain fun.

Trivia...

These are simply fun facts that will give you an extra appreciation of wine and winemaking in general.

DEFINITION

Here we'll define words and terms for you in an easy-to-understand style. You'll also find a glossary at the back of the book with the wine-related lingo.

INTERNET

www.internet.com

We think that the Internet is a great resource for those interested in wine, so we've scouted out some of the best web sites for you to check out.

PART ONE

WINE HAS BEEN HIGHLY VALUED THROUGHOUT HISTORY

WHY WINE?

WE MIGHT ASK, why music? Why books? Why friends? Why conversation? Why good food?

The answer is, of course, because these things are *life-enhancing*. Cut out any one of them and existence would be the poorer. But whereas we learn as children about the pleasures of good food, or books, or music, or friends, most of us don't come to wine until we're grown up. We find then that it's a big subject, and the entrance is not very clearly marked.

Well, here's the entrance. In this part we'll be talking about the culture of wine: the *unique* role it has played – and continues to play – in human civilization.

Chapter 1

Wine Culture

LOOK BACK OVER human civilization – someone, somewhere, will be drinking wine. They may be drinking it while philosophizing; writing poetry or painting; celebrating a marriage; or putting the kids to bed. Whatever the case, it's wine that completes the picture and occasion.

In this chapter...

✓ Wine and civilization

✓ Wine and the intellect

✓ Wine and science

✓ What is wine and what is a spirit?

✓ You don't have to give up spirits

✓ How wine is drunk worldwide

✓ Drinking wine with food

✓ Cooking with wine

THE ENJOYMENT OF WINE IS CENTRAL TO MANY CULTURES

Wine and civilization

WINE HAS ALWAYS *been integral to the most important aspects of human life. At its most basic level, wine is a staple of people's diet, and a useful source of calories. Generally speaking, the poorer the economy of an area, the less fuss is made about wine, but the more vital it is to life.*

Wine as religion

■ **Wine has always** *been considered life-enhancing.*

In richer societies, where people have time and money to spare, wine becomes not a necessity but an icon of good living. That's how most of us approach wine today. But wine has other functions, too. It has been a part of religious ceremony for as long as religions have existed – the ancient Greeks even assigned wine its own god, Dionysus (also known as Bacchus). Wine has also been a medicine – for most of human history wine was a great deal safer than water, whether it was a matter of washing wounds or mixing drugs.

■ **The young Bacchus** *is depicted here with a satyr.*

Wine as cash crop

Wine is also of course an agricultural crop. Even today, whole local economies from California to Catalonia in Spain are built on producing it. In many wine regions of the world, the difference between a cold, wet summer and a warm, dry one is the difference between profit and loss; the difference between financial security and indebtedness.

Wine and people

Wine, you see, is about people. It is made by people, for people, and more than any other agricultural product it reflects the character and tastes of the people who make it. You can't say that about bread, or beef, or milk. Pour a glass of wine and you're tapping into the culture of the person who made it. An Italian wine doesn't (shouldn't, anyway) taste like a French wine; a California wine doesn't taste like a German or a Spanish wine. Yes, it's perfectly possible to make industrial-scale wine that has absolutely no personality and conveys no sense of where it came from. But that is not the kind of wine that interests us. And while there will always be a market for mass-produced wine – just as there will always be a market for battery-farmed chickens, or mass-produced sliced bread – just by picking up this book, you've indicated that you're interested in something better.

Wine and the intellect

THE SENSUAL PLEASURES *of wine are too many to enumerate. But wine engages the brain, too. What this book means to do is not merely celebrate the many and varied flavors of wine, but arouse your interest in how and why they get there. It might be that some of the things you've heard about wine have put you off – perhaps you think you'll never know enough to know the difference between the* vintages, *or that the language wine tasters use is just too ridiculous. Yes, wine has its own terms, but so do computers, and you've probably picked those up easily enough.*

DEFINITION

A wine's vintage *is the year in which it was made. A good vintage is a year in which generally good wines were made in a given region; a poor vintage is the opposite. A vintage wine is the product of a single year's harvest; a non-vintage wine is a blending of wines from two or more years.*

Wine and science

IT'S EASY TO GET *lyrical about wine's place in civilization. But wine also involves science: It took the intellect of Louis Pasteur (the 19th-century French chemist who gave us the word pasteurization) to make clear the mysteries of fermentation, for example. To be a top-level wine grower and winemaker today is to have a university-level understanding of chemistry, microbiology, and horticulture, plus the ability to speak several languages and take a tractor apart and reassemble it. Looking through the microscope to study the differences*

between vine varieties and identify the exact varieties present in the vineyards of the world, as ampelographers do, is a study of the movements of peoples and trade from earliest times.

■ **The place and** *people of each wine-producing area influence the flavor of the drink.*

The secret life of Zinfandel

For instance, Zinfandel is one of California's most famous vine varieties. But until recently, no one knew where this grape came from. Now, analysis of its DNA has proved that it originated on an island off the coast of Croatia. Even now nobody's quite clear how or when it reached California. And if that's true of one vine in the United States, imagine how much more complicated the picture must be in Turkey, say, where there are around a thousand different vines, all with local names, all having arrived there for different reasons, with different people, at different times. Yes, we're back to wine and human civilization again. The truth is, you can't separate the two.

What is wine and what is a spirit?

■ **Wine can be made** *from any fruit or vegetable; in Japan people drink rice wine.*

THE FIRST POINT *is that anything, as long as it contains some sort of sugar, can be fermented by yeast into alcohol. In Siberia you might be offered koumiss, which is fermented mare's or cow's milk. In parts of Africa you'll find palm wine; in Southeast Asia, rice wine.*

VIP *Wine can be made from all sorts of fruit and vegetables, and is, but the sort of wine we are talking about in this book is made only from fermented grapes.*

If you take a fermented liquid and distill it, you get a spirit. Whiskey is made by distilling a ferment of grain, usually barley or corn; vodka and gin normally have a similar base, but are distilled to greater degrees of purity. Distill wine and you get brandy. Most countries have a tradition of producing either fermented or distilled alcohol. The sort of drink that results, and the sort of drink that national traditions are based on, depends entirely on what raw materials are available. And that depends on climate.

■ **Wine in Europe** *and North America is genrally made from fermented grapes.*

Who drinks which, and why?

Wine is a Mediterranean drink. The species of vine used for wine are native to the Mediterranean and Black Sea regions of Europe, and they flourish in that sort of climate. That means mild winters and warm summers. Farther north, where it is too cold for vines, the obvious raw material was grain; farther south, in equatorial Africa, it is generally too hot for vines. But there are plenty of palms.

■ **The vines grown** in the Mediterranean are native to the region, flourishing in mild winters and warm summers.

You don't have to give up spirits

LET'S GET ONE thing clear: Loving and appreciating wine does not disbar you from enjoying other alcoholic drinks. Most wine tasters, at the end of a hard day's tasting (having tasted perhaps a hundred young red wines, one after the other), long for a cold beer. Most wine tasters, faced with the dire choice of wines available in some bars, will opt for whiskey, gin, or vodka. So you don't have to choose between wine and beer or spirits (though, as your parents warned you, injudicious mixing of them can lead to morning-after repentance).

The spice of spirits

What's more interesting is why such a variety of alcoholic drinks exists. We love whiskey, and it comes in a wide variety of styles. We love single malts from Scotland, small-batch bourbons from Kentucky, we love good whiskey from anywhere. But whiskey does not have the infinite variety of wine. Wine changes from vintage to vintage, from vineyard to vineyard, from hillside to plain, from one winemaker to his neighbor across the road. Whiskey is varied, but it can't match wine for variety.

Gin? Gin is a commodity. A delicious commodity, but a commodity. Vodka and tequila, though the producers dress them up in fancy clothes, don't engage the imagination or the intellect for very long.

Wine breeds discriminating taste

Of all the alcoholic drinks, wine holds the greatest fascination. Train your palate to appreciate the finer points of wine, and you'll find yourself being more discriminating about good spirits, too. And, indeed, about everything else you eat or drink. Getting to know wine is like learning to see in color instead of in black and white.

How wine is drunk worldwide

EVEN IN THESE DAYS of globalization, there is no single way of drinking wine. Every country, every region even, has its own traditions. These have to do with the sort of wine each region makes, of course, but they are also based on the local food and the local social customs.

When in Rome

In many wine-producing countries, sweet wines are the most highly prized. They're difficult and expensive to make, and until sugar became cheap and easily available, really sweet things were rare. So in a few parts of Italy it remains traditional to offer guests a glass of sweet white vin santo – named "holy wine" because it is so treasured – as an aperitif.

It's worth remembering, too, that most residents of wine-producing regions prefer to drink their own wines rather than those of other areas. This is the case even when they produce only one basic style and would, you might think, be desperate for a change. Go to Alsace in north-eastern France, where there is a great deal of white wine but not much red of any quality, and you'll be offered white, white, and more white – even when you're eating food that might be better with red. In Italy it is considered odd to drink the wine of one region with the food of another, although restaurants in major cities increasingly offer a wider choice. But when you're there, it does feel strange to drink, for example, the wine of Tuscany with the food of Piedmont; or the food of Rome with the wine of Venice.

How non-wine-producing countries drink wine

Regions that do not produce wines not only have the best range of wines, but they also have the most varied ways of drinking them. Britain is an example, but many states of America come under the heading of non-wine-producers as well, and America has traditionally imported a great deal of wine as well as making its own. Britain can beat the world in terms of arcane wine drinking rituals. Take port – the sweet, red, *fortified wine* from northern Portugal.

When the port appears after dinner it is the tradition in Britain to pass it around the table counterclockwise. Anyone who passes it the wrong way is almost certain to be corrected or frowned upon.

Why is port passed counterclockwise in Britain? Nobody knows. Does it matter? Of course not – except that you'll feel uncomfortable if you get it wrong.

Wine goes global

Globalization, however, is making itself felt. The explosion of new wines from different parts of the world has revolutionized the way we drink wine. New international flavors have emerged, as have new styles of wine to fit the way we live. Fifty years ago, in most places, it would have been considered very odd to ask for a glass of white wine at a party. You would have been served Champagne, sherry, or cocktails. But new winemaking techniques – producing a flood of good, inexpensive everyday wines from parts of the world that nobody ever thought about before – have changed all those attitudes. . . and for the better.

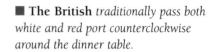

■ **The British** *traditionally pass both white and red port counterclockwise around the dinner table.*

GRAND VIN DE   BOURGOGNE

Mâcon-Chardonnay

APPELLATION MACON-CHARDONNAY CONTROLEE

12,5% vol.   750 ml

MIS EN BOUTEILLES A LA PROPRIETE

Cave de Chardonnay - 71700 CHARDONNAY - FRANCE

PRODUCE OF FRANCE

Wine has become simpler, more democratic, and more standardized. The most popular grape varieties, such as Chardonnay or Cabernet Sauvignon, are grown almost everywhere. Go into a bar or restaurant anywhere from San Francisco to Sicily, say those magic words, and a glass of something good will hopefully appear in front of you.

■ **Chardonnay is one** *of the most popular grapes used in making wine.*

Local and global

Throughout the world these days, there are two ways of approaching wine. One is the international way: International grape varieties made with techniques that can be imitated anywhere to produce a recognizable product. We're not decrying these wines – many of them are top quality. But they are not all there is. The other side of wine drinking is local custom: A glass of vin santo, a wine made from obscure grape varieties you've never heard of, or passing the port counterclockwise. These two sides of wine go together like horse and carriage, like cork and bottle.

Drinking wine with food

WHETHER YOU DRINK wine with food or without may seem so unimportant as to be not worth bothering about. But in fact it's one of the most fundamental changes in the way we approach wine to have occurred in the last 30 years.

The art of drinking and eating

The traditional European way of drinking wine is with food. In Italy, for example, it is taken for granted not only that you drink wine with a meal, but that you have something to eat when you have a glass of wine. In Italy, if you just feel like a drink, you'll probably have something other than wine – beer, or brandy, or whiskey. So the flavors of the wine are designed to balance the flavors of the food. The same is true in most of Europe. The tradition is for wine to have relatively restrained flavors, so as not to overpower what is on your plate.

The art of matching wine and food, which we'll come back to later, developed because wine goes with food so well – better than any other drink. Spirits don't match food well because their high alcohol content can dull your palate, and carbonated beverages are too sweet. Wine and food flatter each other perfectly.

Wine before and after food

In the last few years, however, lots of us have taken to drinking wine just as a beverage, without food. You come home from work and fancy a drink? Pour a glass of Chardonnay or Merlot. You're offering aperitifs before dinner? Chardonnay or Merlot again. And winemakers have responded to this by making wines with less restrained flavors: They're fruitier, more up-front. So there are wines that make perfect aperitifs as well as those that match food.

Wine as an aperitif

The traditional wine aperitifs are sparkling wines such as Champagne, or fortified wines such as sherry. Some fortified wines are sweet

■ **Champagne is** *often drunk as an aperitif.*

and some are not, and it's the non-sweet ones (the dry ones) that make the best aperitifs. The sweet ones are better after meals, when you feel like something rich to round off a good dinner.

You wouldn't normally choose fortified wines to accompany a meal because their alcohol content is too high. It's a bit like not drinking spirits with food: Fortified wines will dull your palate and dominate the food in the same way.

Cooking with wine

COOKING WITH WINE *springs naturally from drinking wine with food. Don't think of it as a big deal. Wine is a seasoning in your food, just like salt or garlic. It's one flavor among many. Don't be afraid of it.*

Some classic French dishes, such as coq au vin, rely on wine for their flavor, just as others rely on mushrooms or oranges or rosemary. Some require wine to be slowly simmered with beef or whatever for a long period, so that the flavors become absorbed and transformed; other dishes, and many sauces, can be given a lift if a dash of wine is added near the end of cooking. If you do the latter, don't overdo the quantity: You don't want the finished dish to taste predominantly of wine, any more than you want it to taste mostly of salt.

■ **Wine is a natural** *seasoning for food as it adds a rich flavor to many dishes.*

The kind of wine to use

There is one absolute no-no here: Don't use any wine that tastes unpleasant. If you've rejected a bottle for drinking because it's stale or otherwise faulty, don't think you can cook with it. You can't.

Any off-flavors in the wine will be concentrated when you cook with it, so keeping a half-bottle of wine in the refrigerator and expecting to cook with it a month later is a shortcut to ruining your dish.

The best way is only to cook with wines that you'd be comfortable drinking. They don't have to be terrifically expensive – in fact, there's no point in using your best wines because their finer points will be lost in the cooking. Generally, unless the recipe specifies otherwise, it's best to use dry wines. The flavor of a sweet white wine might be just what you want in your fish stew – or then again, it might not be. Don't be caught unawares.

Watch the acidity

The other factor to beware of in your cooking is wine with very high acidity. All wine has acidity – it's one of the basic flavors of wine, and wine would taste horrible without it. But some wines have more than others, and that applies to reds as well as whites. Your best bet is to taste the wine before you add it. If you cook regularly you probably have a pretty good idea of what flavors will go with what.

Remember that whatever wine flavor you add to the food will be concentrated in the cooking.

How to use it

Ideally, with confidence. But don't overdo it. Once you've added wine you can't take it out again, and if you don't like what it's done to your dish, too bad. So if you're not sure, add a little to begin with, give it a chance to cook, then taste it and add more if you want. Allow the alcohol to cook off after you've added the wine. You should enhance the flavor of the dish, not serve alcoholic risotto or sauce. If, when you taste the dish, the wine tastes separate and unintegrated, you need to cook it for longer.

■ **Wine is an integral part** *of many wonderful and unusual dishes, such as Champagne risotto.*

GENTLEMEN ENJOYING A WELL-STOCKED WINE CELLAR IN 1813

A simple summary

✓ Wine has been highly valued throughout human civilization. At different times and in different places it has been a food, a medicine, a religious symbol, and an agricultural crop.

✓ For most wine lovers, an appreciation of good wine goes hand in hand with an appreciation of good beer, whiskey, gin, or vodka.

✓ Different nations drink wine in different ways. Wine-producing nations tend to drink lots of their own wine and very little of anybody else's; non-wine-producing nations have a vast choice from around the world.

✓ One of the major changes in recent years has been the growing popularity of wine as an aperitif without food.

✓ Wine is also an essential ingredient in cooking – but don't attempt to cook with any wine you wouldn't want to drink.

Chapter 2
The History of Wine

NOBODY KNOWS who made the first wine any more than anyone knows who baked the first bread. All we know for certain is that people were cultivating grapevines by 5000 B.C. – way back in the late Stone Age. They'd been eating wild grapes – and could have made wine from those, too – for at least three millennia before that. We can't imagine exactly what those early wines tasted like – but they must have tasted better than anything else on offer, or people wouldn't have gone on making them.

In this chapter...

BACCHUS, THE ROMAN GOD OF WINE

Where wine began

THE FIRST CULTIVATED grape pips (seeds) were excavated by archeologists in Georgia (on the Black Sea, not the American South). The area around the Black Sea and the Caucasus Mountains is the source of so much of our civilization that it's not surprising that wine, too, first appeared there. Legend backs up the historical record: Genesis tells of Noah planting a vineyard as soon as the Ark had come to rest on dry land (which suggests that he must have taken vines on board with him from wherever he began). The traditional site of that dry land, Mount Ararat (called Buyuk Agri in Turkish), is in the Caucasus Mountains.

The first wine connoisseur?

However wine began, it was only a matter of time before people began to distinguish between good wine and bad, good vintages and bad. The ancient Egyptians have left us tomb paintings that provide the most detailed picture of viticulture and winemaking anywhere in the ancient world. They were enthusiastic winemakers who had finely honed palates and were as keen on ranking wines by quality as any modern wine critic. When Tutankhamun's tomb was opened in 1922, the wine jars buried with him were found to be labeled with the year and the name of the winemaker and sometimes with a comment like "very good quality."

> Trivia...
>
> How can you tell if a grape pip found in the course of an archeological excavation is from a wild grape or a cultivated grape? Easy – cultivated vines are hermaphroditic, whereas wild vines are either male or female, and the shape of the pips is different.

■ Ancient Egyptian tomb *paintings recount the importance of wine cultivation.*

38

Wine in Ancient Greece

IN GREEK MYTHOLOGY, *the first vine was planted by Orestheus, one of the children of the only couple allowed to survive the great flood sent by Zeus to punish the wicked human race. The Ancient Greeks also discriminated between the production of different years and different vineyard areas. The island of Chios was reckoned to have the best wine; Lesbos and Thasos were also up in the top league. Kos and Rhodes, on the other hand were right down at the bottom, producing the sort of wine fit only for army rations.*

The vine and the olive

The vine and the olive were staples of Greek life. To the Greeks, a people that cultivated vines and olives were civilized; barbarous nations did neither. More-or-less decorous scenes of wine drinking decorate Greek pottery, and are featured everywhere in Greek literature. It was a vital part of that most Greek of occupations, the symposium, in which drinking and conversation, perhaps accompanied by music and dancing, went on long into the evening. But curiously, the Greek habit was to add water to wine, and usually seawater at that. They considered it most uncivilized to drink wine unwatered; spices and other aromatics were also commonly added – which must at least have helped to cover the taste of the seawater.

The wine god

The Dionysus legend sums up the delights and dangers of wine. On one hand he travels the world, spreading wine and civilization. On the other, his followers, the maenads or bacchants, were women – often respectable Greek housewives – who indulged in a sort of mass hysteria or mass intoxication. In one version of the story, the king of Thebes,

Pentheus, refuses to believe in the divinity of Dionysus, and dresses up as a woman to join the crowds and spy on their doings. But the women are intoxicated. Dionysus incites them to attack Pentheus, and they tear him apart, believing that they are hunting a mountain lion. Pentheus's own mother tears off his head. To the Greeks, wine and the gods (not to mention women) could be merciless if mishandled.

A SCENE FROM THE DIONYSUS LEGEND

The vine spreads across Europe

THE IMAGE OF DIONYSUS *spreading the vine across the known world is not so far from the truth, for it was the Greeks themselves who brought the cultivation of the vine to southern Italy. From there it spread northward, helped by trade, and later by the vast empire of Rome: Every city that could afford wine wanted it.*

INTERNET

www.upenn.edu/museum/Wine/wineintro.html

This terrific, well-illustrated site seeks to "live out our past through wine." It charts the origins and ancient history of wine, going back to the Neolithic Age.

But of course trade routes are complicated, and different varieties of vine ended up – perhaps by chance, perhaps by design – in different places. Flourishing, cosmopolitan Greek cities dotted the shores of the Mediterranean, and it's easy to imagine a merchant in one city writing to a colleague at home in Greece for cuttings from a particular vineyard, hoping those vines might do well on the hill behind his house. If the vines succeeded, then his friends in turn might ask for cuttings. Even in the ancient world, people traveled and traded readily and regularly, though not quite as spectacularly quickly as we do now.

From Greek to Roman

The Romans adored Greek wine. But their own viticultural skills increased rapidly, and the Greeks began to favor Roman wine as well. Trade went both ways. Then, as now, imported wine had a certain cachet. And individual vine varieties were valued for their particular qualities, just as they are today.

VIP

Wine growers have always been aware that different vine varieties give wines with different flavors.

The Roman thirst

Ancient Rome had over a million inhabitants – not until the twentieth century was the Mediterranean world able to boast a larger city. And it had an insatiable thirst for wine. Its legions, spread

■ **Romans tending** *their vines, presided over by the god of wine.*

Trivia...

Roman wine merchants seem to have been quite unscrupulous about passing off wines as something better than they were. Falernian was the most fashionable and expensive wine of its day, and the Opimian vintage of 121 B.C. (Opimius was that year's consul) was the highest-rated vintage. People were still claiming to be drinking Opimian Falernian a hundred years later, and far more seems to have been drunk than could ever have been made. So, wine fakery, which still goes on today, started very early on.

throughout the empire, had a daily wine ration that needed to be satisfied, while the citizens of the empire, which stretched as far north as Britain and as far east as Constantinople, enthusiastically adopted the Roman taste. Vines were cultivated in Iberia (Spain) and Gaul (France), and even in England. The Romans were the great civilizers of their day, taming the wild tribes of the north and introducing them to a gentler way of living . . . which inevitably included wine.

The role of the Church

Wine has always been essential to Christian ritual, where it symbolizes the blood of Christ, shed for the redemption of humanity. In Judaism, too, it is a vital part of every religious ritual. These facts alone would have been enough to ensure the survival of vineyards and winemaking throughout the western world. Christian monasteries throughout Europe planted vineyards and made wine. But the monks were far from treating it either as a necessary commodity of everyday life or as simply a part of the Mass. Monks were the most meticulous of vinegrowers, experimenting with soils and sites in a way that a modern viticulturalist would recognize and respect. Monasteries were also the hospitals of their day, the only source of medical care for many people. And wine was always a vital part of medical care, and the safest way of cleaning wounds.

The monks' viticultural talent was important for the development of modern wine. The Cistercians and Benedictines, in particular, seem to have had an eye for a good vineyard. In Germany's Rheingau region it was monks who spotted the potential of a steep, south-facing slope overlooking the Rhine, cleared it of forest and scrub, and planted it. It is still one of Germany's leading wine regions.

In Burgundy, they did what we would today call microvinifications – vinifying small lots of grapes from separate parcels of vineyard – to discover the differences in the *terroir*. They are said to have gone as far as actually tasting the earth to discover how the soil changed from place to place. Today their findings still form the basis of the complicated vinous map of the Côte d'Or, the heart of Burgundy.

DEFINITION

The combination of soil type, climate, degree of slope, and exposure to the sun constitutes the terroir of a vineyard. It is what makes each vineyard subtly different from its neighbor.

■ **Wine is central to** *Christianity, as it represents the blood of Christ in the sacrament of communion.*

HOSPICES DE BEAUNE

This is at once a building, an institution, and a wine auction. As a building it is by far the most famous in Burgundy: Its multicolored tiled roof marks the heart of the old town of Beaune, the main town of the region. It was founded in 1432 by Nicolas Rolin, chancellor of Philippe the Good, Duke of Burgundy, as a hospital for the poor and needy of the region. It was run by the Church and funded by the sale of wine from its vineyards.

Today those vineyards still produce wine, and each November the wine is sold over a weekend in support of the city's modern hospital. The Hospices de Beaune auction is not only the occasion for much celebration and partying by bidders including movie stars and software billionaires, but also an indication for the wine trade of the direction in which prices for the new wine are likely to go.

The first merchants

In the past, people bought their wine differently. The modern wine bottle wasn't invented until the 17th century. Before that wine was transported in amphorae or barrels, and you stored it in that same shipping container at home. (Glass bottles were expensive and fragile, and were rarely used.) Wine was normally served from the barrel in jugs made of leather or metal.

■ **During the Middle Ages** *young wine was the favored tipple.*

Wine merchants existed, of course – there has always had to be a middleman between winemaker and consumer. But the wine people drank in the Middle Ages and beyond was almost always young wine of the previous vintage. (The Greeks and Romans preferred old wine, but we've seen what they added to it.) You bought a barrel of wine every now and again from your wine merchant, kept it in the cellar, and drank it until it was finished. Somewhere along the way it would have turned to vinegar, as wine does when exposed to air. Most of the wine you drank most of the time would have been pretty horrible by modern standards. The invention of the modern wine bottle made better long-term storage of wine possible.

■ **In medieval Europe,** *wine was bought by the barrel and drunk until finished – even if it had turned to vinegar!*

WHAT WAS A WINESKIN?

Wineskins were literally animal skins, cleaned, tanned, and turned inside out so that the hairy side was in contact with the wine. The legs and orifices would be sewn up, but the skin would otherwise retain the animal's shape. The inside would be lined with pitch, which must have imparted a pretty odd flavor to the wine. Even in the last century, these were the common receptacles for transporting wine in Spain. Wineskins were usually made from the skins of pigs – presumably because they were the right sort of size.

But people have also used smaller wineskins throughout history: A leak-proof leather bag for wine would have been part of your baggage when traveling, just as today's tourists clutch plastic bottles of water.

The arrival of the cork

Once the modern wine bottle – made of stronger, thicker glass than had hitherto been possible – had appeared, the only item needed to complete the change to modern methods of wine storage and aging was the cork. Corks – cheap, airtight, and with no effect on the flavor of the wine – make it possible to store wine in bottles, and thus to keep it for longer than a single year. The Romans had known of the virtues of cork for sealing wine – the Romans seem to have known about everything – but it had somehow been forgotten, and not until the later 17th century did anyone think of it again. Until then glass stoppers or wads of cloth had been used. Curiously, the corkscrew doesn't seem to have appeared until several decades later. Quite how they managed in the meantime is not clear.

■ **The rediscovery** *of the cork in the 17th century made longer storage of wine possible.*

Cork quality varies tremendously, with the best corks being used for the best wines. "Best" in this case means longest, smoothest, and freest from flaws. Cheaper corks made from waste and scraps are used for wines that are not going to be kept for long.

But while cork is an impermeable, long-lasting material, it can deteriorate in time, and is sometimes subject to mold that can spoil a wine's flavor.

Corks that have been allowed to dry out and shrink can allow air into the bottle, which is why you should never store wine standing up.

Trivia...

How do you grow cork? First, plant your cork oak tree. Cork oaks like a Mediterranean-type climate, and Portugal is the main source. When the tree is mature, strip the bark – you can do this every nine or ten years. After leaving the bark to dry, you cut corks from it as if you were coring an apple.

Next stop, the New World

WHEREVER WINE-LOVING *nations travel or trade, they take wine with them. So it's not surprising that when Europeans arrived in the Americas one of the first crops they planted was grapevines. The same thing happened when the first European settlers reached Australia, New Zealand, and South Africa. The inhabitants of these countries had their own intoxicants and their own medicines, but wine made from grapes was unknown there until the arrival of Europeans.*

Today, the term "New World" is commonly, if somewhat inaccurately, used by wine professionals and enthusiasts to refer to wines produced outside the "Old World" centers of Europe, the Middle East, and North Africa. New World wine producers may be located in the Americas, Australia, New Zealand, sub-Saharan Africa, or Asia – in countries, in other words, where, unlike the Old World, there hasn't been a continuous history of winemaking over the last millennium.

■ **Lindeman in** *Australia is one of the New World's largest wine companies.*

Missionaries and sacramental wine

The motive for introducing wine to these countries was different in each case. The Spanish missionaries in the Americas wanted wine for the Mass, while the lay settlers wanted wine because it was what they were used to drinking every day. In Australia, originally a British penal colony, wine was favored over locally produced spirits because it was less apt to produce drunkenness and disorder. And the British settlers on North America's East Coast wanted wine simply because, like the Spanish to the south and west, they enjoyed it.

Native vines versus the imports

The making of the first vintage in a new land must have been an event of almost Biblical significance to the settlers. It probably wasn't particularly enjoyable wine, however. The vines would have been whatever had survived the long sea voyage, rather than what was most suited to the terroir, and the winemaking might well have been somewhat improvised. In South and Central America and in California the vine most widely planted by the Spanish settlers was the Mission, alias Pais. It grows prolifically, but the quality of its wine is, to put it kindly, unremarkable. The settlers on the Atlantic coast of North America brought over more interesting and better quality vines, but they all died. Only in this part of the Americas did the vine fail to flourish.

It must have been made even more depressing by the wild vines that were thriving on the East Coast. They were a different species from the European vines the settlers were planting, but they were recognizably grapevines. Why did the wild vines prosper, while anything imported from Europe died? The settlers tried every remedy they could think of. Nothing worked. So they tried making wine from the local wild vines. The wines had a strange, aromatic, pungent flavor not at all to the taste of people reared on the elegant wines of Europe. There seemed to be no solution to the problem of getting a decent drink.

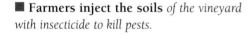
■ **Farmers inject the soils** *of the vineyard with insecticide to kill pests.*

THOMAS JEFFERSON

Thomas Jefferson, as well as being one of the architects of an independent America, was a wine connoisseur and pioneer wine grower. He traveled in France in the 1780s and eagerly shipped home the best wines he could find. Famous wines such as Château Lafite and Château d'Yquem found their way to his cellar, and individual bottles have in recent years occasionally appeared at wine auctions. One of his missions was to persuade Americans to drink wine rather than spirits. To that end he opposed taxation on wine: "No nation is drunken where wine is cheap," he wrote.

But when Jefferson tried to grow vines at his Virginia estate, Monticello, they suffered the same fate as befell the European vines all along the East Coast. Eventually he gave in and concentrated his efforts on finding the best native American vines. Three years before he died, he was sent a bottle of wine made from an American vine named Catawba; and it was Catawba and others like it that were the foundation of the United States' wine industry until California wines seized the lead in the second half of the 20th century.

Phylloxera

THE CAUSE OF DEATH *of those European vines in the eastern United States was almost invisible to the naked eye. It was a tiny insect called* Phylloxera vastratrix, *which, at one stage of its absurdly complicated life cycle, lives and feeds on the roots of vines. Where it bites and sucks on the root, a gall forms; the vine rejects these galls and eventually, over a period of about three years, rejects its whole root system and dies. European vines, all of the species* Vitis vinifera, *had never come in contact with phylloxera before; they succumbed without exception. Native American vines, mostly of the species* Vitis labrusca, *are immune to phylloxera and can happily coexist. But that was only discovered later, after phylloxera had proved a great deal more damaging to vines than anyone could have guessed.*

The death of world winegrowing

It took only a few cuttings, imported to Europe from the New World, to spread the pest. Gardeners always want to experiment with new plants, and vine growers are no exception – show them a new vine and they'll want to try it out. Thus cuttings of native American vines came to Europe, and with them went phylloxera.

In 1863 it was noticed that vines in Provence were dying mysteriously. By 1867 the disease had spread to Bordeaux. It spread to Italy in the early 1870s, and to Spain later that decade. There was no cure, and no prevention, though there were plenty of ideas for both. Some advocated burying a toad under each vine; others tried flooding the vineyards, and this latter method sometimes worked – for a time. Fumigating the soil with carbon bisulfide was effective but killed everything else as well, sometimes including the vines. Not surprisingly the winegrowers, thus deprived of their livelihood, were desperate for a solution to the problem.

Grafting and rebirth

The answer, when it came, also originated in the West. With hindsight it seems obvious: If native American vines are immune to phylloxera, then graft European vines onto American rootstocks.

But this solution took a long time to be accepted. Growers were fearful of the consequences, and they were right to be wary – grafting one species of vine onto another is a science in itself. You have to choose a rootstock that is compatible not just with the vine but also with the climate and type of soil. Some rootstocks, for example, hate lime-rich soil; others may be susceptible to drought or to particular diseases.

In spite of these difficulties, grafting proved the only long-term solution to phylloxera. If you planted ungrafted vines in the vineyards of Bordeaux or Burgundy today they would die, just as their forebears did. Phylloxera never goes away – the louse is remarkably tenacious. Sufficiently resistant rootstock in California was hit in the 1980s and 1990s, and large parts of the state's vineyards have been replanted.

■ **Louis Pasteur's findings** *on the fermentation process were a pivotal point in the history of wine.*

WHAT IS A PRE-PHYLLOXERA WINE?

Strictly speaking, a pre-phylloxera wine is one made in the years before phylloxera reached the vineyards. On special occasions Bordeaux chateau-owners might reach into the darkest recesses of their cellars to unearth wines from the 19th century – we remember tasting an 1874 Château Lafite that was old and frail but still very much alive, made before phylloxera killed the vines.

But the phrase "pre-phylloxera" is sometimes used more loosely than that, to mean wine made from ungrafted vines. There are a few small parcels of ungrafted vines in Europe, for example. Nobody knows why they have not been affected by phylloxera; it's just one of those quirky things. But the phrase pre-phylloxera, used in this sense, doesn't mean that the wine is from the same vines that were there in 1860 or whenever; all these vines were replanted at some point, when they became too old.

We think that using the term pre-phylloxera to mean ungrafted is incorrect. There are many ungrafted vines in the world today: Nearly all the vines in Chile are ungrafted, for example, because phylloxera happens never to have arrived there.

Wine technology

MODERN SCIENCE ENTERED *wine growing in the 19th century, when it solved the problem of phylloxera and, thanks to Louis Pasteur, uncovered the mysteries of fermentation. And once science had entered the picture there was no looking back. Almost every aspect of viticulture and winemaking has been changed by the advent of technology, from the number of vines planted per acre of land to the temperature of fermentation to the stability of wine in the bottle.*

INTERNET

www.geocities.com/Paris /1265/calcohol.html

Here's an enthusiast's quite detailed introduction to winemaking – and the production of mead and beer – and its history. Included are useful details of what can go wrong in the process.

Temperature-controlled fermentation

If we had to point to one technological development that has changed wine more than any other, we would choose temperature-controlled fermentation. We'll go into this when we talk about winemaking in more detail, but basically, if you keep fermentation temperatures cool you retain all the fresh, fruity flavors in wine.

■ **The advance of** *technology has revolutionized the process of winemaking today.*

This one single technological advance – which actually begun only in the late 1970s and early 1980s – has revolutionized the winemaking process all over the world. It's the biggest single reason why so many of the wines that we drink and enjoy today are so much tastier than the wines of the past.

A simple summary

✓ People have been cultivating grapevines since the late Stone Age, and wine seems to have been made first around the Black Sea.

✓ The Ancient Greeks, Egyptians, and Romans were great connoisseurs of fine wine.

✓ The Roman Empire, stretching from Britain in the north to Constantinople in the East and North Africa in the south, helped to spread a love of wine.

✓ Later, in the Middle Ages, the greatest and most innovative winemakers of the day were monastic orders.

✓ The wine bottle and cork were invented in the 17th century.

✓ Missionaries and settlers took vines with them when they traveled to the Americas, Australia, and South Africa.

✓ European vines planted on North America's East Coast invariably died; the cause – only discovered later – was a tiny insect called *Phylloxera vastratrix*.

✓ When phylloxera arrived in Europe, by way of vine cuttings, Europe's vineyards died, too.

✓ The solution was to graft European vines onto rootstocks of native North American vines.

✓ Modern wine production is highly technological.

✓ The advent of controlled-temperature fermentation in the last few decades of the 20th century revolutionized the taste of wine.

Chapter 3

Enjoying Wine Now

AT THE BEGINNING of the 21st century we have a bigger choice of wine than ever before. It comes in a greater variety of styles and from a greater variety of places – and, what's more, it's much better quality than it has ever been before.

In this chapter...

✓ *The importance of a little learning*

✓ *Why quality is better than ever before*

✓ *How not to be a wine snob*

✓ *How much should you pay?*

TODAY WE HAVE AN UNPRECEDENTED CHOICE OF QUALITY WINES TO BUY

The importance of a little learning

GO INTO A WINE STORE *and you may be dazzled by the range of wines available. There could be wines from places you never even knew made wine, and from grape varieties you've never heard of. Yes, you can just pick a bottle off the shelf at random if you want – but it's a lot more fun if you can at least mentally place the wines into styles and categories. It's a lot like viewing art – you might be bowled over by an Impressionist picture you've never seen before, but if you can compare it with a Monet and a Renoir you're well on your way to understanding why it looks the way it does, and whether it's really that good.*

Judge for yourself

A little learning is useful in another way, as well: There's so much hype surrounding some wines that you need to be able to judge for yourself. The more you can put wines into context, the more accurate your assessments can be, and the better value you'll get for your money.

■ **Understanding fine wine** *is like learning to appreciate an Impressionist masterpiece; to begin with you know you like it but do not always know why.*

Why quality is better than ever before

QUITE SIMPLY, *more is understood today about how vines grow and produce fruit, and how that fruit is turned into wine than ever before. In the past, if you were a winemaker, it was probably because your parents made wine, and their parents before them. It was simply a type of farming, and you would do it the way your parents did, just as if you were raising cattle or corn.*

■ **Traditional methods** *of wine-making have been improved upon through a greater understanding of the process.*

Who knows why?

In fact, even in famous regions like Burgundy, until the early part of the 20th century, you'd almost certainly have been farming a few other fruits and vegetables alongside the vines, and tending a few animals. If some wines spoiled in the making while others didn't, you simply accepted the time-honored (and probably wrong) explanations. You didn't stop to think about bacterial infections or lack of hygiene. After all, you probably rarely bathed. Hygiene was not high on your list of priorities.

A wine education

These days, would-be winemakers take university courses and write theses on the action of yeasts on grape juice, or the precise amount of sunlight needed to ripen a bunch of grapes. Wineries are so spotlessly clean that you could eat your dinner off the floors. Science has taken over, worldwide – though we're not saying there's no place for instinct, or creativity.

Great wine will always be a combination of science and art.

■ **Up until the** *early 20th century, grape harvesting was not a very scientific process.*

How not to be a wine snob

A PRIME EXAMPLE of a modern wine snob is the sort of person who will only drink wines that have been rated at 90+ out of 100. (See "Giving Wine Marks" in Chapter 8.) We even heard of someone who'd bought a case of wine, tasted one bottle, and didn't much like it. So he took it back for a refund. The following week it was given a mark of 97 – whereupon he dashed back to the store in a panic and tried to rebuy it.

Keep an open mind

To avoid being this sort of person, simply keep an open mind. People become wine snobs because they know a little but not enough. An example would be those who think it's okay to drink wines from countries A, B and C, but not D. So offer them the most delicious wine from country D and they'll turn it down with scorn – as if you're the person who doesn't know what's what.

People who do these sorts of things aren't real wine lovers. They have no natural curiosity and are only interested in status symbols, not enjoyment. Real wine lovers realize that they will never know all there is to know, and that there are always new discoveries to be made. Real wine lovers are always prepared to change their minds – and they drink wine because they love it, not because they think it's smart.

Don't worry about grades

Another thing: Don't follow the marks given to wines in magazines and newspapers too religiously.

■ **Judge wines by** *their flavor and character, not by what the critics have to say.*

Yes, they can be a good general guide to what's best, and certainly to what's most fashionable. But the critics involved will have tasted perhaps 50, perhaps even 100 wines, one after the other. The wines that come out on top are the wines that stand out for one reason or another: Usually because they're more *concentrated* in flavor. Like beauty queens, they attract attention without necessarily engaging the brain and emotions as strongly as their less "showy" neighbors.

You, at home, will not be drinking wine in this way. You'll be opening a bottle with your pasta or chicken or whatever – and frankly, a massively concentrated wine may not be what you'll enjoy most. Instead, take some time to read the notes that go with the marks. Words such as "subtle" and "balanced" can provide a better guide to wines you'll actually enjoy drinking. The critics took one or two sips and spat them out. You've got to drink it by the glassful.

■ **Learn to appreciate** *real quality by taking time to enjoy classic wines, such as Sancerre.*

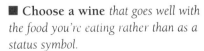

■ **Choose a wine** *that goes well with the food you're eating rather than as a status symbol.*

How much should you pay?

SOME WINES *are extremely expensive because they're extremely good and extremely rare; others are pricey just because they're fashionable. Equally, some wines – fine German wines are an example – are underpriced because outside Germany they're unfashionable. With wine, just as with designer clothes, you can often find yourself paying a premium for the label.*

■ **The cost of producing wine**, *from vine to shelf, is – at least partly – reflected in the price of the bottle.*

There's a right price for every wine – and it may or may not be the price on the bottle.

But remember that while a copy of a Ralph Lauren outfit will be cheaper than the original, it may not be the same quality. A Cabernet Sauvignon from the south of France will be cheaper than a bottle of Chateau Margaux – but it also won't be as good. If you want a certain flavor, a certain quality, and that flavor and quality happen to be fashionable, you have to pay the price.

It costs money to make wine

At the inexpensive end, don't be fooled into thinking that the cheapest wine will be as good as one that costs a few dollars more.

When you pay the very lowest price you're spending a disproportionately high amount on the fixed costs of bottle, cork, label, shipping costs, and tax, and disproportionately little on the wine itself. Paying a bit more can pay dividends in terms of quality. Don't feel pressured into paying more than you can afford – there are good value wines at every price level – but never make the mistake of believing that all wine above a certain price level is a rip-off. Making fine wine costs money, and winegrowers are as entitled to make a profit as anyone else.

A simple summary

✓ Knowing about wine helps you put unfamiliar wines into context – that way you get better value for money, and more enjoyment from your wine.

✓ Greater scientific understanding of the winemaking process, and better educated winemakers, mean that wine quality is better than it's ever been.

✓ Keep an open mind, and select wines because you like them, not because they've scored 98 marks out of a possible 100.

✓ Don't buy the very cheapest wines – they're unlikely to be good value.

✓ Very expensive wines might be pricey just because they're fashionable at the time. Don't feel that you need to pay more than you can afford – but if you want something really fine, don't object to the price.

Chapter 4

Wine and Health

FOR YEARS WINE – and indeed all other forms of alcohol – was a normal part of medical treatment. Only in the 19th century did the temperance movement gain a hold in people's consciousness. And while it is true that alcohol in excess, or wrongly handled, makes you a danger to yourself and to others, it has become clear in recent years that alcohol in moderation is not only harmless, but actively good for your health. The consumption of a glass or more of wine per day has a beneficial effect on the cardiovascular system and can be instrumental in helping you to live a longer, healthier life.

In this chapter...

✔ The good news

✔ The bad news

✔ But remember

WINE CAN HELP COUNTER THE EFFECTS OF A HIGH-FAT DIET

The good news

WINE IS AN INTEGRAL *part of the Mediterranean diet, that combination of plenty of fresh fruit and vegetables, legumes, whole grains, fish, and olive oil that is believed to be the healthiest of all. It is so-called because it is typical of food patterns of the early 1960s in the wine- and olive-growing regions of the Mediterranean. Not only is such a diet low in saturated fat, it's also extremely tasty.*

■ **The Mediterranean diet** *incorporates plenty of fresh vegetables and olive oil.*

These were not rich places in the early 1960s, and medical services were relatively limited. In spite of this, adult life expectancy was among the highest in the world, and there were very low rates of diet-related diseases such as coronary artery disease and certain cancers.

Hearty wines: The French Paradox

But that's not the whole story. Back in the early 1990s Dr. Serge Renaud asserted on *60 Minutes* that it was drinking red wine that kept levels of heart disease in France at a low level, despite a diet famously high in fat. Just think of all that cheese, butter, and cream and you'll know what he meant. This correlation was dubbed the French Paradox, and it has kept researchers busy ever since. It also caused sales of red wine to soar overnight, and was the beginning of the current boom in red wine drinking in the United States. Recent research now suggests that white wine may be just as beneficial.

Moderate drinking is much better than either total abstention or excessive drinking.

If plotted on a graph, increasing from no consumption to overconsumption, a J-shaped curve appears, with rates of heart disease bottoming out with moderate regular consumption of wine. One recent study estimates that an alcohol intake of 30 grams per day results in a 24.7 percent reduction in risk of coronary heart disease.

INTERNET

wine-and-health.com

This not-for-profit site, set up by Robert Joseph, provides a chance for medical experts, wine professionals, and wine drinkers to exchange facts and opinions about all of the effects – good and bad – that are associated with wine.

Alcohol was frequently prescribed by family doctors as a remedy or tonic until well into the 20th century. In the 1950s and early 1960s, alcohol was even available in British hospitals on the National Health Service.

More recent findings, from a group of scientists including the same Serge Renaud who launched the idea of the French Paradox, investigated French men who consumed two to five units of wine per day and found a 29 to 33 percent reduction in overall mortality relative to total non-drinkers.

How it works

Coronary artery disease is caused by the build-up of cholesterol in the arteries supplying blood to the heart. If the arteries are partially blocked, the heart cannot get enough oxygen, and the pain of angina is the result. If an artery is blocked completely, a heart attack occurs.

The cholesterol that blocks arteries is low-density lipoprotein cholesterol (LDP). This is cleared from the blood by high-density lipoprotein cholesterol (HPD). Both are carried in the blood. Moderate alcohol consumption produces a better balance between the two.

In addition, alcohol has an anticoagulant effect which makes blood less likely to clot where it's not supposed to. Red wine, far more than white wine, also has antioxidant properties. It contains a substance known as resveratrol, which seems to be important in the cardioprotective effects of wine.

■ **The news we** *have all been waiting for: Drinking wine in moderation can be good for you!*

Wine and Alzheimer's

Most of the research on the health effects of wine has been on its cardioprotective effects, but there is strong evidence that regular moderate wine consumption can reduce the risk of developing Alzheimer's Disease. Wine also appears to have the effect of slowing mental decline in elderly people, though this is not regarded as proven.

Wine and strokes

A study by a group of Spanish scientists has found that consumption of less than 30 grams of alcohol per day brought about a 42 percent reduction in the risk of stroke. This study declared that alcohol protected against all cerebral infarction and cortical infarction, and was "borderline protective" against deep cerebral infarction. However, the researchers noted that low amounts of alcohol do not protect against hemorrhagic stroke.

■ **Red wine can** *stimulate headaches or migraines in some people.*

The bad news

ANY SENSIBLE PERSON will realize that all these years of research do not mean that everybody should be drinking more wine. Some people, for example, simply can't drink red wine, and all wine drinking appears to carry a slightly increased risk of cancer of the digestive tract, particularly the esophagus. There is also a slightly increased risk of breast cancer. It might be supposed that wine's antioxidant properties would protect against cancer as much as its alcohol content would promote cancer, but studies carried out so far have been largely inconclusive.

Wine and allergies

The most common allergic reaction to wine is a headache after drinking red wine. Some people find that they can't drink red wine at all; others can drink red wine in the evening but not during the day. Red wine can trigger migraines. For sufferers, the serotonin released from the cells by the phenolics in red wine has a role in the onset of migraines. For other people, histamine can produce a headache. Asthmatics can be troubled by the sulfites in wine, and levels of these are being reduced in most countries.

The morning after

Drink too much and you're likely to have a hangover. That applies whether you're drinking wine, beer, or whiskey. The varied but familiar symptoms have been blamed on a number of causes, principally mixing grape alcohol with grain alcohol, drinking port (the port trade invariably disagrees with this) or just overdoing the quantity. Congeners are a factor, and these are present in wine, though they occur in higher concentrations in spirits. Drinking plenty of water can help prevent the dehydration that makes one feel like death; drinking with a meal rather than without food can also help. But in the end, the only prevention is moderation.

> ### DEFINITION
>
> *The impurities in spirits that are distilled below 100 percent alcohol are known as* **congeners**. *They give the spirit its aroma and flavor, and are present, albeit in much lower concentrations, in wine.*

Wine and calories

There is no such thing as non-calorific wine. If you're on a strict diet, a glass of wine may well cheer up a regime of lettuce leaves and carrot juice, but there's no getting away from the fact that wine contains calories, and calories make you fat if you don't burn them up. A standard glass of dry red or white wine contains around 110 calories. Sweeter wine, with residual sugar as well as alcohol, has more calories. Sweet fortified wine, with more of everything, has even more calories. However, the number of slender wine professionals shows that this is not necessarily a problem.

■ **Too much wine** *and you may end up with a hangover the next day.*

But remember

WHEN YOU'VE WEIGHED UP *the scientific evidence for and against wine drinking, you may well decide that a little of what you fancy does you good. Wine has its place in a healthy lifestyle, and you'll probably do yourself more harm by worrying about your health than by having an extra glass of Cabernet. But there are times when alcohol of all sorts should be treated with extra caution.*

Wine and driving

The only sensible answer is that you can't do both. We all know that drinking and driving is foolish; and even a single glass of wine can impair your judgment.

Your liver metabolizes around one glass of wine an hour. If you have to drive home, stop drinking well before it's time to go. Better still, take a cab.

Wine and pregnancy

Excessive drinking in pregnancy is associated with fetal alcohol syndrome (FAS), resulting in abnormal facial features and reduced intelligence in the baby. Although some experts now believe that fears of FAS are exaggerated, consult your doctor before drinking during pregnancy.

Wine in moderation

The beneficial effects of wine drinking come with moderate drinking; excessive drinking can lead to liver disease, brain damage, high blood pressure, nerve and muscle wasting, infertility, and a higher risk of some cancers. The difficulty lies in defining the word "moderate." It is said that a heavy drinker is someone who drinks more than her doctor; most governments try to eliminate such flippancies by defining healthy levels of wine drinking. The United States puts its recommended limits at an average of one drink per day for women and one to two for men. In Britain the recommendations are higher – up to three glasses of wine per day for women, and up to four for men.

■ **Pregnant women** *should consult their physician before drinking alcohol.*

INTERNET

www.wineinstitute.com

This site is the Wine Institute of California's attempt to counter the tide of anti-alcohol propaganda disseminated in the United States, much of it with government support.

Women's recommended alcohol consumption levels are lower partly because they are generally smaller than men and also partly because they absorb more alcohol, glass for glass, than men.

Different enzyme levels in the stomach and lower body water content result in alcohol becoming more concentrated in female body tissues. Women on the contraceptive pill also eliminate alcohol more slowly than women who are not on the pill and most healthy men.

Don't believe everything you read

Wine and health has become a sexy subject for newspapers and magazines, and journalists who hardly know one wine from another find themselves writing would-be authoritative pieces on the dangers or benefits of drinking wine. As a result, an awful lot of red herrings get published. There have been stories alleging that Chilean Merlot is the healthiest wine of all, or that Rioja is healthier still. The best thing to do with these stories is to apply a little common sense. Wine is a great thing, but it won't make you live forever, nor does it contain the secret of eternal youth. The best reason for drinking wine is because you enjoy it. People with a serious interest in wine very seldom abuse it.

A simple summary

✓ There is increasing scientific evidence to show that moderate regular drinking of wine can reduce the risk of heart disease.

✓ There is also evidence that wine can reduce the risk of developing Alzheimer's Disease, or having a stroke.

✓ But it is not all good news. Wine may slightly increase the risk of contracting certain types of cancer. Migraine sufferers may find that red wine is a trigger; and of course excessive drinking gives you a hangover.

✓ You should never drink and drive, and drinking can be risky during pregnancy. Wine can also be fattening.

✓ Moderate drinking will allow you to enjoy wine with the least risk of any ill effects, and greatest chance of benefits.

PART TWO

LEARNING TO TASTE WINE IS AN ENJOYABLE PASTIME

LEARNING TO TASTE WINE

THERE'S NOTHING ALARMING about learning to taste wine. Yes, it's a piece of specialist knowledge – but so is learning to drive a car or handle a computer, and chances are you've mastered those particular skills.

Another point: If you're interested enough in wine to buy this book, you're probably interested in food as well. If you can tell the difference in flavor between beef and lamb, between apples and pears, between chocolate and coffee, then your palate is already well honed. Learning to taste wine simply means adding a range of new flavors and sensations to your repertoire. And the *easiest* way of doing this is by comparing the smells and tastes of wine to those smells and tastes you already know.

Chapter 5

Why Smell and Taste Matter

WHAT DO YOU LOVE MOST ABOUT FRIED BACON? Is it the salty flavor? The crisp or soft texture? Is it that wonderful savory smell? What about freshly ground coffee: Is it just the taste you go for? Or is it the smell that makes it worthwhile getting out of bed on a Monday morning?

You see, you've answered this one already. If what we eat or drink has no smell, we think it's pretty dull stuff. How do you tell if toast is burning, or if vegetables are going off, or if the dog has been rolling in something disgusting? By the smell, of course. Why is it hard to work up enthusiasm for food when we have a cold? Because our sense of smell is knocked out of action.

In this chapter...

✓ Take a look at your sense of smell
_____

✓ What your taste buds actually do
_____

✓ Memories are made of this
_____

✓ How to taste
_____

SNIFFING WINE IS AN IMPORTANT PRELUDE TO DRINKING IT

Take a look at your sense of smell

ONE SNIFF *and you know if something is fresh or stale, sweet or savory, whether it will taste of thyme or rosemary, of cheese or ham, of strawberries or peaches. All your taste buds can tell you is which of four primary flavors – saltiness, sweetness, bitterness, and acidity – are present. If matters were left to our taste buds alone, we would hardly have gotten as far as distinguishing processed cheese from Brie.*

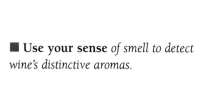

We take our sense of smell for granted so much that we usually only notice when it's not there. But it's far more informative than taste.

What the nose knows

Our sense of smell is a feeble instrument compared to that of a Bloodhound, but nevertheless it can detect some 10,000 different scents. And they don't have to be present in any great quantity, either: Concentrations of as low as one part in 10,000 are sometimes sufficient to enable us to spot aromas.

The part of the brain that registers flavors and scents is the olfactory bulb, and smells reach it via receptors – of which there are about 1,000 – in the nose.

■ **Use your sense** *of smell to detect wine's distinctive aromas.*

You can even detect smells without actually sniffing something: The retronasal passage at the back of your throat carries volatile smells up to where the receptors in your nose can spot them. So you can smell something even while it's in your mouth.

■ **When tasting wine** concentrate on the different flavors as you would when enjoying good food.

What your taste buds actually do

AS WE'VE MENTIONED, your taste buds detect the four basic flavors. Different parts of the tongue, roughly speaking, concentrate on different tastes: sweetness is detected on the front of the tongue, bitterness at the back, acidity at the edges, and saltiness on the front edges. Bitterness, saltiness, and acidity are qualities that don't have smells, and bitterness and acidity are crucial pieces of information about wine . . . which is why the smell of a wine alone isn't sufficient to tell you all you need to know.

■ **When tasting wine**, *always concentrate on the texture of the liquid in your mouth.*

Texture matters

The texture of wine is also important, and only your mouth can tell you about this. Does a wine have a fat, rich texture, like syrup or well-concentrated stock? Or is it thin like water? Is it sparkling? Some wines have a very faint prickle of gas, just detectable on the tongue. Does it taste of *tannin* like strong, black tea? Does it give the burning sensation of very high alcohol? All these questions relate to what is called the "mouthfeel" of a wine, and can only be determined by taking a mouthful of wine. Again, they are vital to your overall judgement of a wine.

DEFINITION

The substance in wine that furs up your gums and makes them feel rough and dry is tannin. *It is derived from the skins, pips, and stalks of grapes, so is usually only found in red wines. Red wine needs tannin if it is to age well in the bottle, so young reds intended for aging can be high in tannin. It softens with age.*

Memories are made of this

SMELLS AND TASTES *are some of the most powerful aids to memory we have. They can transport us back to childhood, or to a distant city, or to a holiday we took ten years ago. A smell of Chinese cooking always reminds us personally of secondhand bookshops, simply because so many of London's secondhand bookshops are near Chinatown, and you can't browse the shelves without getting a whiff of Peking duck. If wine tasters' descriptions of the smells of wine sometimes seem a bit far-fetched, it could just be that they're in the habit of noticing and remembering smells more.*

■ **Château Latour wines** *are noted for the way in which they age.*

Recalling smells and tastes

Noticing, and remembering, smells and flavors is part of learning to taste wine. A wine that smells and tastes of strawberries is, you'll agree, going to be easily distinguished from one that tastes of fruitcake. But both are fruity, so using that simple adjective won't help you remember in the future which was which. But if you take a sniff and think, oh yes, strawberry pie, then you're halfway to identifying that wine next time it comes your way.

If nobody else thinks it smells of strawberry pie, don't worry.

The smells of wine are never simple. They're composed of many different compounds, and a wine can remind you of several things at the same time.

A red might, for example, make you think of plums and blackcurrants and toffee and dark chocolate all at once. In fact, the more smells and tastes are packed into a wine the more complex it is said to be; and complexity in wine is a virtue. It's one of the things that differentiates a high-quality wine from an everyday one.

■ **In great vintages**, *Château Gruaud Larose wines are among Bordeaux's finest.*

How to taste

PROFESSIONAL WINE TASTERS
go through a ritual of sniffing, slurping,
and spitting, and that's what we're
going to look at now. It's not just for
show. Every stage of it, as we've already
suggested, is designed to extract the
maximum information about the wine.

But there's no point in doing any of it
unless at the same time you're thinking
about what you're tasting. Consider
sampling an unfamiliar food. You
probably try and compare it to something
you already know, to give yourself a
benchmark: You might compare the
flavor of a hitherto unknown fruit to
strawberries, and the texture to pears.
That way you put it in context.

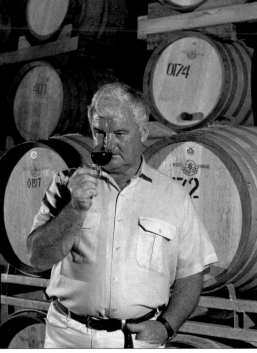

■ **It's easy,** *simply swirl the wine around the glass,*
then take a big sniff . . .

Concentrate on the wine

Wine is no different, but may be more
subtle in its distinctions. Concentrate
entirely on the wine through each step
outlined below. Maybe the nose – the wine
taster's term for the smell – reminds you of
apples or lemons or plums, while the finish,
as wine tasters call the final sensation of the
wine in your mouth as you either swallow
or spit – speaks more of raspberries or
leather or whatever.

■ *. . .* **now take a slurp,** *hold the wine in your*
mouth while sucking air through it and roll the
wine around your mouth to relish the flavors.

DEFINITION

The acidity, tannin, and alcohol in a wine combine to form its structure. A wine with good structure will have a slightly firmer texture and flavor (think of tea or Coca Cola) than one with poor structure, which will taste soft and "flabby" (think of spring water).

When you're more familiar with the flavors of wine you'll find yourself automatically comparing a new wine to wines you already know – because the nose, or the *structure*, or the finish, is similar. Remember a wine by comparing it to flavors you already know.

Hold up your glass – what do you see?

Yes, it's going to be red, white, or pink. But there are almost as many shades of red wine as there are shades of red paint, and white wine is never absolutely water-white.

The color can tell you quite a bit about the wine. Darker shades – the deepest, blackest reds, the most golden whites – tend to come from warm climates. So you can expect something rich and ripe. Lighter colors, particularly in white wines, often mean cooler climates. So you can expect something lighter, less lush.

Color can give you an indication of the maturity of the wine.

With age, red wines tend to lose color, eventually ending up a sort of brick red; white wines, conversely, gain color, becoming golden and eventually browny-yellow. If you tilt your glass over a white background and look at the edge, or rim, of the curve of wine, you can get an idea of how mature it is: On a mature red wine the rim will be fading. On a very young red the color will be dark and intense right to the very edge.

■ **The color of wine** *can tell you a lot, so hold up your glass and look carefully at the shade of the liquid.*

Now take a sniff

A good, hearty sniff, too. First of all give your glass a swirl to encourage the wine to release all its volatile aromas.

When tasting, don't fill your glass more than a third full: You want to leave some air space for those aromas to collect, and you don't want to spill the wine when you swirl it.

Here's where you start "listening" to the nose. If it smells of fruit, try to determine what sort of fruit. You know from experience that strawberries smell very different from fruitcake, or ripe plums smell nothing like strawberries, or whatever smells you have put in your olfactory catalog over the years. A white wine might smell of green leaves, or pineapple, or peaches, or vanilla, or toast-and-butter. A red might smell of blackcurrants, or strawberries, or tobacco, or toffee. Or, of course, a thousand other things.

And now a mouthful

Make it a middling-sized mouthful. Effete little sips are no good, but don't take so much you're afraid you'll burst. Now, holding the wine in your mouth, suck air in though it. Remember what we said about being able to smell something even when it's in your mouth? That's why you're sucking air through the wine: to release as many volatile compounds as possible.

Roll the wine around your mouth for a moment or two, until you think you've got as much information about it as you can. Then either swallow it or spit it out – if the latter, make sure you're tasting by the kitchen sink, or have a bucket handy. It's best to taste wine away from distracting smells, so the kitchen might not be the best place.

Even after you've swallowed the wine or spat it out, keep on listening to the flavors. A really good wine will have a long aftertaste; an inferior wine will be short, and the flavor will fall away quickly.

■ **When tasting red wine** *look out for the flavor of tannin; it will be sure to make you pucker your lips.*

Trivia...

How dark can a white wine be? Some sherries – usually olorosos, or those made from the Pedro Ximenez grape – are practically black in color. Yet technically they're still white wines, because they're made from white grapes. Their color comes from long aging in wooden barrels.

Normally the taste will confirm what your nose told you, but add information about acidity – high? low? – sweetness, if any, and tannin, if it's a red wine. Think about the structure of the wine. Does it feel well structured? Or does it feel a bit limp, a bit too soft? Or indeed too tough – that is, too hard, too tannic?

■ **The color of a wine** *can indicate its country of origin and also its age.*

A simple summary

✔ Your sense of smell is far more informative than your sense of taste.

✔ Your sense of taste detects just four primary flavors: saltiness, acidity, sweetness, and bitterness – but most of these are crucial in wine.

✔ Your mouth will also detect tannin – very important in red wines – and the "mouthfeel" of a wine.

✔ Your sense of smell can detect some 10,000 different aromas.

✔ Compare the smells and flavors you find in wine with other familiar smells and flavors. That's the way to remember them.

✔ To taste wine, look first at the color, which can tell you about the origin and maturity of the wine. Next investigate the nose, then the palate. All three together will help you build up a picture of the wine.

Chapter 6

The Basic Tastes of Wine

WE'VE LOOKED AT HOW EXTREMELY VARIED the flavors and smells of wine can be. Now we're going to simplify them by breaking them down into categories. The basic flavors found in all wines, after all, number just four – fruit, alcohol, acidity, and sweetness (or the lack thereof). The balance of a wine – crucial to its quality – depends on having all these factors present in the right amount.

In this chapter...

✓ Fruit

✓ Alcohol

✓ Acidity

✓ Sweetness

TRY A CHILLED LIGHT WHITE WINE WITH SUBTLE FRUITY TASTES

Fruit

ALL WINE TASTES *of fruit, to a greater or lesser degree. Sometimes that fruit can be juicy and fresh and simple – almost like eating raspberries, perhaps. But more often it is complex and reminiscent of several different fruits – perhaps apple and quince and melon, all at once. Fortified wines often taste of dried fruit such as sultanas, dried figs, or citrus peel. Wines with a lot of bottle age taste less obviously of individual fruits, but should still be fruity tasting.*

■ **If you like your** *wine fruity, why not try a Riesling with the subtle flavor of apple?*

Surprising but true

The one fruit that wine very seldom tastes of is grapes.

This is odd, you'll agree, given that grapes are the only fruit from which wine is made. Cider, after all, tastes recognizably of apples, so why shouldn't wine taste of grapes? The answer is that the fermentation and aging processes involved in winemaking produce an enormous array of chemical compounds, which take the flavor of wine way beyond mere grapes. It's why wine has fascinated the world for centuries and cider hasn't.

But as always with wine, there are exceptions. Wines made from the Muscat grape (of which there are several varieties used for wine) do taste of grapes – ripe, sweet, aromatic grapes, picked straight off the vine.

One woman's strawberry is another woman's banana

Fruits often smell and taste like other fruits. Strawberries and bananas taste quite similar, papayas (custard apples or pawpaws) are quite like strawberries in flavor, and quinces are like a cross between apples and pears. So while it's useful practice to be as precise as you can when describing a wine to yourself, don't be surprised if one day you think of asparagus, and the next day the same wine reminds you of green beans. You're still in the same general family of aromas.

Alcohol

Trivia...

Herb and spice aromas and flavors are quite common in wine, but vegetable aromas are less often found. Green peppers, green beans, and asparagus are common, and mature red wine from the Pinot Noir grape can have a whiff of rotting vegetables and be none the worse for it. But generally speaking, any wine tasting strongly of cabbages should be treated with caution.

YOU CAN'T HAVE WINE *without alcohol. Yes, sometimes you see "de-alcoholized" wines on the market – they're wines from which the alcohol has been removed – but they don't meet most legal definitions of wine. Alcohol is a product of fermentation: yeasts act on sugars present in the grape juice, and alcohol is the result. The main alcohol in wine is ethanol, but higher alcohols, or fusel oils, are also produced. Alcohol helps to give wine its weight and* body. *It contributes to mouthfeel and balance and helps the wine to age gracefully. It also has pleasant effects on the drinker (when drunk in moderation, of course).*

DEFINITION

The sensation of the weight of a wine in the mouth is otherwise known as its body *A full-bodied wine is said to be heavy, or weighty.*

■ **The alcohol content** *of the wine is given on the bottom left of this label.*

■ **Wine tastes** *of different fruit to different people; it may remind you of strawberries while the next person thinks it's quince.*

Why some wines contain more alcohol than others

Because alcohol is the result of the transformation of grape sugars by yeasts, it follows that the more sugar there is in the grape juice, the more alcohol there'll be in the wine. Generally speaking, the riper the grapes the more sugar they contain – so wine from super-ripe grapes will be more alcoholic than wine from grapes that are only barely ripe.

But there are other factors, as well. Some wines, as we've seen, are fortified by the addition of brandy. This can bring their total alcohol content up to 20 or 21 percent alcohol by volume (which is how alcohol in wine is measured). In other wines the fermentation may be stopped before it's complete in order to leave some residual sugar (that is, unfermented grape sugar) in the wine. Some fine German wines may have as little as 7.5 percent alcohol.

The strongest wines don't always taste the most alcoholic

It's a question of balance again.

The importance of good balance to wine can hardly be overstated.

You know when it's there because none of the constituent parts of the wine are obtrusive. You can have perhaps 14 percent alcohol in a wine – which is a lot in an unfortified wine – but if it has fruit and acidity to balance then the alcohol won't strike you as being unusually high. On the other hand, a wine that has 12 percent alcohol – a pretty standard level – can taste too alcoholic if it is short on fruit and acidity.

■ **Some fine wines** *from German vineyards have a very low alcohol content.*

Acidity

ALL WINE MUST have acidity, both for its flavor and for its preservative qualities. It is acidity that makes wine taste refreshing and stops it from being cloying. It balances the fruit flavors and the weightiness of the alcohol, and if the wine has residual sugar it balances that, too. The more alcohol and the more residual sugar a wine has, the more acidity it will need for balance. But the acidity should never taste obtrusive. Wines with a lot of residual sugar, such as dessert wines, have extremely high acidity, but you shouldn't be aware of that when you taste them.

■ **Although high in acidity**, dessert wines, such as Sauternes should be nothing but sweet.

DEFINITION

Very sweet wines are often referred to as dessert wines, because that is the course of the meal with which they are intended to be drunk.

The importance of acidity

Wine will not age well unless it contains sufficient acidity.

Wines with low acidity age much faster; white wines go brown early and reds lose their color, and the flavors become flabby and seem to fall apart in the mouth. So if you buy a wine that is very low in acidity, don't even think of keeping it more than a few months.

Why acidity is not the same as sourness

Sometimes you hear people describing over-acidic wines as "sour," but they're using the wrong word.

Sourness in wine is when wine begins to turn to vinegar as a result of infection by acetobacter bacteria.

Sourness in wine is a very serious fault – you wouldn't want to drink a wine like this.

Where acidity comes from

It's quite simple: Acidity comes mostly from grapes, and partly from the fermentation process. The main acids present in wine are tartaric acid, malic acid, and lactic acid.

Grapes tend to lose acidity as they ripen. Part of the skill of producing well-balanced wine is picking the grapes at the right moment – when they have enough sugar but neither too much nor too little acidity.

This is most difficult to accomplish in hot climates, because acidity levels can plummet when it's very hot. Cooler climates preserve the acidity in the grapes much better, which is why wines from cooler climates have more acidity, and taste fresher, than wines from hot climates.

Acidification – adding acidity to either the unfermented juice or the finished wine – is one of the options open to winemakers in many warm climates. There's nothing wrong with this, and it can improve the balance of the wine, providing it's not done with too heavy a hand.

■ **Modern winemakers** *test the acidity in the grapes – and in the fermenting juice, possibly acidifying when necessary.*

Sweetness

SWEETNESS IN WINE *is optional. Yeast, left to itself, will usually ferment all the sugar present in grape juice and turn it into alcohol. A wine with no residual sugar is said to be dry. Many "dry" white wines have a little residual sugar.*

Sweet wine is wine with obvious residual sugar. It may taste honeyed, or it may have the fruity sweetness of peaches or apples or raisins. Some newcomers to wine look down on sweet wine, because they fear that liking it will make them look unsophisticated. And it's true that the very cheapest sweet wines are aimed at an unsophisticated audience. Yet some sweet wines are among the finest, rarest, and most expensive one can buy.

How sweet is sweet?

Let's define some terms here. Sweetness is measured in grams per liter of residual sugar, but what the figures say and how the wine tastes in your mouth can be two very different things. We're back to that all-important question of balance – a wine with very high residual sugar, and very high acidity to match, may well taste less sweet, and certainly more refreshing, than one with much lower residual sugar but without enough acidity. The lower the acidity in a wine, the more any sweetness will show.

■ **Grapes grown** *in hot climates will produce wine with low levels of acidity.*

■ **This Muscat** *is a medium-sweet wine.*

Wine can be legally and technically dry with up to about 10 grams per liter of residual sugar.

Most dry wines have much less than this, but it's not uncommon for some technically dry California Chardonnays, for example, to have several grams per liter of residual sugar. They don't taste sweet, just softer than they would if they had little or no residual sugar like most Chardonnay from France.

"Medium dry" means a wine with between about 10 and 20 grams per liter of residual sugar. Between 20 and 30 grams per liter means a medium sweet wine. Properly sweet wine has more than 30 grams per liter – sometimes much more.

Why all wines are not sweet

Certain things have to happen for wine to be sweet. As we've seen, yeast will normally gobble up all the sugar present in grape juice. However, when the alcohol level in the juice has risen to a certain point, the yeast will die – yeast can't live in a very alcoholic environment. (The actual alcohol level that kills the yeast depends on the strain of yeast.)

■ **Champagne ranges** *from the bone dry to the lusciously sweet.*

■ **Even though Chardonnay** *is technically a dry wine, the ripe grapes can produce several grams per liter of residual sugar.*

BOTRYTIS CINEREA

The process of producing some of the world's finest, most delicious sweet wines is so bizarre that if it didn't already exist you'd be hard put to invent it. *Botrytis cinerea*, or noble rot, is a fungus, an unattractive mold that with the right climatic conditions, will attack ripe grapes. First individual grapes, then the whole bunch, become affected by this rot. They look like any other rotten grapes – brown, shriveled, and with varying amounts of mold growing on them.

But noble rot has a very precise effect on ripe grapes. It sucks out the water, thus concentrating the sugar and acidity. It also changes the biochemical makeup of the grape, so that wines made from botrytis-affected grapes are not just sweet and intense but have a particular honeyed flavor. Such wines can age in the bottle for many years. Sauternes from France are probably the most famous example, but Germany, Austria, and Hungary produce equally good botrytis wines.

■ **The distinctive** *flavor of Sauternes is produced by* botrytis-*affected grapes.*

■ **Although grapes** *attacked by* Botrytis cinerea *look unattractive, they produce some of the world's finest dessert wines.*

...CONTINUED

Few wine regions make botrytis wines because the fungus requires a rarely found combination of high humidity, morning mists, and warm fall days. It's unpredictable, too, and doesn't arrive every year. You also have to leave your grapes on the vine until late in the fall, risking loss of your whole crop from rain or hail. Making botrytis wines is one of the world's riskiest ways of earning a living.

■ **Noble rot makes for** *grapes that look brown and rotten, but produces wine that tastes delicious and sweet.*

Once the alcohol level rises above the point when the yeast dies, any remaining grape sugar will be left unfermented.

If you want to make sweet wine just by your choice of grapes, then you have to start off with extremely sweet grapes. You can do this by leaving them on the vine to become overripe and shriveled. This way they lose some of their water content, and both the sugar and the acidity is concentrated.

EXTRACT

If you evaporated some wine over a flame, you'd be left with some solid residue. This is known as the extract, or dry extract, of the wine, and it's measured in grams per liter. It consists of sugars, minerals, non-volatile acids, and other substances. It's not something you can taste, but it contributes to the balance and ageability of the wine.

Alternatively, you can stop the fermentation process before all the sugar has been turned into alcohol. One way of doing this is by centrifuging the fermenting juice; another is by adding sulfur dioxide (SO_2) (this is the winemaker's all-purpose disinfectant, used to kill unwanted bacteria and organisms). A third way is by fortifying the wine by adding grape brandy. But the cheapest sweet wines bypass all these techniques, and simply add concentrated unfermented grape juice to dry wine.

■ **You can often** *taste the fresh flavors of apples and strawberries coming through when drinking wine.*

A simple summary

✓ The four basic flavors of wine are fruit, alcohol, acidity, and lastly, sweetness.

✓ All wine tastes of fruit, or should, but wine very seldom tastes of grapes.

✓ Alcohol is produced by the action of yeasts on grape sugars, and helps to give wine its weight and body.

✓ Acidity makes wines refreshing.

✓ Wines from cooler climates tend to have higher acidity than wines from warm climates.

✓ Sweet wines are sweet because they contain unfermented sugar from the grape juice.

✓ The balance between fruit, alcohol, acidity, and sweetness or dryness is crucial to wine quality.

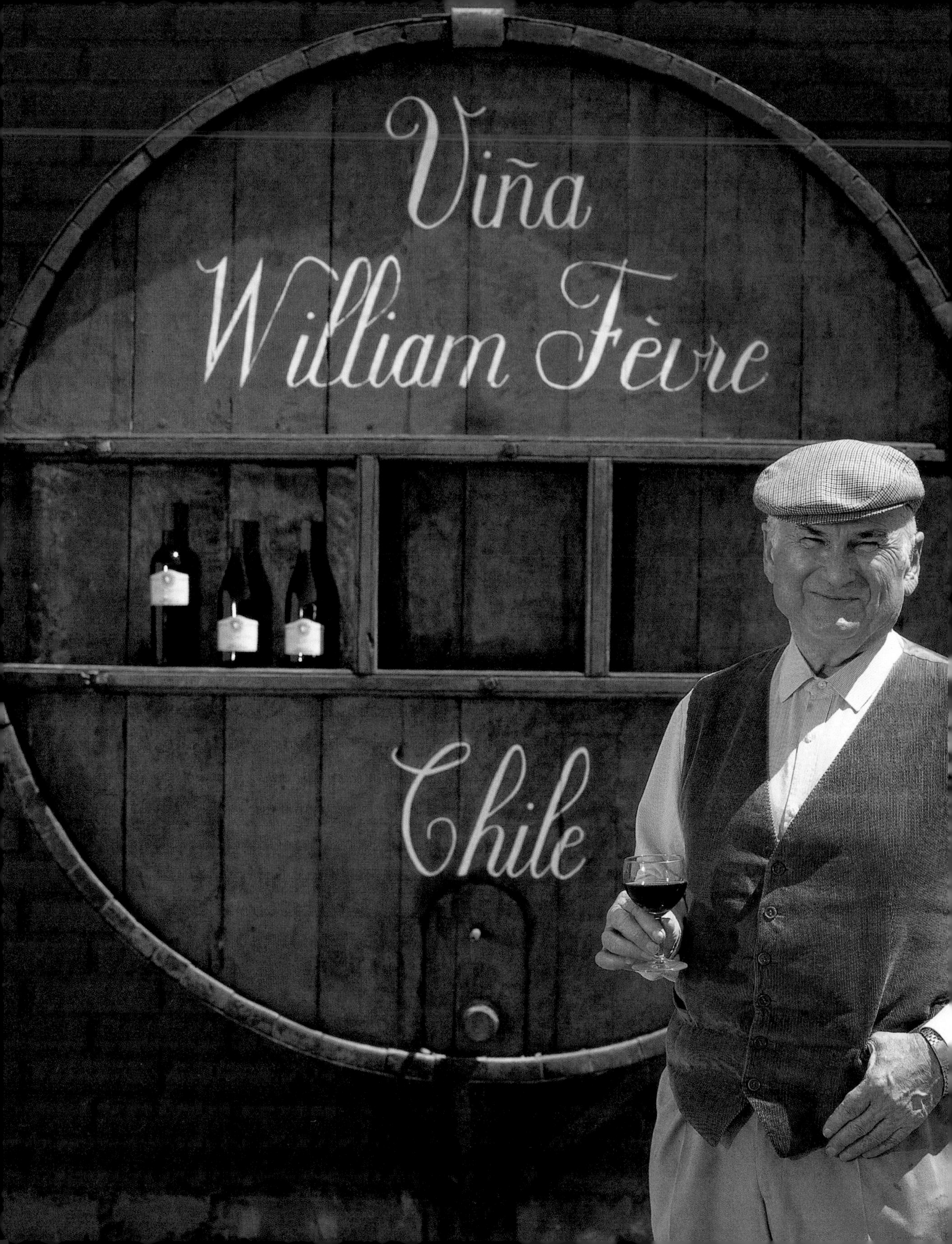
Viña
William Fèvre
Chile

Chapter 7

Other Tastes You Might Find

WE'VE LOOKED AT THE FOUR BASIC FLAVORS OF WINE, those that are present to some extent in every wine you taste. But there are other flavors, as well. The four we're going to look at now – oak, tannin, age, and off-ness – don't occur in all wines. But when they do, they're crucial.

In this chapter...

✓ Oak

✓ Tannin

✓ Age

✓ Off-ness

DON'T DISREGARD ANY HINTS OF FLAVOR WHEN TASTING WINE – THEY MIGHT WELL BE THERE!

Oak

WHY ON EARTH *should wine taste of a particular type of tree?*
Simple – a great many wines are aged in oak barrels.

INTERNET

www.lecoleduvin.com

Here's an online wine school created by the authors of this book.

Wine can be stored in all sorts of receptacles before it is bottled. Stainless steel vats and epoxy-lined cement vats are popular, hygienic, and effective. They impart no flavor to the wine, and the wine will not change or develop while in them.

Wooden barrels are different. They manage to be both watertight and yet sufficiently porous for some exchange of gases through the wood. A certain amount of wine evaporates through the pores of the wood and a certain amount of air gets in. This oxygenation enables the wine to develop and mature.

Why some wines smell like a sawmill

There is, however, an enormous difference between new oak barrels and old oak barrels. The wine can breathe through either, but old oak barrels – four or five years old or more – will impart no oak flavor to the wine. Only new oak barrels will do this. Flavorwise, a barrel of five-years-old is pretty neutral. What the oak does do is allow slight and slow oxygenation through the pores of the wood, and this can give an impression of greater softness and roundness to the wine.

■ **Stainless steel vats** *are used for most modern wines. Some very good wines never go near an oak barrel.*

■ **Cement vats,** *if kept clean, do not impart unwanted flavors to the wines stored in them.*

When people talk about "oaky wines," they mean wine aged in new oak barrels. The flavor given by new oak is unmistakeable. It's primarily vanilla – vanillin is one of the substances extracted from the oak by the wine – but it can be toasty, as well. You can smell it and taste it. But oakiness, just like fruit, acidity, alcohol, and sweetness, should be in balance with the rest of the wine. Winemakers can overdo it.

If a wine smells like a timber yard and the fruit is overwhelmed by the oak, then that wine has been over-oaked.

Barrels and the oak in them

Different oaks impart subtly different flavors to wine.

Winemakers can choose between oaks from several different French regions, such as Limousin or Allier, or they can choose American oak, which tends to have more aggressive vanilla flavors. (These stronger flavors are partly the result of U.S. cooperage techniques: Kiln drying of wood rather than European-style air-drying, and sawing of staves rather than splitting.) Portuguese oak is widely used in Portugal; German, Slavonian, and Russian oaks also all have their fans.

The most fashionable size of barrel for aging wines is the 59-gallon (225-liter) *barrique*, which originated in Bordeaux. Most winemakers find it has the ideal ratio of volume to surface area in contact with the oak, and is relatively maneuverable in the bargain.

■ **The many** *different types of oak from which barrels are made contribute to a variety of different flavors in the finished wine.*

When the chips are down

New oak barrels are expensive, and give the most flavor only in their first year. If you want a wine with a vanilla flavor, but don't want a higher price, there are two main options open to you. You can dunk a bag of oak chips in the fermenting wine, much as you would dunk a teabag; or you can insert planks of new oak, called inner staves, into the fermenting vat. Such techniques give the flavor of new oak, and can be perfectly acceptable for inexpensive wines intended to be drunk young. However, they don't mature the wine in the way that an oak barrel does. For fine wines there's no substitute for the real thing.

Why the oaky taste is only found in some kinds of wines

The vanilla-and-toast flavor you get from new oak barrels has an extraordinary affinity with certain grape varieties. Cabernet Sauvignon suits it perfectly; so does Chardonnay. Both of these wines can blossom with a bit of new oak and gain extra layers of complexity.

But some wines have flavors that seem to fight the flavor of oak. When that happens, the fruit flavors usually lose, and the oak swamps everything. The light, neutral dry whites of Italy are a case in point: Age them in new oak and the oak takes over, to the extent that you can't taste anything else. The Riesling grape, too, is seldom enhanced by the flavor of new oak. So new oak isn't the right choice for all winemakers.

Don't make the mistake of thinking that a wine aged in new oak is automatically better than one that wasn't.

Even the slight oxygenation you get from aging wine in old oak barrels doesn't suit all wines. Some light white and red wines keep their crispness and aroma best if they're stored in stainless steel tanks.

■ **This table wine** *is not aged; there is no date on the label.*

94

Tannin

REMEMBER TANNIN? *It's the astringent, mouth-drying stuff that coats your gums when you drink black tea. It can be pretty noticeable in wine, too – particularly young reds intended for long bottle aging.*

Why all wines are not tannic

Tannin is really only noticeable in red wines, and the color of red wine is itself a type of tannin. Tannin is found mostly in the skins, but also in the pips and stems of grapes, and some red grapes naturally have more tannin than others. The longer you leave the skins and juice to macerate together during and just after fermentation, the more tannin you extract.

What tannin does for wine

In a nutshell, tannin helps red wine to age. Red wines with little tannin are intended for drinking young.

But the sort of red that is meant to go on improving in the bottle for perhaps ten years needs lots of tannin. As it ages, the tannin softens and becomes less noticeable.

Trivia...

Tannin does more than color wines; it can color your teeth, as well. The best way to get purple-gray colored teeth is to taste 50 or so young red wines, one after the other. A good tip for Halloween parties, perhaps. Luckily, it comes off with a good scrub.

Balance matters here, as in everything. In very young reds the tannin can seem very powerful; but you should still be able to sense the fruit lurking behind, waiting to emerge. A red wine that is all tannin and insufficient fruit will never be very good, no matter how long you age it.

■ **The level of tannin** *in wines depends on whether they are supposed to be drunk young or left to mature.*

Age

ALL WINES *have a life span – think of it as youth, maturity, and old age. Flavors change as wines age. Wines improve until they reach their peak, stay there for a while, then gradually decline. Some wines accomplish all these stages within a year or two; others may take 50 years. And just where you think the peak of each wine occurs depends to some extent on personal taste.*

You can't taste age

At least, not in the sense of age being a particular flavor like oak. What you can taste are its effects. Think of cheese for a moment. If you cut into a young Brie cheese its flavor will be fresh, almost milky, whereas an older Brie will be more pungent. One that is past its best will smell of ammonia.

■ **Different types of** *wine mature at different ages. Some may take as long as 50 years!*

Wine ages in much the same way. Young wine smells fresh, and full of juicy young fruit. These are called primary aromas. Later they give way to a more subtle *bouquet*. White wines, for example, may become more cookielike or honeyed. The fruit will still be there, but transformed into something richer and more complex. And then, as wine passes its best, the fruit flavors fade and eventually only the acidity and tannin remain.

■ **This soft, fruity Chorey-Lés-Beaune** *from Burgundy is best drunk within three years of the harvest.*

Why some wines age more gracefully than others

How a wine ages depends on its makeup. It must have sufficient fruit and acidity, and these must be balanced by alcohol and/or extract and/or sweetness. Reds must have sufficient tannin. Wines that will age well may taste pretty substantial in youth, but sheer weight is not an infallible guide. Structure and balance are what really matter.

■ **Sparkling wines** *are sold when they are ready to drink.*

An ability to age well is often taken as the ultimate sign of quality, and to some extent it is. Expensive wines that don't age well generally lose credibility: Fine wines are expected to be able to develop. If you're charging $50 for your wine and it fades within three years, nobody will take you seriously. But one of the joys of modern wine is that there are so many wines that don't need to be aged at all, apart from the half-hour or so it takes to get them home from the store.

Many wines can be drunk young these days. Most are not intended to be aged further, and won't improve. Only a minority have to be laid down for more than a couple of years.

How to tell when a wine is at its peak

A tricky one, this. Normally you only find out for sure when it has just passed it. It's one of the most frustrating things about wine: Lay down a case of good red wine, and every time you open a bottle you'll think, yes, delicious, but it still wants a year or two. And then one day you open a bottle and realize that it was better a year or two ago. That, I'm afraid, is life.

But it also depends on what you yourself consider to be its peak. Some people always like their wine young; others always like it rather old. Each will think the other is totally wrong and missing the point. The French tend to like their wine much younger than the English, to the bafflement of both. American taste is increasingly for youthful wine.

■ **A good mature wine** *does not have a flavor of age but rather of quality.*

97

A QUICK GUIDE TO SLOW AGING

CALIFORNIAN WINES	Age only top wines
RED BORDEAUX	Always age, except the simplest wines
WHITE BORDEAUX	Age top wines, particularly Sauternes
RED BURGUNDY	Age top wines
WHITE BURGUNDY	Age top wines
CHAMPAGNE	Always age; even non-vintage is better with another six months
GERMAN WINES	Age top wines
ITALIAN REDS	Age top red wines
SPANISH REDS	Usually no need to age: They're released ready to drink
PORT	Age vintage Port only
AUSTRALIAN WINES	Age only top wines
NEW ZEALAND WINES	Don't age
CHILEAN WINES	Age only top red wines
SOUTH AFRICAN WINES	Age very top wines a bit

(For more details on these wines, see Part Four.)

■ **Only the best** *of Californian wines should be left to age.*

■ **Spanish red wines** *grown in vineyards, like this one in* Castilla y León, *are most enjoyable in their youth.*

■ **Only the top** *Chilean wines, like this Seña, are worth keeping.*

Off-ness

WINE CAN TASTE wrong because it is unbalanced – too acidic, too oaky, too tannic, too alcoholic. But while these inadequacies are indicative of badly judged winemaking, they are not the sort of faults we are talking about here. Wine faults suggest there is something actually wrong with the wine; they are the reasons you might send a wine back in a restaurant. To take an analogy from apples, you might not have a high opinion of the flavor of Golden Delicious, but you would only describe one as faulty if it were bruised or rotten or maggoty.

■ **Just one sniff** *and the smell will reveal whether your wine is badly oxidized.*

Wine faults

Wine faults can be as simple as oxidation – a lack of fruit and freshness, and sometimes a browning of color, resulting from over-exposure to oxygen – or they can be much more complicated. The most important thing is to be able to spot when a wine is faulty, and not to confuse faults with other non-faulty aromas and flavors.

A wine should smell and taste fresh and clean. If it smells musty or stale, or of drains, it is faulty.

Faults are generally obvious to the nose. If a wine is badly oxidized, one sniff is all you need. But remember that faulty wines are not bad for your health; only for your enjoyment.

Why some wines taste like vinegar and others smell like unused attics

We've mentioned vinegary wines before, in the context of acidity: They are contaminated with *acetobacter* bacteria. These are precisely the bacteria you want if you are in the vinegar-manufacturing business. It's easy to spot an acetic – or vinegary – wine because of that vinegar tang.

More common faults are those that result in a musty smell, like the smell of an attic that nobody goes into. These can be caused by a variety of factors, from oxidation to bacterial infection from a dirty barrel (this shouldn't happen, but sometimes does). Wines that smell "mousy" may be affected by a type of yeast called *Brettanomyces*.

■ **On rare occasions** *wine can be infected with bacteria from a dirty barrel.*

Sometimes faults can be barely noticeable: The nose may just seem flat, without the liveliness and aroma that you expect. Perhaps the wine is slightly oxidized, or slightly faulty in some other way. But beware of confusing this with a wine that just doesn't have much of a nose anyway. Spotting marginal faults such as these is a question of practice.

What precisely is a "corked" wine?

Corkiness is one of the biggest nightmares of every winemaker. We've talked about cork – how it's impervious, neutral, and long-lasting, and therefore the ideal closure for wine. All that is true, but cork is a natural product, and things can go wrong with it.

The main problem is infection by a chemical compound called TCA (2,4,6-trichloranisole). This imparts a horrible musty flavor to wine, known as "corkiness." TCA occurs during part of the production process, and its incidence can be as high as one in 12 corks.

Obviously, that is completely unacceptable: Imagine if one in 12 cars were faulty, or if one in 12 hamburgers tasted disgusting. Not surprisingly, many top wine producers are turning to plastic corks as an alternative. Plastic seems to do the job perfectly well. It may not look quite as authentic, but if it's more reliable, who cares? Plastic corks haven't yet appeared on any really fine Bordeaux, but unless the cork industry finds a solution to TCA soon, they will.

■ **Corks are often** *to blame for spoiling the flavor of good wines.*

But these are not faults

Beware of assuming that everything out of the ordinary is a fault. If, for example, you come across small crystals in the bottom of the bottle, or perhaps attached to the bottom of the cork, don't worry. They are crystals of tartaric acid, also called tartrate crystals. They precipitate out of wine over time, and they're quite harmless. Make sure you leave them behind in the bottle, though, as they'll spoil the look of the wine in the glass.

■ **Be aware of** *the specific lifespans of your wines, because if you leave them too long before opening they may decay.*

Pieces of cork floating in your glass are not a fault. They are not – we cannot stress this too strongly – the same as corkiness, or corked wine. Just fish them out and enjoy the wine.

A simple summary

✓ In addition to the basic flavors we looked at in the last chapter, the flavors of oak, tannin, age, and off-ness can occur in wine.

✓ The flavor of oak is the vanilla-and-toast flavor imparted by aging wines in new oak barrels.

✓ Old oak barrels are also used for wines, and can be more suitable for some wines. These do not impart the characteristic oak flavor.

✓ Tannin comes from the skins, pips, and stems of grapes, and is found in red wines. It helps red wines to age.

✓ You can't taste age itself, but you can taste its effects. All wines have a lifespan (of youth, maturity, and decay), just like cheese.

✓ The majority of modern wine is made to be drunk young, and does not need long aging.

✓ Wine that is off usually tastes vinegary, stale or musty.

✓ Corkiness, caused by a chemical known as TCA infecting wine corks during the cork production process, is a major problem. Such wines smell and taste musty.

Chapter 8

More About the Taste of Wine

WE'VE LOOKED AT THE MAIN COMPONENTS that make wine taste the way it does. Now we want to extend that, and look first at whether wine tasting is objective or subjective, and then at how flavors combine with less easily definable wine concepts such as depth, elegance, or finesse – how, in fact, to judge quality.

In this chapter...

✓ Let's be subjective about this

✓ You don't have to like everything

✓ How to judge quality

✓ Some tasting terms to use

✓ Giving wine marks

✓ Styles of wine

JUDGING THE QUALITY OF WINE IS A TALENT THAT GROWS WITH TIME AND EXPERIENCE

Let's be subjective about this

IT'LL BE OBVIOUS by now that the only way we can describe a flavor is in terms of another flavor. In that respect flavor is like color: You can only describe a shade of blue by comparing it to other shades of blue. And do we all see colors exactly alike? It certainly seems to be the case that we don't all taste flavors, or smell aromas, in exactly the same way. We don't all have the same sensitivity to acidity, for example, or to bitterness or sweetness. Some people demand more salt on their food than others.

We all have our own tastes

How much of this is due to nature and how much to nurture is more difficult to determine. Certainly a practiced wine taster will notice flavors at lower concentration than a beginner. But even practiced tasters can have their weak spots – particular flavors or aromas that they simply don't recognize unless they're obvious.

Some people – entire countries in fact – have a sweeter tooth than others. French wine drinkers, for example, generally like their dry wine to taste drier than their counterparts in America. Similarly, sulfur dioxide, the antioxidant used in almost all winemaking, is more readily noticed by some people than others. If the producer has been too generous with the sulfur, the wine will have a pungent smell of burnt matches. Some people spot it even in tiny concentrations. But we know good tasters who readily admit to being relatively insensitive to the smell of sulfur dioxide.

Trivia...

Even winemakers focus on different aspects and flavors, depending on their training. We know one who is swift at spotting faults in other people's wine, yet produces reds and whites that are so heavily influenced by new oak barrels that they all taste alike.

■ **If there is a smell** *similar to burnt matches from your wine, the producer has used too much sulfur dioxide.*

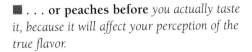
■ **Try not to imagine** *your wine tasting of apples . . .*

The scientific evidence

However, subjectivity is not the whole story. When wine tasters describe wines as tasting, for example, of freshly-cut grass, they're not imagining it. The grassy flavor of white wine from the Sauvignon Blanc grape comes from a family of compounds called methoxypyrazines – and just one part per trillion in water can be detected by the nose.

In fact, the sophisticated gas chromatography equipment used by the food and drink industry to analyze component aromas and flavors can demonstrate that the green pepper flavor sometimes detected in red wines from the Cabernet Sauvignon grape comes from methoxypyrazines, also found in peppers. The same machines reveal the presence of another family of compounds, monoterpenes, in flowers and in "flowery" wines made from Muscat and Riesling grapes.

Wine tasters are open to suggestion

If you give wine tasters two glasses of wine and ask them to describe the differences between them, they will almost always do so even if you've actually poured both glasses from the same bottle. Having been told there are differences, they proceed to find them. (We're as guilty as anyone else.) Here's another trick: Line up half a dozen glasses of white wine and, before you start, think of the smell of pears. Or apples. Chances are you'll find the smell of pears or apples on most of those wines.

This doesn't mean that every time you decide that a wine smells of mangoes or peaches it's just your imagination working overtime. It means that you have to try and empty your mind of autosuggestion and focus on the wine as objectively as you can. And be aware that you can easily be led astray.

■ **. . . or peaches before** *you actually taste it, because it will affect your perception of the true flavor.*

105

You don't have to like everything

INTO THIS COMPLEX MIX *of varying sensitivities and autosuggestion comes the question of personal taste. There are so many flavors in the world of wine that you're as likely to enjoy them all as you are to enjoy all the music played by every radio station in the world. When one of our wine enthusiast friends first tasted a wine made from the Gewürztraminer grape, for example, she hated its characteristic rose-and-litchi smell and flavor. (We'll be looking at grapes and their flavors in Part Three.) She could tell a good Gewürztraminer from a poor one – but she just didn't like the flavor. A few years later, she did, but that's another story; tastes change.*

Taste is a complex thing

■ **The Meursault grape** *creates a complex fine white wine.*

And remember that flavors in grapes are seldom straightforward: Wines tend to taste of more than one thing at a time. For example, we know another taster who dislikes the flavor of blackcurrants. The Cabernet Sauvignon grape typically tastes of blackcurrants, so does he therefore hate all wines made from Cabernet Sauvignon? It would be unfortunate if he did: there are an awful lot of them about. But in fact he loves Cabernet Sauvignon, because the flavor of blackcurrants is tempered by other flavors.

You will inevitably come across wines that you know are perfectly good, yet you just don't like the flavor. Don't worry. Judging the quality of a wine, and deciding whether or not you personally like it, are not necessarily the same thing.

Don't fear that you'll look ignorant if you admit to not liking a wine. "It's a good wine, but it's not for me," is a perfectly reasonable comment.

How to judge quality

The easy answer is that wine quality is the sum total of everything we've looked at so far: fruit, acidity, alcohol, sweetness or dryness, oak, tannin, maturity, and an absence of faults. Inevitably, it's not quite that simple.

Is more always better?

Structure and balance have a great deal to do with quality. Concentration and weight, curiously, have less. That doesn't mean that they don't matter: all good wines are concentrated in flavor. The last thing you want is something wishy-washy and *dilute*. But don't be seduced into thinking that because some oak in, say, a Chardonnay, can be a good thing, more is better. It's not. We're back to balance again.

> **DEFINITION**
>
> *A wine that tastes watery is said to taste dilute. It may have been made from grapes picked during a rainstorm.*

■ **Learn to tell** *the difference between "subtle" and "dilute".*

Likewise, a powerful red wine with massive tannins, huge fruit flavors, and 14.5 percent alcohol is not automatically superior to a lighter wine. The lighter wine may have better balance. While the first wine may seem astonishing when you first taste it, the second wine might be the one you choose to drink.

Some critics reckon the real test of a good wine is whether you want to finish the bottle. Never forget that wine is made for drinking, not for winning competitions.

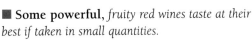

■ **Some powerful,** *fruity red wines taste at their best if taken in small quantities.*

Elegance counts but it's not everything

Elegance, finesse – call it what you will. Naming it is easy. Defining it is trickier. It's tied up with structure and balance, but it goes further, just as elegance in dress is more than simply wearing clothes that fit. It's a certain refinement and stylishness. You'll recognize it when you come across it. To call a wine "elegant" is high praise.

And yet wine can be very high quality without being particularly elegant. Some red grapes and wines are by their nature somewhat rustic and earthy, but at the same time they can have tremendous depth, subtlety, and complexity. There is more than one way for a wine to be high quality.

Some tasting terms to use

IF YOU'VE READ this far you've already become accustomed to a great many tasting terms in common use: Those referring to fruit and vegetable flavors, those referring to body and weight, and those referring to structure, elegance, and balance. Even if you haven't yet come across those particular qualities in the wines you've tasted, we hope that you'll spot them when you do.

Now we want to run through a few more terms, which sound general but have very particular meanings. We're also going to look at whether these terms are used in a complimentary or derogatory sense.

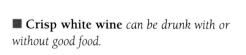
■ **Crisp white wine** *can be drunk with or without good food.*

Crisp, soft

Crisp wine is always white; you wouldn't talk about a crisp red. It means a wine with positive acidity and a certain briskness; refreshing and dry. It's probably a young wine. It implies good quality, though on its own it is nothing remarkable.

Soft can be a compliment or not, according to the context. In white wine it usually implies insufficient acidity, which is undesirable; but in reds it means an attractive mellowness and drinkability.

Hard, firm

To call a wine hard means that you find it austere and ungiving, with high levels of tannin and probably acidity. Young, high-quality reds intended for long aging in the bottle may be hard in youth, and will soften with age;

■ **If a wine has been aged,** *the vintage will be shown on the label.*

but modern winemaking styles mean that even these wines are less hard in youth than they used to be. Hardness is an unfashionable quality, even in wines for the long term.

Firmness is quite different. It implies a good structure, with balanced acidity and, in a red wine, balanced tannin. All wine should be firm; the opposite is flabby.

Closed, dumb

Some wines, before they reach maturity, go through a closed, or dumb stage. It takes practice to detect. Imagine such a wine as a tight flower bud, with everything present, but hidden. The nose and palate are understated – you can sense the fruit and the richness, but it's as though you're seeing them from a long way off. Such wines develop and emerge with further age and possibly after exposure to oxygen. To describe a high-quality young wine as closed or dumb implies no disapprobation.

Green, ripe

"Green" is a word to be used with care. On red wine it implies unripeness. At its worst, greenness can be detected as a nose of green beans or green peppers, and means the wine was made with grapes that were not properly ripe. When applied to white wine it may mean the same thing, but greenness on a young white wine can be attractive, implying youthful acidity.

Ripe is, of course, the opposite. To describe a wine as ripe is always a compliment. It means a rich roundness of fruit; a luscious quality.

Giving wine marks

THIS MAY SEEM *a bizarre thing to do: Do you give meals a grade out of 100? When you go to a restaurant, do you say, "Well, the sushi was a 95, but I wouldn't give the hazelnut torte more than 73"? No, of course you don't. And the truth is that looked at in any normal context, giving wines a mark out of 100 is weird, and misses the point.*

Yet wine critics do it. It was Robert Parker who pioneered the application of the American high school grading system to wine, and because he is the world's most influential wine critic (via his magazine *The Wine Advocate*), everybody else now feels obliged to do the same. Parker is adamant that his marks (anything over 90 is very good) should only be read in conjunction with his tasting notes, and he's absolutely right. The trouble is that it's much quicker and easier to quote a mark – and so wines are sold not just in the United States. but throughout the world with the marks of Parker and other leading critics attached to them.

Not by marks alone

All we can say is this: Don't go by the mark alone. Look for the tasting note.

When you buy a piece of meat, you don't just ask whether it's good meat. You want to know whether it's suitable for roasting, broiling, or stewing, and whether it needs sauce or French fries or what. It's the same with wine. You might buy a mark, but what you drink is wine.

■ **The variety of wine** *available today is vast, so don't rush in – choose carefully!*

Styles of wine

THERE ARE SO MANY *wines available today that it can be helpful to break them down into basic styles. There are young, simple, lighthearted wines; light, elegant, refined wines; more structured, long-lasting wines; bigger, richer wines; and massive, concentrated monsters. In fact, if you think in terms of Hollywood film stars, you'll have an idea of the sort of thing we mean.*

We've simplified things by choosing five movie stars whose characters made sense to us. We'll be referring to all five throughout the rest of the book, but when you are tasting and thinking about wines yourself, feel free to cast your own favorite actors or actresses whom you think have the characteristics we are trying to illustrate.

Shirley Temple wines

These are the lightest and youngest of all. They're not wines to be taken that seriously, but when you want something fresh, simple, and easygoing – perhaps for a picnic – these are your wines. They can be red or white, but either way they'll have masses of youthful, juicy fruit. Red Shirley Temple wines have low tannin, and little or no oak aging; whites are fruity and lively.

■ **Shirley Temple** *wines, although young, are fruity and juicy.*

Audrey Hepburn wines

Audrey Hepburn wines are a bit more grown-up. They're cool and collected, with impeccable balance, but plenty of fruit, too. Reds are fairly light, but with full flavors and the subtlest oak you ever saw. Whites may be oaked or not, but they are never, ever, over-oaked. Audrey Hepburn wines include those that are delicious young as well as those that are sensational 20 years later.

■ **Audrey Hepburn** *wines are not bursting with flavor but they are highly sophisticated.*

Cary Grant wines

Imagine Audrey Hepburn wines with a bit more muscle, a bit more beef, and you have Cary Grant wines. There's plenty of structure here, but you hardly notice it under the supple fruit and seductive richness. These wines are good at any age: in youth they're vibrant, in maturity they become complex.

■ **A Cary Grant wine** *will be sure to seduce you.*

John Wayne wines

Uncompromisingly big, and with something solid about them, these are John Wayne wines. They swagger into your glass and you'd better sit up and take notice – these are not wines to mess around with. They can be red or white: Whites have lots of toasty, buttery oak and high alcohol levels, and reds, too, have been responsible for the depredation of several oak forests. They've got lots of tannin, too, but it's soft, rich tannin. These wines have a soft center, and lots of luscious fruit. They may look tough, but they're cuddly underneath.

■ **You don't need to** *be a cowboy to drink this wine; although tough on the outside, it is definitely soft-centered.*

Arnold Schwarzenegger wines

These are the biggest and beefiest of all. They're all red, and they're all bursting with tannin and alcohol and fruit. They win tastings hands down, because their measurements are just so enormous. Sometimes they can be a bit overdone, a bit bigger than anything you'd actually want to drink. But when they're good they're sensational – as long as they can keep their balance. They age pretty well, too, but they seldom get the chance: They're fabulous young, and people like to bring them out and admire them.

■ **Arnold Schwarzenegger wines** *are heavy and full of flavor.*

A simple summary

✓ Everybody tastes wine differently, and different people may be more or less sensitive to certain flavors and aromas.

✓ The flavors tasters claim to find in wine are not imaginary. Particular groups of chemical compounds found in wine are associated with particular flavors.

✓ You are not obliged to like every wine you taste, no matter how good its quality.

✓ Wine quality is above all a question of structure and balance. Concentration is important, as is elegance, but a wine can be high quality without being elegant.

✓ Be careful how you use some tasting terms. Some always imply approbation, some the opposite.

✓ Simplify the process of selecting the wine you want by thinking in terms of Hollywood film stars.

PART THREE

WHITE OR RED – THAT IS THE QUESTION

HANDLE WITH CARE

THIS PART IS ABOUT THE PRACTICALITIES of wine: How to know what to buy, how to buy it, how to store it, and how to serve it. These things need a little advance *planning*, but no more than you apply to your regular grocery shopping.

Just think of wine as something that you buy conveniently prepackaged and ready to drink. As we've seen, it comes in different *flavors*, but then so does food, and nobody has any problem with that. Later on in this part we'll help you get a grip on flavors by breaking wines down into basic styles. And as for serving: *just keep it simple*.

Chapter 9

Deciding What to Buy

Y OU KNOW WHAT IT'S LIKE. You go into a wine store, and you're faced with bottles of all shapes and sizes, from every place you've ever heard of and a few you haven't. There are wines from California, from New York State, from Tuscany, from Sicily, from Burgundy, from Champagne, from Rioja, from New South Wales, and from Marlborough. All you know is that you need a couple of bottles of something dry and white for tomorrow night, because you've got some friends coming round and you're going to cook salmon. It's a familiar feeling. It's called panic. But we've already seen that it's perfectly possible to break wines down into categories. That already narrows your choice. Here's how to narrow it down further.

In this chapter...

✓ First decide your budget

✓ Are you buying to drink or to invest?

✓ What sort of food do you like to cook?

✓ Don't get carried away

DON'T PANIC – CHOOSING THE RIGHT WINE IS SIMPLE!

First decide your budget

DECIDING HOW MUCH you want to spend on wine is no more difficult than deciding how much you want to spend on clothes or food or CDs, though if you've ever managed to keep to your budget on any of these you're more disciplined than we are. But that's another matter.

It depends on the occasion

Your wine budget isn't ruled only by the current state of your bank account. There's also the type of occasion and the people who will be there. Are you buying wine for a birthday celebration dinner, or for Friday night supper? Remember that you can buy many types of wine at all price levels, and while something simple (for which read "inexpensive") might be terrific to drink around the kitchen table on Friday night, the same wine served at a special dinner is going to look a bit mean, as though you wanted to save money and thought nobody would notice.

It depends on the person

Which brings us to our second consideration: people. There are, of course, plenty of people who really wouldn't notice. We're never quite sure what to give these people. Normally, though, we end up drinking what we'll enjoy, in the hope that, like putting on a favorite piece of music, it might spark some interest in their minds.

If it's the sort of occasion where you're going to push the limits in other ways, then push the limits on the wine as well. The wine should be in proportion to the food, in terms of expense and lavishness.

But you don't have to spend a fortune to get a delicious wine.

Trivia...
We asked an acquaintance, a successful lawyer, how much he would expect to pay for a bottle of wine for a dinner party. His answer was "about $12." This man has an expensive car, state-of-the-art hi-fi, and regularly eats in expensive restaurants. Yet when it comes to wine, his budget is miserly, that of a marginal ambulance-chaser. On the other hand, a hi-fi buff might well find plenty to mock when he looks at the equipment on which a wine enthusiast plays his CDs.

■ **If you are going** *to prepare an extravagant meal, it's worth serving a wine that lives up to the occasion.*

The producer or region currently being hyped everywhere you look and regularly getting marks in the high nineties is not the only wine to serve if you want to make an impression. You've probably gathered by now that we're always a tiny bit skeptical of ratings on a hundred-point scale; they're a guide to what's hot, but not always to what's best to drink. The rule is to buy carefully but not meanly. Pay attention to producers' names, grape varieties, and, especially if you're buying wines from outside the United States, vintages. Read the tasting notes, not just the marks. And don't even consider buying the cheapest possible example of a wine. It won't be the best buy.

■ **An inexpensive wine** *is ideal for a light lunch.*

Are you buying to drink or to invest?

UNTIL NOW WE'VE only talked about buying to drink. But wine can be an investment as well, though it's by no means a certain one. Wine can outpace the stock market, but the fine wine market can crash, and has on occasion in the past. When that happens there's so much fine wine swilling around that you may have to wait years before the excess is drunk and prices begin to pick up again. So feel free to investigate the investment possibilities, but remember that your investment won't automatically make you a fortune.

Ask the experts

If you're buying to invest, there are several points that you must take into account.

When buying wine as an investment, take advice from a specialist wine merchant. They know the wines, and the market, better than you do.

They will tell you, among other things, that only certain wines are considered blue chip, and then only in certain vintages. If you're buying as an investment, only consider the very top wines from Bordeaux, Burgundy, and California, plus the best vintage ports, and only in the very best vintages.

All vintages do not perform equally as investments. Some rise early, and fast, and keep rising. Some trudge along at the same price for ten years, and then rise. Some fall before they rise. Some never rise at all.

You should only buy wines with a proven track record at auction.

Every year there are new wines, sold at megaprices, with promises of absolutely top quality. Be wary of these as long-term investments. The same pundits who give them 100 out of 100 when they're new can easily change their minds when the wines are five years old, and find them unexpectedly disappointing. If that happens, the best thing you can do with your investment is to drink it.

■ **If you're buying** *wine as an investment, get advice from a specialist wine merchant.*

Unlike paintings or jewelry, every wine has a life span, and its resale price will take that into account.

Vintage port, for example, seldom increases its price much in its first ten years. Only when it starts to become drinkable does its price rise – if it is going to. And once a wine is over the hill, too old to be drunk with real pleasure, its price reflects its value as a rarity, a relic – and that may be less than its price at its peak of drinkability. It may eventually be more, but you'll be dead by that time.

■ **The resale price** *of older wine depends very much on its likely lifespan.*

What sort of food do you like to cook?

HAVING SENT *off the investors, clutching their gold cards, to see their specialist merchants, let's get back to buying wine to drink. You can drink wine without food, and we do it all the time, but that's easy. What is far trickier is matching your wine to your food. We'll be looking at this in more detail in Chapter 12. What we want to talk about now is general rules about buying wine.*

Buy wine that goes with your diet

For example, if what you most like to eat is fish and salads, your consumption of tannic, red Napa Cabernet Sauvignon is probably relatively low. In that case, don't be seduced into buying loads of it, no matter how good the offer. White wines or light reds are going to be much more suited to your habits. Conversely, if you're passionate about steak and french fries and eat them on every possible occasion, you may not get through a great deal of light, white Pinot Blanc. It's common sense, really, and no more complicated than buying clothes. If you're a banker, you buy suits because that's what you wear every day. If you're a lifeguard, you may never need to buy a suit at all.

■ **White wine** *is the usual – but not the only – choice for fish.*

Don't get carried away

IN OTHER WORDS, *try to avoid doing what most wine enthusiasts do.*

If you go into a shop to buy a case of Chardonnay, then buy only a case of Chardonnay and come out. That way you'll stick to your budget and have the wine you need.

If you don't, you'll find yourself looking around a little while your case of Chardonnay is being organized.

You'll see a Sauternes and think – hey, that's a terrific year. Perhaps just a couple of bottles? And then you glance at the Italian shelves and see a wonderful Chianti or Barolo, and add that on. And then something interesting from Spain, and one of those promising-looking Burgundies, plus some sparkling wine because it's on sale, and besides, while you're here. . ..

■ **If your budget is tight,** *don't be tempted to buy expensive Champagne.*

■ **When buying** *at discount outlets, it's easy to find yourself carrying home more than you intended.*

■ **If you get** *carried away with your wine shopping, make sure you enjoy it!*

You'll end up with a carful. It was not what you intended. Yes, it's delicious, and no, you probably won't regret your buying spree. You'll always have something unusual to pull out of the rack, and quite often you'll come across wines that you'd forgotten you had, and they turn out to be wonderful. It's not that buying this way isn't fun. It's just that it's probably better to be disciplined and orderly about these things. Probably. We've never tried.

■ **Don't be put off** *by the number of wines available on the shelves, you'll soon find out which one you prefer.*

A simple summary

✓ Before buying wine, first decide how much you want to spend. If you habitually overspend your budget on other things, you probably will on wine as well, but at least you had a budget to start with.

✓ Keep the cost of the food and the cost of the wine in proportion to each other.

✓ You can buy to invest, but take specialist advice before you even think of such a thing.

✓ Buy wine to go with the sort of food you cook and the sort of life you lead.

✓ When you go into a wine shop, don't get carried away. Or, if you do, enjoy it.

Chapter 10

Where and How to Buy

THE RANGE OF WINE OUTLETS seems to be designed to confuse the beginner. Most enthusiastic wine drinkers use, at different times, supermarkets, specialist wine merchants, wine producers, auctions, and the Internet.

In this chapter...

✓ Buying at your local supermarket

✓ Buying at a wine store

✓ When to go to a real specialist

✓ Buying by mail order

✓ Buying on the Internet

✓ Buying at the cellar door

✓ A special case – buying at auction

✓ Buying wine futures

IT'S WORTH TAKING THE TROUBLE TO CHOOSE YOUR WINE

Buying at your local supermarket

THE WAY MANY *people buy most of their wine is at their local supermarket (though some local laws prohibit food stores from selling wine), when they're picking up the rest of the shopping.*

■ **Sometimes the bigger** *chains' buying power enables them to offer wines at bargain prices.*

It depends on the store

How much you might be able to expand your wine repertoire this way depends on the quality of your local store. Supermarkets often have good prices, but tend to limit their ranges to lines that sell fast and are heavily marketed. But they're usually fussy about reliability, and demand that quality meets a reasonable standard.

Beware the bargain hunter

A lot of supermarkets feature their wine selection, and aim to appeal to the wine buff. If you have one of these near you, check it out — particularly if it's the sort of store that's prepared to bother with wines of only limited availability. Others specialize in discounting.

Supermarkets can be great places to find bargains, but tread carefully. For every delicious wine that's being sold at a loss, there could be a poor one that sensible people would not buy.

Pros and cons

It's convenient to stock up on wine in supermarkets, and if you're pressed for time it's quick. The disadvantage is that there's nobody to give you advice. Some supermarkets give you information on styles and flavors via "shelf talkers" and quotes from wine critics, but others don't. And even when they do, they're asking you to rely on what might be the only favorable opinion anybody ever expressed about the wine. So, if you don't know what you're buying, supermarkets can be a bit of a gamble. But then, what is life without an element of chance?

Buying at a wine store

THE ALTERNATIVE is to go to a dedicated wine store. Ideally, the person behind the counter is the proprietor, and knows his or her wines; less ideally it's someone who knows even less than you do. If it's a chain of stores, the latter is likely to be the case. In any event, the same warnings about bargains and specials apply as in the supermarket.

Pros and cons

Advantages and disadvantages? Big chains offer good prices, and often a very good range as well, of both best-selling lines and more rarefied ones. They're great for browsing, and you'll probably end up buying all sorts of wines you never knew you needed. Slip a reference book (perhaps even this one) into your pocket when you go. Nobody will mind you checking vintages and styles, and in fact you'll probably meet lots of new people, because everyone will want to borrow your book to check on the same things. In this sort of store you can come across wines you've never heard of, and they might be unmissable. Never reject a wine just because you've never heard of it.

Getting personal

Smaller wine stores where the proprietor is behind the counter are more personal, and can be more fun if you want to chat and get advice. Don't be afraid of making a fool of yourself.

People who love wine to the extent of opening a store tend to like talking about it, too. If you want suggestions about what to drink with a particular meal, this is the place to come. We've often heard people going into such stores and describing the menu for that evening. The proprietors go into overdrive, they love it. In a store like this the owner not only knows the wine, but knows the other wines like it that aren't in stock, as well. He or she may even have visited the vineyards and be able to tell you the name of the grower's dog.

■ **One of the bonuses** *of shopping in specialist wine stores is that the people who work there will usually know what they are talking about.*

When to go to a real specialist

BY A "REAL SPECIALIST," we mean somebody who focuses on a particular region or country, such as Bordeaux or Burgundy or Italy. They will go there at least once a year to see the producers and taste and buy the new vintage; they will have wines that nobody else has and can describe the soil in a particular vineyard and tell you whether it faces south or southwest. Not only do they know the name of the owner's dog, but they probably have one of its puppies.

■ **Look out for specialist** *stores that focus on wines from particular regions.*

When a region is your passion

The time to go to a real specialist is when you're heavily into a particular region and are prepared to pay top price for the very best wines that region has to offer. Single vineyard Barolo? *Grand Cru* Burgundy from top producers? *First growth* Bordeaux? You probably won't find wines like these at your local supermarket – or if you do, they could well be from vintages nobody wants. At a serious specialist, you will get serious advice from someone who really knows what they're talking about in detail.

Be prepared to pay

And you'll pay for it. Prices are unlikely to be excessive – the wine business is too competitive for that – but top-of-the-range wines cost a lot of money, and if your specialist merchant doesn't take them, another merchant in Tokyo or Sydney or Frankfurt will. When demand exceeds supply there's no room for discounting.

Of course, your serious wine specialist may be an all-round wine merchant as well, with lots of everyday wines.

This sort of store can be ideal if you want to trade up gradually, and get good advice on the way. And here's a tip: Never be afraid to ask questions. You won't get put down. The wine trade is not nearly as snooty as it's made out to be. In fact, merchants are generally delighted to be dealing with somebody who is taking an interest.

Buying by mail order

THIS IS NOT ALWAYS POSSIBLE in the United States, but where local *laws permit, it's the perfect way of accessing all sorts of small specialist operations that just happen to be based at the other end of the country.*

Pros and cons

The minimum order is usually for one case of 12 bottles, which may often be mixed, and delivery is generally charged at cost for orders of just a case or two. Bigger orders may be delivered free.

The disadvantages are that you have to buy a lot of wine at a time. The advantages are numerous: You have the pick of the world's wines – obviously there's no limit to the number of merchants with whom you can deal. Ordering is no longer literally by mail: E-mail, fax, or telephone is quicker and easier. And advice is always available at the end of the telephone.

■ **When buying by mail,** *it's worth looking for firms that offer mixed cases.*

Buying on the Internet

LIKE EVERYTHING ELSE on the Internet, this is a rapidly expanding way of buying wine. All sorts of producers, auctioneers, existing merchants, and newly launched firms are now getting involved. In many ways it's just like buying by mail order, in that you choose your wines, pay, and wait for them to be delivered. It also means that if you want a particular wine that is in short supply, you have stockists all over the country at your fingertips. Indeed, if it's a very special wine, you have merchants all over the world; though if you locate your rare red Burgundy in Sydney or Tokyo you'd better be sure it's worth the cost of shipping.

Do you need a lot of wine?

How much advice you get, buying this way, is pretty much up to you. Lots of merchants' web sites give information about the wines they sell; lots have the facility for you to ask questions and get answers. But because you have to buy a certain quantity at a time (usually one mixed case minimum) it's only practical if you're prepared to spend that much at a time.

■ **Buying directly from** *the producer is a great way to learn about the wine you are purchasing.*

Trivia...

Go to Château Haut-Brion, one of the highest-rated Bordeaux chateaux, and you'll find yourself in the unromantic, unpastoral surroundings of a French suburb. Much of the land around used to be planted with vines, but became more valuable for building. There must be some back gardens here that could grow sensational, world-beating wine; instead they grow roses and geraniums.

Buying at the cellar door

THIS MEANS GOING to the producer to buy your wine. It's the opposite of the high-tech approach to wine buying, but if you want to get to know something about wine from the ground up and, quite possibly the people who made it, this is a great way of doing it.

You have to be there

■ **Sonoma Valley** *is one of the main wine regions within an hour's drive of San Francisco.*

First, obviously, you have to be within reach of a wine region. A lot of wine regions are close to major towns or cities: the Napa and Sonoma Valleys are just over an hour by car from San Francisco, the Hunter Valley is about two hours from Sydney, and the vineyards of Bordeaux are so close to the city of the same name that some of them are actually in the suburbs. So they're usually quite easy to get to even as a day trip from the city.

Beware of getting carried away when you visit a winery, though. Wines bought here can be like vases bought on holidays overseas: They don't always have the same appeal when you get them home.

Call ahead

Most wine producers welcome visitors, though only at the biggest can you expect guides who speak other languages. Usually it's best to telephone or write in advance to make an appointment – if it's the owner who'll be taking you around, he or she may not be pleased if you turn up without warning when they're busy.

Check with the local tourist office before starting out. They often have brochures that indicate what wineries offer tours and/or tastings, which require appointments, and which are open regular hours.

Tour and tasting

The usual format is a tour of the cellars and winemaking facility, plus a small tasting. And while you don't absolutely have to buy anything, you'll probably get the feeling that it's expected. So it's as well to do some homework first, and decide which producers to go and see. Bigger producers, with a special tasting area and shop and lots of merchandise, are the easiest to escape from if you decide you hate the wines and don't want to buy any. In smaller producers, where you're tasting under the eagle eye of the owner and there's no one else about, you need a pretty strong nerve just to say thank you and goodbye.

■ **If wine tasting** *in a cellar, feel free not to buy if you don't like the wine, but don't waste the producer's time.*

A special case – buying at auction

HERE YOU REALLY DO *have to know what you're buying. Wine auctions are held in major cities, such as London, New York, Sydney, Geneva, and Hong Kong, and over the Internet. The international auction houses (chiefly Christie's and Sotheby's and their associates) have customers all over the world. You can bid on the Net, by telephone, in writing, or in person.*

The bad news

Auctions are not designed for browsers. There may be a small tasting before the sale, but it will only be of selected lots. The majority of the wine sold at auction is sold sight unseen, and if it turns out to be corked or oxidized or too old, that's your hard luck. If you buy a wine from a wine merchant and it's corked, you can take it back. If you buy a corked wine at auction, tough.

A trustworthy auctioneer raises your chances of getting a good bargain.

Other points to beware are that you don't know how the wine has been stored. For fine wines that age a long time in the bottle the conditions of storage are crucial, as we'll see in the next chapter. Wines that appear at auction may indeed be from the cellar of a private collector, perfectly cared for since they left the producer; but they may also have come from much less perfect storage conditions, or just be a wine merchant's leftovers. Beware, too, of a growing number of forgeries in modest wines with fake labels.

■ **If you are having difficulty** *finding a specific rare wine, try visiting an auction as some are devoted solely to selling fine and rare wines.*

The good news

But if buying at auction were all risk and no reward, nobody would do it. The advantages are that you have access to a huge range of rare and not-so-rare wines at all stages of maturity. Some auctions are devoted to fine and rare wines; others are of much more everyday (but still good) bottles. And you can pick up bargains: an end-of-season sale, when the wine trade itself is not seeking more stock, can be a good way of buying a case or two of mature red at less than you'd have to pay in the stores.

What you pay

Because wine auctions are both frequent and sensitive to market fluctuations, the current auction price of a wine is taken to be the most accurate indication possible of its market value. But auction prices vary.

■ **Maybe that bottle** *of Bordeaux you've been hanging onto for years will suddenly become fashionable again and increase in market value.*

It all depends on market demand, and that depends on fashion, the state of the economy in New York or Singapore or Frankfurt, or half a dozen other factors. For example, a few years ago a red Bordeaux called Le Pin suddenly became the subject of a bidding war between a handful of customers in the Far East. Within a matter of days its price had risen to a staggering $36,800 for a case of 12 bottles of the 1982 vintage. Four days later, five cases of the 1983 and 1985 were bought for $83,360 by somebody else. The next day the same bidder paid $103,408 for ten cases of the 1988, 1989, and 1990. Yet not long before you could have picked up the same wine for a fraction of those prices. Did prices stay at that high level? They did not. Not enough bidders were prepared to pay that sort of money, and over the ensuing months the price subsided to less crazy levels.

Bear in mind that at auction you can pay totally different prices for the same wine on different days. It's the luck of the draw.

The fine print

Whatever you bid, you will probably have to pay a tax imposed by the auction house, called the buyer's premium. (Sellers pay a similar tax, called the seller's premium.) It is a percentage of the hammer price, and you have to be very quick indeed at mental arithmetic to work out the premium and bid at the same time. Much better to set your top price in advance, and work back from there to what your top bid can be. And having set it, don't go above it. It's all too easy to get carried away in the heat of the moment, and bid more than you intended.

133

Buying wine futures

WHAT ARE WINE FUTURES? *Quite simply, buying wine futures means buying young wine in the spring after the vintage, long before it is bottled, and taking delivery of it only a year or 18 months later, when it leaves the producer's cellar.*

Only certain wines are sold as wine futures. Red Bordeaux is the most common example, but certain others have followed Bordeaux's lead. You can buy Burgundy like this now, or the best Rhône wines. Top Australian and Californian producers also sell wine futures.

Why you should consider buying futures

The advantage is that you make certain of obtaining your share of wines that may be scarce or even unobtainable later. Prices may be lower at this stage: If it develops as a very good vintage, worldwide demand will be high, and prices may later rise dramatically.

And why you should take care

The disadvantage of buying wine futures is that you have to buy wine that you probably will not have tasted yourself, or will at best have tasted at such an early stage of its development that predicting how it will turn out in 10 or 15 years time is extremely difficult.

Wines can change dramatically while they age, and vintages that look extremely promising in youth may not turn out to be all that exciting after all.

Prices, too, can stay stable or even occasionally fall if economies are shaky. If you've paid a high price for your wine futures it can be frustrating to see that in spite of all the predictions there is a glut of wine on the market, and you could have picked up the same wine later for less.

■ **If you want to** *invest in futures, why not try one from a top Australian producer?*

If you do buy wine futures, make sure you buy through a long-established, reputable wine merchant. If your merchant should go bust (perish the thought, but it can happen) between your paying for the wine and receiving it, you can have problems getting your hands on it. So ensure that you have all the paperwork that establishes your ownership of the wine; don't take anything for granted.

■ **Established wine merchants** *often provide a convenient and reputable service, and are your safest bet if you're considering buying wine futures.*

A simple summary

✓ You can buy wine from a store, by mail order (except in some states), over the Internet, at the cellar door, and at auction, or you can buy wine futures.

✓ Different sorts of wine stores have different sorts of wine. Supermarkets carry mostly best-selling lines; chains will have a more interesting range; and specialist merchants will have the finest and rarest. You can use all

types at different times, according to what you want. Each has its advantages and disadvantages.

✓ You can buy at auction, but beginners really should take care here.

✓ Buying wine futures can ensure that you get the wine you want, but it won't automatically save you money, and you may not want to commit so early.

VAVASOUR
1990 RESERVE
Cabernet Sauvignon/
Cabernet Franc
PRODUCED AND BOTTLED BY VAVASOUR WINES LIMITED.
REDWOOD PASS, AWATERE VALLEY, MARLBOROUGH.
PRODUCT OF NEW ZEALAND
12.5% Vol

Chapter 11

How to Store Your Wine

WE INCLUDED THIS CHAPTER BECAUSE we're guessing that just as you keep groceries in the cabinet so that you don't have to buy salt or rice every time you want to cook a meal, so you'll want to keep a supply of wine. And just as you wouldn't keep salt somewhere damp, or eggs somewhere warm, so there are ways of storing wine that are better than others.

In this chapter...

✓ The crucial points

✓ Which part of your home to choose

✓ What if you're really short of space?

✓ How long to keep it

STORE YOUR WINE CORRECTLY AND AT THE RIGHT TEMPERATURE TO ENSURE IT TASTES ITS BEST

The crucial points

FIRST OF ALL, *you don't have to have a proper wine cellar. If you have one you're extremely fortunate and we wish you joy of it, but if you live in a third-floor apartment you need not despair.*

There are just five basic points to remember in storing wine: It must be stored lying down, at as even a cool temperature as possible, in darkness, in reasonably humid conditions, and away from strong smells. Most of us can find somewhere on the premises that fits the bill.

If you plan on drinking it soon, you don't need to be as rigorous as if you plan to keep it for several years. However, even a few days of very hot weather can do irreparable damage to a bottle of wine, so it's worthwhile finding somewhere suitable even for short-term storage. For the sake of convenience we're going to call this storage place your cellar, even though it's more likely to be a closet or a garage.

INTERNET

www.goodwineguide.com

The online site of Robert Joseph's annual Good Wine Guide.

Lie down, now

Wine is stored lying down to keep the cork wet. If the cork dries out it shrinks, and air gets in; the wine then oxidizes. You'll notice that wine merchants keep their better wines lying down even in the store. If you think a bottle of wine in a store has been standing up for a long time (check for dust), don't buy it. It may be all right, but it would be less risky to buy something else.

(Incidentally, wines with plastic corks – of which there's an ever-growing number – don't need to be kept horizontal. Plastic corks don't dry out.)

Temperature

The warmer your cellar, the faster your wine will age. It may seem on the face of it that a warm cellar is therefore rather useful – you can enjoy your wines sooner, without that tedious wait. But this, we're sorry to say, is not how it works. Wine ages much better if it ages slowly, with time to develop complexity. Allow a wine to age too quickly and it simply won't be as good.

■ **Wine should always** *be stored lying down so that the cork stays wet and doesn't dry out.*

If storing wine in a cellar watch out: High cellar temperatures can actually damage wine, and make it taste cooked and tired. The threshold at which wine can suffer is about 77°F or 25°C.

Leave it for long at that temperature and you risk spoiling it. Ideally your cellar temperature should be around 50–60°F or 10–15°C. And there should be as little variation as possible from winter to summer. A variation of about 20°F or 10°C will be all right, but your wine will be happier if the temperature change is very gradual. Wine doesn't like sudden temperature fluctuations.

Conversely, don't keep it too cold. If you keep it in the garage or the garden shed, there's a danger it could freeze in the winter (wine freezes at between 18°F and 25°F or -4°C and -8°C, depending on its alcohol content). If it freezes, the least that will happen is that the cork will be pushed out, which is the end of your bottle of wine. Anybody who has tried to chill a bottle fast by putting it in the freezer, and then forgotten about it, will have discovered that if the wine freezes solid the bottle can break.

■ **Store your wine** *in a dark area, as it should not be exposed to sunlight for a long period of time.*

Let there be darkness

Leave your wine in the sun, and it will deteriorate. White wines suffer the most; reds are more robust. The effects of a period of sunbathing on a bottle of white are similar to the effects of a hot day: The wine tends to *maderize* and acquire a cooked, stewed flavor. Whites can acquire a brown tinge. Let's not exaggerate: this won't happen overnight from the effects of light alone. But keep your wines in bright light for a few weeks and you're running a risk. Incidentally, this helps to explain why most wine bottles have traditionally been made out of dark green or brown rather than clear glass.

Humidity

Humidity is good for your bottles of wine in the same way that it's good for your furniture: It stops wood from drying and shrinking, and it does the same for corks.

Trivia...

Early in his career, one of the world's best-known wine critics lost thousands of dollars worth of great wine that a friend had stored for him in an old railway car in his backyard (don't ask why). When the coldest cold snap in 30 years set in, he turned into the proud owner of the world's most expensive Popsicles.

If the humidity is very low, corks can shrink at one end even if the bottle is lying down. Humidity of around 75 percent is generally regarded as ideal, but little research has been done on precisely what levels are best. In most modern houses central heating is the main enemy, drying out the air, as well as keeping the temperature higher than your wine would like. Air conditioning is also a problem, unless you have a humidifier.

■ **Humidity prevents** *the cork from shrinking in the bottle.*

Humid is not the same as damp

However, the last thing you want is actual dampness. Some cellars, especially the traditional underground sort, can be extremely damp. The wine itself probably won't be harmed by such conditions, but the labels can deteriorate. Leave a wine too long in a cellar like this and you may find yourself having to guess at the identity of your wine. Cardboard cases can also collapse if a cellar is damp. If you're buying wine with a view to reselling it later you should be aware that wines with damaged labels tend to fetch less at auction than bottles with labels in pristine condition.

If you have a really damp cellar where labels tend to become moldy or to fall off, you can protect the labels by spraying them with hair spray.

No unpleasant smells, please

This guideline for storage is essentially unproven. If you store your wine in your garage next to the chicken fertilizer, will it pick up the smell? We don't know, because we've never wanted to take the risk. It is always said that you should never keep wine for long periods anywhere with permanent, strong smells, but whether these really can permeate the cork and affect the wine is, we think, unproven.

Certainly it doesn't seem to work the other way. If you go into a bottle cellar there is no smell of wine. Logically one would think that if strong smells get into the wine, then the smell of wine, which is itself pretty strong, could get out. It's up to you. Take the risk if you want to. We're not going to.

■ **Cellars usually provide** *the optimum conditions in which to store wine successfully.*

Which part of your home to choose

OBVIOUSLY, THE BIGGER your home the more choice of places you have in which to store wine. And the more rooms you have the more likely you are to be able to find somewhere that has approximately the right conditions. But even if you live in one room, don't despair: Wine is surprisingly compact. You won't be able to keep cases and cases of the stuff, but a couple of cases should be no problem. You will probably have to settle for conditions that are less than perfect, but then if your space is limited you're probably not going to be keeping bottles for years on end.

Keeping it outdoors

Let's start with near-ideal conditions and work down. A garage can be excellent, provided that it doesn't suffer from huge temperature fluctuations. If it freezes in winter and cooks in summer, your wine is better off indoors. Consider also the security question – if you keep your wine in any sort of outbuilding, make sure you can lock it properly. Wine is extremely stealable.

> ### Trivia…
>
> *It is sometimes said that vibration is bad for wine if you plan to keep it a long time. There is no scientific proof of this one way or the other, but we suppose that very old and fragile wine might suffer if you happen to live right next to a railroad track. For young wine it is unlikely to be a problem.*

Moving indoors

A favorite indoor spot for storing wine is the closet under the stairs.

This is only applicable if you have a staircase. If you live in an apartment with no stairs, or a one-story house, skip this paragraph. The closet under the stairs is dark, and both convenient and out of the way. Unless you live somewhere subtropical or arctic, the temperature is probably reasonable. Basements are ideal, but only if yours is generally cool, suitably dry, and not given to major temperature and humidity fluctuations.

Failing that, a closet in a spare bedroom can be good, as long as you feel you can trust your guests. (If their luggage clanks on the way out, run up and count your bottles.) If you have no spare bedroom, look in your closets. There may well be some space on the floor, or in a cupboard above, that would take some bottles.

The worst place to keep wine is usually the kitchen. At the very least it's going to be too warm for storing wine safely.

Acquiring the racks

Racks are the most convenient way of storing wine. We have a few corners with bottles just piled up in them, but the bottle one wants is always at the bottom and one has to take the pile apart to get at it. Besides, pile up too many bottles like this and the weight can be too much for those at the bottom. Result: broken bottles, a horrible mess, and a waste of wine. Racks are safer.

They're easy to buy. Wine merchants and home-decorating stores generally sell them, either ready-made or for self-assembly. If you're good at carpentry you could make your own, but be sure they're strong enough to take the weight. We know a wine lover with shelves fitted along the walls of a dark corridor: they're just like bookshelves, but closer together. That works well, too.

■ **When storing your** *wine, avoid putting the wine rack in the kitchen as it is usually too warm.*

Storage cabinets

If you're really worried about heat or temperature fluctuations, there are special temperature-controlled cabinets you can buy. They come in different sizes, but four- or five-case capacity is about the maximum. They're expensive to buy, but efficient.

Refrigerators are not satisfactory for storing wine. Even at their warmest setting, they're too cold.

Building a proper cellar

Creating your own wine cellar is a big investment, but perfectly possible to do. A spare room in the house or space in your basement or garage can be converted into a temperature-controlled cellar complete with racking.

■ **If you really love** *wine, you could convert your guest room into a wine cellar to store your bottles.*

Keeping track of your bottles

This we're definitely better at talking about than doing. If you have lots of wine in the house it is hard to remember everything you've got. Did you drink that last bottle of Sauternes, or is there another one? Is there any Cabernet for drinking, or is it still too young? Didn't I buy some Rioja a while ago? If so, where did I put it? Keeping a record of what you have can, in theory, eliminate these dilemmas.

■ **Create a** *computer file to organize all your wine data.*

You can either keep a cellar book, or have a program on your computer that does the same thing. You make a note of the name of the wine you have bought, plus the number of bottles, the price, date of purchase, and seller. Each time you open a bottle of that wine you note the date and the occasion, what food you drank it with and, most importantly, you write a tasting note. You note especially whether it was young, mature, or needed drinking up.

If all you want is to be able to locate your bottles of wine quickly and see at a glance what you have, then bottle tags could be your answer.

They're just tags that you slip over the necks. On them you write the name of the wine and the vintage, so you can glance along your racks and find the bottle you want without pulling out every single bottle to check the label.

What if you're really short of space?

IF YOU HAVE *a small apartment and a big wine collection, or if you just have nowhere suitable at home to keep your wine, it's time to investigate storing it with your wine merchant. Usually only the bigger specialist merchants can help you with this. It means renting space to store your wine in a commercial cellar, which may be many miles from your home. The rent is not usually high – a few dollars per case per year – but it's obviously only worthwhile if you have a lot of wine, and plan to keep it for some years. Your wine won't be accessible at short notice, either. You'll have to give several days' warning if you want to move it, and you certainly can't take out a bottle or two at a time.*

If you opt for storing your wine with a merchant, make sure your cases are clearly marked with your name as owner. It's unlikely that your wine will go astray, but such things have happened.

143

How long to keep it

WE'VE SEEN THAT different wines mature at different rates, and that most wines we buy today can be drunk young and need no further aging. These are the wines most of us drink most of the time. They will probably comprise the majority of the wine you have in the house. You're unlikely to want to keep these wines more than a year, or two at the most. Keep an eye on what you have, and make sure you drink it before it gets too old. It's just like keeping food in your freezer: It's there for convenience, not because it's going to improve. Don't leave it there to get old and tired.

However, take the case of Champagne. It's worth buying even non-vintage Champagne six months or so before you're going to want to drink it: that extra bottle age helps to round it out. Vintage Champagne will need even longer, usually several years.

Have a plan

If you've bought a few cases of wine for the long term, you probably have some idea of when they might begin to be ready. Either your wine merchant will have advised you, or you keep an eye on vintage charts like the one at the end of this book.

■ **Most wines** nowadays
are intended for immediate
consumption; don't let your
wine age unnecessarily.

144

To find out if your case of wine is ready to drink, open a bottle at the beginning of the anticipated maturity period, and see how it's getting on. If it's too young, leave it another year or two before trying another bottle, and so on.

It means that you'll drink a lot of your fine wine when it's too young, but there's no way around that. If you want to invent a sensor that can detect the maturity of the wine without opening the bottle, we'll be the first to buy it.

■ **A cellar really** *is the ideal place to store your wine.*

A simple summary

✔ Wine should be stored lying down. The ideal place to store wine is somewhere cool and of even temperature, dark, reasonably humid, and away from strong smells.

✔ You can store wine either indoors or in an outbuilding such as a garage. If the latter, beware of winter cold.

✔ Wine racks are inexpensive and easy to buy. Proper temperature-controlled cellars can be installed in or under your house, but the financial investment is greater.

✔ Keep track of the contents of your cellar with a cellar book or on your computer.

✔ You can rent storage space in commercial cellars, but this is appropriate for long-term storage.

✔ Most wine will need drinking within a year or two. If you have wines laid down for the longer term, taste them at intervals to judge their progress.

Chapter 12

The Right Way to Serve Wine

IF YOU GET THIS PART WRONG, you can undo a lot of the effort you've put into choosing wine. But it's actually much easier to get it right than wrong. Trying too hard is the most common mistake. Keep it simple, and the wine will practically serve itself.

In this chapter...

✓ Glassware

✓ Corkscrews and other tools

✓ What temperature to serve wine

✓ When to decant

✓ Wine with food

✓ Serving wines in order

✓ Wine in restaurants

LEARNING TO SERVE WINE CORRECTLY IS FAR SIMPLER THAN IT APPEARS

Glassware

THINK OF ALL *the different sorts of wine glasses you've seen on sale. Cut ones, colored ones, trumpet-shaped ones, ones with tiny round bowls teetering on top of an impossibly long stem. Now think of a trash bin. Or better yet, a recycling bin. Consign all these glasses to it. Bang down the lid, and make sure it's tight. You won't be using any of them.*

A big bowl

When serving wine use glasses that are utterly simple.

A wine glass should have a good big bowl, not some little tiny thing that takes a thimbleful of wine. You want a bowl big enough to be filled just half full and still look properly generous. We've seen that the best way to release the nose of a wine is to swirl it gently in the glass. Try that with some of the abominations sold as wine glasses, and you'll have wine all over the table and all over you.

A curved rim

You also want a rim that curves gently inward at the top. This will help to contain the aromas in the glass. A flaring, trumpet-shaped glass will dissipate the aromas, so that you miss half the pleasure of the wine. Colored glass disguises the color of the wine and cut glass, too, makes it difficult to see the color clearly.

Do I need a different glass for every wine?

It's up to you. If it's a fancy occasion and you're going whole hog in every other way, you'll presumably have a different wine with every course of the meal. In an ideal world, different wines have different-shaped glasses. Sparkling wine is served in tall, narrow flutes, because wide saucers allow the bubbles to escape too quickly. Red wines generally benefit from bigger glasses than white, and fortified wines such as port are served in smaller, tulip-shaped glasses.

■ **Wine glasses** *come in a large variety of shapes and sizes.*

What if I want to start off with one basic wine glass?

Nothing is easier. Choose a fairly big glass – nothing too small or mean-looking.

Remember that the thinner the glass and the finer the rim, the more pleasant it is to drink from.

And make sure you buy enough of them: Glasses get broken, and when you want more the store doesn't stock them any longer.

■ **When choosing** *wine glasses for the first time, choose relatively big ones to suit a variety of occasions.*

A basic wine glass, of the best quality you can afford, will see you through pretty well all occasions. If you're fond of sparkling wine you may want to invest in flutes as well, if only because they hold less. Expensive sparkling wine poured into big wine glasses seems to disappear at alarming speed.

Corkscrews and other tools

WHICH CORKSCREW *you choose is a matter of taste and physical strength as much as anything else. Personally we prefer the sort that does the job with minimum effort and fewest broken corks. The Screwpull is good on both these fronts. Some people like the kind known as the waiter's friend, but they're not as easy as a Screwpull.*

Whatever kind of corkscrew you choose, make sure that it has a wire spiral rather than one that looks like a large screw. The wire spirals grip the cork better, and a solid screw will just rip straight through an old or poor quality cork.

Sensible gadgets you might need

There are masses of other gadgets on the market, most designed to be given as presents rather than actually used. Some people insist on using special foil cutters (we just rip the foil off with the point of the corkscrew). But some can be handy. Champagne cork grips can be useful to help remove recalcitrant sparkling wine corks.

■ **Corkscrews like these** *vary enormously in quality.*

*The most useful gadgets of all are the ones that
preserve wine once you've opened the bottle.*

There are two basic methods of doing this.
One is to remove the air from the bottle,
leaving a vacuum – if there's no oxygen in
contact with the wine, the wine can't oxidize,
and it will stay fresh for several weeks. The
other is to put some inert gas into the bottle. Being
heavier than air, this will immediately sink down and
rest on the surface of the wine, thus preventing contact
between wine and oxygen. Ask your wine merchant
about gadgets available to do these jobs.

■ **Cradles may look**
*impressive, but realistically they
are of no use at all.*

Gadgets you can live without

Decanting cradles that tilt the bottle for you and pour the wine into a decanter. Port
tongs that you heat up and apply to the neck of a bottle of vintage port to break the top
off. Little rings to slip over the neck of the bottle, or foil circles to roll up and put inside
the mouth of the bottle, to stop drips. Thermometers to check that your wine is at
precisely the right temperature. You really don't need these, and you shouldn't give them
to your friends and family as gifts. They don't need them either.

What temperature to serve wine

SOME PEOPLE *get obsessed with this, hence the availability of wine
thermometers. All we will say on the matter is this: Too cold is better than too hot.*

A cooling off period

It's true that different wines are ideally served at different temperatures. Sparkling wines,
dry white wines, and sweet white wines need about an hour in the refrigerator. Red wines
are best not at the traditional room temperature – the phrase was coined before central

heating became common – but somewhat cooler. If you're storing your
wine somewhere cool, just bring it to the table half an hour or an hour
before you want to serve it – unless it's midsummer or you live in the
tropics, in which case serve it at cellar temperature. Light red wines with
little tannin can also benefit from a brief time in the refrigerator – perhaps
20 minutes or half an hour.

CHAMPAGNE IS BEST SERVED CHILLED

And remember

If wine is served too warm it becomes too volatile and you get lots of alcohol vapors coming off. It will taste soupy and won't show at its best.

Conversely, if it's served too cold it will not be volatile enough, and will taste dumb and hard. Red wines served too cold taste unapproachable and harsh. But wine will warm up in the glass. What it won't do is cool down.

When to decant

AGAIN, THIS IS *a subject that causes people a disproportionate amount of angst. There are actually very few wines you have to decant. Only if the wine has a sediment deposit do you have to decant, and only red wines that have been in the bottle for quite some years do this.*

■ **Wine can be** *decanted into a jug and poured back into the – rinsed – bottle.*

Separating the dregs

If you're drinking 20-year-old Cabernet Sauvignon, it may well have *thrown a deposit*, and the idea of decanting is simply to separate the wine from the deposit. Otherwise, every time you pick the bottle up and pour from it, the deposit will get mingled with the wine. The wine will look cloudy and you'll get bits at the bottom of your glass.

DEFINITION

If a bottle of mature red wine has a layer of dark gritty solids at the bottom it is said to have thrown a deposit. The deposit consists of tannins and coloring matter precipitated out of the wine. It is harmless.

Get some air

There are other occasions when you might choose to decant a wine.

Red and even white wine that you want to drink, though they could probably do with a bit more bottle age, can benefit from decanting – the aeration helps the flavors to open up.

151

Alternatively, you may just choose to decant wine because it looks so handsome on the table. We often decant for just that reason. And while it's customary to decant red wines but not white, in previous centuries people often decanted white as well. So if anyone tells you you're wrong to decant a Sauternes or a Chardonnay, tell them you're following 18th-century practice.

Don't worry too much about how long before serving to decant a wine. We usually decant wine immediately before we sit down. If you're serving a very old wine, it's best not to decant it too early, anyway; fragile old wines can fade away completely before you ever get to them.

■ **Decanters** *can make impressive center-pieces for your table.*

What sort of decanter to use

Up to you. There are no rules here. Glass shops (and wine shops) often have good selections of decanters and wine jugs. Some have handles, some have stoppers, and some have both. Choose whatever you fancy. Antique ones are beautiful and can be good value compared to modern glass.

Decanter care

Rinse the decanter out after every use with clean water.

Never use any kind of detergent on your decanter.

If you find it's getting stained on the bottom with red wine, try squashing a cloth inside and pushing it round. Alternatively you can get little metal beads like ball bearings that you swirl round inside to get the staining off. Always let a decanter dry thoroughly inside before putting the stopper in. And don't leave a wet stopper in for long periods or it'll get stuck.

Wine with food

THIS IS ONE *of our favorite subjects. If you're a cook interested in good food it will become one of your pet subjects, too. You know the pleasure you get out of mixing flavors and textures in a dish? Add wine to the equation and you immediately widen your scope. It's like an artist discovering a completely new color.*

■ **The traditional** *rule to follow is simple – red wine with red meat and . . .*

The traditional rules

These are perfectly simple and sensible – red wine with red meat, white wine with white meat and fish, sweet wine with desserts. It's all to do with the weight of the wine, and its tannin.

Richer, heavier foods demand richer, heavier wines; light foods demand light wines.

The tannin in red Bordeaux cuts through red meat brilliantly, but clashes with fish. And sweet foods need sweetness in wine. Try eating pecan pie with a light dry Chardonnay and with a sweet Sauternes, and see which you prefer.

Traditionally, people also drink white wine before red, younger wine before older, and dry wine before sweet. Again, the reason is that wine tastes better that way. If you drink a tannic red and then go on to a white, the white can taste thin; go from an old, subtle, delicate wine to a young, vigorous one and the young wine will seem brash in comparison; move from a sweet wine to a bone dry one and the dry one will be uncomfortably acidic and angular. Most people will opt to eat steak before chocolate mousse rather than afterward for the same reasons.

So we would say, remember the traditional rules but don't follow them slavishly. There's a great deal of common sense in them. Food and wine are much more varied than they used to be, so there's plenty of scope for making new rules.

■ *. . .* **white wine with** *white meat or fish.*

153

The new rules

These are really an extension of the old rules, but with a slightly different focus. We eat less plainly roasted meat these days and more dishes that depend on a variety of flavors. That means not only must we take into account the flavor of vegetables and sauces when matching wines, but the flavors of Asian cooking, or Mexican, or Middle Eastern. All these have invaded our cookbooks and made them infinitely more varied. The flavors of lemon grass and cilantro, ginger and anise, chilies and cumin have to be taken into consideration.

Wine with spicy foods

Luckily, as our food has become more varied, so new wine flavors have come along to match. So there's no longer a problem drinking wine with Chinese or Japanese or Thai or Indian cooking. You just have to look beyond the traditional rules.

As a very general rule, very tannic reds clash with chili. But a lot of Asian food is spicy and subtle rather than blazingly hot, and if the tannins are soft enough the combination can be successful.

We find that rich soft reds often work well with Indian dishes, and with Mexican foods. Off-dry Riesling and aromatic whites such as Sauvignon Blanc are good with spicy foods, as well; indeed, Sauvignon Blanc is particularly successful with Thai dishes.

Round spicy-tasting whites, especially Pinot Blanc, Pinot Gris, and Gewürztraminer (we'll look at the flavors of these grapes later, in Part Four), are particularly good with Chinese food. Riesling is also excellent with Chinese food. Japanese dishes are harder to match, but Sauvignon Blanc is a good standby for sushi or tempura. Just lay off the wasabi – it's an absolute wine-killer. And be careful of new oak in the wine. A lot of Asian flavors are very complex and delicate, and are not improved by being cudgeled by too much wood.

Wine with vegetarian foods

Generally speaking, vegetarian dishes do not need high levels of tannin. You're looking principally at Shirley Temple and Audrey Hepburn wines, with a dash of Cary Grant. Arnold Schwarzenegger wines and a vegetable terrine are not going to be comfortable companions.

When you're eating vegetarian dishes there's no excuse for not thinking carefully about the flavors of the vegetables. Are they bitter, like Savoy cabbage or chicory? Or sweet, like celeriac or parsnips or sweet potato? Corn-on-the-cob is very sweet. Peas and broad beans are sweet but delicate. Green beans have a fresh, light flavor. With sweet vegetables, just a touch of sweetness in the wine – a barely perceptible level of sweetness, even – can work extremely well. Rosé wines can have this (white Zinfandel can be too sweet). California Chardonnay can have this sweetness, too. Or think about Pinot Blanc or Pinot Gris. For warming, wintry vegetarian foods with lots of root vegetables, think about soft reds such as Merlot. Tomatoes, on the other hand, have high acidity. We've never found a better match than unoaked Sauvignon Blanc for tomato dishes.

Wine with fish

If you eat fish, you can break one of the old rules and try light reds, providing the flavors of the fish are strong enough. Salmon and Pinot Noir, for example, can be a match made in heaven. The general principles, you see, are exactly the same as ever – think about the weight of the food, and don't overpower light dishes with heavy wines, or vice versa. And think closely about your flavors: Wine is just one of the ingredients with which you create a good meal.

GOOD WINE AND FOOD COMBINATIONS

ASPARAGUS	Sauvignon Blanc
CONSOMMÉ	Dry sherry
EGGS	Difficult to match with wine – try light whites or soft reds
MAYONNAISE	Light, dry whites
PASTA	Match the wine to the sauce: Sauvignon Blanc for tomato sauces, pesto, or seafood; soft Merlot reds for meat sauces or mushroom sauces
PIZZA	Light red with some tannin
PROSCIUTTO	Light dry white

■ **Sauvignon Blanc** is the perfect accompaniment to many types of pasta dishes.

FISH

GRILLED SOLE	Chablis
SALMON	Pinot Noir, Sauvignon Blanc, or Chardonnay
SCALLOPS	Mature Chardonnay, dry Riesling
TROUT	Mosel Riesling
FRUITS DE MER	Muscadet
FISH IN CREAMY SAUCE	Good, rich Chardonnay
TUNA	Pinot Noir, good Chardonnay, or Sauvignon Blanc (not too much oak)

■ **Chardonnay and salmon** is perfect for a light lunch . . . mmm!

Meat and Poultry

BARBECUES	Young, gutsy red
BEEF CASSEROLE	Rich Cabernet Sauvignon, Merlot, Shiraz, or Zinfandel
ROAST CHICKEN	Goes with almost anything: match the sauce or other trimmings
COLD MEAT	Good dry white is better than red
DUCK	Rich white
GAME BIRDS	Good Cabernet Sauvignon, Pinot Noir, Shiraz, Zinfandel, or Merlot
LAMB	Cabernet Sauvignon

■ **With a hearty lamb** *dish, try Cabernet Sauvignon or Shiraz for a rich finishing-touch.*

Desserts

FRUIT-BASED DESSERTS (with peaches, apricots, apples, strawberries, raspberries)	Sauternes, late-harvest Sauvignon Blanc, late-harvest Riesling, sweet Vouvray
MERINGUES	Good Champagne with bottle age
CHOCOLATE	Sweet Muscat, tawny port, sparkling Moscato from Italy

Cheese

Almost all cheese is better with white wine than with red

STILTON	Port
GOAT'S CHEESE	Sauvignon Blanc
ROCQUEFORT	Sauternes
BRIE	Not-too-oaky Chardonnay, or young Merlot
CHEDDAR	Cabernet Sauvignon

■ **Sauternes, when served** *with Rocquefort, creates the perfect after-dinner treat.*

Serving wines in order

WE'VE ALREADY *touched on this, but it's probably clearer now why the rule of white before red, young before old, and dry before sweet was ever invented. It wasn't dreamed up to trip the uninitiated; a meal is generally better if it progresses from light flavors to richer flavors to sweet flavors, and so wine follows the same pattern.*

But of course we drink wine differently now. Lots of people like a glass of red wine before a meal. Does that mean they can't go back to white? And how literally must you take the young before old rule?

The answer is that you should take nothing too literally. If somebody wants to drink a rich red before drinking white with the meal, that's fine. Remember that a classic French first course is foie gras with a glass of Sauternes. You can break any rule in the book, provided you do it with style, and it tastes good.

Wine in restaurants

CHOOSING WINE *to serve at home is one thing. Choosing in a restaurant, when perhaps four people are all eating different things and the wine list is limited, is another thing altogether.*

SAUTERNES GOES VERY WELL WITH CHEESE

■ **Don't spend too** *much time deliberating over the wine list. It is best to allocate someone with the role of wine chooser!*

157

Choosing from a wine list

The first point is that somebody has to be appointed, or appoint themselves, the Official Chooser of the Wine.

What you can't do in a restaurant is hand the wine list to everybody in turn and ask them what they'd like. This is no time for democracy.

Instead, ask them to decide what they're eating, and then ask them to tell you. And remember, if you want to order two or three or four different wines and have them all open at the same time, for different people to drink with different courses, that's fine. It's often more fun that way than trying to find one wine that will suit everybody.

A wine problem to solve

So let's suppose, out of our imaginary foursome, that one person is kicking off with duck, and then having roasted cod, and can't drink red wine. Another is having chicken liver salad, then fennel risotto, and will only drink red wine. Another is having pasta with pesto, then lamb. You, choosing the wine, think you're going to have a nervous breakdown, followed by roasted red peppers and then venison.

Easy. Here's what you do. The venison and the lamb demand a decent red – perhaps a good Cabernet Sauvignon. That will deal with the chicken liver eater as well. The red peppers and the pesto will be terrific with Sauvignon Blanc. If you get one with just a touch of oak it'll be all right with the duck, too. You get a bottle of each, and when they're gone, you get some more.

■ **If everyone is having** *completely different meals, order combinations of reds and whites to meet each individual's needs.*

Ask advice

The modern habit of listing wines by grape variety has made life a great deal easier for the Official Chooser of the Wine. It's true that lots of traditional restaurants still don't do this, and you have to remember the differences between, say, Nuits-St-Georges and Châteauneuf-du-Pape. But that is what wine waiters are there for. They're paid a salary – so make them do more than just hand you the wine list.

■ **Don't be afraid** to return a wine you think is faulty.

A good wine waiter has tasted the wines on his or her list, and can advise you on which ones will go with the dishes you have chosen.

The wine waiter should always suggest wines at a range of prices, not just expensive ones, and he or she should never, ever be patronizing or suggest that you don't know what you're doing.

Sadly, good wine waiters are probably in the minority. In that case, don't worry, because by the time you've read this book you'll know more than they do anyway. And if you've got a really dud waiter, don't give a tip.

The wine ritual

When the waiter brings your bottle, it should be presented to you so that you can check the label. Make sure it's the wine you ordered, and that the vintage is the one you ordered. Lots of restaurants don't bother to change the wine list when they run out of a vintage. If it's the wrong vintage, say so. If you don't want the vintage they're offering – perhaps it's too young, or not such a good year – ask for the wine list back, and choose something else.

■ **If the waiter doesn't** *bring the wine that you ordered, be sure to reject it and ask for the original bottle.*

> ### Trivia...
> *We've talked about good and bad wine waiters, but there are even worse ones. We came across one once who, when we sent the wine back (it was dreadful), apologized, took the bottle away, and brought the same bottle back, with a great show of uncorking it as he approached. Not surprisingly, it tasted exactly the same.*

The waiter will uncork the wine in front of you and pour a little into a glass for you to taste. Here's where you put your knowledge of tasting into practice. Swirl it around and sniff it. It doesn't matter if it's a wine you've never tasted before: you're checking for faults. It should smell clean and sound. Take a mouthful; it should taste clean and sound, as well. If it does, tell the waiter it's okay and she'll pour it. But if it doesn't, what then?

■ **Wine has long been** *the perfect accompaniment to an excellent meal, often represented as a serene element of romantic scenes.*

How to send it back

What you don't want to do is throw your weight around and spoil the evening for everyone else. Just say, "I think we've got a problem here. This smells extremely musty (or whatever)." A good wine waiter will then taste the wine and, if it's faulty, will apologize and get another bottle. A bad wine waiter will argue and tell you you're wrong. Usually sending a faulty bottle back is no problem, providing that you do it with courtesy. If the waiter makes it into a problem, remember that you have the final word, in the form of the tip (or lack of).

■ **Wine always tastes** *better when it is served at the correct temperature.*

A simple summary

✓ Glasses should be as simple as possible: no cutting, no colors, no fancy shapes.

✓ Some corkscrews are easier to use than others. Screwpulls are pretty idiot-proof, which is why we like them.

✓ Gadgets for preserving half-drunk bottles of wine are extremely useful. They work by preventing contact between the wine and the oxygen that will damage it.

✓ Serving temperatures should be lower for white wines than for red.

✓ To serve a wine too cool is better than to serve it too warm.

✓ There is no need to decant a wine unless it has thrown a deposit. However, you may wish to decant a young wine in order to aerate it, or you may just decant a wine because it looks nice.

✓ The traditional rules about serving wine with food are red wine with red meat, white wine with white meat and fish.

✓ Remember there are lots of new influences in modern food, from Asia, from Mexico, and from the Middle East.

✓ Match the wine to the whole dish, not just the main ingredient. And match the weight of the food to the weight of the wine.

✓ The traditional order of serving wines is white before red, young before old. Because lifestyles have changed; this doesn't have to be taken too literally.

✓ Choosing wine in a restaurant is usually a compromise between what you would like and what's available. A good wine waiter will be able to give advice, and shouldn't mind if you send the wine back because it's faulty.

PART FOUR

PICKING GRAPES IN THE BEKAA VALLEY IN LEBANON

WHAT MAKES WINE TASTE THE WAY IT DOES

YOU MAY WELL BE WONDERING by now where all these varied flavors come from. After all, wine is only grape juice plus yeast. How can one wine taste of gooseberries while another appears to taste of blackberries and chocolate?

This is where you find out. In this part we'll be looking at the factors that give wine its hugely different *flavors*. They range from the particular type of grape grown in the vineyard, to the whereabouts of that vineyard, its climate and how it is cultivated, to the wishes of the winemaker, molding all these different *elements* into the final result.

AD
SUPERIOR
WINE OF ORIGIN COASTAL REGION
Bellingham
SHIRAZ
Vintage 1985

Chapter 13

The Grapes

T HE GRAPE VARIETY IS THE BIGGEST SINGLE influence on the taste of a wine. It's extraordinary that these rather boring fruits (wine grapes are generally less appetizing than table grapes) are transformed by fermentation into something so magical.

In this chapter...

✓ Grapes galore

✓ Fruity and soft, light- to medium-bodied reds

✓ The Bordeaux varieties

✓ The spicy reds

✓ Moda italiana

✓ National costume

✓ White grapes: To oak or not to oak?

✓ Sweet or dry

✓ The perfumed whites

✓ Other shades of white

EACH DIFFERENT GRAPE WILL GIVE A WINE ITS OWN IDENTIFIABLE FLAVOR

Grapes galore

THERE ARE THOUSANDS *of different grape varieties grown for wine across the world. Most of them are frankly not very interesting. Some have great potential yet to be spotted. Some are not favored by winemakers because they are tricky to grow. The result is that most of the wine we drink comes from a fairly small number of grape varieties. Some of these are grown in almost every winemaking country; others are confined to their native lands, but all of them contribute to the flavor of the wine.*

Now take a deep breath, because we're going to look at the grapes you're most likely to come across. We'll look at red grapes first, then whites. In each case we've divided them into the styles of wine they normally produce. We'll also be referring to the main places they grow. For more information on the wine regions of the world, see Part Five.

Fruity and soft, light- to medium-bodied reds

IF WE'RE THINKING *of film stars, we're at the Shirley Temple end of the spectrum, ranging to Audrey Hepburn.*

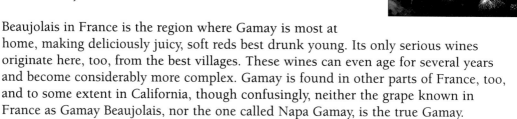

■ **Gamay gives** *Beaujolais its flavor.*

Gamay

This is pure Shirley Temple. Gamay does sometimes manage to make a serious wine, but when it does it invariably complains of being misunderstood – a bit like a composer of film scores who writes a symphony and then finds that nobody takes him seriously.

Beaujolais in France is the region where Gamay is most at home, making deliciously juicy, soft reds best drunk young. Its only serious wines originate here, too, from the best villages. These wines can even age for several years and become considerably more complex. Gamay is found in other parts of France, too, and to some extent in California, though confusingly, neither the grape known in France as Gamay Beaujolais, nor the one called Napa Gamay, is the true Gamay.

Dornfelder

Just as people produce new crossings of roses or carnations, so they produce new vine crossings. Most are unsuccessful; only occasionally does a new vine crossing turn out to make rather good wine.

Dornfelder is one such. It was first produced in 1956 in Germany, and Germany is still about the only place it grows. But that's not because it lacks style. On the contrary, it produces dark-colored, soft, chocolatey wines that are among Germany's best reds.

Pinot Noir

If you thought red wines had to be big and beefy to be really good, then Pinot Noir is the grape to convert you. It's the red grape of the heart of Burgundy, and its wine is so seductive, so silky, so perfumed, and so wretchedly difficult to make, that winemakers all over the world see it as some kind of holy grail that they must achieve.

■ **Red Burgundy** *is made from the Pinot Noir grape.*

A typical Audrey

Red Pinot Noir is the epitome of the Audrey Hepburn wine: Elusive, hard to pin down, and like nothing else on earth. It tastes of strawberries and game, incense and rotting cabbage, all bound together with the most wonderfully silky texture possible. At least, that's the ideal. Most Pinot Noirs fall short of this, just as putting your hair up and wearing little black dresses doesn't provide a sure-fire way to look like Holly Golightly in *Breakfast at Tiffany's*.

Where it's produced

Carneros, Santa Barbara, and the Russian River are among California's top regions for Pinot Noir, with Monterey showing some promise too. Oregon farther north, and New Zealand much farther south, have produced some impressive examples – but not as many as the hype might lead one to expect. The grape loves cool climates and just tastes jammy and cooked if you plant it somewhere too warm. In Australia, Yarra and Mornington are among the best regions, though new areas such as Pemberton are attracting interest from Pinot Noir producers.

Pinot Noir also makes good sparkling wine. It's one of the grapes in the Champagne blend, and is planted in most countries where winemakers want to make really good fizz.

■ **Every vineyard** *has a different terroir – the soil, climate, and slope angle.*

The Bordeaux varieties

THESE ARE SOME OF THE MOST *widely traveled grapes in the world. Because everyone, but everyone, likes red Bordeaux, everyone, but everyone, wants to grow its main grape, Cabernet Sauvignon.*

Because most Cabernet Sauvignon is better with just a little of some other grape added to round out its sometimes lean flavor, the other Bordeaux grapes, Merlot and Cabernet Franc, have come along as part of the baggage. And now Merlot is a star in its own right, too.

Cabernet Sauvignon

■ **Cabernet Sauvignon** *typically tastes of blackcurrants and cedarwood.*

Think Cary Grant. Elegance, structure, a certain debonair style – that's Cabernet Sauvignon. It's the most polished traveler possible. Plant it pretty well anywhere and it will make wine of at least reasonable quality, and taste recognizably of itself. No wonder growers love it.

The classic flavor of red Bordeaux is black currants and cedarwood, and that's basically the flavor of Cabernet Sauvignon. In warmer spots such as California's Napa Valley it is bigger and richer; in cooler places such as New Zealand it tastes a bit green, like green peppers. That's not so desirable. Australia's Coonawarra is as classic a region as Napa for Cabernet – you get beautifully balanced, minty-tasting wines from here. In Italy Cabernet Sauvignon is often blended with Sangiovese, and it takes spectacularly well to being blended. Chile, Spain, Eastern Europe, Lebanon, Mexico, southern France, Washington State, and just about anywhere else you can think of has Cabernet Sauvignon, either bottled on its own or filled out with a touch of something else.

Merlot

In parts of Bordeaux, Merlot takes over as the main grape in the blend, usually stiffened with a little Cabernet Sauvignon or Cabernet Franc to give it a bit more backbone. It makes a softer, more toffeeish wine than Cabernet Sauvignon, with lusher, plummier fruit, but it doesn't usually age as well and can taste dull. The two grapes together can be a perfect marriage, and more and more growers of Cabernet Sauvignon across the world are seeing the virtues of blending in some Merlot.

Thanks to the international reputation and low price of top Pomerol Merlots such as Chateau Petrus and le Pin, the grape is increasingly taking center stage in regions with very different soils and climates.

Washington State and California have some fine Merlots, as does New York State, while Chile makes some of the best moderately priced examples in the world, though many of these are in fact made from the Carmenère grape. Central and Eastern European Merlot is of a more everyday kind, and all but the finest Italian Merlot tends to be very light-bodied.

Cabernet Franc

You won't often see a varietal Cabernet Franc, although a few do exist in Australia, New York State, Washington State, and South America. The Loire Valley in France is where it is most widely grown for its own merits: The reds of Chinon, Saumur-Champigny, and Bourgeuil are what to look for. It has a grassier, lighter, more raspberryish flavor than Cabernet Sauvignon. In a blend – especially with Bordeaux – it adds perfume and elegance. The great Chateau Cheval Blanc in Bordeaux contains a lot of Cabernet Franc.

The spicy reds

THERE ARE SOME *delicious flavors here. Tastes of earth, smoke, leather, coffee, minerals, and yes, spice. These are substantial reds, ranging from John Wayne right up to Arnold Schwarzenegger, and they have rich, opulent fruit at their hearts.*

Syrah/Shiraz

Why the dual name? Because while in France's Rhône Valley the grape is known by its French name of Syrah, once it crosses to Australia it is known as Shiraz. Those are its two main homes, although it is rapidly catching the attention of winemakers elsewhere, and you'll find Syrah or Shiraz in Italy, Chile, Mexico, California, Spain, southern France, South Africa, New Zealand, and even Switzerland. The last is the biggest surprise, because this grape really does like a warm climate.

■ **Traditionally grown** *in France and Australia, the Shiraz grape is becoming popular in other wine-growing countries such as the US and South Africa.*

INTERNET

www.syrah.com

This site is for lovers of wines produced from the Syrah grape in the Rhône and elsewhere.

The variety of tastes

In the Rhône it is smoky and minerally; in Australia it becomes richer and softer, more leathery and blackberryish. Californian examples usually lean toward the Australian prototype, and it is proving successful in Washington State. Syrah/Shiraz ages very well, and good ones really need some years in bottle to show their best. This is not the same as the Petite Sirah sometimes found in California and Mexico.

Grenache

This is another heat-loving grape. Plant it where it can bake, and it will reward you with a smell and flavor that may remind you of freshly ground black pepper plus plums and toffee. In cooler spots, it turns out pallid and thin and far less attractive. It's found all over southern France from the Rhône down to the Mediterranean, and in Spain. Its love for heat recommends it to lots of growers in California and Australia, too, but it's not as fashionable as Shiraz. Its softer in texture, and tends not to age as well. The exceptions are some of the newest, best wines of Spain.

From the remote, mountainous region of Priorato, northeastern Spain, you'll find real Arnold Schwarzenegger Grenaches (or Garnachas, the Spanish name). These are heavyweights, full of tannin and alcohol, and with massively rich fruit to match. In some parts of Italy it is known as Cannonau.

Pinotage

This South African crossing between Cinsaut, a vine that gives soft, fruity, but not particularly distinguished wine in southern France, and the aristocratic Pinot Noir, also used to be grown in New Zealand. Now, however, it is rarely found outside its South African homeland where it can make anything from light, early drinking fruity wines to more structured ones. Few are of truly great quality, however.

■ **The Pinot Noir** *grape, shown here, was crossed with Cinsaut to create Pinotage.*

Tempranillo

Over to Spain, now. There is hardly a more Spanish grape than Tempranillo. It's grown all over that country, although different parts of Spain confusingly give it many different local names.

If you come across the names Cencibel, Tinto Fino, or Ull de Llebre, what you've got is Tempranillo.

It's a pretty classy grape, too: Its wine is dark, well-structured, and laden with flavors of spice and tobacco, and it forms the heart of Rioja as well as many other reds around the country. Its absolute peak of quality is in Ribero del Duero, where it makes wines that last for years. But it can make soft, simple wines for drinking young, too.

The odd thing is that other countries have taken so long to discover this grape's quality. But Australia's winegrowers have recently begun to plant it with enthusiasm.

Zinfandel

California's specialty red grape probably originated, as we saw in Part One, on an island off the Croatian coast. It's the same as the Primitivo vine that grows in southern Italy, and yet Primitivo has yet to make any wine as good as a top Zinfandel. Most vines have their own favorite corners of the world, where they produce their best wine – and it is often chance that leads them to be planted there.

Zinfandel makes every possible style from the pink and sweetish "White" or Blush Zinfandel, which should be drunk as soon as it's bought, to big strapping reds full of tannin and spice. The latter can age very well in the bottle; the best of them are among California's top reds. Outside California Zinfandel is making an appearance in Australia, and it's bound to spread farther.

INTERNET

www.zinfans.com

Enthusiasts of Zinfandel can exchange information here.

Mourvèdre

This southern French and Spanish grape produces structured, robust, gamey wine with a good dark color. In Spain it's known as Monastrell; in Australia, where there's quite a lot of it, it's called Mataro and seldom taken very seriously. California growers are beginning to plant it and take it as seriously as the French and Spanish; and rightly so, because it makes wine of considerable interest. It's not usually bottled as a varietal. Even in Bandol in southern France, where it must by law form most of the blend, there are other grapes in there as well. In California it is favored by the growers known as Rhône Rangers, because of their passion for the grapes of the Rhône Valley.

Carmenère

If you made wine in Bordeaux 150 years ago or more you'd be very familiar with Carmenère, because it was grown very widely there then. These days you'd have to look very hard to find a single Carmenère vine in Bordeaux: After phylloxera destroyed the vineyards they were replanted with Cabernet Sauvignon, Merlot, and Cabernet Franc, with Carmenère hardly getting a look in. Like the Malbec, which also used to be popular in Bordeaux, the Carmenère has been dropped because it seems to grow very unreliably in this part of France.

Chile's Carmenère

Fortunately, many cuttings of Carmenère were taken from Bordeaux to Chile and planted in the vineyards there.

Chile is awash with Carmenère, although until a few years ago it was all thought to be Merlot.

A lot is still sold (quite legally) as Merlot, but more and more companies are sorting out their vineyards and working out which vines are Merlot and which Carmenère. They look very similar: It takes an expert to tell them apart. But they taste quite different. Carmenère has low acidity and lots of rich fruit: Its best wines are peppery and lush. They are often labeled as "Grand Vidure."

Petite Sirah

This has nothing to do with the much more famous Syrah or Shiraz grape. It's mostly found in California, Mexico, and South America, where it makes dark, dense, spicy reds. It's not clear where it originally came from, or whether it is cultivated under a different name elsewhere in the world.

■ **Italy has** *grape varieties all of its own.*

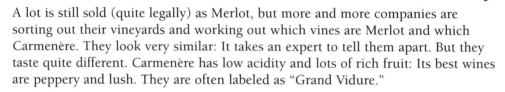
Moda italiana

ITALY HAS SOME *red grapes of sensational quality. Winemakers in other parts of the world are suddenly wild to grow them, and Nebbiolo, Sangiovese, Barbera, and others are becoming as fashionable as grapes can be. But it's proving difficult to make wines as good as top Italian reds – yet.*

Sangiovese

This grape is named after the Blood of Jove, and you can't get much grander than that. It's the main grape of Chianti, and is found all over Tuscany and central Italy, and in much of the south as well. It has high acidity and a flavor reminiscent of tea, black cherries, and sometimes plums. Add to that a good tannic backbone and you have a wine that can last for many years. It also makes simpler wines that are for early drinking.

California versions of Sangiovese are still at an early stage, and are often blended with other grapes to fill out the flavor. Argentina is now producing some good value examples and Sangiovese vines are being planted in Australia.

■ **Monterigioni, Italy,** *is a 13th-century walled town where excellent Chianti is made.*

Dolcetto

A northern Italian grape that makes relatively soft, early drinking wine. We say "relatively soft" because Italian red wine grapes are generally noted for their high acidity; Dolcetto's acidity is not as low as that. Its wine has delicious cherry fruit and a bitter twist on the finish; it can be quite tannic, and the best examples can mature in the bottle for several years. Most is made to be drunk within a year or two. A few wineries in California and Australia are succeeding with it, but it's early days yet.

Nebbiolo

Nebbiolo is northern Italy's most majestic red grape. It makes the fascinating, tar-and-roses-scented wine of Barolo and the only slightly lighter Barbaresco, as well as a host of lesser wines, more mixed in quality. Barolo and Barbaresco are extremely long-lived, dense, concentrated wines of enormous complexity, and there's no question that they are among the greatest reds in the world.

IMBOTTIGLIATO DA VIETTI CASTIGLIONE FALLETTO ITALIA
ANNATA 1985

Vietti

BAROLO

DENOMINAZIONE DI ORIGINE CONTROLLATA E GARANTITA
DELLA LOCALITA' ROCCHE
DELLE 6020 BOTTIGLIE QUESTA E' LA

R.I. 220 / CN
incisore gianni gallo

75 cl. e

14% VOL.
stampatore gianni cozzo

■ **Barolo,** *made from the Nebbiolo grape is regarded as one of the world's greatest wines.*

> ### Trivia...
> *Nebbiolo takes its name from the fog, or "nebbia," that swathes the Piedmontese hills in the fall, when the late-ripening Nebbiolo grape finally ripens.*

So it's strange that it's not more widely planted outside northern Italy's Piedmont region. Growers in both North and South America, and in Australia, are currently experimenting with it, and it is proving to be a difficult nut to crack. It's fussy about where it grows, and it seems loath to produce wine of the same quality that it does in Barolo.

Barbera

In its native Italy this produces good, sometimes exceptionally good, wine. In North and South America, it has long been regarded as an everyday workhorse grape best at producing large quantities of ordinary wine. But opinions are now changing, and more and more growers in California and Australia are taking Barbera seriously. It has good acidity and makes wines that range from light easy-drinking reds to extremely powerful and complex ones that take well to new oak. In California it is so far the most successful of the Italian varieties. Look out, too, for examples from Argentina.

Lambrusco

Hang on a moment. Shouldn't this sweetish bubbly wine, made from the grape of the same name, be categorized as a soft and juicy Shirley Temple? Well, no, it shouldn't. Okay, that's what an awful lot of Lambrusco tastes like outside Italy. But real Lambrusco is a very different beast: Low in tannin, yes, but dry, full of strawberry fruit, high in acidity, and with a pungent twist of bitterness on the finish. Exactly the sort of wine that goes well with a lunch of prosciutto and salami and good bread and perhaps a few olives. There's a medium-dry version as well, and a white version. All are for drinking young and not taking too seriously, but real Lambrusco is a much more interesting wine than most export versions. Specialist Italian merchants will know the difference.

National costume

HERE'S WHERE WE ADDRESS *the grape varieties that haven't yet been discovered by the international set; the grapes that are still confined to their countries of origin. That doesn't make them of lesser quality, only of lesser fame. And wonderful though Cabernet Sauvignon is, there are times when one wants a totally different flavor. That's when Portuguese or Greek grapes come into their own. For years the winemaking in some of these countries was pretty old-fashioned; over the last few years techniques have shot into the new century, and it's become clear that there are some terrific grape varieties here.*

Portuguese red grapes

The best known, and possibly the highest quality grape here is Touriga Nacional. If you've never heard of it, that's because it's usually part of a blend, and is only starting to appear on labels. Like Cabernet Sauvignon, it can benefit from being partnered by a softer flavor to fill it out. On its own it has great structure

■ **When seeking** *a different tasting wine, try one made from an unfamiliar Portuguese grape.*

and richness, high acidity and elegance; a slightly grassy nose when young, with spicy, herby fruit and a plummy flavor. It's one of the key grapes in the blend of fortified port wine, and the same blend is now being used to make unfortified table wines as well. Touriga Nacional ages extremely well but is also rich and lush in youth. Other key port blend grapes include Touriga Francesa, Tinta Roriz, Tina Barroca, and Tinto Cão.

Non-port varieties

Baga is grown farther south in Portugal. It is the main grape behind the red wines of Bairrada. Its keynote is plenty of tannin and plenty of acidity – and plenty of fruit to match. Big, gutsy wines, in other words.

Periquita, alias Castelão Frances, is grown pretty well all over southern Portugal and finds its way into umpteen blends. Sometimes you'll see it on a label. It has masses of cherry fruit and goes well with oak flavors.

Central- and Eastern-European red grapes

It's true that Eastern Europe has acres and acres of international grape varieties like Cabernet Sauvignon, Merlot, and Pinot Noir. But it also has lots of vines that are not found much elsewhere.

The problem in some of the Eastern European countries is distinguishing the quality of the vine from the quality of the winemaking: Good grapes can be let down by old-fashioned techniques in the cellar.

Hungary and Austria

The Kékfrankos of Hungary is known in Austria as Blaufränkisch, and so far the Austrian versions are in the lead, quality-wise. The wine is peppery and lightly plummy, and best drunk fairly young. Austria's St. Laurent makes rich velvety reds that can have considerable concentration; a crossing of Blaufränkish and St. Laurent, called Zweigelt, seems to have both the former's acidity and the latter's richness, a good combination.

Bulgaria and Montenegro

The Mavrud of Bulgaria is tannic and concentrated, usually quite rustic. Vranac, from Montenegro, makes robust solid wines that seem to suit oak aging.

Greek red grapes

Xynomavro, Limnio, and Aghiorghitiko are among the leading red vines here. The first two have high acidity, the third rather lower acidity, but all have good fruit and richness. They're usually blended, either with each other or with other grapes, for wines of considerable character.

White grapes: To oak or not to oak?

THIS ISN'T SO MUCH OF A QUESTION with red grapes. Most red grapes respond well to oak aging, provided that they have enough concentration and structure to start with. The decision on whether to age a red wine in oak is one of style and economics rather than possibilities. Aging in new oak costs more.

With white grapes the situation is different. Some white grapes go beautifully with oak; others are spoiled by it.

The flavors of some white grapes simply don't sit happily with the flavors of new oak, and either the flavor of the grape is swamped by the oak, or you get a feeling of two flavors fighting it out on your palate. Opinions vary, of course. Winemakers love to experiment, and just because we happen to prefer a particular variety unoaked doesn't mean that every winemaker does – or that you will.

■ **California produces** *some of the best Chardonnays.*

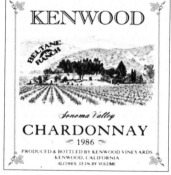

KENWOOD

BELTANE RANCH

Sonoma Valley
CHARDONNAY
~ 1986 ~
PRODUCED & BOTTLED BY KENWOOD VINEYARDS
KENWOOD, CALIFORNIA
ALCOHOL 13.1% BY VOLUME

Chardonnay

Finding somebody who doesn't like the flavor of the Chardonnay grape would be pretty difficult. Most people like the vanilla of new oak barrels too, and the oak goes with the Chardonnay as well as strawberries with cream. So finding examples of Chardonnay that have not been in new oak outside some more traditional Burgundy cellars and a few pioneers in the New World can

be pretty tricky. At its best, oaked Chardonnay has a lovely buttered-toast character. But like most things, the oak can be overdone. If all you can smell is buttered-toast then you'd be entitled to ask for a little more wine with your oak. Ideally, the oak balances and enhances, but doesn't dominate. And winemakers in Chablis prove that top-class Chardonnay can be successfully produced without any oak at all. One style is not automatically better than the other.

■ **In Chablis,** *Chardonnay is often made without using oak barrels.*

The taste

Defining what Chardonnay actually tastes like is more difficult. The truth is it doesn't have a terribly strong flavor of its own. Instead, it obligingly takes on the style indicated by its site and climate, and the flavor wanted by the winemaker. Rich versions are full of tropical fruits such as pineapple and mango; middleweight Chardonnays are nuttier and more cookielike; lightweight ones, especially those made with no oak at all, are crisp, even steely. It's an unusually wide spectrum of flavor.

To age or not to age

Chardonnay can be capable of aging for many years, but most examples are made to be drunk young. White Burgundy is the classic Chardonnay made for aging. It's a popular grape in sparkling wine, too. It's a major part of the classic Champagne blend, and is grown for sparkling wine in greater or lesser quantities in most winegrowing countries.

Sauvignon Blanc

This is another grape that can be made with or without oak, but if you want the pungency, the freshness, and tang that has made it so popular, then you have to eschew oak. The essence of Sauvignon Blanc is its green, herbaceous, gooseberry and asparagus flavor; its smell of newly cut grass and, in the more assertive (and less ripe versions), its smell of cat's urine.

■ **The smoky, flinty** *flavor of the Sauvignon Blanc grape is brought out by the flinty chalk of the best vineyards in the Loire; Pouilly-Fumé is the result.*

A cool grape

This benchmark style comes from France's Loire Valley and from New Zealand. Similar, though less pungent versions come from Chile, South Africa, and the cooler parts of Australia. This is a grape that likes cool climates. If the weather is too chilly, however, the green, cat's-urine character can – for many people – become quite offensive. Grow it anywhere too hot and it loses acidity and turns flabby. Oaked versions are often labeled "Fumé Blanc," especially in the United States, where California is a major producer. Washington State has arguably been more successful with it.

Sweet Sauvignon

Sauvignon Blanc also makes extremely good sweet wines – its naturally high acidity makes for excellent balance. Sweet Sauvignon Blancs, often called "late harvest" on the label, can have great intensity and concentration. It is a part of the blend in Sauternes, where it adds acidity to the Semillon, the other main grape used.

Sweet or dry

ACTUALLY, THIS IS A SLIGHTLY arbitrary distinction, because many white grapes can make sweet or dry wine according to the circumstances. Sauvignon Blanc, as we've just seen, can make sweet wine; so can other grapes we'll come to later, such as Muscat, Gewürztraminer, or Pinot Gris. We'll excuse ourselves for the inconsistency by saying that the three grapes we're looking at here are especially versatile.

Riesling

Some say that this is the finest white grape in the world, with more complexity and finesse than Chardonnay. It's an Audrey Hepburn of a wine if ever there was one. Yet in terms of popularity it's way behind. It dominates the best vineyards of Germany, is a star in France's Alsace, in Austria, and in Australia's Clare and Eden Valleys. In North America, Washington State, Oregon and New York state seem particularly suitable, but lack of consumer demand means that Riesling is not that big a player. In Canada it makes terrific *ice wine*.

■ **France's Alsatian Riesling** *is richly ripe and a favorite with critics.*

DEFINITION

If you leave healthy grapes on the vine until midwinter, and wait for them to freeze solid when the nighttime temperature drops to 20°F (-6°C), then pick them while they're still frozen and press them quickly so that the ice stays behind and only very sweet viscous juice emerges from the press, you can make ice wine. The Germans, who invented it, call it Eiswein. It is intensely sweet, with high balancing acidity.

A versatile wine

Riesling has structure, high acidity, elegance, complexity, peachy fruit in youth that matures over the years to a fascinating honeyed kerosene nose and palate. It goes well with food, particularly the sort of spicy East-meets-West food that is one of the current modes. It makes everything from bone dry to richly sweet (but never cloying) wine.

Riesling? No thanks

Why don't more people want to drink it? There are several reasons, and none of them are good ones. It's associated with German wines, and German wines are associated with low quality by those who do not know them – or who have been unlucky enough to be exposed to too many cheap examples. Riesling is not the easiest of grapes to understand; in youth it

■ **Erroneously, German** *wines are associated with low quality.*

can be closed, lean, and dumb, and German Riesling in particular needs several years to emerge from its shell. And finally, it doesn't take well to oak, and oak has been so fashionable for so long now that any grape that doesn't suit it has a built-in disadvantage.

INTERNET

www.r-for-riesling.com

Meet and chat with other lovers of riesling at this site.

But did you know?

However, if you feel like taking the plunge, here's some guidance on styles.

German Rieslings can be anything from absolutely dry to intensely sweet, though most occupy a medium-sweet middle ground, with high balancing acidity.

Alsace Rieslings can be equally dry and sweet, but have higher alcohol so they always feel weighty, whereas German Rieslings, with lower alcohol, generally feel much lighter. Austrian Rieslings are mostly dry and light. Australian Rieslings have a lovely lime and toast essence and are broader in flavor, though still with good acidity and good ageability, and New Zealand can produce some brilliant examples. North American Rieslings rarely have the complexity of any of these and, sadly, the tendency at present is to uproot the vines to replace them with Chardonnay.

Semillon

This underrated grape is the major part of the blend in the great sweet wine of Sauternes, and is often used for similar sweet wines elsewhere, also in conjunction with Sauvignon Blanc. Semillon provides lush fruit and a rich, silky, almost waxy feel; Sauvignon gives acidity and lightness.

■ **Australia's Hunter Valley** *has perfect conditions for growing Semillon.*

As a dry wine Semillon reaches its heights in Australia, where the Hunter Valley is the classic region, though Semillons from the Barossa Valley or the Margaret River can also be excellent in their richer style. In France most of the best dry white Bordeaux contain a large proportion of Semillon, again blended with Sauvignon Blanc. Elsewhere in the world it is found in small quantities in Spain, Chile, New Zealand, and South Africa, and in rather larger quantities in Eastern Europe. California has quite a lot of Semillon, used for good quality so-called *Meritage* blends, in mixtures with Chardonnay, and for rare sweet Sauternes-styles. So far, though, this is not a popular variety with most California producers and better examples are to be found farther north in Washington State.

DEFINITION

California's Meritage wines are Bordeaux-style blends. That means reds made from Cabernet Sauvignon, Merlot, and Cabernet Franc, and dry whites made from Sauvignon Blanc and Semillon.

Chenin Blanc

Chenin Blanc is so unfashionable that it makes Riesling look popular. And it's easy to see why. Grow it somewhere too hot, allow it to yield too generously, and you'll get a pleasant but not remotely exciting wine. Grow it somewhere too cool, so that it doesn't ripen properly, and you'll get wine that is harshly unripe, coarse, and unpleasantly green-tasting. It's widely grown in California for cheap jug wines that are perfectly drinkable but often completely unmemorable. South Africa makes better sweet examples.

A wine to work at

The magic happens when you get it just right. (The Loire Valley is the only place in the world where this happens, so far.)

Plant Chenin Blanc in the right site, in the right climate, and treat it like a serious grape without new oak, and it responds with wine that is at once honeyed, minerally and waxy, and full of apples and peaches and steel.

It is susceptible to Botrytis cinerea, or noble rot, and when thus affected can produce dessert wines of immense concentration. And they live, it seems, almost forever. The best dry Chenins can live a fair while, too. Simple ones, it's true, are best drunk within a couple of years. But dry Savennières, from the Loire Valley, really needs ten years to show much beyond high-tensile acidity. Vouvray is bigger and richer, whether it's sweet or dry, and also needs five years plus for the dry wines, and a decade or so for the sweet ones.

■ **Savennières should** *be left for ten years to develop its flavor fully.*

Such requirements don't make a grape very commercial. It can be an unfriendly wine when you first encounter it. But persevere, because it's worth the effort.

The perfumed whites

THESE GRAPES HAVE SOME *of the most exotic flavors you'll ever come across in a wine. These wines are seldom aged in new oak, because oak just masks the perfume.*

■ **Delicate, dry Muscats** *are best drunk young.*

Muscat

This is not just one grape but a whole family. They share strong aromas, but some have more elegance and finesse, some are clumsier, some smell more of roses, some more of oranges, some more of spice – or of all three together.

Some are white, some black. It's a grape that mutates astonishingly easily, too, so a vine that produces white grapes normally may suddenly decide to produce black ones.

Types of Muscat

Muscats can be dry or sweet. Dry ones are in the minority: You'll find them in Alsace, Portugal, Austria, and Australia, though they're rare everywhere.

Sweet ones are far easier to find. California makes some fine ones, as does Greece (especially Samos), Slovenia, and much of Eastern Europe. Sweet fortified ones come from southern France in the form of Vins Doux Naturels – something of a misnomer because these wines are not wines at all in the normal sense, and could hardly be called natural. Nevertheless, they are utterly delicious, light, and elegant. Richer heavier darker ones come from Spain. Really heavyweight fortified Muscats come from northeastern Victoria in Australia, where the wines are thick and viscous, brown and raisiny, and unlike anything you've ever tasted before. They're real Arnold Schwarzeneggers, and are, incidentally, the perfect thing to drink with ice cream. There are also Shirley Temple-ish sparkling Muscats, especially from northern Italy. Light, delicate Asti or Moscato Spumante is just the thing for a hot summer's day.

Gewürztraminer

Gewürz is the German word for spice, and this grape lives up to its name. Open a spice cupboard, with mingled aromas of cloves and cinnamon and ginger, overlaid with rose petals and lychees and even a hint of expensive face cream, and you've got Gewürztraminer. Sounds weird? It is. It also goes extremely well with Chinese food, and lots of other subtly spicy dishes, but it's not a wine that goes with everything. We wouldn't recommend it with steak, for example.

■ Gewürztraminer's *spiciness does not go with every dish.*

A rich Alsatian

Gewürztraminer's home is in Alsace, in eastern France, where it produces wines of a richness, almost oiliness, that is found nowhere else. They range from dry to ultra-sweet and botrytis-affected, and can sometimes lack acidity; Gewürztraminer needs acidity to balance all that perfume. But when it has acidity it can age for several years.

It's not widely grown elsewhere in the world. Italian versions are leaner, lighter, and less headily perfumed. German versions are seldom of remarkable quality, and while it is grown throughout Eastern Europe, it is frankly not very interesting there. New Zealand and the U.S. Pacific Northwest are far more promising, producing elegant wines with refined aromas and good structure. South Africa occasionally gets it right, and there are a few good ones in Chile.

Viognier

A few years ago it looked as though Viognier was dying out, even in its homeland of France's Rhône Valley. Now it's one of the most fashionable grapes around, though there's still not much of it about. What a turnaround.

In the Rhône it is grown in Condrieu and Château Grillet for wine that smells of apricots and spring flowers, costs an arm and a leg, and is best drunk young. New plantations in southern France are making less fearsomely expensive wines that have the apricot scent and flavor, though less of the complexity that makes Condrieu worth its price. South America, Australia, and California have some extremely good Viognier, and plantings are increasing.

■ **France's Rhône Valley** *is traditionally the home of Viognier.*

Albarino/Alvarinho

Another dual-nationality grape, this time growing either side of the border between Spain and Portugal. It makes light acidic wine with an elegant apricot aroma. In northern Spain it is usually bottled as a varietal, and commands high prices – especially when it has been aged in new oak barrels. In Portugal it forms part of the Vinho Verde blend, but is increasingly bottled alone there, as well.

Albarino is a delicious wine, but only the very best examples are worth aging.

Other shades of white

WHITE GRAPES ARE MORE VERSATILE *in their flavors than red. We've seen how white grapes can make wines redolent of roses and spice, apples and peaches, citrus fruits or butter. They can be toasty or minerally, buttery or steely. Now we're going to look at some grapes that don't have such obvious aromas, but are important for other reasons.*

■ **White grapes** *are more versatile than red grapes, giving wine a variety of flavors.*

INTERNET

www.anythingbut
chardonnay.com

This site is for those interested in unusual wine styles.

Pinot Gris

This is another Alsace grape that makes rich dry or sweet wine in its homeland, but much lighter styles elsewhere. It has a broad, sometimes oily, sometimes spicy, sometimes earthy flavor; with a few years' bottle age it can take on a mushroomy flavor.

Pinot Gris is an extremely useful wine for matching with food, because its richness and spiciness can cope with all sorts of spicy dishes.

Outside Alsace, good examples are mostly found in Italy (where it is called Pinot Grigio), Oregon, and on a smaller scale in New Zealand. Germany (where they know it as Grauburgunder), Austria, Slovenia, and Romania all have large plantings of it, and quality is often very attractive.

Grüner Veltliner

Austria is this grape's base, though it's also found over the border in Hungary, and in other parts of Eastern Europe. It makes a light peppery white that is the staple everyday wine in much of the country, though if yields are kept low it can make much more concentrated wine that ages well in the bottle.

Müller-Thurgau

Müller-Thurgau is not by any stretch of the imagination a top quality grape. But it's very widely grown in Germany and Eastern Europe for light, sweetish, vaguely spicy wine of no distinction. It's a crossing of Riesling and Silvaner, without any of the quality of either parent. It used to be the main variety in New Zealand, and New Zealand examples, like those from Oregon and Washington State, make wines with considerably more freshness than those of Germany. Müller-Thurgau from these places is about as good as it gets.

Baden
Bodensee
1995
MEERSBURGER
Fohrenberg
Müller-Thurgau

A.P. Nr. 033 30 96
Qualitätswein
Erzeugerabfüllung
Winzerverein
Meersburg eG
D-88709 Meersburg

WINZERVEREIN
MEERSBURG EG
SEIT 1894

0.75l · 11%

■ **Müller-Thurgau** *grows well in Germany and Eastern Europe.*

Pinot Blanc

This makes light everyday wine in Alsace, where it has some Brazil-nutty richness but less spice than most other grapes in this region. In northern Italy (where it's called Pinot Bianco) it produces easy-going daily-drinking wines, and it makes respectable wines in Slovenia, Croatia, Germany (where it's known as Weissburgunder), and elsewhere in Eastern Europe. In the New World it is generally ignored in favor of Chardonnay, which has a similar flavor profile but more glamour. Some California wines labeled as Pinot Blanc are good (including a few that are actually made from the Melon de Bourgogne, another variety altogether), and some are extremely good. It's always a bit of a Cinderella grape when Chardonnay is around, but it can be useful with food.

Silvaner

A light neutral-flavored grape that makes everyday wine in Alsace (where it is spelled "Sylvaner") and sometimes something more interesting in parts of Germany. In Franconia it can gain earthy flavors.

Trebbiano/Ugni Blanc

This is a remarkably neutral variety. As Trebbiano, it is grown over great swathes of central Italy, and quality-wise much depends on the particular clone: Trebbiano di Soave is considered much better than Trebbiano Toscano, for example. Trebbiano plays a part in most central Italian white wines: Soave, Verdicchio, Orvieto, Frascati, and Lugana are all more or less dependent on it.

As Ugni Blanc it is grown in southwest France for distillation into Cognac and Armagnac. It's used in the south of France for blending into the local white wine, but nobody boasts about it.

Palomino

This Spanish grape is hardly ever used for table wine. When it is, it's usually so soft and toffeeish and low in acidity that you wouldn't particularly want to drink it. The reason we mention it here is that it is the main, and often the only, grape of sherry.

■ **Palomino** is widely used to make sherry.

Allow Palomino to grow flor, the Saccharomyces yeast that in the sherry region lives on the surface of the wine and feeds on it, changing its flavor and its biochemical makeup; age it in wood for many years, fortify it, and it acquires extraordinary richness and complexity. You'd never think it from tasting that dreary table wine.

Chasselas

Once widely grown in France (in regions such as Pouilly Fumé where the Sauvignon Blanc has generally replaced it) the Chasselas is hard to find now outside Switzerland, where it's known as the Fendant and is the everyday white. Its flavor can be very neutral, yet good ones made with care reflect their "terroir" more than most wines, and can taste earthy or flowery or steely depending on where they were grown.

THE CABERNET SAUVIGNON GRAPE

A simple summary

✓ The choice of grape variety is the single most important element in the flavor of a wine.

✓ Of the thousands of grape varieties that exist, only a few dozen are widely grown for wine.

✓ Some grape varieties are used by themselves; others usually go into blends.

✓ Some grape varieties make many different styles of wine, others make just one or two basic styles.

✓ Fruity and soft, light- to medium-bodied reds can be made especially from Gamay, Dornfelder, and Pinot Noir.

✓ Cabernet Sauvignon, Merlot and Cabernet Franc are planted in most winegrowing countries for wines in the Bordeaux style.

✓ Syrah or Shiraz, Grenache, Pinotage, Tempranillo, Zinfandel, Mourvèdre, Carmenère, and Petite Sirah all make spicy reds.

✓ Italy has a range of great grapes: Sangiovese, Nebbiolo, Dolcetto, Barbera, and Lambrusco.

✓ Portugal, Central and Eastern Europe, and Greece also have grapes that are found nowhere else, and that give a distinctive flavor to their wines.

✓ Some white grapes can be made with new oak or without: Chardonnay and Sauvignon Blanc are among the most versatile.

✓ Riesling, Semillon, and Chenin Blanc are all just as good at making sweet wines as dry ones.

✓ Some of the most perfumed wines in the world come from Muscat, Gewürztraminer, Viognier, and Albarino or Alvarinho.

✓ Some white grapes make a virtue of their lack of obvious aromas. These include Pinot Gris, Grüner Veltliner, Müller Thurgau, Pinot Blanc, Silvaner, Trebbiano or Ugni Blanc, Palomino, and Chasselas.

Chapter 14

The Vineyard

G RAPES ARE A TRICKY FRUIT. They lull would-be winemakers into thinking they're very easily grown in wildly different locales – which is why you can find them in places ranging from Hampton Court in the cool and often rainy south of England to the sun-baked, near-desert conditions of Israel. But if you want to turn those grapes into wine that tastes good, you have to choose your vineyard carefully. The type of soil, the direction and angle of the slope, the average rainfall, and even the difference in the temperature between day and night all have an influence on the style and quality of the drink that ends up in the bottle.

In this chapter...

✓ Climate

✓ The slope

✓ Soil

✓ Vine growing

✓ Take your pick

CHARDONNAY GRAPES IN BURGUNDY, THEIR HOMELAND

Climate

LET'S START with the most important factor of all – the climate in which the grapes are grown. Like any other fruit, grapes need to bask in the sun if they are going to ripen properly. Really chilly places such as Alaska are simply too cold for vines and, after a cool, cloudy summer, even traditional regions in northern Europe can produce wine with the unmistakable "green" flavor of unripe grapes.

But just as sunbathers become dozy if they soak up too many rays, when grapes get too hot, the wine they produce will taste dull. The best most mouthwatering apples come from cooler regions, and much the same can be said for wine grapes. This is why the hotter parts of North Africa have yet to produce memorable reds or whites. The ideal spot for a vineyard might well be a compromise: The sunniest part of a relatively chilly region (the best slopes in Chablis in northern Burgundy, for example) or the coolest part of a warm one (say, Carneros in California or the Adelaide Hills in Australia).

Some like it hotter than others

Some grapes, such as the Riesling, perform best in cool climates; others, like the Zinfandel, need warm ones. Some are relatively tolerant of a broad range of climates; others, such as the Pinot Noir, are fussier, demanding conditions that are neither too warm nor too cool (which helps to explain why this variety is only found in very specific parts of any region). And the climate can vary widely even within the same region and in the same year.

Never assume that every wine from a particular year and place is going to taste the same.

But "cool" or "warm" is only part of the story. The weather can, perversely, be too steady. Florida may produce delicious oranges, but the absence of winter – so appreciated by the people who buy their retirement homes there – is no good for vines, which need chilly weather so they can undergo a dormant period. Even in places that seem to have more appropriate conditions for grapes, the word "climate" can be an unhelpfully broad term – like "health."

■ **Vines are dormant**
during the winter season.

Unexpected weather

For just as you can be consistently healthy or unhealthy, a region can have a consistently good or bad climate for wine. Chile, for example, has weather patterns that barely change from one year to the next. But, like people who suffer from occasional bouts of ill health, wine regions can have the climatic equivalent of a bout of flu – too much rain, or not enough, for example. They can, more rarely, break a leg – be hit by a hailstorm that tears the grapes from the vines – or even, very occasionally, lose a limb altogether – when frost conditions are so severe that vines die and have to be uprooted and replanted.

■ **The Napa Valley** in California, where frost can devastate the vines.

Fighting back

Severe frosts can hit vineyards in all of the world's most famous regions. Champagne, Chablis in Burgundy, Bordeaux, and the Napa Valley have all, at some time, been devastated by the effects of an unusually cold night. If you pay a visit to frost-prone vineyards in the winter and early spring (cold snaps can threaten vines until early May in the Northern Hemisphere), you may see oil burners, sprinklers, or windmills being used by grape growers to protect their crop.

Even when hail doesn't rip the grapes from the vines it can rupture their skins, leaving them vulnerable to pests, birds, or disease. The only way to avoid the injustice of these storms, which can create havoc in one plot while leaving its neighbors unscathed, lies in flying over the clouds and seeding them with pellets to make their hail fall elsewhere. Some winegrowers are unwilling to pay the cost of the airplane and pilot and, in Europe, where plots are often very small, the ones who are ready to pay quite fairly resent having to protect their tightwad neighbors. So these are generally good regions in which to set up shop as an insurance salesman.

The not-so-gentle rain

The climate can also be too wet – or too dry. An excess of water at best makes for grapes and wines with a diluted flavor and, when associated with warm temperatures, also increases the risk of rot ruining the flavor of the stuff in the bottle. Short of covering the vines in plastic (an expensive option that is used occasionally in Britain but is illegal elsewhere), the only way anyone has discovered to protect grapes from the rain is the one pioneered by Christian Moueix, one of the top wine producers in Bordeaux. In one very wet year, he hovered over the pickers at Château Petrus in a helicopter, which worked like a giant hair dryer to blow all the moisture off them and the crop. This option may have been appropriate for Château Petrus, which makes tiny amounts of wine that sell for hundreds of dollars per bottle, but we suspect it is unlikely to be widely adopted elsewhere.

Trivia...

The first person to make a broad analysis of the relationship between climate and wine was A.J. Winkler, a Californian scientist who in the 1920s devised a system of "heat units" to measure the average temperature of any region during the growing season. Today, Winkler's scale is still widely respected, though modern experts have realized that the difference between day and night temperatures can be as important as the average figure on the thermometer.

When vines get thirsty, they go on strike and the grapes stop ripening. In places where a lack of rain is a constant problem, irrigation systems are used, which range from the crude ditches traditionally used in South America to the computer-operated networks of pipes buried beneath the earth in California and Australia. The only drawback to watering vines – from reservoirs, rivers, or the snow-melt from nearby mountains – lies in the potential for overgenerosity, and the dilute wines it will bring. Think about adding too much water to a pot of soup, and you'll get the idea.

Irrigated wines

In much of Europe, where drought is a less frequent hazard (though one that may be growing because of global warming), irrigation is actually against the law. In such places, wines from irrigated vineyards are dismissed as being "industrial." In the 1990s, the illegality of giving a gasping vine a drink contributed to countless wines in regions such as Bordeaux being far less tasty than they might have been. Hot dry summers made for late ripening and for harvests that coincided with rainstorms, which diluted the juice.

■ **There are now** *more instances of poor-quality wine being produced due to irrigation being illegal in much of Europe, including Bordeaux.*

The slope

AS LONG AGO AS *the 9th century A.D., the emperor Charlemagne, whose territory stretched across much of modern Europe, showed a keen interest in wine (in those days mostly made by monks). On a visit to Burgundy, in the heart of his empire, he is said to have noticed that the snow melted earlier in the day on one part of a slope than elsewhere.*

He reasoned that the warmth of the sun was as effective in ripening grapes as it was in transforming snowflakes into water, and he declared that particular patch of vines to be among the best in the region. The vineyard was named Corton Charlemagne after the emperor and today, more than a millennium later, its wines still regularly win higher points when they are tasted "blind" against ones produced from grapes grown in nearby plots. The particular conditions of the Corton Charlemagne provide one of the earliest examples of a microclimate – a piece of land with its own weather.

Facing the sun

The rules of where best to plant a vineyard are quite simple. First, as Charlemagne understood all those years ago, and the makers of solar heating panels know today, an angle facing the sun (southward in the Northern Hemisphere, northward on the other side of the equator) gives your plants the best access to the available heat and light.

■ **The slope and aspect** of a vineyard will affect the taste of the wine produced.

So, some of the greatest wines in France and Germany come from vines grown on ludicrously steep slopes that call for near-mountaineering skills on the part of the pickers. Altitude, of course, also has a role to play: The higher up the hill you go, the cooler the temperature. Flat land can be a fine home for vines, too – after all, much of Bordeaux and the Napa Valley are remarkably flat. But it has its own disadvantages. The heavy rain that drains from the hills can sit in a lake on the flat land – and vines, just like human beings, don't like to stand around with wet feet. While vines grown on valley floors are sheltered from the wind, they can be at risk from frost, as pockets of cold air can often settle.

Soil

OPEN ANY BOOK on gardening and you'll find advice on which type of plant grows best in which type of soil. One of the reasons that bourbon tastes so different from Scotch whiskey is that the early American settlers discovered that rye and corn were easier to farm than the barley they were used to back home. Vines are less choosy, helpfully thriving on unfertile land that is often of little use for other types of farming. Even so, there are distinct differences between the types of soil favored by the different grape varieties.

■ **Although vines** prefer unfertile soil, different grape types prefer different specific soil types.

Chalk, clay, slate, or gravel

As long ago as the 15th century, the Duke of Burgundy issued edicts to outlaw the growing of the Gamay grape in the best vineyards of his region. Today, those bits of land are still planted with the Pinot Noir favored by the Duke, while the Gamay is used to produce the wines in the granite soil of Beaujolais a little farther south. Chardonnay and Sauvignon Blanc, for example, are both at their best on the chalky soil of Burgundy and the Loire, while Riesling produces some of its best wine on slate. The Merlot likes clay – which is why it does so well in the clay soil of Pomerol and St. Emilion – while the Cabernet Sauvignon prefers vineyards that are covered with gravel – which explains why part of Bordeaux is called Graves, after the French name for these little stones.

But there are more subtle variations, too. In Burgundy, where the best reds are made exclusively from the Pinot Noir, shifts in the earth have created subtle differences between the soil in small neighboring plots of land. Each of these plots has its own name and identity. If you look at a handful of earth taken from two that are only separated by the narrowest of tracks, you might find that one is slightly different in color, more granular, or richer in a particular kind of fossil.

Variations in the soil and the microclimates can produce flavors that are sufficiently different to allow experienced tasters to identify the precise vineyard from which a wine has come, irrespective of the producer and the vintage.

Who has the best soil?

Centuries of successful winegrowing have encouraged French wine experts to claim that their country has the best vineyard soil in the world. But vines, like people, can adapt to new conditions – as winemakers have proved by planting European varieties such as the Pinot Noir, Chardonnay, and Merlot in North or South America or Australia. Unfortunately for their national pride, even some of those French experts cannot differentiate between wines from

■ **French wine experts** *have often, wrongly, claimed they have the best soil for growing wine.*

their country and ones from, say, California, in blind tastings. This has led some producers in the New World to believe that soil has little real influence on a wine's flavor. But such tastings are the exceptions to the rule, and the New World's best winemakers now readily admit the importance of the soil of their vineyards.

OLD VERSUS NEW

Vieilles Vignes, a term sometimes found on the labels of French wines, literally means "old vines." It refers to the fact that the longer a plant has been growing and the deeper its roots have gone in search of water, the more intense and complex will be the flavor of the grapes it produces. Under French law, grapes from young vines – under five years old – are not allowed to be used for quality wine, and most vines are uprooted and replaced after 50 years or so, as they become less productive. The devastating effects of the phylloxera beetle at the end of the 19th century ensured that Europe has very few vines older than 100 years. Some vineyards in Australia, however, such as Château Tahbilk in Victoria and Hill of Grace in South Australia, are over 130 years old.

Vine growing

THE WAY VINES *are grown can vary enormously, too. Firstly, there is the question of whether they are planted directly in the soil or grafted onto phylloxera-resistant rootstock. These days, ungrafted vines are rarely found outside Chile, Argentina, and parts of Australia that have so far escaped the attentions of the louse. In Europe, Noval's Nacional in Portugal, Bollinger's Vieilles Vignes Française in Champagne, and a few sandy vineyards of southern France (phylloxera lice hate sand) are among the only vines to be grown on their own roots.*

Different kinds of rootstock suit different grape varieties and conditions.

Unfortunately, as the winegrowers of California's Napa Valley discovered in the 1980s, one of these rootstocks turned out to be less resistant to the louse than it ought to have been. More than 75 percent of the vineyards had to be uprooted and replanted.

Picking from ladders

In parts of Italy and Portugal, where grape growing was historically something of a sideline, the plants are sometimes trained on high trellises to allow cabbages and other vegetables to be cultivated beneath them. Where other harvesters have to bend double, pickers in these vineyards must climb ladders to gather the grapes. Elsewhere, in places such as Beaujolais, Australia, and the Rhône, vines are still sometimes grown as bushes – as has been done for hundreds of years. Nowadays, however, most vines are trained on wires by a number of methods, each devised to suit particular climatic conditions and the yields the producers seek to harvest from each plant. These factors will also influence the number of vines that are grown per acre.

The size of the harvest

The ideal yield per acre depends on the grape variety, soil, and climate, but two simple rules generally apply:

The warmer the weather, the riper the flavor and bigger the harvest, but too big a crop means less flavor and complexity in your wine.

GOING ORGANIC

Grape-growing in the second half of the 20th century was transformed by the development of chemical fertilizers and an arsenal of products to protect grapes from vine disease and pests. The beginning of the 21st century, on the other hand, saw a vociferous movement toward organic and biodynamic farming. Organic winemakers prefer to use manure rather than chemical fertilizer and try to fend off fungus with natural substances such as copper, sulfur, and lime. Pests are fought with bacteria-based insecticides, and so-called "good" bugs are encouraged to kill off or deter the "bad" ones that damage grapes.

Biodynamic farmers go further, believing that the soil is a living thing whose natural bacteria and compost, if allowed to develop without chemical interference, can both protect vines and help them to grow good grapes. Some of the biodynamic winemakers' practices might seem unusual. It takes a lot of faith to believe that sprinkling the vineyard with tiny amounts of dung previously buried in a cow's horn, on a date determined by the phase of the moon, can improve wine quality, but there is no denying that the list of wines produced in this way includes some of the finest in the world. At the turn of the century, only one percent of French wine could be described as organic or biodynamic, but 15 to 20 percent of California's vineyards have already been converted to these more environmentally friendly methods.

Thus, quality-conscious producers may choose to plant their vines twice as densely as their neighbors – while harvesting the same weight of grapes. They may also prune the plants more severely at the beginning of the growing season, leaving fewer buds on each vine in an effort to limit the number of bunches of grapes. But the size of the harvest can be difficult to predict or control. Nature doesn't tend to publish its annual production targets and estimates on a notice board, and vinegrowers sometimes have to resort to a so-called "green harvest" – removing a proportion of the partly ripe grapes a few weeks before the harvest – to reduce what might otherwise be too generous a crop.

Pests and disease

Vines and grapes are vulnerable to pests, ranging from birds and rabbits that are common in France and grape-loving spiders and kangaroos in Australia and the phylloxera lice that devastated the world's vineyards at the end of the 19th century. Larger beasts can be deterred by scarecrows, nets, and shotguns, but insects can be harder to discourage. Modern insecticides, though effective against spiders, provide no protection against the phylloxera louse, which will destroy any vine that has not been grafted onto resistant rootstock. Disease is another hazard. Vines fall prey to nasty fungal infections. Modern fungicides are effective against these, but are unpopular with organic and biodynamic wine producers.

■ **Nets placed** *on top of the vines protect the fruit from birds.*

Take your pick

NO TIME IN THE WINEMAKER'S YEAR *is more stressful than the period just before and during the harvest. Pick too early and the wine will taste "green," but leave it too long and it could have a "stewed" jammy flavor. These days, the decision of when to pick is largely based on the readings of devices that test the natural sweetness and acidity in the grapes, but many modern producers still prefer to rely on their own taste buds, biting into the fruit to assess its flavor. Besides all this tasting, you also have to listen to the weather reports – and maybe decide to start the harvest before a predicted storm, or wait until it is over.*

Man versus machine

■ **Throughout the world,** *grapes are usually harvested by hand.*

Of all the activities associated with winemaking, none is more wrapped in romantic imagery than grape-picking. The picture of men and women bending almost double to cut the fruit from the vines and carrying it in baskets on their backs has barely changed in two millennia, and harvest suppers in the Napa Valley can look remarkably similar to those depicted by the Greeks and Romans. But this tradition is under threat.

Although grapes are still harvested by hand in most of the world's vineyards, as labor costs rise, winemakers are turning to machines to do the job. These huge, tractor-like devices that straddle the vines, shaking the fruit from its stems, offer a number of advantages over human beings. They give the winegrower greater freedom to choose when to start picking, allowing him or her to rush the grapes in before rainstorms are likely to arrive. They are fast – a machine can work faster than 20 men – and they work uncomplainingly over weekends and right through the night.

Keeping cool

Harvesting grapes in the dark, when temperatures are low, is preferable to the middle of the day, when the freshly picked fruit can be "cooked" by the sun and lose its potential to make fresh-tasting wine. But, though it may be difficult to hire human pickers to work through the night, for top-quality wine there is no substitute for the skill of human beings, who can avoid rotten fruit and leave unripe bunches to be picked a few days later.

At the best estates and wineries, the grapes are inspected by hand as they arrive and substandard ones are removed. This level of care obviously cannot be applied by producers who make millions of bottles of wine.

THE GROWING YEAR

Northern Hemisphere / Southern Hemisphere
January / July: Vine pruning begins.
February / August: Vine pruning continues.
March / September: Time to till the soil to aerate it and remove weeds. The first buds may appear.
April / October: Leaves, shoots, and embryo bunches of grapes appear, giving an idea of the possible size of the crop. Cold weather or rain can cause "millerandage" – seedless grapes that never grow to maturity – while weather that is too warm may lead to "coulure" – the sap feeding the leaves rather than the grapes, which then fall off the plant.
May / November: Soil tilling and weeding, and – for non-organic growers – adding of chemical fertilizer and spraying to protect against mildew and fungus.

June / December: The vines are flowering now. Poor weather can slow the process, making for uneven ripening later. Some shoots are trained to the wires. Others are removed.

July / January: The grapes "set" – become recognizable berries within the bunches. If the crop looks over-generous, some bunches may be removed. Spraying and weeding continue.

August / February: The grapes become sweeter and the black ones undergo "veraison" – changing color. A combination of rain and warm weather at this stage can allow rot to set in, especially if the bunches are overly shaded by the leaves. For this reason some foliage may be removed to allow access to fresh air and sunlight. Drought now will slow down ripening, so if the law permits, the irrigation sprinklers may be turned on.

September / March: Harvest time! Early in the month in California; far later in France, where growers may have removed some bunches a few weeks before beginning to pick. Rain and hail are unwelcome hazards.

October / April: Still picking in Europe – indeed the harvest is only just starting for sweet wines. Once the crop is in and pressed, the residue of skins, pips, and stalks – the "marc" – is spread among the vines.

November / May: Still picking the last of the grapes for very sweet wines. Time to tidy the vineyard.

December / June: Producers of ice wine in Germany and Canada may still be picking. Some others may begin pruning. Otherwise, this is the moment to sell the wine you made last year – and take a well-earned break!

A simple summary

✓ Every grape variety has an appropriate soil.

✓ Soil can vary in neighboring vineyards.

✓ It is important to harvest grapes when they are neither under- nor over-ripe, and when it is neither too hot nor raining.

✓ Warm weather gives you richer but possibly less interesting flavors. A cool climate makes for wine flavors that can be refreshing or green and unripe.

✓ Vines are best grown on slopes facing the sun.

✓ Over-generous crops make for dilute wine.

✓ Vines and grapes need to be protected from frost, pests, and diseases.

Chapter 15

The Winemaker

GIVE THREE COOKS THE SAME INGREDIENTS and chances are they'll come up with three distinctly different dishes. Winemakers are just the same. It takes skill to make wine, and this skill is responsible for the variations found between wines produced from the same grape variety and region. Compare a range of Napa Valley Chardonnays or Champagnes and you will see how important it is to take note of the producer's name on the label. So what makes one producer better than another?

In this chapter...

✓ Back to basics

✓ Basic winemaking

✓ Red wines

✓ White wines

✓ Pink wines

✓ Jazzing up the basic pattern

EVERY WINEMAKER CAN PUT HIS OWN STAMP ON THE WINE HE PRODUCES

Back to basics

■ **The raw** *material of wine production.*

LET'S TAKE ANOTHER look at our raw material.
To the consternation of those who like to believe that God created fruit but it was the Devil who invented alcohol, grapes really do seem to be specifically designed for the production of wine. Just try crushing a handful into a bowl and letting the sweet juice come into contact with the yeast contained in the fine coating of dust on the skins. Leave the bowl in a warm kitchen for a few days and, hey presto, you'll have a mixture of pulp and fizzy, vaguely wine-like, alcoholic liquid. If the grapes were black, the natural pigment in the skins will have dyed the stuff in the bowl pink; if they were white, it will have some of the green-yellow hue of white wine.

Increase the volume of grapes, invest in a press to squeeze the juice out of them, buy a few barrels or tanks in which to ferment and store your wine, and you can call yourself a fully fledged winemaker. The only problem is that, while your end product will be liquid, alcoholic, and possibly legally describable as wine, the chances are it will taste so bad that you'd hesitate to use it for vinaigrette.

And that's the point: While there are good yeasts that want to turn grapes into wine, there are also bad yeasts — bacteria — that want to turn wine into vinegar.

But don't be too downhearted. Your first amateur effort will probably be no worse than the beverage hundreds of thousands of professional peasant-winemakers around the world have annually produced over the last few millennia. To be blunt, until the arrival of modern technology and know-how and the competitive wine market in the late 20th century, most producers regularly got away with selling low-quality wine to people living near their vineyards who never had the opportunity to taste anything better.

Art and science

While there were, of course, plenty of more skillful winemakers in every region and a succession of influential *enologists* producing impeccable wines, these were the exception to the rule. The general quality did not improve until production took off in California and Australia in the 1960s, 70s, and 80s and universities began to examine why and how wines tasted the way they did. Their aim, simply stated, was to shift the responsibility for a wine's quality (or lack of it) from God or nature to man; to eliminate faults, and to convey as much as possible of the grape's flavor to the wine. Working in places where the sun shone reliably, they soon realized the essential paradox of wine: Warm weather ripens the grapes, but also makes life difficult when it comes to turning the juice into wine. Almost from the outset, they adopted equipment that cooled the fermenting juice. Their training also made them wary of the armies of bacteria that threaten juice and wine, so they started using easy-to-clean stainless steel vats and new oak barrels rather than the old wooden vats and casks that were still generally the order of the day in Europe.

New and old

It did not take long for the competition provided by the wine "technocrats" of the New World to spark a response in European universities such as Bordeaux and Montpellier in France and Geisenheim in Germany. Often, professors on opposite sides of the globe taught very similar lessons, but were philosophically divided between an exaggerated reverence for tradition and a similarly exaggerated passion for technology.

The Old-World team, like parents indulging a gifted but badly behaved child, were often too tolerant of avoidable faults they confused with "character." As for the New Worlders, they were sometimes so obsessed with "controlling" every stage of the production process, they produced "faultless" wines with as much personality as an android designed to replicate a supermodel.

How far can you go?

But there was another way of defining the difference between the two camps. The New World producers were like composers with a clear idea of the kind of music they wanted to create. If the piano concerto needed a bit more trumpet, well, they could add it. And if they wanted to include a melody from a previous composition, well, they could go right ahead and do that too. By the same token, if a Napa Valley Chardonnay could be improved with a little Sauvignon – or some Chardonnay from a previous vintage or another region – well, that's what would happen.

The Old-World producers saw their role as that of conductor rather than composer. You can speed up or slow down a performance of the *Symphonie Fantastique*, but you can't tinker with the score. So, however much a little Bordeaux might improve your Burgundy, or even mixing a little 1999 with the 1998, you would, in France at least, be breaking the law.

■ **Unlike winemaking** *in the New World, French producers favor traditional methods of wine production.*

Skills of the kitchen

Just as a good chef can transform poor ingredients into a passable dish, so, with a bit of care, a top producer can turn even quite poor grapes into an acceptable wine. But it's as easy to waste the potential of great grapes as it is to turn prime steak into overcooked shoe leather. Most winemaking skills may be learned, either from studies or simply by watching the older generation at work. But, just as some gardeners are undeniably green-thumbed, so some people genuinely seem to bring natural gifts to the kitchen or winery.

INTERNET

www.winetitles.com

This Australian site offers samples from its print publications that are aimed at professional grape growers and winemakers.

Trivia...

In the 1980s and 90s, British retailers became frustrated by the inability or unwillingness of European wineries to offer the fruity, modern, inexpensive wines sought by their customers. So they decided to take matters into their own hands. They contracted so-called "Flying Winemakers" – usually young Australians, whose vintage is six months earlier than the one in Europe – to make the wine for them using the European wineries' grapes and equipment.

By the same token, while a great cook can perform miracles with a simple stove, a pan, and a knife, a bad one can use all manner of gadgetry and turn out a dish the dog might prefer not to eat. There are plenty of grubby little cellars in Europe whose untutored owners produce wine of extraordinary quality – and plenty of high-tech wineries in California and Australia where white-coated graduates churn out a characterless beverage that just happens to be made from grapes. Give a skilled producer the right grapes and the right equipment, and you will have the wine equivalent of a "dream team," which should offer the best possible chance of making truly great wine.

Basic winemaking

NO MATTER WHAT style of wine you are trying to make, there are a few key facts to understand and rules to remember. Every grape you use will naturally contain sugar, acid, yeast, water, and flavor compounds. The riper the grape, the more sugar it will contain.

The limits of alcohol

Left to its own devices, the yeast might go on converting this sugar into alcohol until the strength reaches 15 percent or so, at which point the yeast will be knocked out by the alcohol it has helped to create.

This is why you will rarely find a wine with more than 15 percent alcohol unless, like port and sherry, it has been fortified with a little brandy (see below). Stated simply, if there is any unfermented sugar left, the wine will be sweet. If not, it will be dry.

INTERNET

www.oenotec.com

This new site is dedicated to professional grapegrowers and winemakers.

■ **The Shiraz** *grown in the Barossa Valley, Australia, benefits from the region's warm climate.*

Grapes with enough sugar to make a 15 percent wine are rare, however. They are occasionally grown in warm regions such as the Sierra foothills in California where they make great dry red Zinfandel and in the Barossa Valley in Australia where they produce delicious Shiraz. Some Italian winemakers in less intensely sun-drenched areas such as the Veneto in the northeast and in Tuscany maximize the natural sugar in their grapes by letting them shrivel into raisins, laying the bunches on mats, or hanging them in barns. (Wines made in this way are sold as Recioto or Vin Santo, of which we will learn more in Chapter 17.) The sweetness of grapes in regions like Sauternes and Germany is increased by leaving them on the vines until they have been affected by noble rot or until they freeze and can be turned into ice wine.

A spoonful of sugar

Most grapes contain enough sugar to produce a dry wine with a strength of 12 to 13.5 percent alcohol. If there is less than this, as is often the case in French regions such as Bordeaux and Burgundy, producers are legally allowed to use sugar to raise the final strength of the wine by up to 2 percent.

This is done by a process known as "chaptalization," which is regularly resorted to even by some of the very finest winemakers in France. Winemakers in warmer regions such as California and Australia – where adding sugar is both unnecessary and illegal – have sometimes mocked chaptalization as "cheating."

■ **Unlike many of their** *European counterparts, Californian winemakers do not need to add sugar to their grapes.*

Trivia...

Chaptalization – the practice of adding sugar to fermenting grape juice – was named after Dr. Jean-Antoine Chaptal, professor at the Montpellier School of Medicine and Napoleon's minister for agriculture, who effectively clarified and legalized the process. It has been practiced in cooler regions of France for centuries.

But those mockers could be accused of throwing stones from glass houses. Grapes short of sugar rarely – by definition – lack another essential wine component, acidity. But grapes with lots of natural sweetness can be decidedly short of acidity. Anyone who has ever compared a sweetly dull Golden Delicious apple with a crisp tangy Granny Smith will appreciate the role acidity plays in flavor. The sweeter the grape and wine, the more acidity needed to balance this sweetness. This was understood by the creators of Coca Cola, who included huge amounts of acid in their recipe. New World winemakers don't add such large volumes, but they often have to do a bit of cheating of their own when they boost their grapes' insufficient levels of natural tartaric acid.

Yeast of Eden

Another bit of cheating concerns the third essential component of the grape: The yeast that is contained in the waxy dust on the surface of the fruit. Without yeast there can be no fermentation, but yeasts can be difficult to manage. There are millions of subtly different strains and, while some are more active than others, all eagerly compete with their neighbors. The anarchic behavior of these wild or native yeasts can make for an unpredictable fermentation – starting late, halting for a while, and taking a long time to finish.

■ **Yeast is contained** *in the waxy dust on the surface of the grapes.*

New World winemakers tend to avoid this unpredictability by killing wild yeasts with sulfur dioxide and using their own cultured yeasts, developed for their efficiency just like the ones you buy to make bread. For most Old-World producers, however, and a growing number of their counterparts in the New World, wild yeasts give wines a more interesting flavor than cultured ones.

A modern addition

Sulfur dioxide is used at various stages of winemaking to protect the wine from bacteria and the risk of oxidation.

Modern winemakers who prefer the control they get from cultured yeasts use sulfur dioxide to knock out good but unpredictable natural yeasts and bacteria. Other producers prefer to leave these natural yeasts unscathed.

Don't worry too much over warnings about sulfites on labels. Almost every wine you drink will have been protected against bacteria by a small amount of sulfur dioxide – probably to a lesser extent than most dried fruit and canned vegetables.

Red wines

THE FIRST CHOICE *when making red wines concerns the stalks. Do you remove them, or leave some or all to go into the fermentation vat? Traditionally, producers have often left them on, because they believed that a long-lived wine needed the tannin they provide. Their modern counterparts who seek more immediately drinkable wines prefer to discard them. You also have to decide whether or not to crush the grapes before they go into the fermentation tank. Your decision will be based on the kind of wine you want to make. Most rich deep Cabernet Sauvignons, for example, will be made entirely from grapes that have been crushed.*

On the other hand, producers of lighter fruitier wines, such as Beaujolais, prefer to chuck the fruit straight into the vat. The process these uncrushed grapes go through is known as carbonic maceration which, without getting too technical, involves a mini-fermentation that takes place within the grape itself. Wine made in this way is immediately appealing, but it is rarely worth keeping for very long (think of Beaujolais Nouveau). Modern Pinot Noir, which combines richness with fruitiness, is often made using a combination of crushed and uncrushed grapes.

■ **Not all grapes** *are crushed before fermentation, but richer reds like Cabernet Sauvignon are.*

The cooking process

Now that you've filled the vat, you need to watch out for two things. First, there is the temperature. The process of fermentation creates heat, but it needs a bit of warmth to get going. So, especially if you are relying on unpredictable natural yeasts, you may need to heat the contents of the vat to jump-start them into action.

Once fermentation has begun, the danger lies in overheating. Above 90°F (33°C), the yeasts become sluggish and stop transforming the sweet liquid into alcohol. If this happens, the half-fermented juice is vulnerable to bacteria that could turn it into vinegar. Too cool a fermentation, though, will fail to extract the grapes' full flavor and color.

Bathing bliss

The other danger is that the "cap" of skins that naturally floats to the surface may dry out. One traditional method of avoiding this is to get into the fermenting juice and swim around. In Burgundy, this was said to be one of the few baths the peasant winemakers ever took. The experience is pleasant enough given the warm temperature of the liquid and the fruit-jam smells it produces. Unfortunately it is also dangerous, as it is all too easy to become asphyxiated by those fumes and drown.

These days, producers prefer to break up the cap with a wooden or mechanical paddle, or to sprinkle it with fermenting juice that has been pumped up from the bottom of the vat. Alternatively, they can use rotary fermenters, which operate like giant cement mixers to keep the cap constantly moist, although they are not generally used for the very finest wines.

Checking the fermentation

During fermentation, which can take from a few days to a couple of weeks, daily readings are taken to assess how much sugar is left and how much alcohol has been made. At this stage the winemaker, like a cook adding salt to a soup, may make up for inadequacies in the grape – depending on local regulations and his or her respect for them – by adding sugar or tartaric acid to the vat.

■ **During fermentation** *sugar levels are checked daily.*

Press wine and free-run

Once the sugar has all been converted into alcohol, the liquid and solids are usually left in contact with each other for a little longer. This allows color to be extracted from the skins and tannin to pass from both skins and pips into what is now technically wine. Once this stage has been completed, the wine is drawn off and the solids go into a press. This might be as basic as the traditional basket-presses still favored by some winemakers in Australia, or as high-tech as the computerized presses that work by gently squeezing the contents of a huge rubber bag.

The liquid that is drawn from the press – called the "press wine" – will be more intensely colored and flavored and more tannic than the "free-run" – the wine that has come from the tank. Some, but perhaps not all, of the press wine will be blended with the free-run. But take care – too much press wine and the final wine could be too tannic.

The second stage of fermentation is called malolactic fermentation. If this process doesn't start of its own accord, it may be necessary to kick it off with specially cultured yeasts.

In the vat

Depending on its style, the wine will now be in large stainless steel or epoxy-lined cement tanks, wooden vats, or barrels. Some or all of the barrels may be made of new oak, although wine for immediate consumption will rarely see the new wood. Not only would this give it too much of a vanilla flavor, it would also greatly increase its cost, because new barrels can carry price tags of several hundred dollars apiece. When

■ **Vats can be** *made from a variety of materials such as stainless steel* (above), *cement lined with epoxy, or wood.*

producers want to give inexpensive wines an oaky flavor, they can add strips of oak (staves) or bags of small oak pieces (chips) to the vat. These are, however, generally illegal in countries such as France.

The barrels or tanks must be kept topped up, because too much oxygen allows bacteria to spoil the wine. Also, the wine must be transferred occasionally from tank to tank, or barrel to barrel, to make sure it doesn't grow stale. In some regions, wines from different grape varieties and vineyards are blended and a selection made of the best wine, which may be bottled and sold separately. The length of time between fermentation and bottling varies from region to region, from a few weeks for Beaujolais Nouveau to as long as seven or eight years for ultra-traditional wines in Spain.

Is it ready yet?

■ **The length of time** *between fermentation and bottling may vary.*

By the time it is ready for bottling, the wine should look perfectly clear. It is usually "fined" with egg white, milk protein, or earth, all of which drop through the liquid and drag any remaining solids along to settle at the bottom. The last step is to filter the wine. This makes sure that it is absolutely free of bacteria, although some producers, who know that fining and filtering remove flavor, prefer to skip one or both stages.

White wines

The only essential difference between black and white grapes is their skins. The color and tannin found in those skins are essential components for red wines, but they have no role at all in whites. So, whatever the style of white wine you are making, the skins need to be discarded before fermentation begins.

Ripen and rot

If you want to produce a high-quality, lusciously sweet wine, you need to leave the grapes on the vines to ripen further and possibly develop noble rot. For a cheaper sweet wine you could cheat by sweetening a dry wine with a little grape juice – legal in some areas, such as Germany. But doing so elsewhere might mean breaking the law.

■ **The grape varieties that** *do not benefit from contact with oak are fermented in stainless steel vats.*

Oak or steel?

Where the juice and skins of black grapes are pumped into large vats, makers of white wine have the choice of fermenting the juice in vats or in the barrels in which the wine will mature. Most grape varieties – especially aromatic ones such as Riesling and Gewürztraminer – have nothing to gain from even the most fleeting contact with new oak. They will be fermented in stainless steel tanks or in vats made from old wood that give the wine no flavor at all.

Fermenting in barrels is limited to the few grape varieties such as Chardonnay that benefit from the flavor of the wood, and to producers who are prepared to take the trouble to tend large numbers of barrels, all like pots on a range, cooking at their own speed. Bigger companies usually ferment the wine in tanks and transfer it into the barrels afterward.

Trivia...

The only place where small quantities of white wine are made with the skins is Georgia in the Caucasus. The resulting liquid is deep gold and oddly nutty in flavor, with a mouth-drying texture reminiscent of heavily stewed tea. Understandably, few bottles leave the region.

When is it done?

Whatever the container in which white wine is fermented, though, keeping an eye on the temperature is just as important as it is for red.

DEFINITION

The lees are the dead yeasts left over from fermentation. They're prized by producers of some types of wine such as Muscadet and Chardonnay for the way they can keep wine fresh and add a "cookielike" character.

Winemakers who want to make a tropically fruity wine for early drinking can ferment white juice slowly at temperatures as low as 54°F (12°C) – temperatures that would be far too cool for red wine.

Similarly, while all red wine goes through malolactic fermentation, producers who want to make a more tangy style may use sulfur dioxide to prevent or curtail this process.

Early-drinking white wine will be bottled early – possibly within three months of the harvest. Wines for longer aging will be matured in barrels or larger casks. In the case of richer wines such as Chardonnay, the *lees* that fall to the bottom of the barrel may be stirred to give the wine an attractive, subtly nutty flavor and texture.

GRAPES BEING PUMPED INTO A FERMENTATION TANK

Pink wines

WHAT THE FRENCH and much of the rest of the world call rosé wines are often called "blush" or, more curiously, "white" in the United States. The explanation for this is simple. In the late 1970s, once-popular semisweet Portuguese pink wines such as Mateus and Lancers were going out of fashion. Rosé, it seemed, was no longer flavor of the month. Red wines made from the Zinfandel grape had also lost their appeal – so much so that some producers were even uprooting their vines. Fortunately for lovers of the grape and of pink wines, the winemakers at the Sutter Home winery cleverly created a market for both – simply by making rosé Zinfandel and renaming it "white."

How it gets that blush

The way rosé is produced is, in fact, very similar to the method for making red wine – except for the fact that the juice is drawn from the vat while it is still fermenting and before it has had the chance to draw too much color from the skins. Winemakers then have a choice. They can either allow it to ferment only a little further before stopping the process and bottling the wine as a semi-sweet pink wine, such as Anjou rosé. Or they can let it ferment completely as though it were to become a dry white.

Rosé made by either method is very unlikely to go into a new oak barrel, and nowadays is almost certainly fermented and stored in stainless steel tanks before being bottled within a few months of the harvest. A few, highly exceptional rosés improve with age. Most are best drunk as soon as they are bought.

VIP It can be very difficult to know whether a pink wine is sweet or dry. It is fair to assume, however, that California pink wines labeled as rosé will be drier than ones labeled as white.

Jazzing up the basic pattern

THERE IS MORE to the winemaker's art than the basic grape and the basic fermentation process. A number of things can be done to wine to make it different or more exciting.

Blending

One of the words that wine drinkers often treat with suspicion is "blend." After all, if the purest gold carries the highest price tag and a single malt whiskey is more prestigious than a blended scotch, surely the finest wine must be made from a single grape variety grown in a single vineyard in a single year. Far from it.

If you were to line up a selection of the very best wines in the world, you would find plenty that owe their quality to the skill of a blender.

■ **Pinot Noir** *and Chardonnay grapes are used to produce red and white Burgundy respectively.*

Blending grapes

First, there is the matter of the grapes. Red and white Burgundy are, respectively, made exclusively from the Pinot Noir and Chardonnay, and Barolo is purely produced from Nebbiolo, but these are the exceptions to the rule. Most wines, including such famous examples as Bordeaux, Chianti, Rioja, and all but a very few Champagnes, will be blends of two or more varieties. Even in the New World, where the label might lead you to suppose that a bottle contains nothing but Cabernet Sauvignon, Merlot, Chardonnay or whatever, up to 25 percent of the wine might, depending on local rules, have been produced from another variety altogether. White Zinfandel, for example, often contains a generous dose of Muscat.

When two grape varieties are mentioned on a label, the wine will have been made with equal quantities or, more usually, with a larger proportion of the first of the two.

Different vineyards

In Burgundy and in other parts of France, there is a tradition of making wines from grapes grown in single plots – the so-called Premiers and Grands Crus. But wines from top Bordeaux châteaux such as Château Margaux, Lafite, and Mouton Rothschild are blends of different varieties of grapes grown in vineyards that may well be more than a mile apart. Similarly, Australia's top red, Penfolds Grange, is a mixture of Shiraz grapes grown in various parts of South Australia. Great Champagne such as Roederer's Cristal and Moët & Chandon's Dom Perignon are marriages of Pinot Noir and Chardonnay grapes, which are grown in villages scattered across the region of Champagne.

■ **Roederer's famous Cristal** *is made from blending Pinot Noir and Chardonnay grapes.*

Different years

These prestigious Champagnes have vintages, and are thus the product of a single harvest, but most Champagne – including pricy bottles from Krug – is actually a non-vintage blend of wines from several different years. This kind of mixture is an exception to the rule in France, where legislation strictly forbids the blending for rosé without bubbles. But other countries – including most in the New World – take a more relaxed view. So that delicious 1999 Napa Valley Cabernet Sauvignon you enjoyed may well legally contain a little 1998 Merlot from another region altogether – and be none the worse for it.

■ **Top Champagnes** *are usually made from a single harvest; others contain a mix of vintages.*

■ **Sparkling wine** *can vary in price from reasonable to very costly.*

Sparkling wines

Sparkling wine – from the cheapest stuff on the shelf to the most prized bottle of Dom Perignon – shares one essential characteristic with Coca Cola, Budweiser, and Perrier. They are all liquids in which carbon dioxide has been dissolved and trapped. Open the can, twist the cap, or remove the cork, and the gas is released as bubbles. The difference between these drinks lies in the way the carbon dioxide got into the liquid. In the case of soft drinks and very, very cheap sparkling wine, it is simply injected from a large cylinder.

Beer and quality sparkling wines get their bubbles as a by-product of fermentation. Unlike beer, though, which is only fermented once, sparkling wines go through the process twice. The first fermentation, which follows the pattern we've already seen, produces a *still wine* with a low alcoholic strength. This is then given a shot of yeast and sugar and transferred to a sealed container – a cuve close (sealed tank) in the case of cheaper wine and Asti Spumante, or a bottle, in the case of Champagne or a premium sparkling wine. Re-fermenting the wine in the small confines of a bottle gives it a naturally yeasty flavor and the fine bubbles associated with good Champagne and good sparkling wine from elsewhere.

> ### DEFINITION
> Still wine *is simply wine without bubbles.*

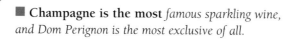

■ **Champagne is the most** *famous sparkling wine, and Dom Perignon is the most exclusive of all.*

THE HISTORY OF SPARKLING WINE

Success, they say, has many fathers while failure remains an orphan. Champagne – the sparkling wine from the region of that name in northeastern France – and the growing number of quality sparkling wines around the world, have become so successful over the centuries that it is hardly surprising that several different regions are staking a claim to their invention.

No one can say for certain whether the first intentionally sparkling wines were made in Champagne, in southern France at Limoux, or in Spain. Or whether they might not, in fact, have first been devised in England. What is known is that, in 1662, a full three decades before the first report of bubbly wine being made in Champagne, an English writer called Christopher Merret wrote that "wine coopers of recent times use vast quantities of sugar and molasses to make them [sic] drink brisk and sparkling."

The English certainly were crucial to the development of sparkling wine. This was partly because of their introduction in 1623 of coal-fired furnaces that enabled them to produce stronger glass than ever before, and partly because of their use of corks to seal bottles, as opposed to the hemp-covered wooden bungs favored by the French. Without these airtight stoppers, any sparkling wine would have simply gone flat. And without the robust glass, a well-sealed bottle would have exploded under the pressure from the bubbles.

Even if the English can take the credit for the bottle, stopper, and method, the prize for creating good-tasting sparkling wine has to go to Dom Perignon. A 17th-century abbot of Hautvilliers Abbey in Champagne, Dom Perignon experimented with blends, and discovered that a fine white sparkling wine could be made from a blend of black and white grapes grown in a variety of vineyards. His wine, though, in common with every other one of his time, came with a load of the yeasty gunk that had caused the fermentation. Getting the wine, but no gunk, into a glass must have called for skill.

This area of human learning was thankfully made superfluous at the beginning of the 19th century. This was when the woman we now know as Veuve Clicquot – the widow of a Champagne producer – experimented with her cellarmaster Antoine de Muller to develop a technique to remove the gunk. It was Mme. Clicquot and M. de Muller who discovered that the yeast could be shaken down into the neck of the bottle, frozen, and removed. And that's the way it is still done today – though the men who traditionally did the shaking, or remuage, have now generally been replaced by machines that do the job just as efficiently. The next development may be the introduction of recently invented yeast "beads" that do away with the need for remuage completely.

Getting rid of the sludge

Wherever it takes place, the second fermentation simultaneously creates both the gas and more alcohol. Unfortunately, while the sugar and the carbon dioxide dissolve in the wine, the powdered yeast remains inconveniently present, as an unattractive sludge. If the now-fizzy liquid is in a tank, it can be bottled directly, leaving the sludge behind. But so-called bottle-fermented wines such as Champagne present more of a challenge. In these cases, the yeast has to be shaken by hand or machine down to the neck of the bottle, whereupon the liquid is frozen. The bottle is then unsealed (it usually has a beer bottle-type cap rather than cork at this stage) and the frozen sludgy pellet allowed to fly out, leaving a crystal clear, bone dry, sparkling wine.

Finally, the bottle is topped up – usually with a slightly sweeter wine – and resealed with the final cork. This fiddlesome process has been so automated in recent years that the transfer method, which involved transferring the bottle-fermented wine into a tank from which it was then bottled, is no longer widely used.

Secrets of the cork

Corks for sparkling wines are made from three or more layers of cork.

There is a tough agglomerate of tiny cork fragments around the outside in contact with the bottle and a springy layer that comes into contact with the wine. It is the elasticity of this last layer that gives these corks their characteristic mushroom shape when they are removed from the bottle.

Fortified wines

While most wines weigh in with a strength of 14 percent or less, there are some that turn the scales at 15 to 20 percent. These heavyweights are the exception to the rule that the alcohol in wine comes from the grape – or from a little extra sugar added by chaptalization. Their strength comes from the addition of brandy, usually during the fermentation process. The brandy in question is not the tasty, barrel-aged, golden stuff we're used to sipping from balloon glasses, but a freshly distilled colorless liquid with almost no flavor. Wines made in this way range from the light grapey Muscats and salty dry fino sherries of Spain to raisiny Marsala from Italy, rich plummy port, and tangy marmaladey Madeira.

■ **Port is produced** *in the Duoro Valley, Portugal.*

THE HISTORY OF FORTIFIED WINES — A HAPPY ACCIDENT

In the 17th century, wine merchants were aware that dry wines produced in warm regions tended to become vinegary when they were transported in their barrels. Furthermore, sweeter wines actually caused casks to explode in the hold of ships. By trial and error, the merchants and producers came to understand that the more alcohol any drink contained, the more robust it seemed to be. Cognac at 40 or 50 percent could be stored for years in its barrels, while red wine at 10 percent tended to lose its flavor or turn sour.

Among the wines that suffered in this way were the rustic reds of the hot region of the Douro in Northern Portugal. This might not have mattered had the English not, in one of their periodic spats with France in 1674, decided to ban the importation of Bordeaux or any other French wine. The fortified wine from the Douro in northern Portugal – which the English called Port – became an instant success and by the late 18th century, nearly 36 million bottles were being imported into Britain. Where port went, sherry, Marsala, and Madeira followed – as, later, did fortified wines of southern France such as Muscat de Beaumes-de-Venise.

A simple summary

✓ Winemakers control style, flavor, and quality.

✓ Ripe grapes make sweeter or stronger wines.

✓ The temperature at which the juice is fermented must be just right as it will affect the wine's flavor.

✓ Wine can be fermented with natural or cultured yeast.

✓ Some types of wine are best fermented and aged in stainless steel, while others benefit from being in oak barrels.

✓ Wine can be re-fermented to make it sparkle.

✓ To fortify wine, simply add neutral brandy.

PART FIVE

WINE IS NOW PRODUCED IN DIVERSE CLIMATES

WHERE WINE COMES FROM

HAVING LEARNED ABOUT THE ROLES played by grapes, soil, climate, vinegrowing, and winemaking, the next factor to consider is the *influence* of the place where a wine is made. As *globalization* has led to the universal availability of once-regional dishes like hamburgers, pizzas, and  kebabs, producers in very different places are using the same varieties of grapes and winemaking methods to produce very similar wines. Even so, climates, soils, traditions, and cuisines ensure the wines retain a *regional* flavor and style. Here we will discover why French wines taste different from those made in Italy – and why California wines from Carneros are distinct from those from in Mendocino, farther up the highway.

Chapter 16

France: Home of the Classics

OUR FIRST PORT OF CALL IS FRANCE, the country that offers the world's broadest range of classic flavors.

In this chapter...

✓ What is it about French wine? ✓ Bordeaux

✓ Burgundy: the patchwork quilt

✓ Champagne: the most famous wine of all?

✓ Rhône Valley: the spice jar   ✓ Loire Valley

✓ Alsace: the best of both worlds

✓ Eastern France: Jura and Savoie

✓ Southwest: land of tradition

✓ The south: meeting point of the past and future

✓ Vin de pays and vin de table: the bargain basement

EVERYONE ADORES THE FRENCH CLASSICS

What is it about French wine?

THE ANSWER lies in France's soil, climate, and history – and the philosophy of its winemakers. If you look at a New-World wine label the most important elements will be the names of the grape varieties and of the winemaker (think of Robert Mondavi Cabernet Sauvignon or Rosemount Chardonnay).

Village people

Now look at a French bottle. The biggest word on the label will be the name of the region, town, or village where the wine was produced (think of Bordeaux Rouge, Gevrey Chambertin, or Châteauneuf du Pape). French wines, their producers stress, are not simply about grape varieties any more than movies are simply about actors and actresses. Just as a good film must have a decent plot, a wine must, they believe, have the flavor of the place where it was produced. To them, it's almost a matter of faith – a faith that has its own Bible in the shape of the legal structure on which their entire wine industry is based.

INTERNET

www.wine-france.com

This site provides a friendly guide to French wines.

You've got to know the system

France's most basic wines are *vin de table* – table wines – whose labels legally cannot refer to grape variety, region, or vintage. Next come *vins de pays* – country wines from large regions – which very often do declare their grape varieties. Then there are the *appellation contrôlée* wines. This designation covers all of France's best known wines, from regions such as Champagne and Bordeaux to little villages like Vosne Romanée in Burgundy, and even the tiny "la Romanée" vineyard within that village. Some regions, such as Burgundy and Alsace, also rank their best vineyards as *Premier* and/or *Grand Cru*; some parts of Bordeaux, by contrast, rank their estates – their châteaux – in a class system of their own. Many areas, including such famous places as Pomerol in Bordeaux, get by with no classifications at all.

When confronted by all these different systems, even experienced wine experts might be forgiven for sympathizing with the American humorist who, while accepting that people in other countries might choose to speak a foreign language, wondered why they couldn't all speak the same foreign language. All we can say in France's defense is that these systems have grown up over time. Like the private jokes and language to be found in any household, they simply take a little getting used to.

■ **On French wine** *labels the largest word is the name of the region or town where it is produced.*

The Appellation rules don't simply guarantee where the grapes were grown, they also cover the types of grapes – white Burgundy, including Chablis, has to be made from Chardonnay, a variety that would be illegal for, say, white Bordeaux. And it limits the amount of wine that can be made per acre and the method by which the wine is produced (ensuring, for example that a sparkling wine from the Loire is made in the same way as Champagne).

Strength in numbers

■ **In France a large number** *of individual winemakers may grow their own grapes on the same land.*

Another key difference between France and, say, California, lies in the number of people who are involved in producing wine. There are fewer than 1,000 wineries in the whole of California. Some 500 individual estates and merchants could legally produce and sell wine from Gevrey Chambertin, a village whose total annual output is far smaller than that of just one of California's bigger wineries. France's wineries take a number of very different forms, however.

AS ELSEWHERE IN EUROPE, WINES CAN BE FROM:

✓ Individual producers (viticulteurs, vignerons, récoltants) that have estates (domaines, châteaux) in whose vineyards they grow their own grapes and make and sell their own produce.

✓ Cooperatives that make wine from grapes purchased from grower-members.

✓ Merchants (négociants) that buy, blend, mature, bottle, and sell wine from estates and cooperatives.

Who's who

Good wine is produced by growers, cooperatives, and merchants, but so is plenty of bad and even more mediocre wine.

The difference between good and bad lies in luck, raw materials (the quality of the grapes), skill, equipment, and integrity. The key to getting the best examples of any wine style (in France or anywhere else, as we've said before) lies in remembering the name of a producer, merchant, or cooperative whose wines you enjoy – as well as that of the name of the region in which they were produced.

So, let's set out on a tour of France's wine regions to see just how varied they can be – and the differences that set them apart from each other.

Bordeaux

WE'LL BEGIN, almost inevitably, with Bordeaux, the region whose red wines include some of the best-known and most sought-after in the world.

The class system at work

If you wanted a modern image of Europe's traditional class system, you could do worse than look at Bordeaux. At the top of the pile there are the aristocrats, the hundred or so big-name estates (châteaux) whose wines are to be found in the cellars of collectors and restaurants and may well be included in the lists of *Crus Classés* Most of these genuinely taste aristocratic; some, like the tapestries to be found in a number of Europe's castles, and now look decidedly motheaten.

Next there are the more workaday middle classes – a few hundred châteaux including some that are actually categorized as Cru Bourgeois.

Finally there's the proleteriat – the thousands of small producers whose wines might be sold under the name of their château, or, depending where the vines are situated, quite simply as Bordeaux or under a regional designation such as Médoc or St. Émilion. The existence of these regional appellations reveals that the area shown on a map as Bordeaux actually includes a large number of smaller regions, each of which produces wines with their own characteristic style. Bear in mind that a bottle labeled as Bordeaux could come from anywhere in the entire region.

■ **The quality of** *Bordeaux is much sought after and sold in prestigious shops, such as this Maison du Vin.*

Keeping cool

The climate of Bordeaux is relatively mild, but certainly not warm by Californian or Australian standards. Grapes rarely ripen sufficiently to produce the 12 to 13 percent strength to be found in most bottles, so chaptalization is common. The principal five grapes are the Cabernet Sauvignon, Cabernet Franc, and Merlot (for red wines), and the

Sémillon and Sauvignon (for whites). Variations in the soil (mainly between clay and gravel) and a desire to make wine with complex flavors explain why wines are almost invariably blends of these varieties.

Some things to keep in mind

The tannic – cold tea – character of red Bordeaux comes from a combination of the Cabernet Sauvignon grape (and, to a lesser extent, the Merlot), the climate, and the belief of most producers that the tannin is a necessary component of any red wine that is intended to age. Ideally, the tannin should soften to allow a Cary Grant stylishness to emerge; unfortunately, all too often, this doesn't happen.

Even quite small differences in soil and aspect can have a huge influence over both the flavor and quality of wines, especially when the weather is less than ideal. This enables better-situated estates such as Château Margaux regularly to make better wine than their neighbors. In poor – rainy or cold – vintages, the most famous châteaux also have the best equipment and know-how, and the means to discard sub-standard grapes.

■ **The tannin in** *Bordeaux comes from a combination of grape and climate.*

Lesser châteaux, which produce decent wine when the weather is good, will have had a far harder time in bad years, so buy wines from the humblest châteaux in good vintages, and from the smartest châteaux in lesser years.

Beware of confusing similarly named châteaux (Château Yquem and Eyquem for example, or numerous versions of Château Latour), which have nothing to do with each other.

Try to find the "second label" wines produced by top châteaux from grapes not quite good enough to go into their main "grand vin."

Wines such as les Forts de Latour, les Carruades de Lafite, and Pavillon Rouge de Château Margaux, like second quality clothes from top designers, can offer a more affordable taste of their producers' style. The wines' only drawback is a lesser degree of complexity and longevity.

A tour of Bordeaux: the reds

Our visit to the red wine-producing vineyards of Bordeaux starts at the northern end of the Médoc, in the commune of St. Estèphe. The wines here tend to be tough and slow to mature. Some never soften – especially in cool years – but estates such as Cos d'Estournel, Montrose, and Haut Marbuzet make wines that are always worth buying.

First among equals

INTERNET

www.bordeaux.com

Take a virtual tour of Bordeaux at this site.

If Bordeaux were a Monopoly board, Pauillac – our next commune – would be the best corner, Park Avenue, or Boardwalk. If you own property here, you're doing okay; if you don't and you want to buy a bottle of the gloriously complex blackcurrant wine here, it's going to cost you serious money. Especially if it is from one of the three first growths – Châteaux Latour, Lafite, and Mouton-Rothschild. The best second growths here, such as the confusingly named Pichon-Longueville-Comtesse-de-Lalande and Pichon Baron-Longueville, often make wine of first growth standard and have consequently been nicknamed "super-seconds." Château Lynch-Bages is a fifth growth that can also produce wine that competes with the best in the region.

St. Julien, a bigger appellation than Pauillac, has no first growths, but several "super-seconds" such as Châteaux Léoville Lascases, Léoville-Barton, and Ducru-Beaucaillou. As the wines here mature, they develop the characteristic smell and flavor of cigar boxes. Margaux, which is larger still, is a mixed bag. At one end of the scale, there is the sublime Château Margaux – the only château to share its name with its appellation – and the third growth Château Palmer, but there are plenty of châteaux here that produce pretty ordinary wines. These trade on Margaux's prestige to sell at higher prices than they deserve. Better value is to be found in wines such as Châteaux Chasse Spleen and Poujeaux from the less famous region of Moulis-Médoc. Nearby Listrac's wines are tougher and more tannic and tend to attract traditionalists.

Basic fare

Médoc wines that fall outside these communal appellations are sold as Médoc or Haut-Médoc. Some Médocs from good producers – such as la Tour de By, Loudenne, Patache d'Aux, and Potensac – are worth buying, but they are the exception to an often disappointing rule. Haut-Médocs such as Beaumont, Cantemerle, and

■ **Buying a good** *Médoc at source can often prove to be difficult.*

Sociando-Mallet are a better bet. The most famous – and best – Haut-Médoc is Château la Lagune, a Third Growth that, unusually for a Cru Classé, doesn't have a communal appellation.

When buying wines from the Médoc and Haut-Médoc, watch for wines with the words Cru Bourgeois on their label. This designation is not always a reliable indication of quality, but it may tip the odds in your favor.

INTERNET

www.hautbrion.com

This brilliant site details the history of Chateau Haut-Brion, one of the top estates in Bordeaux.

Graves

Bidding farewell to the Médoc, we next go south, to the historic region of Graves and the smaller appellation of Pessac Léognan, home of Château Haut Brion, the estate whose wine in the 17th century so enchanted Samuel Pepys (chronicler of the Great Fire of London). This region's name refers to its gravel soil, which favors the blackcurranty Cabernet Sauvignon. Other great châteaux here include la Mission-Haut-Brion, Pape-Clément, Domaine de Chevalier, and Haut-Bailly.

Crossing the water

Bordeaux's other important red wine regions, St. Émilion and Pomerol, are on the other side of the Gironde and Dordogne rivers. There is a lot of clay in the soil here, which helps to explain why the major grape variety is the Merlot, rather than the gravel-loving Cabernet Sauvignon. St. Émilion, like Margaux, is another mixed bag, with sublime, plummy, spicy wines – and dull earthy stuff with little identifiable flavor. Tread carefully when buying here, and don't place too much trust in wines labeled St. Émilion Grand Cru. "Premier Grand Cru

■ **A label bearing** *"Premier Grand Cru Classé" is a good indicator of a better St. Émilion.*

Classé" – a quite different classification – is much more reliable. Alternatively, explore nearby supposedly lesser regions such as Montagne St. Émilion, which often offer better value for money. The top St. Émilion is Château Cheval Blanc. Others to look for include l'Angelus, Ausone, and Figeac Pomerol, which has no classification system, makes lovely, cherryish wines that can have a mineral character. This is the place to find tiny superstar estates such as Château Petrus, Clinet, Certan-de-May, Vieux-Château-Certan, and le Pin. Pomerol is never cheap; for a more affordable taste of its style, try a wine from the neighboring appellation of Lalande de Pomerol. Other worthwhile regions that can offer value for money include Fronsac, Côtes de Bourg, Côtes de Blaye, and Côtes des Francs.

■ **Sémillon grapes,** *such as these, are mixed with Sauvignon to make Pessac-Léognan.*

The whites

A few of the top estates in the Médoc – Châteaux Margaux, Talbot, and Lynch-Bages – make white wine, but these are luxurious exceptions to the rule and there are no white St. Émilions or Pomerols. For the best dry whites, we have to head back to Pessac-Léognan, where the Sémillon and Sauvignon are blended and usually fermented and matured in oak barrels to produce wine with a rich peachy flavor all its own. Whites labeled as Graves can be good, as can some Premières Côtes de Bordeaux and Entre-Deux-Mers, but lots of very ordinary Sauvignon Blanc is sold under these appellations, and as Bordeaux Blanc.

Finally, there are the great sweet wines of Sauternes and its neighbor Barsac, which owe their existence to a quirk of geography that encourages mist to gather over the vines in the fall, and noble rot to develop on the grapes. The best wines from these appellations are sublime, honeyed, and apricotty. Producing them calls for luck, skill, and commitment. Sadly, plenty of very poorly made Sauternes can be found on the market.

Things to remember about Bordeaux

✔ Almost all wines are blends (principally Cabernet Sauvignon, Cabernet Franc, and Merlot for red wine; Sauvignon Blanc and Sémillon for whites).

✔ Wines vary enormously in quality. Cheap Bordeaux is often poor value for money.

✔ Bordeaux Supérieur is made from slightly riper grapes. It won't necessarily be a better wine.

✔ The fact that a wine label bears a château label – or the words "Mis en Bouteille au Château" (Château-bottled) provides no quality guarantee.

✔ The system of Crus Classés varies from sub-region to sub-region.

✔ Wines from good châteaux in less well-known regions, such as Fronsac, Côtes des Francs, Loupiac, and the Premières Côtes de Bordeaux can be a good buy.

✔ Vintages vary greatly, some being better for one sub-region or style than another. Some years' wines last a lot longer than others.

■ **Remember that** *most Bordeaux wines are blended.*

■ **Bordeaux wines** *vary enormously in quality – do your homework and try before you buy.*

227

BORDEAUX TO BUY – AND WHEN TO DRINK IT

Top producers:

✓ Bordeaux Rouge/Blanc: B&G 1725, Ch. Bonnet, la Cour Pavillon, Dourthe No. 1, Maître d'Estournel, Michel Lynch, Sirius.

✓ Affordable fine red Bordeaux: Châteaux Angludet, Beaumont, Bel-Air (Lalande de Pomerol), Canon (Canon-Fronsa, Cantemerle, Cardaillan, Chasse-Spleen, la Gurgue, Labégorce-Zédé, Maucaillou, Monbrison, Patache d'Aux, Potensac, Poujeaux, de la Rivière, St. Georges (St-Georges-St-Émilion), Ségonzac, Sociando-Mallet, Thieley, Tournefeuille (Lalande de Pomerol)

✓ Affordable fine dry white Bordeaux: Châteaux Chantegrive, Dom. de la Grave, Landiras, Rochemorin, du Seuil

✓ Top red Bordeaux: Châteaux Angélus, Ausone, Beauregard, Belair, Bon-Pasteur, Calon-Ségur, Canon, Canon-la-Gaffelière, Carbonnieux, Cheval-Blanc, Domaine de Chevalier, Clinet, la Conseillante, Cos d'Estournel, la Croix de Gay, la Dominique, Ducru-Beaucaillou, Certan de May, l'Eglise-Clinet, Clos René, l'Evangile, Figeac, la Fleur-Pétrus, Gazin, Gruaud-Larose, Haut-Bailly, Haut-Brion, Issan, Lafite, Lafleur, Lagrange, Langoa-Barton, Larmande, Larrivet-Haut-Brion, Latour, Latour à Pomerol, Léoville-Barton, Léoville-Lascasses, Lynch-Bages, Pichon-Longueville-Comtesse-de-Lalande, Pichon Baron-Longueville, Magdelaine, Margaux, la Mission-Haut-Brion, Montrose, Mouton Rothschild, Ormes-de-Pez, Palmer, Pape Clément, Pavie, Petit-Village, Pétrus, de Pez, le Pin, Prieuré-Lichine, Rauzan-Ségla, Talbot, la Tour du Pin Figeac, Troplong-Mondot, Trotanoy, Valandraud, Vieux Châteaux Certan

✓ Top dry white Bordeaux: Châteaux Carbonnieux, Clos Floridène, Couhins-Lurton, Domaine de Chevalier, Fieuzal, Haut Brion, Laville-Haut-Brion, la Louvière, Pape-Clément, Smith-Haut-Lafite

Top sweet white Bordeaux: Châteaux Climens, Coutet, de Fargues, Doisy-Daëne, Gilette, Guiraud, Haut-Peyraguey, Raymond-Lafon, Rayne-Vigneau, Rieussec, Suduiraut, Yquem

Lifespans: Drink basic Bordeaux within five years of the vintage; affordable Bordeaux from good vintages, within ten; Top red, dry, and sweet white Bordeaux from good vintages within 25, 15, and 25 years respectively. Drink wine from leser vintages earlier.

Good vintages:
✓ Good red vintages: 1982, 1985, 1988, 1989, 1990, 1995, 1996, 1998 ✓ Good dry white vintages: 1993, 1994, 1996, 1997, 1998, 1999.
✓ Good sweet white vintages: 1995, 1996, 1997, 1998.

Burgundy: the patchwork quilt

BURGUNDY VARIES *in many ways from Bordeaux. Here, there's no blending of grape varieties – the reds are made exclusively from the Pinot Noir while the whites are produced from the Chardonnay. There are almost no grand châteaux, either. While the big aristocratic estates of Bordeaux survived the French Revolution, Burgundy's vineyards were taken back from the Church and redistributed as small parcels to the region's peasants. Because they had no reputation of their own, these new owners sold their wine under the name of the village or the vineyard in which the grapes were grown.*

■ **Unlike other** *regions, Burgundy's wines are not blends of different grapes.*

Today, while the labels of Bordeaux's wines tend to bear the names of the châteaux where they were produced, Burgundies generally carry the names of the commune where they were produced – such as Nuits-St-Georges or Beaune.

Premier and Grand Crus

Over the years, in some cases, the best vineyards within these communes have developed such a reputation for the wine they produce that they have become as famous, and even on occasion more famous, than the village in which they are situated. These vineyards are known as Premier Crus (first growths) and Grand Crus (Great Growths), respectively the better and best vineyards in a commune.

Not all communes have Grand Cru vineyards. The ones that do add the name of the vineyard to their own – so Meursault Charmes, for example, comes from the Charmes vineyard in Meursault.

Grand Crus are so grand that their labels don't have to mention which commune they are from. So there is no way to tell from the label of a wine from the La Tache Grand Cru vineyard that it is has been produced in the appellation of Vosne-Romanée. Confusingly, the names of vineyards that are not Premiers Crus also legally appear on labels sometimes. Meursault les Tessons is one example.

Don't confuse non-Premier Cru wines with genuine Premier Crus, whose labels should (but won't always) include the words "Premier Cru."

Meet the maker

As generations have come and gone and families have intermarried, estates have been created that now consist of small plots spread across various village appellations. So, while a Médoc château may annually produce 25,000 cases of the same wine, the Burgundian winemaker might not only produce a tenth as many bottles, but he'll divide that production among several different appellations. Occasionally, he might only make as little as one barrel – 300 bottles – of a particular wine.

If one estate makes wines from several villages and vineyards, the reverse is also true. The famous 125-acre Clos Vougeot Grand Cru, once a single estate that belonged to a monastery, is now split among over 70 producers, all of whom can make their own wine from the grapes they pick there and print Clos Vougeot on their – often very similar – labels. They can also sell their wine to merchants who will blend it with their own or other producers' Clos Vougeot. And sell it under yet another label.

Producers' names are often confusingly similar (there are, for example, four separate members of the Rossignol family making wine in the village of Volnay), but the quality of their wine can vary dramatically. So take care to read and remember the name of the estate or merchant.

A tour around Burgundy – the whites

Our trip begins around 100 miles south of Paris in the region of Chablis, where some of the leanest, driest, most minerally Chardonnay in the world is produced. Some producers here ferment and/or age their wine in new oak barrels; others take pride in the fact that their Chablis has no oak character at all. It is worth paying extra for a Premier Cru or Grand Cru Chablis, which will have come from one of the best vineyards. These can be among the quintessential Audrey Hepburn wines. Humbler wine labeled as Petit Chablis can be good too, but rarely impressive.

■ **Chablis produces** *some of the world's driest Chardonnays.*

In the Côte d'Or – the Hill of Gold – 124 miles or so farther south, we come to some more Grand Crus in the villages of Aloxe Corton (where the famous Grand Cru is the Corton Charlemagne), Puligny, and Chassagne Montrachet (which share a vineyard called le Montrachet). The Côte d'Or's other most famous white-wine village, Meursault, doesn't have any Grand Crus, but wines from Premier Cru vineyards such as Les Perrières and Les Charmes are worth buying. The keynote of Côte d'Or whites is a combination of nutty, buttery richness, plus a hint of the mineral that is found in Chablis. Wines from this region are never cheap but Pernand-Vergelesses, Monthélie, St. Aubin, and St. Romain can all offer affordable good value.

Heading south, there are good whites in the Côte Chalonnaise from Mercurey, Rully, and Montagny – and some interesting examples of Burgundy's little-known Aligoté grape in Bouzeron. The biggest source of (relatively) inexpensive white Burgundy, though, is the Mâconnais region to the north of Lyon. Much of the Mâcon-Villages wine produced here is dull stuff made by cooperatives to be sold in supermarkets. There are some good examples of Mâcon-Viré and Mâcon-Clessé, but for interesting wine you should head for the hills where the (somewhat) more reliable St. Véran and Pouilly Fuissé (and its neighbors Pouilly Loché and Pouilly Vinzelles) are produced. There are no Premier Cru or Grand Cru wines here, but there are good wines from individual vineyards.

Burgundy reds

There are a few light reds produced (in the village of Irancy) near Chablis, but for the good stuff we'll go back to the Côte d'Or. The Côte de Nuits, as the northern part of this region is known, is the home of many of the most intense longest-lived Burgundies, in villages such as Gevrey-Chambertin, Morey-St-Denis, Chambolle Musigny, Vougeot, and Nuits-St-Georges. The flavors here range from raspberry to blackcurrant and licorice.

■ **Gevrey-Chambertin** *can produce long-lived Burgundies.*

As we head south into the Côte de Beaune, to the appellations of Chorey-les-Beaune, Aloxe-Corton, Pernand Vergelesses, Ladoix, Savigny les Beaune, Beaune, Volnay, Pommard, Chassagne-Montrachet, and Santenay, the raspberry comes to the fore – sometimes accompanied by some lovely floral plummy characters. The finest wines – the Grands Crus such as Corton, Chambertin, and Clos de la Roche – can improve over decades. Lesser wines are at their best in the decade after the harvest.

Mercurey and Rully, in the Côte Chalonnaise, often offer more affordable value than some of the villages of the Côte d'Or, but the Mâconnais is a source of generally unimpressive rustic red made from the Gamay grape.

Beaujolais: the exception to the Burgundy rule

For a real taste of what the Gamay can do, you need to go to the granite hills of the Beaujolais, where growers use the Maceration Carbonique to bring out its cherry-and-banana-and-chocolate flavors. These are generally wines to enjoy in their youth: Shirley Temple in a glass.

Beaujolais actually comes in five forms. Setting aside Beaujolais Blanc – a Chardonnay rarely seen nowadays – there is basic Beaujolais that could come from anywhere in the region, and Beaujolais-Villages which, like any French wine with "villages" tacked onto its name, will have been made from grapes grown in better vineyards. Both Beaujolais and Beaujolais-Villages are also produced as nouveau – literally "new" – a style that goes on sale in November, a few weeks after the harvest. Beaujolais Nouveau, which makes up around half the region's total production, can be tastily fruity stuff to drink chilled with friends in a bar, or with plenty of cold meat. It can also be perilously close to vinegar. Which you get will depend entirely on the quality of the vintage and the producer.

Beaujolais' best wines come from ten "Cru" villages whose labels probably won't even mention the fact they are from Beaujolais at all.

Of these, the best are probably Morgon, St. Amour, Fleurie, and Moulin à Vent. Unlike standard Beaujolais, they can be worth keeping for five years or longer.

Things to remember about Burgundy

✔ Red wines are made from Pinot Noir; whites are mostly made from Chardonnay. Beaujolais is made from Gamay.

✔ Red Burgundy is generally lighter in color and style than most other red wines.

✔ Quantities are much smaller than in Bordeaux.

✔ "Basic" red Burgundy costs more than equivalent red Bordeaux, but is generally a better buy. Also look out for wines such as Côtes de Beaune Villages, Côtes de Nuits Villages, and, in good vintages, Hautes Cotes de Beaune and Hautes Côtes de Nuits. White Burgundy is less reliable.

✔ Wines from less well-known villages such as St. Romain, Savigny lès Beaune, and Auxey Duresses can be better value than from "big name" ones such as Gevrey Chambertin and Nuits-St-Georges.

✔ Wines are generally sold under the name of the region (e.g., Burgundy or Beaujolais) or commune (e.g., Chablis, Nuits-St-Georges) and/or vineyard (e.g., Meursault-Charmes and le Chambertin).

✔ When looking for quality, the name of the winegrower or merchant is as important than that of the appellation.

✔ Vintages vary greatly, some being more successful for one style than another. Burgundy has good vintages in years when Bordeaux has poorer ones – and vice versa.

■ **When looking** *for quality Burgundy wines, the name of the winegrower is just as important as the appellation.*

BURGUNDY TO BUY — AND WHEN TO DRINK IT

Top producers:

✓ Chablis: Jean-Marc Brocard, Pascal Bouchard, La Chablisienne, Jean, Réné & Vincent Dauvissat, Jean-Paul Droin, Joseph Drouhin, William Fevre, Laroche, Long-Depaquit, Dom des Malandes, Durhup, Louis Michel, Louis Pinson, François Raveneau, Servin, Verget, Vocoret & Fils

✓ Côte d'Or: Bertrand Ambroise, Guy Amiot, Dom. de l'Arlot, Comte Armand, Robert Arnoux, Dom. d'Auveney, Denis Bachelet, Bertagna, Simon Bize, Blain-Gagnard, Jean-Marc Boillot, Bonneau du Martray, Bouchard Pere et Fils, Louis Carillon, Coche-Dury, Robert Chevillon, Marc Colin, Michel Colin-Deleger, Jean-Jacques Confuron, Confuron-Cotetidot, Joseph Drouhin, Drouhin-Laroze, Claude Dugat, Dom. Dujac, Rene Engel, Faiveley, Fontaine-Gagnard, Jean-Noel Gagnard, Vincent Girardin, Etienne Grivot, Gros Frere & Soeur, Henri Gouges, Louis Jadot, Jayer-Gilles, Francois Jobard, Michel Lafarge, Domaine des Comtes Lafon, Laleure-Piot, Hubert Lamy, Latour-Giraud, Dominique Laurent, Dom., Leflaive, Olivier Leflaive Freres, Dom. Leroy, Maroslavac-Leger, Meo-Camuzet, Ch. de Meursault, Alain Michelot, Michelot-Buisson, Monthelie-Douhairet, Bernard Morey, Pierre Morey, Denis Mortet, Pierre Morey, Michel Niellon, Ponsot, Dom. Pousse d'Or, Jacques Prieur, Ch. de Puligny-Montrachet, Ramonet, Daniel Rion, Dom. de la Romanee-Conti, Emmanuel Rouget, Guy Roulot, G. Roumier, Etienne Sauzet, Serafin, Tollot-Beaut, de Vogüé

✓ Côte Chalonnaise: Cave de Buxy, Juillot, Steinmaier, de Suremain

✓ Maconnais/Beaujolais: Dom. de la Bongran, Duboeuf, Ferret, Guffens-Heynen, Chateau Fuissé / Vincent

Lifespans: Basic reds and whites should be drunk within five years or so. As you climb the quality scale, longevity rises to 20 or 30 years – but only in top vintages from top producers.

Good vintages:

✓ Red: 1978, 1985, 1989, 1990, 1992, 1995, 1996 1997, 1998, 1999.

✓ White: 1989, 1990, 1992, 1993, 1994, 1995, 1996 1997, 1998, 1999

Champagne: the most famous wine of all?

CHAMPAGNE BREAKS all the rules we've learned so far. A number of entire villages admittedly enjoy Premier Cru status, but these words rarely appear on labels. There are small estates like those in those other regions that produce and sell their own wine, but most wine is made and marketed by big companies such as Moët & Chandon and cooperatives that supply Champagne to retailers and restaurants who like to have their own names on the label.

■ **The word Champagne** *exudes decadence, luxury, and wealth.*

What's in a vintage?

In other words, when buying Champagne, we tend to rely on the brand. Like the couture houses with which many of them are associated, each brand will have a recognizable "house style." Champagne is only given a vintage on its label in the best years. Most of the Champagne that any of us are likely to drink is a blend – not only of vintages but also of grapes from different parts of the region. Champagne with a vintage on its label is only made in the best years.

The quality of the year is only one of the factors that sets vintage Champagne apart. This wine gets much better treatment from its producers than non-vintage. Where some non-vintage Champagne is rushed onto the market within 18 months of the harvest, vintage Champagne is allowed to rest in the bottle for three or four years with the yeast that helps to create the bubbles. This prolonged yeast contact helps to give the wine a cookielike richness that should set it apart.

The best so-called "prestige" Champagnes such as Dom Perignon and Roederer Cristal, like the best sports cars, warrant the premium price they command, but beware of ordinary Champagne in fancy packaging.

■ **White Champagne** *is often made from black grapes.*

Trivia...

It is no accident that many Champagne houses are under the same ownership as perfumiers and couturiers. Like a scent, a Champagne is chosen by style. For example, Winston Churchill favored the Pol Roger brand. James Bond's preference for Bollinger may have something to do with that (excellent) film producer's marketing budget – in the original novels, he preferred another brand.

234

While Champagne producers all claim that their non-vintage and vintage wine is ready to drink the day it hits the street, almost every good example will benefit from being kept in a cellar for at least one year and possibly five years or longer.

Things to remember about Champagne

✓ Most wines are "non-vintage" blends of different years' harvests.

✓ Vintages are only "declared" in years of higher quality wine.

✓ Champagne is sold under the name of its producer.

✓ Red (Bouzy Rouge), pink (rosé de Riceys), and white (Coteaux Champenois) wines without bubbles are also produced in the Champagne region. They are always expensive and rarely represent good value for money.

■ **Pinot Noir** *is the key black grape in Champagne.*

CHAMPAGNE TO BUY — AND WHEN TO DRINK IT

Top producers:

Paul Bara, Billecart-Salmon, Bollinger, Gimonnet, Deutz, Gosset, Alfred Gratien, Charles Heidsieck, Henriot, Jacquesson, Krug, Lanson, Laurent-Perrier, Moet & Chandon, Pol Roger, Pommery, Roederer, Ruinart, Salon, Taittinger, Veuve Clicquot

Lifespans: Champagne is supposedly sold ready to drink, but it can benefit from being cellared. Non-vintage wine from good producers can be kept for up to three years or so, vintage wines for 10 to 15 years, and Prestige Cuvées for 25 years or longer

Good vintages: 1989, 1990, 1991, 1992, 1993, 1995, 1996, 1997, 1998

Rhône Valley: the spice jar

THE HOTTEST COMPETITION NOW FACING *Bordeaux and Burgundy comes from the region that follows the Rhône river southward from the city of Lyon. The combination of the grape varieties grown here, highly individual vineyards, and a warm climate, make for reds and whites that have one common characteristic: a spicy perfumed quality rarely found anywhere else. If France makes John Wayne wines, this is the place to find them.*

In the northern part of the region, the Syrah works solo to make smoky-spicy intense reds like St. Joseph, Hermitage, Crozes Hermitage, and Côte-Rôtie. While in the south, wines like Côtes du Rhône, Gigondas, Vacqueyras, Lirac, and Châteauneuf du Pape are usually blends in which the more peppery Grenache is joined by a cast of other varieties including the Syrah, Mourvèdre, and Cinsault.

There are no Premier or Grand Crus in the Rhône Valley, but individual vineyard wines in the northern region — those from the La Landonne in Côte Rôtie, for example — are sold at prices equal to top Bordeaux and Burgundy wines.

■ **Châteauneuf du Pape** *is made of many different grapes, including the peppery Grenache, Syrah, and Cinsault.*

In Châteauneuf du Pape, however, there is a combination of vineyard and château and domaine names.

White spice

The whites, though still spicy, vary too, as you follow the river south. Condrieu and Château Grillet are made from the floral and apricotty Viognier, while Hermitage is made from the Roussanne and Marsanne. Just as important are the marmaladey sweet fortified wines made from the Muscat in places such as Beaumes de Venise. The pink wines of the Rhône can be among France's best, but ignore the advice from the producers of Tavel to let their wine age: it's at its juicy peppery best within a year or so of the harvest.

The dry sparkling wines of the Rhône – St. Péray and Crémant de Die – are often fairly dull, but the Muscatty, grapey, sweet Clairette de Die Méthode Ancestrale can be a refreshing delight.

But with the popularity and prestige of red wines such as Hermitage, Cornas, Côte-Rôtie, and Châteauneuf du Pape has come higher prices. For an affordable taste of the Rhône, try a Côtes du Rhône or Côtes du Rhône Villages (which comes from the best part of the Côtes du Rhône region), a Côtes du Ventoux, or a wine from St. Joseph in the northern Rhône, or a Rasteau or a Cairanne from farther south.

Things to remember about the Rhône

✓ Reds and whites should taste spicy.

✓ Reds from the northern Rhône are made from pure Syrah; those from the south will mostly be blends that include the Grenache and other grapes.

✓ White Rhônes are good very young – and after five years or so. In between, they can taste dull.

✓ Even some of the best producers often prefer not to use new oak barrels.

✓ While there is no official ranking to indicate the best vineyards, the finest wines generally come from the best producers' best vines in Hermitage, Côte-Rôtie, and Châteauneuf (for reds), Condrieu and Cornas (for whites).

RHÔNE TO BUY – AND WHEN TO DRINK IT
Top producers:

✓ Northern Rhône: Thierry Allemand, Ch. d'Ampuis, Guy de Barjac, Bernard Burgaud, Gérard Chave, Delas, Guigal, Auguste Clape, Clusel-Roche, J-L Colombo, Dom. Courbis, Yves Cuileron, Jean-Michel Gerin, Alain Graillot, Grippat, Jean-Paul & Jean-Luc Jamet, Robert Jasmin, Jean Lionnet, André Perret, Marcel Richaud, R. Rostaing, Marc Sorrel, Tardieu-Laurent, Georges Vernay, Vidal-Fleurie, Alain Voge

✓ Southern Rhône: Ch. Beaucastel, Ch. Beaurenard, Dom. de la Janasse, Font de Michelle, Ch. Mont-Redon, Dom. de la Mordoree, Ch. La Nerthe, Ch. Rayas, Vieux Télégraphe (northern and southern Rhône) Chapoutier, Delas, Guigal, Jaboulet

Lifespans: Basic dry and sweet whites are best within three to five years of the harvest and rosés should be drunk within a year. Condrieu can last for seven years or so but easily loses its floral appeal. White Hermitage and other dry top whites should be drunk within three to five years and after ten; between these ages they can be dull. Top Northern Rhône reds and Chateauneuf du Pape can last 20 to 30 years, but lesser years and examples of these wines need drinking within a decade.

Good vintages: ✓ Red: 1989, 1990, 1994, 1995, 1996 1997, 1998
✓ White 1994, 1995, 1996, 1997, 1998

Loire Valley

NONE OF FRANCE'S regions can begin to compete with the variety of wines to be found along the river Loire as it flows westward from the middle of France to the Atlantic coast at Nantes. There are some very individual reds made from the Cabernet Franc and the Pinot Noir, but the focus here is on white wine – dry, sweet, and sparkling.

■ **A huge variety** of wines is produced along the Loire.

Dry whites

Best known of the dry wines are the steely gooseberryish Sauvignon Blancs of Sancerre and Pouilly Fumé. Less famous and cheaper, but often similarly worthwhile, are the wines made from this grape in Menetou Salon, Quincy, and Haut-Poitou.

If you find the flavor of Sauvignon Blanc too pungent and want an alternative to Chardonnay, you could try Muscadet, the dry, lemony, often slightly sparkling wine made from an undistinguished grape called the Melon de Bourgogne near the Atlantic coast. To appreciate Muscadet at its best, accompany it with oysters.

The most interesting white wines of the Loire, though, are made from the Chenin Blanc. Vouvray single-handedly demonstrates what this versatile variety can do, producing bone-dry, appley versions, honeyed demi-sec, luscious late harvest Moelleux, and creamy Champagne-method sparkling wines. Montlouis offers a more minerally version of the Vouvray style. Dry Chenin Blancs worth seeking out include Jasnieres and Savennieres (especially the Grands Crus Coulée-de-Serrant and Roche-aux-Moines), and sparkling Saumur, like Crémant de Loire, can be good value sparkling wine. The finest of all the Loire's wines, however, have to be the great sweet whites of Coteaux du Layon – especially pineappley licoricey Bonnezeaux and honeyed spicy Quarts de Chaume. These communes have been classed as Grands Crus.

River reds

We can't leave the Loire without tasting the reds – the light berryish Pinot Noirs of Sancerre and the fresh blackcurrant Cabernet Francs of Anjou,

■ **Muscadet should** *taste dry and lemony, and be slightly sparkling.*

Chinon, Bourgueil, and St. Nicolas de Bourgueil. The Cabernet Franc is also used to make pink Cabernet d'Anjou, which can be deliciously berryish – and a far better bet than the sugar-watery stuff unashamedly sold as Anjou Rosé.

Things to remember about the Loire

✓ The major grape varieties are Sauvignon Blanc, Chenin Blanc, Cabernet Franc, and Pinot Noir.

✓ Vintages vary widely.

✓ Sparkling wines can be good value.

✓ Sweet wines are among the longest lived in the world.

✓ Moelleux means "sweet" while demi-sec is semisweet and sec is dry. Even so, some Vouvray may prove to be sweeter than you might expect.

LOIRE TO BUY – AND WHEN TO DRINK IT
Top producers:

✓ Middle Loire: Ackerman-Laurance, Bouvet-Ladubay, Cailleau, Chateau Chamboureau, Champalou, Clos de la Coulée de Serrant, Couly-Dutheil, Dom. Bizolière, Dom. des Aubuisières, Dom. Echarderie, Chateau de Fesles, Filliatreau, Foreau, Gratien & Meyer, Huët, Joguet, Langlois Château, Mabille, Vincent Ogereau, Olga and Jean-Maurice Raffault, Rene Renou, Richou, la Roche aux Moines

✓ Upper Loire: Henri Beurdin, Bourgeois, Chateau de Chatenoy, Crochet, Didier Dagueneau, Alain & Pierre Dézat, Gitton, Jolivet, Ladoucette, Lafond, Serge Laporte, Henri Natter, Chateau de Nozet, Pabiot, Dom. Pellé, Pichard, Pinard, Jean-Max Roger, Rouzé, Teiller, Jean Thomas, Chateau de Tracy, Vacheron, Jean Vatan

Lifespans: Muscadet is at its best within a year or so of the harvest – as is all but the very best Loire Sauvignon Blanc. Dry Chenin Blancs (Vouvray etc age better and good sweet examples from good vintages last forever. Reds vary enormously but are generally best within five to ten years or so

Good vintages: ✓ Red: 1989, 1990, 1995, 1997 ✓ White (late harvest wines): 1979, 1985, 1986, 1989, 1990, 1995 ✓ White (dry): 1997, 1998, 1999

Alsace: the best of both worlds

ALSACE IS THE EXCEPTION *that proves the rule of French wine. This is the only major region that can fairly be described as almost exclusively white wine country; the few reds produced here could best be described as "sidelines." The tall green bottles seem to have far more in common with the ones used on the other side of the Rhine in Germany. Now take a look at the label. France's wines are mostly sold by the name of the village, vineyard, or region, except in Alsace, where grape names such as Riesling, Gewurztraminer, and Pinot Gris are emblazoned across the label as boldly as Chardonnay might be on a bottle from California. There are a number of Grand Cru vineyards that earn a mention too, but the village appellations of the kind we've become used to in Burgundy, the Rhône, and Loire are nowhere to be found.*

■ **Wines from the** *Alsace region are predominantly white.*

Grape expectations

Of the six principal grapes grown in Alsace, the most typical, if not always the source of the best wines, is the floral, spicy, litchi-ish Gewurztraminer. The Pinot Gris (also known as Tokay-Pinot Gris) can be spicy too, but less overtly so, while the Pinot Blanc is creamier and richer and more reminiscent of a Chardonnay without oak. Alsace's Muscat offers a rare opportunity to sample dry examples of this, naturally the grapeyest of grapes, while the Sylvaner provides an earthy taste of how wines used to be. For most producers, though, the finest longest-lived Alsace wines are made from the Riesling.

Style counsel

Most Alsace wines are supposedly dry, but many have an unmistakeable touch of sweetness. Confusingly, unless you know the style favored by the producer, there is no way to tell until you have pulled the cork.

■ **The Pinot Gris** *grape produces a mildly spicy wine.*

Vendange Tardive, however, will always be decidedly sweet, while *Selection de Grains Nobles* should be as luscious as the finest Sauternes. Wines labeled *Edelzwicker* or *Gentil* will be blends of different grapes, while the Pinot Noir usually produces raspberryish reds that are sometimes almost pale enough to qualify as rosé.

DEFINITION

Vendange Tardive means late-harvest, while Selection de Grains Nobles refers to a wine made from selected nobly rotten grapes.

Things to remember about Alsace

✓ Wines are mostly labeled according to the grape variety from which they are made.

✓ The best quality wines should come from Grand Cru vineyards (such as Hengst, Rangen, and Sporen).

✓ Wines can be dry or sweet.

■ **Pinot Blanc** *gives a creamy, rich-tasting wine.*

ALSACE TO BUY — AND WHEN TO DRINK IT

Top producers:

Adam, Albrecht, Blanck, Bott-Geyl, Albert Boxler, Ernest, J & F Burn, Cattin, Deiss, J-P Dirler, Dopff au Moulin, Dopff & Irion, Eguisheim cooperative, Faller, Hugel, Josmeyer, Kientzler, Kreidenweiss, Meyer-Fonné, Mittnacht-Klack, Muré, Ostertag, Pfaffenheim cooperative, Rolly Gassmann, Schaller, Schlumberger, Schoffit, Sick-Dreyer, Bruno Sorg, Trimbach, Turckheim cooperative, Weinbach, Zind-Humbrecht

Lifespans: Drink basic Pinot Blanc and Gewurztraminer within three years or so. Grand Cru dry wines easily last for a decade or so and late-harvest examples can improve over 20 years. Most Alsace reds are for early drinking.

Good vintages: 1989, 1990, 1992, 1993, 1995, 1996, 1997, 1998

Eastern France: Jura and Savoie

IT IS EASY TO UNDERSTAND *why the wines of Jura and the skiing country of Savoie have been pushed into the shadows. Many of the grape varieties grown here – such as the Mondeuse, Poulsard, Jacquère, Altesse, and Savagnin – are largely unknown outside the region. Some of the styles are decidedly unfashionable. There are few brands, and the presence of all those well-heeled skiers – the wines' greatest fans – helps to make for prices that keep the bottles away from the bargain shelves.*

While they are close to each other on the map and usually treated as a pair of regions, Jura and Savoie are really quite different. The Jura has some pleasant Pinot Noir and Chardonnay, but the distinctive wines are the Vin Jaune, whose nutty character comes from the effects of a yeast that is allowed to develop on the surface of the grapes while they are in the barrel (we'll find out more about this when we take a look at the way sherry is made in Spain), and the sweet raisiny Vin de Paille made using the traditional method of allowing the grapes to dry out on straw – paille – before they are crushed. At their best, Savoie's wines are light, fresh, and either floral (white) or berryish (red).

Things to remember about the wines of Jura and Savoie

✔ Wines are made from Pinot Noir and Chardonnay (Jura) as well as other varieties rarely found elsewhere, such as the Savagnin and Poulsard (Jura), the Mondeuse, Altesse/Roussette, and Jaquere (Savoie).

✔ Arbois' Vin Jaune is France's answer to dry sherry. Vin de Paille gets less recognition but can be a very good buy.

■ **Winemakers in Jura** *use the Pinot Noir grape as well as unfamiliar local varieties.*

EASTERN FRANCE – WINE TO BUY – AND WHEN TO DRINK IT

Top producers:

✓ Jura: Lucien Aviet, Jean Bourdy, Frutière d'Arbois, Ch. d'Arlay, Christian Beaulieu, Ch. l'Etoile, Dom. Grand Freres, Jean Macle, Andre & Mireille Tissot, Jacques Tissot

✓ Savoie: Dominique Allion, Grande Cave de Crépy, Maison Mollex, Royal Seyssel, Varichon et Clerc

Lifespans: Light Jura whites and reds are generally at their best within five years of the harvest and Savoie examples need drinking within a year or so. Vin Jaune and Vin de Paille, however, can be worth cellaring for 10 to 20 years.

Good vintages:
✓ Jura: 1985, 1989, 1990, 1995, 1996
✓ Savoie: 1997, 1998, 1999

Southwest: land of tradition

HISTORY HAS BEEN *ungenerous to this, the area that is still producing some of France's most traditional wines. But for an accident of geography and local chauvinism, wines such as Bergerac and Monbazillac might have been included as part of Bordeaux, whose wines they resemble. Then there are once-famous wines such as Gaillac, Cahors, and Jurançon, which have the misfortune of being made in relatively small quantities from grapes that are unknown or unfashionable elsewhere. These are, in short, wines to seize upon when traveling in France or when visiting restaurants or wine stores with an unusually enterprising selection of bottles.*

■ **Bergerac has produced**
wine since Roman times.

Things to remember about the southwest

✓ The wide range of wines made here are produced from a wide range of grape varieties. These include the ones used in Bordeaux (Bergerac, Buzet, Monbazillac, Duras, Pecharmant), as well as Malbec (Cahors), Tannat (Madiran), Petit and Gros Manseng (Jurançon, Pacherenc du Vic-Bilh), and Gamay (Gaillac).

✓ While some wines seem tough and rustic, many offer flavors found nowhere else (Jurançon, Cahors) and can represent good value and characterful drinking.

THE SOUTHWEST — WINE TO BUY AND WHEN TO DRINK IT

Top producers:

✓ Jurançon: Bellegarde, Bousquet, Brana, Bru-Baché, Cauhapé, Clos Guirouilh, Clos Lapeyre, Clos Uroulat, Cru Lamouroux

✓ Cahors: Ch. la Caix, la Caminade, du Cèdre, Clos la Coutale, Clos de Gamot, Gatoul, de Hauterive, Haute-Serre, Lagrezette, Lamartine, Latuc, Paillas, Rochet-Lamothe, Clos Triguedina

✓ Bergerac/Monbazillac: Ch. Belingard, Ch. Court-les-Mûts, des Eyssards, Ch. de Gueyze, Ch. de Monbazillac, Dom. Richard, Ch. Tour des Gendres

✓ Buzet: Vignerons de Buzet

✓ Pacherenc/Madiran: Barréjat, Ch. Bouscassé, Crampih, Montus, Peyros, Pichard, Plaimont

Lifespans: Most dry whites and light reds (such as Bergerac) should be drunk within five years of the harvest. Good Cahors, Madiran, and late-harvest Jurançon can be kept for twice that long.

Good vintages: ✓ Cahors: 1989, 1990, 1995, 1996
✓ Jurançon: 1995, 1996, 1997, 1998

The south: meeting point of the past and future

THE WARM SOUTH OF FRANCE – *what is now known as Provence and Languedoc Roussillon – has been making wine for over 2,000 years. But until the recent arrival of technology, investment, and self-confidence, it rarely offered much competition to the famous more northerly regions. The traditionally rustic wines of Minervois, Corbières, and Fitou are improving fast as producers take more care over the way they use grape varieties such as the Carignan and the Syrah. Other wines worth looking out for include Faugères, St. Chinian, Côteaux de Languedoc, Collioure, Bellet, and Côtes du Roussillon, which can compete with many offerings from the Rhône. The best single-estate wines from these appellations are increasingly competing with efforts from more famous regions.*

Red, white, and fortified

Although most of the best wine is still red, there are some good Chardonnays from Limoux, some spicy whites from Cassis, and a raft of rosé de Provence that can be good when well made and caught young. Another specialty are the sweet fortified wines such as the dark plummy Banyuls and Maury that French critics compare to vintage port (of which we'll learn more in Chapter 17), and the various grapey Muscats such as de Frontignan and Rivesaltes. Blanquette de Limoux is an improving Champagne-method sparkling wine.

One word of warning: labels that include the word "Tradition" will be more to the taste of those who like their wines to taste earthy rather than fruity. In other words, if you enjoy California Merlot, avoid most "Tradition" wines from the south.

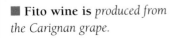

■ **Fito wine is** *produced from the Carignan grape.*

Things to remember about southern France

✓ A broadening range of wines are produced, from the traditional rustic reds and whites of Corbières to spicy alternatives to the Rhône (Pic St-Loup).

✓ Grape varieties include Carignan (Minervois, Corbieres, Fitou), Syrah (Pic St-Loup), Merlot, Cabernet Sauvignon, Grenache, Chardonnay.

✓ Reds are generally far more successful than whites.

✓ Some of the best wines are vin de pays (see opposite).

■ **In Southern France**, *red wine is always the flavor of the day.*

THE SOUTH — WINE TO BUY AND WHEN TO DRINK IT

Top producers:

Gilbert Alquier, Ch. de Caraguilhes, les Caves du Sieur d'Arques, Clos Bagatelle, Etang des Colombes, Ch. l'Espigne, Força Real, Dom Gauby, Ch. Grézan, Ch. de Gourgazaud, Ch. Héléne, Ch. de Jau, Ch. de Lastours, Ch. Malviès, Dom. du Mas Amiel, Mas de Bressades, d'Oupia, Clos des Paulilles, Piccinini, Prieuré de St Jean de Bébian, Producteurs de Mont Tauch, Pech-Latt, Ch. de la Peyrade, Ste. Eulalie, la Tour Boisée, la Tour Vieille, Vignerons Catalans, Villerambert-Julien, la Voulte Gasparets

Good vintages:
✓ Red: 1989, 1990, 1991, 1992, 1993, 1994, 1995, 1996 1997, 1998, 1999
✓ White: 1989, 1990, 1991, 1992, 1993, 1994, 1995, 1996 1997, 1998, 1999

Vin de pays and vin de table: the bargain basement

SOME WINES FALL *outside of the appellation controlée rules. First, there's a curious designation of VDQS – Vins Délimités de Qualité Supérieure (Wine of a Superior Quality) – that covers a few specific areas such as Sauvignon de St.-Bris near Chablis. Second, there are the far larger vin de pays (country wine) regions whose wines are often sold under the name of the varietal from which they are made and can represent very good value alternatives to varietals from the New World.*

Vins de pays

Most vins de pays are made by big producers, some of whom – Fortant de France and Val d'Orbieu, for example – offer wines ranging from basic daily-drinking fare to ambitious reds and whites that win prizes in international competitions. Individual estates such as Mas de Daumas Gassac make red and white vin de pays de l'Hérault as good as – and sold at the same price as – well-known wine from Bordeaux.

■ **Some of the largest** *French wine producers are situated in the Languedoc-Roussillon.*

Vins de table

Finally, there is the basic table wine – vin de table – that you get in restaurant pitchers but rarely see in serious shops. Vin de table labels cannot legally mention grape varieties, regions, or vintage. Good examples are very rare.

■ **Vins de table** *could be made anywhere in France.*

Things to remember about vins de pays and vins de table

✔ Vin-de-pays wines vary enormously depending on the region and producer. A Chardonnay from the cool Jardin de France region in the Loire will be very different to one from the warm south, sold as Vin de Pays d'Oc.

✔ A few producers, such as Mas de Daumas Gassac, Fortant de France, and Val d'Orbieu, are making vin de pays that are as good as many appellation controlée wines.

✔ Vintages are almost irrelevant for most vins de pays. Drink the youngest examples you can find.

■ **Mas de Daumas Gassae**, *the top wine from Hérault, is generally sold at the same price as Bordeaux.*

VIN DE PAYS TO BUY — AND WHEN TO DRINK IT

Top producers:

Clos Centeilles, Dom. de Clovallon, Font Caude, Fortant de France, Galet, Grange des Pères, HDR (Hugh Ryman), James Herrick, Mas de Daumas Gassac, Domaines Rothschild, VVO – Val d'Orbieu (top wines), Dom. Virginie

Lifespans: Most Vins de Pays should be drunk as soon as they are bought. Wines like Mas de Daumas Gassac, which can improve over a decade, are the exceptions to the rule

Good vintages: 1997, 1998

A simple summary

✓ Most of France's wine regions produce individual styles that are not found in other parts of the country.

✓ A combination of climate, soil, choice of grapes, and appellation contrôlée rules dictate what can be made where and how.

✓ Throughout many parts of France, hierarchies exist establishing which vineyards (usually the Grands Crus and Premiers Crus) have the potential to produce the best wine. The structure of these hierarchies varies confusingly from one region to another.

✓ Appellation contrôlée may guarantee a wine's regional and stylistic authenticity – but not its quality.

✓ France's best dry white wines mostly come from the northern half of the country – Alsace, Burgundy, and the Loire.

✓ France's best sweet whites mostly come from Bordeaux (Sauternes, Barsac, the Loire (Vouvray, Bonnezeaux, Quarts de Chaume), and Alsace (Vendange Tardive, Selection des Grains Nobles).

✓ Some regions specialize in making wines with single varietals (Chardonnay for white Burgundy and Pinot Noir for red; Syrah for red northern Rhône, Sauvignon for Sancerre and Chenin for Vouvray; Riesling, Pinot Gris, and Gewurztraminer in Alsace) while others use blends (Cabernet Sauvignon and Merlot in red Bordeaux, and Sauvignon Blanc and Sémillon in white; Grenache and Syrah in the southern Rhône).

✓ Vintages can vary enormously, from year to year, from region to region, and even from style to style within a single region.

✓ The producer's name may be the most important element of a wine label (bad producers can make bad or simply ordinary wine in the most famous regions and vineyards).

Chapter 17

Italy: Different Grapes and Styles

FROM FRANCE, WHOSE REGIONS such as Bordeaux and Burgundy seem to have more or less hogged the limelight over the last millennium, we take a tour of the sunny regions of southern Europe. Italy and Greece had vineyards that were famous 2,000 years ago. Today they are back in the headlines – along with their neighbors such as Spain, Portugal, the countries of the Eastern Mediterranean, and North Africa. We'll begin in Italy.

In this chapter...

ITALY MAKES SOME OF THE MOST DISTINCTIVE WINE IN THE WORLD

Legal labyrinth

ANY WINE ENTHUSIAST who pretends not to be confused by Italian wine is either trying to kid you or kid themselves. This is, without question, the most complicated wine country in the world. There are countless regions and denominations – the Italian equivalent of France's appellations contrôlées – an army of different grapes, some of which change name, depending on where they are grown, and a glorious band of producers who persist in challenging the system by constantly creating wholly new styles of wine.

The official rules

However, because our aim in this book is to try to keep things simple, we'll make as much sense of this labyrinth as we can. Let's start with the official rules.

Until quite recently, there were three levels of quality. Basic wines were vino da tavola (table wine). Next came denominazione di origine controllata (DOC), Italy's version of France's appellation contrôlée. Then there were a few supposedly better areas, which were declared to be denominazione di origine controllata e garantita (DOCG), such as Chianti Classico.

■ **The countless rules** governing Italian wine production are hard to follow.

Unlike France's appellation system, however, Italy's doesn't offer any indication of the best vineyards in any region – but this hasn't deterred producers from proudly printing vineyard names (sometimes preceded by Cru) on their labels.

Getting around the rules

This is far from the only way innovative winemakers have unilaterally taken control of Italy's wine industry. In particular, while France's producers happily or reluctantly live with legislation that dictates the grape varieties they may use in their wines, some of Italy's best estates decided to sidestep their country's laws completely. They simply created new blends, which they labeled as *vino da tavola*, the designation we met on p. 247–48 that covers the stuff that is served by the pitcher in restaurants.

The reputation of the producers and the quality of the wines was good enough for the new *vini da tavola* to sell at several times the price of DOCG wines. Inevitably, the authorities eventually had to separate these high-quality *vini da tavola* from the pitcher wine. They did this by creating a totally new designation called *Indicazione Geografica Tipica* (IGT), but complications – and high-quality *vino da tavola* – still exist.

A look at the regions

Italy's wine regions differ from those in France in one significant way – their names rarely appear on wine labels.

So, while you can buy bottles of Burgundy, Bordeaux, and Champagne, you can't fill your wine rack with Tuscany, Piedmont, or Umbria. Whatever the region, though, as in France, a wine could come from an estate (e.g., Azienda, Podere, Cascina, or Tenuta), a cooperative (e.g., Cantina Sociale), or a merchant.

INTERNET

www.wine.it

This commercial site is dedicated to Italian wine.

■ **The region where** *a wine was made can be hard to find on Italian labels.*

Northwest Italy: all quiet on the western front

WE'LL START OUR *tour of Italy in the northwest, in Piedmont, home of a wide range of very different wines. The most famous and probably, despite competition from Chianti, Italy's top wine of all, is Barolo. Like Burgundy, its very different soul mate in France, this wine, supposed to be made from a single grape variety (the Nebbiolo), was traditionally often blended with stronger, less flavorsome wine from farther south. It was also frequently made in a heavy-handed way that concealed the fruit flavors and accentuated the tannin.*

Barolo and Barbaresco

Then, along came a new generation of producers who, with a few of the best of the old guard, helped to jettison the rustic image of both Barolo and Barbaresco, its kid brother. It was as though a role played by John Wayne had been taken over by Cary Grant. Good examples of Barolo and Barbaresco are worth keeping for at least a decade. Simpler Nebbiolos for early drinking are sold as Spanna.

■ **Nebbiolo grapes,** *grown in the Piedmont region, make the wine of Barolo.*

Trivia...

Today, few wine experts would question Barolo's role as one of the world's great dry red wines. At the beginning of the 20th century however, it must have proved popular with lovers of Coca Cola, because back then it used to be sweet and slightly sparkling. Today, the giant Banfi winery still makes a fizzy red in Piedmont called Brachetto.

Barbera

The other major red grape of the region is the Barbera. Grown throughout Italy, but arguably at its best here in Barbera d'Alba, it can have a really stylish Audrey Hepburn character. There are blends of Barbera and Nebbiolo, and even the occasional Pinot Noir, as well as characterful wines made from the Freisa, Dolcetto, and Grignolino. Another place that uses the Barbera as a component is Lombardy, where it partners the local Bonarda grape to make wine that tastes like not-quite-ripe plums. This area also produces some distinctively light floral reds called Valtellina in the mountains near the border with Switzerland.

Nearby Liguria, the region around Genoa, produces light floral reds known as Rossesse that apparently were popular with Napoleon. The steeply sloping vineyards of the tiny area of Valle d'Aosta grow interesting local grapes such as the Fumin and Petit Rouge, and use the Nebbiolo to make violetty wines labeled as Donnaz.

The whites

Most of the more exciting wines of both Liguria and Valle d'Aosta are, however, white. Valle d'Aosta has delicious Muscats, Chardonnays, and Pinot Grigios. Liguria has fascinating spicy wines made from the local Pigato and herby ones from a grape called the Vermentino, which – this being Italy – is not the same variety as the Vermentino of Sardinia. Lombardy makes a wine called Lugana that can be an attractively subtle alternative to Soave – and lots of Franciacorta sparkling wine.

Piedmont's top white grape is the Arneis, which produces lovely aromatic spicy dry wines, but the white wines you are most likely to come across outside Italy are the Muscats: the sparkling Asti Spumantes and semi-sparkling and lower alcohol (four to five percent) Moscato d'Asti. The perfect warm-weather drink.

Things to remember about the northwest

✓ The key grapes are Nebbiolo (used for Barolo, Barbaresco, Spanna), Barbera, Muscat (Moscato, Asti Spumante), Arneis.

✓ Individual vineyard wines such as Gaja's Sori Tildin are worth looking out for.

✓ Barolo can be drunk younger nowadays, but good examples still deserve to be kept for a decade before they are opened.

✓ Moscato and Asti Spumante are best drunk young while they are still fruity.

Northeast Italy: the mysterious east

HEADING EASTWARD, we get to a set of very different regions, a range of Italy's most distinctive wines, and some more confusion. Some wine books include a wine region called the Sud Tirol; others have the Alto Adige. Both are in fact the same place: The lederhosen-wearing, German-speaking inhabitants close to the Austrian border prefer the former, while the authorities in Rome favor the latter. The best reds here are the berryish Dunkels and Schiavas made from the local Lagrein grape. Trentino, to the south of this region, offers reasonable but rarely exceptional Cabernet, Merlot, and Pinot Noir, and more interesting wines from the spicy Teroldego to the mentholly Marzemino.

■ **White wines** *are the most interesting ones produced in the northeast region.*

The reds

The eastern part of the region, Friuli-Venezia Giulia, nudges up against the border with Slovenia and confuses everybody by not boasting a single style of its own. At the last count, there were at least 70 different kinds of wine being made here, ranging from familiar grape varieties such as Merlot and Cabernet Sauvignon to local grapes rarely found elsewhere, such as the Refosco and Schioppettino.

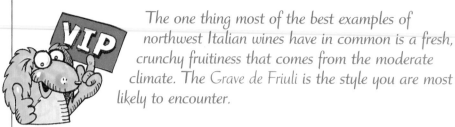

The one thing most of the best examples of northwest Italian wines have in common is a fresh, crunchy fruitiness that comes from the moderate climate. The Grave de Friuli is the style you are most likely to encounter.

The most famous reds in the northeast, though, are the Valpolicellas and Bardolinos of the Veneto. Most of these are pretty ordinary wines for drinking very young. But when they are good, they can have wonderfully cherryish flavors found nowhere else.

There is a serious style of Valpolicella that is worth traveling a long way to find.

Recioto, as it is known, is made by one of the most traditional methods of all. Like France's Vin de Paille, it involves drying the grapes until they have almost become raisins before crushing and fermenting them. There are two kinds of Recioto, the dry Amarone and the sweet Amabile. Both are, unsurprisingly, wonderfully raisiny and go brilliantly with Parmesan cheese. Ripasso is another intermediate style that tastes like a cross between good standard Valpolicella and Amarone.

■ **Good wines from the** *Veneto can have a powerful cherry flavor.*

The whites

There are a few other good reds in the Veneto – such as the local Raboso and Macullan winery's delicious Cabernet Sauvignon – but the whites are better known. The one you've most probably come across is the white equivalent of Valpolicella, the usually very ordinary but sometimes deliciously almondy Soave. Sweet raisiny Recioto di Soave can be as delicious in its own way as Recioto di Valpolicella.

■ **Recioto di Soave** *has a delicious raisiny taste to it.*

*Many Veneto wines can be very disappointing. Avoid basic examples of Soave and Valpolicella. Instead, look for wines labeled as **Classico**, made by smaller producers such as Pieropan from individual vineyards.*

A sweetie

The Friuli-Venezia Giulia region makes a fine honeyed sweet wine too, called Picolit, that has been compared (though only by Italian critics) to top Sauternes. Of the dry whites from the northeast, we'd recommend Bianco di Custoza (often a better buy than Soave) from the Veneto, Chardonnay, Muscat, Riesling, Pinot Gris, and Gewürztraminer from the Alto Adige. Two producers from Friuli-Venezia Giulia, Jermann and Gravner, make all sorts of brilliant blends, including the local Tocai Friulano and Ribolla.

Things to remember about the northeast

BRUNELLO DI MONTALCINO
DENOMINAZIONE DI ORIGINE CONTROLLATA E GARANTITA
IMBOTTIGLIATO NELLE CANTINE DI PALAZZO ALTESI
DALL'AZIENDA AGRICOLA ALTESINO, MONTALCINO
€ 0,75 ℮ℓ   68 Sl   VOLUME 13%

Riserva 1983

■ **It is the names of** *vineyards that are most commonly found on Italian wine labels.*

✔ This is a very varied region, with indigenous grapes such as the Tocai Friulano and the Raboso and international varieties such as the Merlot and Chardonnay.

✔ The most interesting wines in the region are the Recioto wines of Valpolicella and Soave. Basic versions of both these wines can be very dull.

Central Italy: classical performances

THE ROAD SOUTHWARD *takes us to the center of Italy, the cities of Florence, Rome, and Sienna – and the regions of Tuscany, Emilia-Romagna, Latium, Umbria, and the Marches. This is the home of such familiar wines as Chianti, Brunello di Montalcino, Orvieto, and Montepulciano d'Abruzzo, as well as a flood of cheap Lambrusco and top-class IGT reds that sell for the same price as top-class Bordeaux.*

Chianti

Chianti, Tuscany's most famous red, has come a long way since it cast off its straw-covered flasks and began to be sold in "serious" Bordeaux-style bottles (the ones with the high shoulders). The contents changed, too. Chianti used to be light, herby red wine to be drunk young; today, better winemaking has made for far more interesting, longer lived, tobaccoey, fruity flavors. There are now huge numbers of castles and palaces among the hills offering high-quality examples of Chianti and Chianti Riserva wine.

DEFINITION

As in Spain, Italy's winemakers have always treasured wines that have been matured in (usually old) oak barrels. The word Riserva on a label provides an official indication of barrel-aging.

The vine-covered hills of Chianti are divided among several sub-regions. Producers in Chianti Classico, the most famous – and, in theory, the best – use a black cockerel as their logo while those in Chianti Rufina prefer a little cherub. The Colli Senesi and Colli Fiorentini sub-regions are less well known. Good and poor wine is produced in all these sub-regions. Here, as elsewhere, the name of the producer is more important than the region.

Chianti Classico can now be – and indeed often is – made with as much as 10 percent Cabernet Sauvignon. Another Cabernet-influenced red made nearby is Carmignano. The Bordeaux grape is still excluded, however, from Vino Nobile di Montepulciano and Brunello di Montalcino, the Tuscan wines that are often claimed to be Italy's finest. There are great examples of both denominations – and plenty of over-priced and disappointing ones.

■ **The wonderful Tuscan** *countryside is home of many great Chiantis.*

Vin Santo

Vin Santo is another style that varies wildly in quality. This nutty, sweet or dry wine made from dried grapes is Italy's answer to sherry. At its best, this can be delicious raisiny stuff to be sipped after a meal. Cheaper versions are given away in restaurants with cantucch (almond cookies), which are often tastier than the wine.

A new wave breaks

Rosso di Montalcino and Rosso di Montepulciano are lighter, fresher, and cheaper than the classic wines of central Italy.

And often a better buy. The more recent denomination of Bolgheri is an increasingly worthwhile source of well-made reds. Look out too for the numerous inventive reds that used to be sold as *vino da tavola* but now usually carry the letters IGT. The best of these are known as "Super-Tuscans." Good modern fruity reds are also produced farther south in Torgiano in Umbria.

When looking for more traditional flavors, we arrive at yet another of Italy's confusing traps for the unwary. You could be forgiven for imagining that the Abruzzi region's Montepulciano d'Abruzzo might have something in common with the Vino Nobile di Montepulciano we met earlier. Well, they are both red and from central Italy, but that's where the resemblances end. The Tuscan wine is produced in the village of Montepulciano from the Sangiovese grape, while the Abruzzi wine is made from another variety altogether called – logically enough – the Montepulciano. Add in very different conditions offered by the mountainous vineyards of the Adriatic coast and, hardly surprisingly, you get some quite different flavors. Montepulciano d'Abruzzo, like Rosso Conero – the Marches red that's also largely made from Montepulciano – can be very tasty chocolatey wine.

Two styles in one

Leaving the best known, if not best, till last, we come to Lambrusco. This is schizophrenic stuff from the region of Emilia-Romagna. On the one hand, there's the sweet carbonated beverage in screw-cap bottles made for people overseas who prefer their wine to taste like Coca Cola; on the other, there's the weird and wonderful bone-dry Lambrusco-with-a-cork that tastes just like unripe plums and needs to be enjoyed with fatty, herb-flavored food.

The whites

The whites of central Italy are a very mixed batch. Galestro, produced around Chianti, is pleasant but unmemorable. Tuscany's tangy Vernacchia di San Gimignano is far more worthwhile. So is the honeyed nutty wine of Orvieto in Umbria (often at its best in Amabile sweet versions). Frascati, the fuel that sometimes seems to keep the wheels moving in Rome, can be terrific too – but only when wine producers include more of the Malvasia del Lazio grape than the laws allow. Otherwise, it tends to be flabby and flavorless. Verdicchio, by contrast, varies between deliciously rich (such as the oaked Casal di Serra) and green and unripe.

Things to remember about central Italy

✓ There are lots of varied styles, but the key red wine grape is often the Sangiovese (Chianti, Brunello di Montepulciano, Vino Nobile di Montepulciano, Sangiovese di Romagna). Other interesting varieties include the Montepulciano (Rosso Conero, Montepulciano d'Abruzzo). The best whites are Verdicchio, Frascati, and Orvieto, but the quality of these varies widely.

✓ This is the part of Italy where many of the most innovative *vino da tavola* and IGT wines are produced.

✓ As elsewhere in Italy, quality is improving rapidly, but producers are more important than denominations.

Southern Italy: a beaker of the warm south

■ **New technology** *has led to improvements in wine production in southern Italy.*

The ankle or foot of Italy, and the islands of Sicily, Lipari, and Sardinia, have hardly been known for great wine. Until recently, a combination of a hot climate, limited ambition, and primitive methods and equipment generally conspired to create thick, dull, alcoholic red wine and sweet Marsala to use in the kitchen.

During the last years of the 20th century, however, new technology and a modern approach in this and other sunny parts of the Old World, have exploited the flavors of traditional grapes such as the Aglianico, Piedirosso, Negroamaro, Greco, and Fiano, both neat and in blends with imported varieties like the Cabernet Sauvignon, Merlot, and Chardonnay.

The reds

The best southern Italian reds include the beefy, traditional, chocolately Ciro from Calabria, Aglianicos from Campania,

Basilicata (especially from Taurasi and the slopes of Mount Vulture), and the Castel del Monte (made mostly from the Montepulciano) from Puglia.

Salice Santino, Squinzano, and Copertino form a trio that gives the characterful and aptly named "bitter-black" Negroamaro grape a chance to show what it can do. Sicily's most interesting reds include Corvo from the Casa Vinicola Duca di Salaparuta and the wines of the Regaleali winery.

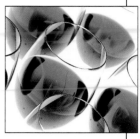

■ **Red wines from** *southern Italy tend to be heavy and chocolatey.*

The whites

Dry whites from the south need careful buying. There's still plenty of dull stuff to be found – including most examples of Lacryma Christi – but Fiano di Avellino from Campania can have an attractive honey and plum character, while good Greccheto in Umbria can be both creamy and rich. The interesting grape, though, is the widely-grown Greco, used for peachy Ciro Bianco and spicy Greco di Tufo.

This grape is also responsible for the delicious sweet Greco di Bianco from Calabria (Umberto Ceratti produces a particularly good one). Other fine sweet wines include Carlo Hauner's Malvasia di Lipari, de Bartoli's raisiny Moscato Passito di Pantelleria Bukkuran, and Florio's Morsi di Luce.

Sweet wines

Marsala ought to be Italy's answer to top-class port, Madeira or sherry. Sadly, unlike the serious wine laws covering those wines, Italy's rules allow Marsala to be made from almost any grape variety and bottled at almost any age.

Florio and De Bartoli are good examples of Italian sweet wines, but they are exceptions to the rule that recommends you avoid most basic Marsala.

Sardinia's sweet sticky Cannonau, made from the grape the French know as Grenache, can be good, but Sella e Mosca's Sardinian port-like Anghelu Ruju is a more reliable alcoholic red.

Things to remember about southern Italy

✓ Once the source of poor cheap wine, this is the part of Italy to look to for exciting modern winemaking – and value.

✓ There are also often interesting "classic" wines such as Salice Salentino and Taurasi that show what traditional grape varieties can do.

ITALIAN WINE TO BUY — AND WHEN TO DRINK IT

Top producers:

✓ Emilia-Romagna: Baldi, Cavicchiolo, Fattoria Paradiso, Il Moro, Vallania, Vallunga

✓ Friuli-Venezia-Giulia: Bidoli, Collavini, Dri, Marco Felluga, Gravner, Jermann, Puiatti, Schioppetto, Zonin, Italy

✓ Latium/Umbria: Antinori, Bigi, Boncompagni Ludovisi, Cantina Colacicchi, Italy la Carraia, Covio Cardetto, Decugnano del Barbi, Fontana Candida, Lungarotti, Palazzone

✓ Marche/Abruzzi-Molise: Barone Cornacchia, Castello di Salle, Farnese, Illuminati, Marchetti, Masseria di Majo Norante, Mecvini, Pepe, Tatta, Tenuta S. Agnese, Tollo, Umani Ronchi, Valentini, Villa Pigna

✓ Piedmont/Lombardy/Liguria: Altare, Batasiolo, Borgogno, Ca. dei Frati, Ca. del Bosco, Ceretto, Chiarlo, Clerico, Aldo Conterno, G. Conterno, Conterno Fantini, Eredi Lodai, Fontanafredda, Gaja, Bruno Giacosa, Elio Grasso, Longhi de Carli, Marcarini, G. Mascarello, B. Mascarello, Pio Cesare, Pira, Poggio, Prunotto, Ratti, Rocca Ripalta, Sandrone, Scavino, Vajra, Eraldo Viberti, Vietti, Roberto Voerzio, Gianno Voerzio

✓ South, Sardinia and Sicily: de Bartoli, Ceratti, Corvo, Florio, Fratelli d'Angelo, Hauner, Mastroberardino, Planeta, Regaleali, Rivera, Sella e Mosca, Taurini, Terre di Ginestra

✓ Trentino/Alto Adige: Appiano, Cavit, Conti Martini, Fedrigotti, Ferrari, Foradori, Gaierhof, Grai, Hofstatter, Alois Lageder, Maddaena, Maso Poli, Pojer & Sandri, San Leonardi, Teifenbrunner, Vallarom, Vinicola Aldeno, Viticoltori Alto Adige, Roberto Zeni

✓ Tuscany: Altesino, Antinori, Argiano, Avignonesi, Badia a Coltibuono, Biondi Santi, Casale-Falchini, Castell'in Villa, Castellare, Castello dei Rampolla, Castello di Volpaia, Catelli di Ama, Fattoria dei Barbi, Felsina Berardenga, Frescobaldi, Isole e Olena, Luce, Marchese Incisa della Rochetta, Monte Vertinie, Pergole Torte, Il Poggio, Rocca di Castagnoli, Ruffino, Selvapiana, Talenti, Teruzzi & Puthod, Val di Suga, Villa di Capezzana, Vinattieri

✓ Veneto: Allegrini, Anselmi, Bertani, Bolla, Boscaini, Conte Loredan Gasparini, dal Forno, Guerrieri-Rizzardi, Maculan, Masi, Mazzi, Pieropan, Prà, Quintarelli, Italy le Ragose, Santa Sofia, Serego Aligheri, Tedeschi, Villa Spinosa, Zenato

Lifespans: Ageability depends on the region and the winemaker. As a rule, basic Soave, Valpolicella, Barbera, and Chianti are for early drinking. Better, single vineyard examples can be kept for longer. Top Chiantis, Brunellos, and Super Tuscans can last for 10 to 20 years and Barolo and Barbaresco may need this long.

Good vintages: ✓ Red: 1989 (Piedmont), 1990 (Veneto and Oiedmont), 1991 (Chianti and Veneto), 1993 (not great for Chianti), 1994, 1995 (especially Veneto), 1996 1997, 1998

A simple summary

✓ Italy's red wines have a characteristic herby, tobaccoey character that helps them to marry well with Italian food.

✓ Italy's white wines tend to be light and sometimes quite neutral in style.

✓ Many of Italy's best wines are IGTs that fall outside the traditional system of regional DOC and DOCG designations.

✓ While Italy uses some of the same grapes – Cabernet Sauvignon, Cabernet Franc, Merlot, Muscat, Chardonnay, Pinot Noir, Gris, and Blanc – as France and the New World, its best wines are mostly made from local varieties such as the Nebbiolo, Sangiovese, and Barbera.

✓ The same grapes are grown in different regions under different names.

✓ "Classico" refers to the best part of a wine region (but does not necessarily guarantee better quality wine).

Chapter 18

Spain: Viva el Vino

A T FIRST GLANCE THE ITALIAN and Spanish languages can sometimes appear quite similar, but they are very different. The wines of these two southern European countries, like their music and cuisine, have even less in common. Unlike Italy, which has cooler regions, most of Spain is pretty warm. So, until modern winemaking methods came along, this was not a great place to produce fresh dry white wine.

In this chapter...

✓ A love of age

✓ The northeast

✓ The northwest

✓ Central Spain

✓ The south and the islands

SPANISH WINE IS MUCH MORE DELICIOUS THAN SANGRIA DRINKERS IMAGINE

A love of age

THE RED WINE *they liked best was old – stuff that ideally had been aged and softened for several years in wooden barrels, picking up vanilla flavor from the oak, and stored for a while in the bottle. In another variation from Italy and France, the woody flavor of Spanish wine tends to be more apparent. This is explained by the traditional use of oak from American forests, barrels associated with flavors of coconut, vanilla, and buttermilk, rather than the subtler French oak.*

■ **Spanish winemakers** *favor storing their wine in American oak barrels so that they create the desired vanilla flavor.*

The Spanish system

In recognition of this national preference for long-aged wine, Spain has created a unique appellation system and set of terms that reveal how long the wine has been stored.

The word Crianza on a back label means that the wine will have been aged for at least two years in a cask. (By contrast, Crianza on a back label for white wines means it's aged at least six months.) Red Reserva and Gran Reserva wines spend a minimum of a year and two years in barrel respectively and can't be put on the market until they are at least three and five years old.

Vino Joven – literally "young wine" – will have not been in a barrel at all and is intended to be drunk young. Apart from these terms, Spanish wine labels may include the words *Vino de Mesa* (table wine); *Vino Comarcal*, Spain's answer to France's Vin de Pays; *Vino de la Tierra*, up-market Vino Comarcal; *Denominación de Origen* (DO), Spain's equivalent of Italy's DOC; or *Denominación de Origen Calificada* (DOC, the Spanish version of Italy's DOCG). As we have seen elsewhere, these provide no guarantee of quality

■ **By reading the label** *you can learn whether the wine should be drunk young.*

INTERNET

www.filewines.es/
english/default.htm

This guide to Spanish wines has news of the latest releases and sales.

Holding on

One of the not-widely-known rules laid down by the Spanish appellation system is a requirement for wineries that want to label and sell their wine as Reserva or Gran Reserva to hold a pretty hefty amount of each vintage. This rule helps to explain why, unlike Italy's countless tiny estates, Spain has a far smaller number of far larger bodegas – wineries.

Not too many grapes

Also unlike Italy, with its baffling array of grape varieties, Spain keeps things simple by making most of its wines from a fairly limited range – but then it complicates them again by using different names depending on where they are grown. So, while Cabernet Sauvignon and Merlot are being introduced (especially in regions such as Penedes, Navarra, Somontano, and Costers del Segre) if a red wine tastes soft and plummy, it is probably made at least partly from the Tempranillo. And if it's peppery and juicy, it will more than likely contain a fair amount of Garnacha (the grape grown in the Rhône as Grenache).

The northeast

THE FACT THAT *Spain's most famous wine region is tucked away near the border with France is no coincidence. The foundations of Rioja's wine industry were laid in the 1860s by Frenchmen who crossed the Pyrénées in flight from the phylloxera louse that was devastating their vines in Bordeaux. The variety they grew at home and brought with them – Cabernet Sauvignon – was also used here for a while, before being expelled in favor of local varieties. Today, Cabernet Sauvignon is quietly being reintroduced, but very slowly and only as a small part of a blend dominated by Tempranillo and Garnacha.*

■ Wines from Rioja
Alta are blended with ones from other parts of Rioja.

Regions and sub-regions

Unlike French and Italian blends, which come from individual vineyards or villages, most top quality Riojas are mixtures from two or three sub-regions: Rioja Alta, Rioja Alavesa, and Rioja Baja.

There are single-estate wines such as Campillo, Remelluri, and Baron de Ley, but these are exceptions to the rule.

Many of Rioja's wines are made by big companies that are coasting along on reputations gained half a century ago – and on the local acceptance of these firms' Gran Reserva wines that have been allowed to dry out in the barrel.

Beware of over-priced smartly packaged bottles. A good producer's Crianza will taste better and cost less than a poor one's Reserva or Gran Reserva.

■ **Navarra-produced wine** *is increasing in popularity.*

Up-and-coming Navarra

Navarra, Rioja's next-door neighbor, produces very similar wines but with the difference that here, foreign varieties such as Cabernet Sauvignon and Chardonnay are also widely used by themselves. Another thing that sets Navarra apart is its specialization in producing pink rosado wines. The dynamism of traditional and varietal wines from producers like Chivite is rapidly helping to make this a region to watch.

The whites of Rioja and Navarra

Until recently, the quality Spanish white wines one would most likely see outside Spain were traditional Riojas made from the local Viura and Malvasia grapes and aged for a long time in oak barrels to develop a savory nutty character that was all their own. Nowadays, these old-fashioned characterful wines are hard to find. Marques de Murrieta still produces one, as do the Cune and Tondonia wineries, but most white wines are clean, light, and relatively characterless. Navarra does better with its whites and produces some tasty Chardonnays.

Towers of power – Miguel Torres and the Penedes

If Navarra is gaining a reputation for its "imported" varieties, the region that first introduced the notion of straying beyond Hispanic tradition was the Penedes in Catalonia. And the family-owned company that got the ball rolling in the Penedes was Torres, whose current head, Miguel, deserves credit for introducing many aspects of modern winemaking to Spain.

■ **Miguel Torres,** *champion of modern Spanish wine.*

For Miguel Torres, who had studied the wines of other countries (and also went on to develop vineyards in Chile), the varying climates and altitudes of this region provided a wonderful place to experiment. At up to 2,500 feet above sea level, in the hills of the Penedes Superior, he could produce fine Riesling, Gewürztraminer, and Chardonnay – and even bring out more flavor from the local Parellada than this local variety usually has to offer. The warmer Medio Penedes at around 6,800 feet above sea level, on the other hand, offered ideal conditions for grapes ranging from the local Garnacha and Tempranillo to Pinot Noir, Merlot, and Cabernet Sauvignon.

Sparkling success?

Others have followed in Torres's footsteps, but the region as a whole is still best known in Spain for its Cava sparkling wines. Popular internationally because of their low prices, these Champagne-method wines can be attractive enough when young, but rarely match their French or New World counterparts because they are traditionally made from the local Parellada, Macabeo, and Xarello varieties, none of which is noted for its fruity flavors. The introduction of the Chardonnay by modernists such as Raimat and Codorniu has given the wines a fresher appeal – and caused huge controversy among traditionalists, who oppose such innovation.

If you like fresh sparkling wine, avoid older Cavas. To non-Spaniards, they can taste earthy and dull – and have a bigger price tag.

New directions

Of the other significant regions in this part of Spain, the most important is Priorato, where a California- and Bordeaux-trained winemaker called Alvaro Palacios is leading the switch from thickly tough alcoholic reds to exciting international-quality reds made from grapes such as Cabernet Sauvignon and Syrah. Conca de Barberá and Campo de Borja also have some attractive, if more modest, new-wave reds. Cariñena offers some bigger and softer Garnacha-based wines. Somontano and Costers del Segre produce modern examples of both Spanish and imported grape varieties.

Things to remember about the northeast

✔ The key region here is Rioja, but Priorato, Navarra, and Somontano are all places to watch.

✔ Wines are highly variable in quality, but the best examples are among Spain's finest and most age-worthy reds.

✔ Avoid the trap of believing that highly priced old bottles are generally worth their price.

A RIOJA WINERY

269

The northwest

HEADING WEST from Rioja and Navarra, close to the northern frontier between Spain and Portugal, we move from world-famous red-wine country to Galicia, a cool, damp region that produces a spicy, dry white wine with a cult following. The most significant area here is the Rias Baixas, which owes its reputation to the Albariño, a brilliant floral-spicy variety that is also grown on the other side of the border with Portugal, where it is known as the Alvarinho. Some Albariños develop interesting flavors with age, but the best advice is to drink most as young as possible. Nearby Valdeorras is a region that may attract more attention in the future thanks to the peary-appley wines that are being made from its indigenous white Godello grape, but the whites made in Ribeiro from the Torrontes and Treixadura are rarely exciting.

Another really promising region for white wine is Rueda, which has attracted a number of top producers such as Marquès de Griñon and Marques de Riscal from Rioja. The climate here, Sauvignon Blanc, and the local Verdejo grape, and modern winemaking are all coming together to produce delicious fresh peary wines that taste equally good with and without the influence of oak barrels.

■ **Rueda has all** *the right elements to make it a wonderful and successful winemaking region.*

Spain's top red

The main focus of interest in this part of Spain, though, is Ribera del Duero where rich gamey reds are produced. This is where you'll find Vega Sicilia, Spain's priciest wine. Confusingly, while this estate has earned a reputation for the region as a whole, its own wine is unlike those of its neighbors. Where other Ribera del Duero reds (and this is a red-only region) are made from Tempranillo (here known as Tinto Fino), the Vega Sicilia blend also includes the red varieties of Bordeaux. This would be illegal for anybody else, but Vega Sicilia gets a special dispensation because they've been playing by their own rules since 1864.

■ **Home of Spain's** *most expensive wine: Vega Sicilia.*

Vega Sicilia divides its wines into three categories, ranging upward in quality from Valbuena to Unico Reserva (only produced in the best vintages) and Reserva Especial.

This last is a wonderful non-vintage wine, releases of which can be differentiated from each other by means of a lot or code number on the label.

Alternative Ribera del Dueros to look out for include Vega Sicilia's sister property Alion, its best-known competitor Pesquera, plus Pago de Carraovejas and Dominico de Pingus. Some of Ribera del Duero's other wines taste rather rustic, but the general quality is improving – as it is in Toro, where the Fariña winery's Gran Colegiata is a good buy.

Things to remember about the northwest

✓ The spicy dry whites of Rias Baixas, particularly Albariños, and Rueda have developed a cult following.

✓ The quality of Ribera del Duero reds has been improving.

✓ The pricey Vega Sicilia is the only Ribera del Duero wine produced from Tempranillo and red Bordeaux varieties.

■ **Bottle-aging** *cellar of Bodegas Vega Sicilia.*

Central Spain

THE HEART OF SPAIN is hot dry flat country punctuated by the gleaming white windmills that so mesmerized Don Quixote. You can grow olives here – or vines. But not much else. Until recently, the variety of grapes grown on those vines was the extraordinarily neutral-tasting Airen, but European Union grants, new forms of irrigation, better grape varieties, and more modern methods of vinegrowing and winemaking are changing things dramatically.

Getting better and better

The most interesting regions here include Valdepeñas to the south, where some good, soft, old reds are offered by Felix Solis at prices far lower than asked for poorer examples from Rioja. Jumilla has some good daily-drinking reds with a slightly spicy flavor that comes from the use of the Mourvèdre grape (here known as the Monastrell). In Almansa, Piquera is the producer to look for, while Ochoa's efforts from Yecla can sometimes be worthwhile.

The cheap stuff

Even though good winemaking has arrived in these regions, there is plenty of dull stuff still available.

Beware of attractively-priced old-fashioned examples of La Mancha, Jumilla, Yecla, and Valdepeñas. The chances of getting good wine labeled as Alicante, Bullas, Mentrida, Utiel-Requena, or Vinos de Madrid are small – despite the proud words Denominación de Origen on all these regions' labels.

Valencia does reliably deliver inexpensive flavorsome wine – provided you stick to the fresh, grapey, ludicrously cheap, sweet white Moscatel. Otherwise this region has little to offer at the moment, but Swiss investment may bring a wider range of choice.

Things to remember about central Spain

✓ Wines from central Spain may be cheap and plentiful, but they are often dull.

✓ Valdepeñas produces some decent inexpensive reds.

The south and the islands

THE ISLAND OF *Mallorca claims a long wine history, and certainly has grapes that aren't found elsewhere in Spain. Most of the best vineyards are around Binissalem, a village that has a denomination of its own, but there are few wines that stand comparison in quality and value terms with the better efforts of the Spanish mainland. They generally look good, however, when set alongside the stuff that is produced in the volcanic Canary Islands. The true wines to linger over in southern Spain are the sherries produced around the town of Jerez de la Frontera in Andalusia.*

■ **Sherry production** *is a local tradition that dates from Roman times.*

Sherry amor

If one style of wine deserves to be more widely known, it is sherry. It was appreciated 2,000 years ago by the Romans and 600 years ago by Geoffrey Chaucer. But the history of the sherry we know today began by accident in the 18th century when producers noticed that some barrels of white wine developed an ugly white scum on the surface. To their surprise, the scum, which turned out to be a peculiar kind of yeast, did not spoil the wine, but actually seemed to protect it against bacteria that would turn it into vinegar. The scum also improved the wine's flavor. The Jerezaños called the yeast *flor* ("flower") and the wine it affected *fino* ("fine").

Unlike most other wines, sherry almost never has a vintage. This is because the best Fino is a blend of young and mature wine designed to ensure that the drink in your glass always tastes tangily fresh.

Using a process known as the Solera system, barrels of varying ages are stacked on top of each other. Each year's wine is topped up with one from the following year in such a way that the sherry in the oldest barrels – which might be a century old – attains a kind of immortality.

■ **Sherry is made in** *many stages; care must be taken to get each one right.*

The quality of dry sherry depends on the quality of all of the wines in the chain and the care that is taken to maintain the Solera. Companies such as Lustau, Barbadillo, and Gonzalez Byass are particularly reliable.

Drink up

While Fino is the most famous dry sherry, very similar but more delicate styles are produced a few miles from the town of Jerez, in the coastal towns of Sanlúcar de Barrameda (where it is called Manzanilla) and Puerto de Santa María (where it is known as Puerto Fino). Sherry lovers find a saltiness in Manzanilla, that is usually explained by the influence of the sea.

■ **The Solera system** *sees old and new wines blended in barrels.*

All sherries are supposed to taste tangily fresh. Dry sherry loses its freshness far more quickly than most people imagine. Don't let your sherry hang around to grow stale. Buy it from a busy shop that won't have left it to gather dust on the shelf. Keep it in the fridge and aim to finish the bottle within two weeks.

Leave these dry wines in a barrel for a while and they turn into something else. Fino becomes steadily nuttier and is described by stages as Fino-Amontillado – after eight years or so – Amontillado. Genuine Amontillado is deep gold and at once bone dry and raisiny, but examples for export can be sweetened to please foreign palates. Some aged Fino develops into a different golden-colored and deliciously savory style called Palo Cortado, while the Manzanilla equivalent of Fino-Amontillado is Manzanilla-Pasada.

The flor and the finos

All of these styles began with wine that had been affected by flor. So what happened to all the casks of sherry that didn't have any flor? Well, they went through their own Solera system and developed very different flavors. While the flor kept the finos and amontillados fresh, protecting them from full-scale oxidation, these flor-less *olorosos*, as they are known, became much nuttier, more raisiny, more concentrated, and more fragrant – which is literally what "oloroso" means.

With time, these can become some of the finest sherries of all. Stuff to be sipped at by themselves or enjoyed with cheese. Usually the best examples are bone dry when they are sold, but some are slightly sweetened (and are labeled *dulce* – sweet). Some more basic oloroso is given more generous sweetening and is sold as "cream" or "milk" sherry.

If you want top-class sweet sherry, though, the stuff to go for is the glorious plum-puddingy Pedro Ximénez, made like an Italian Recioto from Pedro Ximénez grapes that have been dried in the sun before being crushed and fermented.

Montilla: the poor relation

Amontillado takes its name from Montilla, a similar – but traditionally unfortified – style produced farther inland, to the northeast. Today, Montilla-Moriles – as it is properly known – is usually seen as a cheaper more basic alternative to sherry, but good well-made examples are actually a better buy than many undistinguished sherries on the market.

■ **The Montilla region** *gives its name to Amontillado and Montilla-Morities.*

Things to remember about southern Spain and the islands

✓ Wines from Mallorca are generally preferable to those of the Canary Islands.

✓ A layer of yeast called flor protects the wine in the barrel and gives it a distinct flavor.

✓ Fino dry sherries are generally blends of young and mature wines that ensure a fresh, tangy taste.

✓ Besides the famous Fino sherries of Jerez, other, more delicate sherries are produced in Sanlúcar de Barrameda (Manzanilla) and Puerto de Santa María (Puerto Fino).

✓ Sherries aged eight years or more in the barrel are termed Amontillado.

✓ The nuttier and more fragrant oloroso sherries are produced without flor. These are often sweetened and called milk or cream sherry.

■ **Amontillado sherry** *is left to age for eight or more years.*

SPANISH WINE TO BUY — AND WHEN TO DRINK IT

Top producers:

✓ Catalonia, etc.: Albet i Noya, Can Feixes, Can Ráfols dels Caus, Castellblanch, Cavas Hill, Chandon, Codorníu, Juve i Camps, Jean León, Marqués de Monistrol, Masia Bach, Puig Roca, Raimat, Rovellats, Sergura Viudas, Torres

✓ La Mancha/Valdepeñas: Marqués de Griñon, Senorio de los Llanos, Felix Solis

✓ Navarra: Agramont, Castillo de Monjardin, Chivite, Guelbenzu, Nekeas, Ochoa, Palacio de la Vega, Señorio de Sarria, Vinicola Murchantina

✓ Rias Baixas: Lagar de Cervera, Martin Codex, Pazo de Barrantes, Salnesu, Valdamor

✓ Ribera del Duero: Allion, Arroyo, Balbas, Hermanos Sastre, Mauro, Pago de Carraovejas, Pedrosa, Pesquera, Pingus, Valtravieso, Vega Sicilia

✓ Priorato: Clos I Terrasses, Clos Mogador, Mas Martinet, Alvaro Palacios, Scala Dei, Vilella de la Cartoixa

✓ Rioja: Amézola de la Mora, Ardanza, Artadi, Baron de Ley, Berberana, Breton, Campillo, Campo Viejo, Contino, El Coto, CVNE, Lopez de Heredia, Marqués de Cacerés, Marques de Griñon, Marqués de Murrieta, Marqués de Riscal, Marqués de Vargas, Marqués de Villamagna, Martinez Bujanda, Montecillo, Navajas, Palacio, Remelluri, La Rioja Alta, Riojanas

✓ Sherry: Barbadillo, Caballero, Diez-Merito, Domecq, Gonzalez Byass, Hidalgo, Lustau, Osborne, Valdespino

Lifespans: Most whites are for early drinking, but top-class white Rioja and ambitious Chardonnays such as Torres's Milmanda will last for a decade or more. Reds vary depending on the producer, region, and personal taste. Spaniards enjoy mature wines more than many people in countries like the United States, so they may opt for a mature Gran Reserva Rioja while the foreigner chooses a younger, fruitier Priorato. Wines are traditionally sold when they are more-or-less ready to drink. As a rule, therefore, do not expect to store a Crianza red for longer than three years or so after purchase. A Reserva may last for five years.

Good vintages: ✔ 1990, 1991 (Penedés), 1994 (particularly Ribera del Duero), 1995, 1996 1997, 1998

■ **Although Spain** *produces some good whites, the finest Spanish wine is mostly red.*

A simple summary

✔ Spain is a conservative country, most of whose winemakers have been quite slow in adopting modern technologies. But things are now beginning to change quite fast.

✔ Most of the best wines are still red – though the Albariños of Galicia, the whites of Rueda, the Muscats of Valencia, and traditional white Rioja are all worth looking for.

✔ Reds are less varied than in France and Italy because the same grapes – Tempranillo and Garnacha – are grown in a large number of regions.

✔ The emphasis on long-aged wines is reducing now, but the influence of American oak barrels is still one of the hallmarks of Spanish red wines.

✔ There are far fewer producers here than in France or Italy, so there's less of a jungle to hack through when you set out to find and remember a producer whose wines you like.

Chapter 19

Portugal & Eastern Mediterranean

OUR TOUR NOW TAKES US TO less well-known, but no less ancient, wine-growing regions of southern Europe. The wines of Portugal, the Eastern Mediterranean, and North Africa vary enormously, with a great many regions resisting the trend toward international styles by growing indigenous grape varieties.

In this chapter...

✓ Portugal

✓ Eastern Mediterranean

✓ North Africa

PORTUGAL AND THE EASTERN MEDITERRANEAN COUNTRIES ARE NO NOVICES TO WINEMAKING

Portugal

MENTION PORTUGUESE wine to most people, and the chances are that they will think of decanters full of vintage port or bottles full of sweet fizzy Mateus Rosé. Unless they've traveled to Portugal or one of its former colonies, they are unlikely to have had much contact with most of this country's red and white wines. London and New York sport far fewer Portuguese restaurants than French or Italian (or even Spanish) ones. Portugal's wines are mostly made from grape varieties that are rarely found elsewhere – and, unlike their neighbors on the other side of the Spanish border, the reds aren't given the universally-popular vanilla flavor that comes from time spent in American oak barrels. So, when it comes to wine, this remains a largely undiscovered country. Let's go ahead and discover it.

■ **Traditional harvesting** *methods are still practiced in Portugal.*

The legalities

One bit of the map we won't need is the list of DOCs – *Denominçãos de Origem Controlada*. Supposedly the best of Portugal's wine regions, they may be taken seriously in Portugal, but neither they nor the slightly humbler IPRS – *Incaçaos de Provência Regulamentada* – will help us find genuinely good wine. Indeed, some of Portugal's best modern reds are legally designated as supposedly more basic *Vinhos Regionãos* (country wines) and *Vinhos de Mesa* (table wines).

■ **Most Portuguese** *wine is made from indigenous grapes.*

A perfect example of the failings of the DOC system is the northern region of Dão, which has a reputation for producing some of Portugal's top reds – despite the fact that most of them taste dull and earthy. Fortunately, a dynamic company called Sogrape has used California-influenced winemaking and better grape varieties to make fruiter, tastier versions. The nearby region of Bairrada is known in Portugal for its sparkling wines, but the herby-plummy reds here – made from the local Baga grape by producers such as Luis Pato and Aliança can also be first class. The other DOC region beginning to offer impressive reds is the Douro – home of vintage port and Portugal's most famous red, Barca Velha. It also boasts a growing number of delicious wines from port producers such as Quinta de la Rosa and Quinta do Crasto that owe some of their damsony rich flavors to the efforts of Australian-born winemakers who have settled in Portugal.

THE FAMOUS WINERY OF JOSÉ MARÍA DA FONSECA

A scattering of quality

Delicious new-wave red wines can be found in various other regions spread throughout the country. So the Alentejo to the east has producers like Sogrape, JP Vinhos (whose Quinta da Anfora is a regular prize winner), Quinta do Carmo (which belongs to Château Lafite), and the attractive commercial wines of Esperào. The firm of José María da Fonseca produces a range of reliable wines in the regions of Setubal and Terras do Sado, close to Lisbon, including *Vinho de Mesa* wines such as Camarate, Pasmados, and TE. Two other deliciously cherryish wines, Periquita and Pedras do Monte, both showcase the Castelão Frances grape, which is also known as the Periquita.

Whites

Portugal's most famous white – Vinho Verde – is actually more usually red. But the aggressive, unripe-plum style of this red wine makes it an unlikely winner with non-Portuguese customers. White Vinho Verde, however, can be delicious, slightly sparkling, dry, and appley. Made from local varieties such as the Alvarinho (which we met in Spain as the Albariño) and Loureira grapes (picked from vines that are grown overhead to allow vegetables to be grown on the ground), these are not only among the most distinctive wines in the world, they are also some of the least alcoholic, with strengths of just eight or nine percent. Confusingly, while Vinho Verde is traditionally dry, some widely-available brands are semi-sweet. Solar de Bouças and Casa de Sezim are typical dry examples. Other Portuguese dry whites are a very mixed bag – too many are dull and flabby. Look for modern wines from the Bright Brothers, Sogrape, and José María da Fonseca. The sweet Moscatel de Setubal, however, is delicious grapey honeyed stuff.

Port

Portugal's two famous fortified wines both owe their existence to Britain and, more specifically, to one of the periodic spats the British had with France in the 18th century. A ban on French wine created a thirsty vacuum that had to be filled. No country was better placed at the time than Britain's long-time ally Portugal. The only problem was that the warm summer climate in the Douro provided the right conditions for wine to be spoiled by bacteria. One way to protect it was with alcohol – by fortifying the fermenting juice with brandy. The resulting sweet, plummy, strong drink was an immediate success and the British love affair with port began.

A matter of taste

From the outset, the port drinkers discovered that this thick dark wine was best left for a few years to soften before drinking, that it was best decanted to separate the liquid from the powdery deposit that settles in the bottle, and that fine port could only be produced when the climate was right – roughly once every three or four years. Like Champagne – the other region with "declared" vintages – the best port is usually a blend of wines from various parts of the region. And like Champagne, port is bought and sold on the "house-style" of its producers. So, just as some people prefer Bollinger to Roederer Champagne, there are port drinkers who choose to drink Graham's rather than Taylor's.

The style of port

But vintage port is only one of the styles that are produced. The most basic stuff is ruby: young spirity wine that used to be drunk in Britain with lemonade. One step up the scale from ruby is "Vintage Character," as its name suggests, supposed to taste like vintage port. Well, maybe it does – but not like good vintage port. Next comes Late Bottled Vintage (LBV), which is closer to vintage port in that it is produced in a single year. On the other hand, the year in question is rarely a great one. As you might infer from this style's name, LBV is bottled much later (up to two years later) than vintage port. This extra time in the barrel softens the wine, permitting it to be drunk earlier. To make life even more convenient, most of the producers of LBV also filter it to remove the deposit. This helpfully saves the trouble of having to use a decanter. Unfortunately, wine made this way tastes less interesting and does not age as well.

■ **The terraced vineyards** *of the Douro are laid out in a way the Romans would have recognised.*

If you want a flavorsome LBV port with a bit more character, look for traditional versions from Warres and Smith Woodhouse, which will not have been filtered.

Generally better than "non-traditional" LBV are two rarer styles. Crusted (or crusting) port is a blend of different vintages, bottled early without filtering, so it will need to be decanted. Good examples can give true vintage style at an affordable price.

■ **Tradition dies hard in** *the steeply sloping vineyards of the Douro where port grapes are still picked by hand.*

"Single Quinta" ports break the traditional vintage-port rule by being produced at individual estates (quintas) rather than blended from a number of different vineyards. Quinta de Vargellas, Quinta do Panascal, and Quinta de Cavadinha belong respectively to the big port houses Taylor's, Warre's, and Fonseca. Others such as Quinta de la Rosa are independent. Quinta de Vesuvio, under the same ownership as Dow's, Graham's, and Warre's, is particularly worth looking for. Single Quinta ports tend to have shorter lives than the best vintage ports but their quality can be very comparable.

The varying shades of port

All of the ports we have looked at so far are a dark, plummy red. But port comes in other colors. First, there's white port, which is sadly usually little better than basic ruby. Indeed, even its producers prefer to take it with ice and tonic water – but Churchill makes a more serious, nutty example that shows what could be done.

Next, there's a really shameful golden-pink style produced by blending ruby and white. Confusingly described on its label as "Tawny," it is actually a cheap, dull-tasting version of genuine tawny port, which owes its bronze hue and delicious marmaladey flavor to prolonged aging in barrels.

INTERNET

www.symington.com.

This is the site of the Symington family, producers of such famous ports as Dow's, Graham's, and Warre's.

Aged tawny port

How do you know whether you are getting real barrel-aged tawny port rather than the cheaper stuff? The answer lies in the flavor of course, but if you have to choose a tawny port from its label, look for a reference to age. A tawny that describes itself as "10 Year Old," for example, will be the genuine item.

The traditional port producers have mostly resisted selling tawny port from a single year, supposedly fearing that to do so would cause confusion. (Though, given the other confusing names and labels they have exploited for their wines, this is decidedly hard to believe.) So most tawny is sold as 10, 20, or 30 years old. Some producers, such as Noval and Niepoort buck that trend, however, and offer delicious "Colheita" tawny ports with vintage years. These can, in their way, be every bit as good as vintage port.

Tawny port looks pretty in a decanter but does not need decanting. It keeps for several days once it has been opened and, when well-chilled, can be a delicious drink on a warm summer afternoon. (This is actually the way it is often enjoyed in the Douro.)

Madeira

Far less fashionable than port, Madeira has a similar history – and a long tradition of being drunk by 19th-century landowners in the southern United States. Produced on the island of Madeira, not far from the coast of North Africa, this fortified wine owes its

distinctive style to an accident of history. Sailing ships traveling from Britain south across the equator routinely used to carry casks of Madeira's wine as ballast. Eventually a thirsty sea captain with keen taste buds noticed that it tasted better toward the end of the trip than at the beginning. The high temperatures in the hold as the ship passed through the tropics had evidently contributed to the wine's flavor, giving it a nutty orangey tang.

Today, sailing ships are less easy to come by, so producers replicate the cooking process of their hold in special ovens known as *estufas*.

■ **Bual Madeira** *has a distinctive smokey-nutty flavor, and is sweet in taste.*

The styles of Madeira

Madeira comes in four basic styles: Sercial, Verdelho, Bual, and Malmsey. Sercial, the palest, driest, and most lemony, is made from a grape called the Esgana Cao (literally "dog strangler"). Verdelho is deeper in color, with a flavor that can be very like lime marmalade – but less sweet. Next comes Bual which is deeper, sweeter, and more green-brown in color, and tastes smokier and nuttier. Last, with flavors of honey, treacle, and old-English marmalade, comes Malmsey.

All these styles of Madeira can be delicious by themselves, with nuts and raisins or cheese, or – in the case of Malmsey and Bual – with rich fruitcake.

Things to remember about Portugal

✓ Portugal's most interesting wines are its reds and its fortified wines – but look for good examples of Vinho Verde and Muscat.

✓ Indigenous grapes help to produce rich unusual flavors not encountered elsewhere.

✓ Modern winemaking is improving quality rapidly. But, as in Spain, there are relatively few good producers.

✓ Do not trust the DOC system. Look instead for good producers – and bottles they have labeled "Garrafeira" or "Reserva" to indicate that they are among the best they have produced.

■ **When buying** *Portuguese wines, don't ignore good examples of Vinho Verde and Muscat.*

PORTUGUESE WINE TO BUY — AND WHEN TO DRINK IT

Top producers:

✓ North: Aliança, Barca Velha, Boas Quintas, Casa de Santar, Cava de Insua, Duque de Viseu, Palacio de Brejoeira, Luis Pato, Porta dos Cavaleiros, Quinta da Aveleda, Quinta da Cotto, Quinta de Gaivosa, Quinta de la Rosa, Quinta do Crasto, Quinta do Serrado, Quinta dos Roques, São João, Sogrape, Solar das Bouças

✓ South: Cartuxa, Carvalho, Caves Velhas, Esperão, J.M. da Fonseca, J.P. Vinhos, Margaride, Quinta do Bacalhoa, Quinta do Carmo, Ribeiro & Ferreira

✓ Port: Dow, Fonseca, Graham, Guimaraens, Niepoort, Noval, Quinta da Vargelas, Quinta de la Rosa, Quinta do Bomfim, Quinta do Crasto, Quinta do Vesuvio, Ramos Pinto, Smith Woodhouse, Taylor, Warre

✓ Madeira: Artur Barros e Souza, Blandy, Cossart Gordon, Henriques & Henriques, d' Oliveira, Rutherford & Miles

Lifespans: Port, depending on the vintage and producer can last for three or four decades. Most is best drunk within 20 years, however and white port as soon as it gets to your home. Portuguese white wines should be drunk soon after purchase, while reds can be stored for a decade or so but – in the case of some traditional examples – stand the risk of becoming fruitless.

Good vintages: 1990, 1991, 1992, 1993, 1994, 1995, 1997, 1998

Eastern Mediterranean

THE FINAL SECTION *of our southern European tour takes us to the Eastern Mediterranean. The birthplace of wine, these countries have, until quite recently, produced little of interest. The trouble was that the indigenous and expatriate wine drinkers were far too undemanding – and there was no need to sound out the opinions of foreigners.*

■ **In the Eastern Mediterranean,** *Cabernet Sauvignon grapes have been imported to improve local wines.*

Greece

One of the slowest countries to join the wine revolution that has swept the rest of the world, Greece has finally begun to show that it can offer more than tired bottles of Retsina and dull red Taverna Red. A new generation of producers such as Boutari, Kourtakis, Hatzimichalis, and Strofilia is exploiting traditional local grapes and imports such as Chardonnay, Cabernet Sauvignon, and Merlot to make wines that combine local character with the kind of fresh fruit flavor sought by drinkers throughout the world. Regional designations are far less important than producer names (some of Greece's best wines carry no appellation at all), but good dry reds and whites are being made in Agiortikos, Limnos, Naousa, and Nemea. Among the local grapes, the most interesting are the Roditis, Xynomavro, Agiorgtiko, and Assyrtiko for dry wines, while the Mavrodaphne and Muscat are both used to make delicious sweet wines.

Cyprus

The winegrowers of the island of Cyprus have a history of selling overseas. Unfortunately, the exports took the form of a cheap alternative to sherry and concentrated grape juice that was diluted and fermented to produce an often disgusting drink known – with double inaccuracy – as "British Sherry." Today, the KEO winery is producing perfectly acceptable light red, white, and pink wines, most of which are drunk in Cyprus.

Turkey

Winemaking is improving in Turkey, and it certainly needed to. Even now, famous wines such as Buzbag are stale and fruitless and only worth drinking if nothing else is available.

Lebanon

Credit for the fact that Lebanon has any wine industry at all after the years of turmoil through which it has lived recently can be attributed to the efforts of Serge Hochar, who managed to make his Chateau Musar in the midst of the hostilities. His wine is a rich, earthy, spicy, plummy blend of Rhône and Bordeaux grapes that varies fascinatingly – if sometimes alarmingly – from one vintage to the next. It is almost always worth keeping for a decade or so. Chateau Kefraya also produces a good blackcurranty red. Whites are not as interesting.

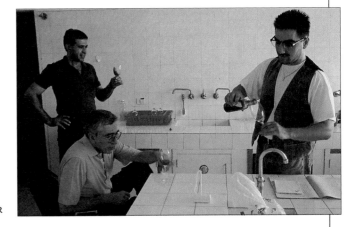

SERGE HOCHAR (CENTER) AT CHATEAU MUSAR

Israel

It was the market for kosher wine that originally encouraged early Israeli settlers to try to produce wine in sun-baked, irrigated vineyards. Despite heavy investment from overseas, the quality of most of the wine was extraordinarily poor. It didn't improve until the 1980s, when winemakers from California helped to launch a new wave of wines from the cool, high-altitude Golan Heights. The Golan Heights Winery's Cabernet Sauvignons, Merlot, Sauvignon Blanc, and Muscat are all worth buying. Wines from Askalon and Barkan wineries are also worthwhile, while those from the Carmel winery are perfectly acceptable.

■ **These wine barrels** *are from the Carmel winery, where much of Israel's wine is produced.*

North Africa

A CENTER OF WINEGROWING *before the Romans built their empire, the warm countries of North Africa still held a place in the wine world of the early 20th century. Until the gradual introduction of* appellation contrôlée *in France and elsewhere in Europe, French settlers made thick alcoholic wine in Algeria that was used to add alcohol, color, and flavor to feeble examples of Bordeaux and Burgundy.*

Good news and bad

The Coteaux de Mascara still has both an appellation and pride in its potential that dates back to those days, but the French legacy of uninspiring Carignan grapes, a lack of technology, and state control and interference have done little to produce attractive modern wine, and religious fundamentalists have hardly been inclined to encourage winemaking.

Morocco makes some pleasant earthy reds, including one rejoicing under the memorable name of "Rabbi Jacob," but little of real note. Tunisia, though, probably offers the best wines of the three countries, including good Muscat – sweet and dry – and pleasant Minervois-style reds from producers such as Domaine Karim.

EASTERN MEDITERRANEAN AND NORTH AFRICAN WINE TO BUY — AND WHEN TO DRINK IT

Top producers:

✓ Lebanon: Chateau Kefraya, Chateau Musar

✓ Israel: Barkan, Binyamina, Castel, Dalton, Golan Heights (Yarden, Gamla), Margalit, Segal, Tishbi, Tzorsa

Lifespans: The best reds can be kept for up to a decade, but most wines are best drunk young

Good vintages: 1997, 1998

A simple summary

✓ Local wine legislation is helpful as a guide to where a wine has been produced, but reveals little about its quality or even – on occasion – its style.

✓ For better or worse, wine styles and flavors still reflect local tastes and traditions.

✓ The warm climate of most of this region has, until recently, handicapped winemakers' attempts to produce fruity modern wine. Now, investment, regional pride, new equipment, and skills imported or learned from the New World are all helping to revolutionize quality. But some countries and regions are still making wines that taste stewed and dull.

✓ As a general rule, red wines and sweet whites are still much more successful than dry white wines.

Chapter 20

Northern and Eastern Europe

Turning our back on the sun, we go north to Germany, Austria, and Switzerland, to the surprising vineyards of Great Britain and the slowly up-and-coming countries to the east of the old Iron Curtain.

In this chapter...

GOOD WINE CAN BE PRODUCED IN COLDER COUNTRIES TOO!

Germany: from bone dry to ultra sweet

THE UNCHALLENGED *home of the Riesling grape, Germany produces some of the most sublime white wines in the world. Unfortunately, over the last few decades, while German cars, cameras, and computer equipment have been internationally synonymous with expensive reliability, German wines have found few fans in other countries. In this section, we'll take a look at why Germany's best wines taste the way they do – and how to find examples that are worth buying.*

INTERNET

www.germanwines.de

This official site is dedicated to German wines of every kind.

A basic overview

The first and most obvious thing to be said about Germany as a wine-producing country is that it is in northern Europe, where the climate is far too cool to produce big, richly flavorsome red wines. There are some German reds – at their best, delicate Audrey Hepburn-style efforts – but most wines are white. Next, there's the tricky question of sweetness. Ask most people how German wine tastes and the chances are that they'll answer that it's sweet. And they're partly right: Lots of it is pretty sweet. Some, indeed, is intensely sweet, thanks to being made from grapes that have been affected by noble rot or picked while frozen. But there are some delicious drier and bone dry wines too.

Where is it from?

The key to whether the contents of the bottle you are opening are going to be sweet or dry will lie on the label. Unfortunately, unless you are an experienced German wine drinker, you may find deciphering that label to be something of a struggle. Let's take it stage by stage, beginning with the place where the wine was produced.

HARVEST TIME IN BADEN

Germany's version of the appellation system doesn't – yet – recognize any vineyards as intrinsically better than others, but it divides the wine-producing areas up into large regions (*Anbaugebiet*) such as the Rheingau, Mosel-Saar-Ruwer, or Baden, whose name will appear somewhere on the label.

Within each *Anbaugebiet* there are sizeable districts (*Bereich*) which could be as big as the *Anbaugebiet* itself. Next comes a set of vineyards (*Grosslage*) before we finally get to the single vineyard (*Einzellage*). So how do these elements fit together to make a wine name? Well, most German wine names include a word that ends in "er," such as Bernkasteler, Piesporter, or Niersteiner. This indicates that the wine has some relationship with the wine-producing commune of Bernkastel, Piesport, or Nierstein. This rule won't always work, but it's pretty reliable. So far, so (relatively) simple.

■ **These vineyards are** *in the Rheingau region of Germany.*

The nature of the relationship

Now we have to establish the nature of the relationship. And this is where it gets more complicated, we're afraid. The communal name will be followed by another place name. This could be a *Grosslage* (some of which are good, others decidedly poor) or an *Einzellage* (which ought to be better). Unfortunately, unless you've done your homework or have a German wine guide on hand, you won't know that Piesporter Michelsberg comes from the big, unreliable *Grosslage* of Michelsberg while Piesporter Goldtröpfchen is from the great Goldtröpfchen *Einzellage*.

Because you probably won't have that wine guide, we've listed some of the best vineyard names – and ones to treat with caution – as well as the names of estates whose wines can generally be relied on, wherever their origin. One bit of immediate advice though.

Whatever you do, avoid any wine with the word *Bereich* on its label (such as Bereich Bernkastel). It could come from almost anywhere in a really huge area and will almost always be cheap and nasty.

What grapes are used?

Having gained some idea of where the wine was made, the next stage is to check the grape variety. Most of Germany's best wines are Rieslings, but there are good examples of grapefruity Scheurebe and Rivaner, creamy Weissburgunder (aka Pinot Blanc), spicy peary Grauburgunder or Ruländer (both aka Pinot Gris), earthy Silvaner and berryish red Spätburgunder (Pinot Noir), and Dornfelder. Recently developed varieties such as Ortega, Optima, Reichensteiner, Bacchus, and Muller-Thurgau are rarely used to make great wine.

INTERNET

www.r-for-riesling.com

This lively site is home for Riesling enthusiasts.

The absence of a grape variety on a German wine label is a bad sign.

Is it sweet or dry?

Now, we'll look at the sweetness. Germany's wine law grades wines according to the ripeness of the grapes, ludicrously implying that a sweeter or more alcoholic wine is intrinsically better than a drier or lighter one, regardless of where it was produced. *Qualitätswein* (quality wine) defines any wine that reaches a minimum level of ripeness. This minimum figure will then have been boosted by added sugar (chaptalization) and the finished wine will usually, but not always, have been sweetened with a dose of grape juice.

So, a wine labeled Qualitätswein will always be semi-sweet, unless the word Trocken (dry) or Halbtrocken (off-dry) appears as well.

The double-arch insignia of the CHARTA organization also indicates a dry wine. Dry German wines are very popular in Germany, where they represent well over half the production. These dry styles have proved less popular in other countries.

One of the attractions of Germany's sweeter wines is their often modest levels of alcohol. Despite having as much flavor as many California and Australian wines with strengths of 13.5 percent or more, sweet Kabinett and Spätlese wines can have a strength of 9 percent or less. Drier wines and reds will be more alcoholic (the sweetness having been fermented into alcohol) but even these rarely exceed 12.5 percent.

Quality consciousness

Sweet or dry *Qualitätswein* from a good producer can live up to its quality name, but bear in mind that this term is also the one that's shamelessly used on millions of bottles of sugar-watery Liebfraumilch and Hock. Riper grapes are used to make wines of various ripeness levels that are collectively known as *Qualitätswein mit Prädikat* (QmP) – quality wine with distinction. There are dry, *Trocken*, and *Halbtrocken* versions of these too. But, again, unless these words appear, a QmP will be sweet. The proportion of QmP wines that are produced depends on the quality of the vintage. In lesser-quality vintages, the vast majority of wines will be designated as *Qualitätswein mit Anbaugebiete* (QbA) – quality wine from a particular region.

QmP wines, which cannot legally be chaptalized or (apart from Kabinett) sweetened, are classed according to their ripeness (and, usually, sweetness). The least sweet will be Kabinett, which should have the flavor of a just-ripe apple. Spätlese – as sweet as a just-ripe peach – comes next, followed by Auslese, which should be sweeter still and have a little of the

■ **Spätlese should** *taste like a sweet, just-ripe peach.*

dried-apricot character of grapes that have been affected by noble rot. Beerenauslese will be more curranty – more noble rot here – while Trockenbeerenauslese, made from individually picked nobly rotten grapes, will be intensely luscious and honeyed. Finally, there's Eiswein (ice wine), made from grapes that are picked and pressed when they are frozen, producing the most intensely sweet and concentrated wines of all.

But there's a problem

■ **Eiswein, meaning** *ice wine, is one of the most deliciously sweet German wines.*

This all seems fairly straightforward, but there are two problems. First, there's an overlap between the natural sugar content for each of the ripeness levels, so what one producer might legally label as Spätlese, his neighbor could call a Kabinett. And second, there's the fact that the figures vary from region to region, so a Pfalz Kabinett can taste sweeter than a Mosel Kabinett.

Beneath all of these designations are two that are often forgotten: *Landwein* (country wine) and *Tafelwein* (table wine). In theory these are both more basic than *Qualitätswein* (which, we'd remind you, includes very, very basic wine), but, on occasion, top-class producers use these terms for good wine that simply falls outside the rules.

Numbers, prizes, and names

Whatever the quality-level of a wine, at the foot of the label you will find an *Amtliche Prüfungsnummer* – the official AP number which, if you had access to the appropriate government code books, might be deciphered to reveal the identity of the producer, and the place and date of bottling. The Germans are very proud of the system, which requires every wine to undergo a strict tasting before it can receive its AP number. Unfortunately, the wine only has to score 1.5 points out of five – hardly a very demanding task.

A similarly generous attitude prevails among the judges responsible for giving the prizes and seals that often adorn German bottles.

Do not trust the yellow, green, or red neck labels of the Deutsches Weinsiegel or the medallions handed out by the Bundesweinprämierung. They provide no guarantee of quality.

Where to turn

So, if you can't rely on the AP numbers and prizes to guarantee quality, as elsewhere, you are going to have to trust the producer. The German terms for winery are *Kellerei* and *Weinkellerei*, while *Weingut* and *Domäne* signify a wine estate. Similarly, the word *Schloss* – as in Schloss Johannisberg – is the German equivalent of the French term *Château*, and will indicate an estate rather than a merchant or cooperative (*Winzergenossenschaft*).

A *Staatsweingut* or *Staatliche Weinbaudomäne* is a wine estate that belongs to the state; some of these produce very good wine. Another indication of higher-quality estates is the presence on the label of the black eagle insignia of an organization called the *Verband Deutscher Prädikats und Qualitätweingüter* (VDP). Dry wines with the CHARTA insignia should also be of a decent standard.

The Mosel

One of the world's most exciting wine rivers, the Mosel produces Germany's most floral, delicate wines. All of the sweeter styles are produced successfully, but for many people, the Mosel's finest offering can be its appley sweet-but-not-too-sweet Kabinett. Nothing is more refreshing drunk by itself on a warm summer's day – and few wines go better with Chinese food. If you prefer dry wine, go for a *Trocken* or *Halbtrocken Qualitatswein* or Spatlese. Dry Kabinett wines from the Mosel tend to taste raw.

Things to remember about the Mosel

✔ This is Riesling country. Be wary of wines produced here from other varieties.

✔ The weather here is cooler than elsewhere in Germany, so dry (*Trocken*) wines made from Kabinett grapes tend to taste raw and are fortunately rarely seen outside Germany. Semi-sweet Kabinett Riesling can, however, be delicious, and features among Germany's finest wines.

■ **A picturesque** *valley in the Mosel, where Germany's most subtle and floral wines are produced.*

The Rhine

If we set aside the Mittelrhein – which offers plenty of picturesque tourist villages but few really worthwhile wines – and the Ahr, whose light red wines are mostly drunk on the spot, the Rhine is made up of four main regions. The most famous is the Rheingau region, which is where you will find a number of big-name estates with historic reputations – and wines that often sadly fail to live up to them. But there's no denying the potential for great wine here that the emperor Charlemagne spotted over a thousand years ago.

SIGNS FOR WINE CELLARS IN HATTENHEIM IN THE RHEINGAU REGION

The taste of the Rhine

The flavor to expect in good Rheingau Riesling is a combination of apples, grapes, and honey – with a little less of the floral character we found in the Mosel. Late harvest Spatlese, Auslese, Beerenauslese, and Trockenbeerenauslese wines from top producers here can be sublime. German wine drinkers tend to look to the Rheingau for dry wines, however. Many of these have until now been recognizable by the word CHARTA and its insignia on the bottles and labels. CHARTA is an association of leading growers in the Rheingau, dedicated to improving the quality and standing of *Halbtrocken* (half-dry) Riesling. It recently merged with the VDP, the nationwide association of top growers. It may continue alongside the VDP as a parallel organization, or it may be subsumed into it. At present, the future of the CHARTA association is far from clear.

Sifting the wheat from the chaff

The Rheinhessen is less interesting. There are fine wines produced in a set of towns including Nackenheim, Oppenheim, and Nierstein, but sadly, large amounts of very dull stuff is sold – some of it as Niersteiner Gutes Domtal. The Nahe is another place to find smart-sounding poor wines – and some rare delights – so we'd recommend you focus your attention on the Pfalz, where a combination of a warm climate and go-ahead producers make for extraordinary spicy wines.

Baden and Franken

The other two regions of greatest interest are Baden, where dry Chardonnays, Rieslings, Pinot Blancs, Pinot Gris, and Pinot Noirs are made, and Franken, where the Silvaner grape makes characterful – if often rather earthy and fruitless – wines that are sold in the same shape bottles as Mateus Rosé.

Things to remember about the Rhine

✔ The Rheingau is home to the great estates, but the Pfalz is the region with the exciting new-wave producers who are making spicy wines, including excellent examples of the Scheurebe and Rivaner grapes.

✔ Red wines are made throughout the Rhine with varying success. The place that does best with red wine is the warm region of Baden.

GERMAN WINE TO BUY — AND WHEN TO DRINK IT

Top producers and merchants:

✔ Mosel-Saar-Ruwer: Bischöfliches Priestseminar, Bisschöfliches Konvikt Trier, J.J. Chiastobel, Eitelsbacher Karthauserhof, Freiher von Heddesdorff, Friedrich-Wilhelm Gymnasium, Grans-Fassian, WilliHaag, Immich Batterieberg, Jakoby-Mathy, Weingut Karlsmuhle, Karp-Schreiber, Heribert Kerpen, Lauerberg, Dr Loosen, Mönchhof, Egon Muller-Scharzhof, Peter Nicolay, Pauly-Bergweiler, J.J. Prum, S.A. Prum, Max Ferd Richter, Schloss Saarstein, Seslbach-Oster, Bert Simon, H. Thanisch, Von Kesselstadt, Von Schubert/Maximin Grünhaus, Wegeler Deinhard

✔ RhinBalbach: Georg Breuer, Bruder Dr Becker, Bürklin-Wolf, Crusius, Kurt Darting, Armin Diel, Domdechant Werner'sches, Hermann Donnhoff, H.H. Eser, Graf Von Plettenberg, Gunderloch, Hehner Kiltz, ToniJost, Keller, Kruger-Rumpf, Künstler, Lingenfelder, Müller-Cattoir, Neckerauer, Balthasar Ress, Carl Sittman, Staatliche Weinbaudomäne Nahe, Von Bretano, Von Simmern, Heinrich Weiler, Winzergenossenschaft Heimersheim

✔ Franken: Baden, Württemberg etc Adelmann, Bezirckskellerei Markgräflerland, Bürgerspitall, Castell, Dautz-Able, Dörflinger, Durbach, Heger, Johner, Juliusspital, ErnstPopp, Staatliche Weinbau Lehrund Versuchsanstadt Weinsberg, HansWirsching

Lifespans: Drink basic QbA within three to five years of the vintage, most Kabinett, Spätlese, Trocken, and Halbtrocken wines within ten.

Good vintages: 1985, 1988 (Mosel), 1989 (Rhine), 1990, 1992 (particularly Rhine), 1993 (particularly Mosel), 1994, 1995, 1996, 1997, 1998

Switzerland

OFTEN OVERLOOKED BY WINE DRINKERS distracted by bottles from vineyards in neighboring France, Italy, and Germany, Switzerland tends to keep its wines to itself. This is made easier by the strength of the Swiss franc, the high costs of farming steep slopes, and a distinctive national taste in wine. The climate is warmer than you might expect, so grapes ripen well, but the wines rarely taste richly fruity as the Swiss favor grape varieties that do not lend themselves to producing rich fruity flavors. Subtlety is the key here.

Red and white

The Chasselas, or the Fendant as it is also known, is Switzerland's most widely planted variety. The wines it makes range from light and neutral to light and floral, depending on the soil in which the grapes are planted. The Sylvaner is earthier, while the Müller-Thurgau (usually called the Riesling-Sylvaner) makes light wines whose styles range from floral to vegetal. The most interesting varieties are the Amigne and Petite Arvine, but these are relatively rare. Reds are produced from the Gamay, Merlot, Syrah, and Pinot Noir.

The Swiss system

Switzerland has its own appellation contrôlée system that acknowledges cantons (the most important are Valais, the Vaud, Geneva, Neuchâtel, and Ticino) and Premier and Grand Crus sub-regions. Confusingly, Valais producers can also label their better wine as Appellation Contrôlée d'Origine rather than Appellation Contrôlée.

SWISS WINE TO BUY — AND WHEN TO DRINK IT

Top producers: Ch. d' Auvernier, Bonvin, Dubois, Dom. du Mont d'Or, les Perrières, Porret, Provins, Rochaix, André Ruedin, Ch. de Vaumarcus

Lifespans: As a general rule, drink Swiss red and white wines young, though local wine buffs like the flavor of aged Chasselas and some top-quality New Wave reds will improve with keeping.

Good vintages: 1998, 1999

Austria

DESPITE – OR PERHAPS THANKS TO – *the setback of a scandal in the early 1980s caused by the adulteration by a few winegrowers of their wine, Austria has quietly developed one of the world's most exciting little wine industries. The climate in some regions – most notably Burgenland – is warm enough to ripen black grapes from which rich reds can be made, while in others such as Styria, it is cool enough to produce steely dry Sauvignon Blancs and Chardonnays (here known as Morillon). Alongside these, there are Austria's two calling cards: spicy dry wines made from the local Grüner Veltliner and late-harvest, gloriously nobly rotten whites.*

The Austrian system

Finding your way around Austria's wines is not made easier by an appellation system that is like a slightly distorted version of the one applied on the other side of the frontier in Germany. Actually, it's a far better system – especially since it was tightened up after the scandal – but it takes getting used to.

■ **The climate** in Burgenland lends itself to the production of rich red wines.

Stated simply, as in Germany, the Austrians also label their wines as Kabinett, Spätlese, Auslese, Beerenauslese, and Trockenbeerenauslese, but often use these terms for riper grapes than the Germans.

They also have two words of their own: *Ausbruch* for a sweetness level that is beyond Trockenbeerenauslese and *Strohwein* or *Schilfwein* for wines that, like France's Vin de Paille and Italy's Recioto, are made from grapes that have been dried on straw mats.

Apart from the Cabernet Sauvignon, Merlot, Chardonnay, Riesling, Sauvignon Blanc, Pinot Blanc (known as Weissburgunder), and Pinot Gris (labeled as Rülander), other grapes that are grown here include the peppery white Grüner Veltliner, used for dry wines, the relatively neutral Bouvier (at its best in sweet, late-harvest wines), and the Blaufränkisch and the St. Laurent, both of which can produce Pinot Noir-like, raspberryish red wines.

Liquid gold

Austria's most exciting wines are unquestionably the late harvest and Strohwein wines produced in the region of Neusiedler See, a huge shallow lake where mists regularly form in the fall, facilitating the formation of noble rot. No other region in the world produces so much high-quality sweet wine so reliably. Prices are often lower here than in Germany, but when looking for bargains, bear in mind that wines made from Bouvier or Welschriesling will taste less interesting than ones produced from Riesling on the other side of the border. International fame has allowed top estates such as Alois Kracher, Alois Lang, and Willi Opitz to charge luxury rates for their luxury wines.

■ **Late harvest** and Strohwein wines are referred to as liquid gold because of their rich, sweet flavor and high quality.

AUSTRIAN WINE TO BUY – AND WHEN TO DRINK IT

Top producers: Brundlmayer, Feiler-Artinger, Freie Weingartner, Juris, Knoll, Kollwentz, Alois Kracher, Alois Lang, Munzenrieder, Nicolaihof, Willi Opitz, Pichler, Prager, Ernst Triebaumer, Johan Tschida, Umathum

Lifespans: The ageability of Austrian wines varies widely. Gruner Veltliner whites evolve (but don't necessarily improve) with time and St. Laurents can benefit from five years or so in the cellar. The wines to keep, though, are the best, sweet, late-harvest examples.

Good vintages: 1990, 1993, 1995, 1996, 1998

Great Britain

THE ROMANS, as British winemakers rarely tire of pointing out, used to make wine in Britain. Well, maybe they did. Soldiers grow thirsty and it was, after all, a very long way to transport terracotta amphorae full of the fruits of their own vineyards. On the other hand, even assuming that we were to share the Romans' taste in wine (which they tended to dilute with sea water), there is no evidence that they were remotely as impressed with what they produced in this colony as they were with the stuff they made on the other side of the Channel in France.

Location, location, location

Apart from a climatic hiccup in the Middle Ages, which apparently gave the region of Yorkshire a brief sunny heyday, Britain has had the kind of weather that its latitude would lead one to expect. In simple terms, if winemakers in northern French regions such as the Loire and Champagne often have a hard time ripening grapes, their British counterparts were hardly likely to find it much easier several hundred miles closer to the North Pole.

Britain's keen band of 20th- and 21st-century winemakers combat this rather fundamental handicap with grape varieties such as the Bacchus, Ortega, Rivaner, Schönberger, and Reichensteiner that have been developed specifically to grow in chilly weather. The Seyval Blanc also works well, but is frowned on because it is a hybrid between *vinifera* and *labrusca* grapes. Some stubborn producers also try to use more internationally popular varieties such as the Pinot Blanc and Pinot Noir – but rarely to much avail.

Southern advantage

Vines are planted surprisingly far north (there are vineyards in Durham and Cheshire), but the best wines are produced in the south, southwest, and East Anglia. Most are light and fruitily dry, with flavors of grapefruit and gooseberry, but the sparkling and late-harvest wines show particular promise. There is no useful appellation system, but an English Vineyard Association (EVA) sticker should indicate a better wine.

INTERNET

www.denbiesvineyard.co.uk

This is the site of one of Britain's most dynamic vineyards.

■ **It's easy to see** *why producing wine in Britain is often difficult!*

Most estates are small (with an average of seven acres) and largely focused on selling their wine to visitors and local customers. Finding a wide range of English wine is not easy in London, let alone overseas. Names worth looking out for include Breaky Bottom, Chapel Down, Chiddingstone, Nyetimber (sparkling wine), Three Choirs, and Valley Vineyards.

BRITISH WINE TO BUY — AND WHEN TO DRINK IT

Top producers: Adgestone, Astley, Berwick Glebe, Biddenden, Bodenham, Breaky Bottom, Bruisyard, Carr Taylor, Chilsdown, Chiltern Valley, Ditchling, Elmham Park, Headcorn, Nutbourne Manor, Penshurst, Pilton Manor, Pulham, Shawsgate, Staple, Tenterden, Thames Valley, Three Choirs, Wickham, Wootton, Wraxall

Lifespans: England's light, dry whites can be kept for up to five years or so.

Good vintages: 1998, 1999

Eastern Europe

LONG THE SLEEPING GIANT *of the wine world, Eastern Europe and Russia boast historic vineyards that were producing fine wine centuries ago – before being cast for a while into darkness by the Communist system. Prime vineyards that were once carefully tended by their owners – or their employees – were taken over by cooperatives whose bureaucratic bosses often treated wine as a commodity to be traded with Moscow, liter-for-liter, for gasoline.*

Democracy has brought Eastern Europe back into the mainstream of the wine world, but the process of privatization and modernization in the 1990s was slow and unsteady. This is particularly unfortunate, because this was precisely the time when the wine industries of countries like Chile and Argentina were being galvanized by investment.

Hungary's Tokaji

The one success story of Eastern Europe is the region of Tokaji near the Hungarian frontier with Slovakia. The smoky-dried-apricotty Tokaji (also known as Tokay) wines

Wines produced *in the cellars of Tokaji are amongst the finest in the world.*

produced here from local grapes such as Furmint and Hárslevelü are among the finest longest-lived sweet whites in the world. Under Communism, most wine was produced by a cooperative and standards dropped woefully, but the 1990s brought heavy investment, particularly from France, and recognizable bottles with terms such as "5 Puttonyos" and "Aszú" are now appearing on shelves and restaurant wine lists throughout the world.

So what do these Hungarian terms mean on a label? They refer to the unique way Tokaji is produced and the level of sweetness it has achieved in that particular label.

Instead of following the same procedure as the makers of other unfortified sweet wines — by fermenting late-picked or partially dried grapes — the producers of Tokaji turn their nobly rotten grapes into a sweet paste — known as Aszú. This is then added in varying proportions to dry wine.

Sweet and sought-after

Traditionally, the Aszú was measured in 55-lb. (25-kilo) hods called Puttonyos. This term is still used to indicate sweetness, which ranges from 60 grams of sugar per liter in a 3-Puttonyo wine to the intensely sweet 150-gram 6-Puttonyo and 180-gram Aszú Eszencia. Also produced is an even sweeter, stickier, barely alcoholic Tokaji simply — and confusingly — called Eszencia, which has over 700 grams of sugar per liter and tastes as though it ought to be spread on toast. It is rumored to be an aphrodisiac and sells for silly prices.

The styles and qualities of Tokaji vary widely, with the new investors favoring fresher less oxidized flavors. We agree with them. Royal Tokaji, Disznókö, and Château Megyer are all first-class modern producers.

The blood of Hungary

Hungary's other best-known wine used to be called Bull's Blood and is now more often labeled as Egri Bikavér. It owes its memorable name to the strength it is supposed to have given to 16th-century Hungarian defenders against a besieging Turkish army.

Lightweight recent efforts have usually been little better than simple rustic red wine, but Vilmos Thummerer is a producer that is justifying this wine's reputation.

■ **Most Bulgarian wines** *are fairly basic, but keep your eyes open as the quality of the reds will improve in the near future.*

Egri Bikavér, like many of Hungary's other reds, is largely made from the local Kadarka grape. Another local variety that is widely grown is Kékfrankos – though rarely to great effect. Merlot and Cabernet Sauvignon have been used with some success, along with the Chardonnay, Sauvignon Blanc, and Pinot Gris. Most good examples have been from visiting winemakers, or from wineries making-to-measure for foreign clients.

Bulgaria

Long the source of inexpensive varietal Cabernet Sauvignon, in the Communist era, Bulgaria was the beneficiary of a barter-deal set up to enable Pepsi Cola to sell its wine here. Pepsi Cola was swapped for wine, whose quality was brought up to scratch by consultants flown in from California.

A SELECTION OF TOKAJI WINES FROM HUNGARY.

That, however, was before alternative sources of good value came along. Today, as Bulgaria struggles to get its vineyards back into order, its reputation still rests on mostly basic "international style" reds and whites that are sold cheaply and produced by flying winemakers or (possibly) recently privatized cooperatives. In the future, more interesting reds should be made using the local Mavrud and Gamza grapes.

An appellation system exists but means little in quality terms and has been made even more confusing by the trend of cooperatives in one region producing wine from another and using both regional names on their labels. Areas to watch for, though, include Oriachovitza, Pavlikeni, Plovdiv, Rousse, Stambolovo, Suhindol, and Yantra. The most reliable producers are Iambol, Stara Gazora, Lovico Suhindol, and Svischtov.

Elsewhere in Eastern Europe

At least Hungary and Bulgaria are showing signs of repairing their industries. The other countries of Eastern Europe are in a far sorrier state. Romania makes soft attractive reds that are sold as Pinot Noir but may turn out to be made from another variety altogether. Commercial Chardonnay is made – under the Kirkwood label – in Hincesti in southern Moldova. Otherwise, few wines currently travel far beyond their own borders – and even fewer foreign importers are showing much interest in changing this situation. Some day however, when we've grown bored with a diet of Chardonnay and Merlot, we'll hopefully get the chance to explore well-made examples of hundreds of different grape varieties that are still only to be found in Eastern Europe.

EASTERN EUROPEAN WINE TO BUY – AND WHEN TO DRINK IT

Top producers: Hungary

✔ Tokaji: Bodvin, Chateau Megyer, Chateau Pajzos, Disznókö, Hétszölö, Lauder-Lang, Neszmély, Oremus, Royal Tokaji Wine Co., Istvan Szepsy

✔ Table Wines: Balatonboglar, József Bock, Tibor Gál, Attila Gere. Bulgaria: Dom. Boyar, BVC, Haskovo, Iambol, Khan Krum, Oriachovitza, Pleven, Rousse, Sakar, Sliven, Stabolovo, Stara Gazora, Suhindol, Svichtov

Top producers: Romania: Paulis

Lifespans: Apart from Tokaji, which can be kept for decades, and the occasional better-than-average Bull's Blood, drink Eastern European wines within five years.

Good vintages: Tokaji: 1990, 1993, 1995

Georgia, the region with the strongest claim to be the cradle of winemaking 5,000 years ago, grows no fewer than 1,000 different varieties. Unfortunately, none of these grapes are turned into wine most of the rest of us want to drink.

A simple summary

✓ When buying German wine, look for the grape variety on the label. Be wary of wines that don't mention one. Most of the finest wines are made from Riesling.

✓ Vintages vary greatly, some years favoring the production of sweet wine more than others.

✓ Germany's reds (usually made from Pinot Noir or Dornfelder) tend to be light, but can be attractively berryish.

✓ The suffix "er" in a wine name lets you know where a wine is from (so Niersteiner comes from the town of Nierstein).

✓ Wines labeled *Qualitätswein mit Pradikat* (QmP) are supposedly finer than ones with simply *Qualitätswein*.

✓ But . . . one producer's Spatlese may be sweeter than another's Auslese.

✓ And, whatever other words appear on the label, *Trocken* (dry) and *Halbtrocken* (just off-dry) will take precedence.

✓ Wines from Switzerland are generally overlooked yet some good light, floral wines are produced there.

✓ Austria has many exciting wines, especially the late-harvest and Strohwein wines

✓ Wine produced in Great Britain may not have the best reputation, but there are some worth trying. Look out for names such as Chapel Down, Three Choirs, and Valley Vineyards.

✓ Tokaji is the one success story of Eastern Europe. Wines produced from grapes such as Furmint and Hárslevelü are among the finest longest-lived sweet white wines in the world.

Chapter 21

North America: States of the Art

L EAVING THE OLD WORLD BEHIND, we move on to the Americas, where regional styles are apparent just as in Europe.

In this chapter...

✓ **Wine in the United States: more than meets the eye**

✓ California dreaming

✓ The Pacific Northwest

✓ New York State

✓ Other Northeastern states

✓ The South, Southwest, and Hawaii

✓ Canada

✓ Mexico

THERE ARE PLENTY OF WELCOME SURPRISES WITH WINES FROM THE NEW WORLD

Wine in the United States: more than meets the eye

WINE IN NORTH AMERICA at the beginning of the 21st century is a little like a piece of sculpture whose appearance changes depending on your viewpoint. People in other countries often imagine that most North American wine – and certainly the best and most interesting stuff – is produced in the Napa Valley and Sonoma County. This is a view that a fair few wine producers in those smallish regions in northern California are happy to encourage. After all, it's good for their bank balances.

It's not just Napa and Sonoma

But move around a bit and you find lots of other parts of California that produce wine of similar and even higher quality. Some of it is actually made by the same companies we'll meet in Napa and Sonoma. Now stand back a little to get a wider view, and you'll be reminded that California is not the only part of North America to grow vines. In fact, there are more than 40 other American states, plus both coasts of Canada.

■ **These vineyards** are in *Glenora on Senaca in New York!*

In recognition of the explosion of winemaking over the last 25 years, a system of over 125 regional appellations, called American Viticultural Areas (AVAs) has been established covering vineyards throughout the United States. Some of these are huge: "American" or "United States" cover the whole country, while a wine from the Ohio River valley, for example, could come from Kentucky, Illinois, Indiana, Ohio, West Virginia, or western Pennsylvania. Others are far smaller, referring to a county or a small hillside on which there is only a single vineyard.

Unlike most European appellations, in the United States AVAs are often based on political boundaries that may not have any particular climatic or geological coherence. Nor are any restrictions placed on the styles of wine that are made there.

Not all it seems?

Another key distinction between the United States and other countries lies in the allowance given to producers to include up to 25 percent of wine from a different region in a bottle bearing a regional appellation. A Bordeaux must be made exclusively from grapes grown in Bordeaux; a Napa Valley wine may legally contain as little as 75 percent of grapes from that county. American winemakers are also allowed to blend in limited amounts of wines made in other vintages or from other grape varieties.

When looking for wines from particular U.S. AVAs bear in mind that winery names can be very confusing, not to say misleading. Beware – wines with names like Napa Ridge, for example, may legally be blends that contain no wine from the Napa Valley.

Local charm

In many states, the production and consumption of wine tend to be limited and local. You can buy California wine just about everywhere in the country, but to find a Connecticut red, well, you may have to go to Connecticut.

Some parts of North America are so successful at making particular styles of wine that they are sold all over the world – even without the support of the California image and the marketing budgets of some of the bigger California brands.

So, you'll find Australians drinking Oregon Pinot Noir and Britons enjoying Washington State Merlot. You can be sure we won't be missing out on exciting wines like these as we take our tour around the vineyards of the United States.

California dreaming

INEVITABLY THOUGH, *we'll start out in California, where the global wine revolution first began in the second half of the 20th century. It was, after all, the pioneer winegrowers of the Napa Valley and the researchers at the University of California-Davis who first asked questions about why wine tastes the way it does – and how to make it taste better.*

INTERNET

www.winecountry.com

This site is a comprehensive gateway to California wine.

The missionary position on wine

Winegrowing in California can trace its roots back to 1769, when the Franciscan monk Father Junípero Serra planted vines brought from Mexico at the San Diego Mission shortly after its founding. The first winery in California was built at the San Gabriel Mission east of Los Angeles in 1771, and it remained the largest of the mission wineries for many years until secularization in the 1840s. (Mission grape vines are still found there, though they were replanted in 1861 and are not descendants of the original vines planted by the Franciscans.) By North American standards, the missionaries were late-starters – wine had been made in Canada, Mexico, and Florida 200 years earlier – but their wine and the wine produced by their fellow missionaries began to attract attention.

Among the people whose interest they aroused was a Frenchman living in California, appropriately named Jean-Louis Vignes, who realized that California's wines would taste better if they were made from the European grape varieties grown in France instead of the rather basic Mission or Criolla grape. So, in the 1830s, he imported vines via Cape Horn and Boston and set up California's first commercial winery near downtown Los Angeles, almost precisely on the site of Union Station.

This seems familiar

Vignes was not the only person to plant European vines in North America, but he was the first to do so in California. Others had tried on the East Coast but were defeated by the cold winters or vineyard diseases.

California offered the closest approximation to the kind of climate the vines were used to in Europe.

In simple terms, the secret of California's climatic success lies in the interplay between plentiful sunshine – which is similar to that of southern Italy – and the cooling effects of fog that rolls in from the Pacific.

Commercial winemaking really took off when Hungarian immigrant Agoston Haraszthy established the Buena Vista winery in 1857 to produce premium wines. In 1861, he traveled to Europe to buy vine cuttings. By experimenting with different varieties and soil types, he helped establish the Sonoma and Napa valleys as California's premier wine-making areas. Haraszthy is known as the father of California's wine industry.

THE BUENA VISTA WINERY, SONOMA VALLEY, CALIFORNIA

The legacy of Schoonmaker

At first, the early winemakers used whatever grapes they had on hand to mimic styles that were sold in Europe, describing them as "Burgundy" or "Chablis," for example. So-called varietal labeling began in the 1940s when a New York wine merchant named Frank Schoonmaker decided to treat California wines as seriously as his European imports – on the proviso that they described themselves honestly, using the names of the grape varieties from which they were made.

Schoonmaker's legacy is to be seen on millions of bottles of Chardonnay, Merlot, and Cabernet Sauvignon produced all over the world. Sadly, however, the bad old days linger on in American liquor stores, where cheap sweet American "Champagne" legally stands alongside the French original and pink sugary "Blush Chablis" unblushingly rubs shoulders with the dry white French original.

Labels such as these would be illegal in most other wine-drinking countries, including Europe, Australia, and South Africa.

Wine outlaws

Europe's strict laws ensure that the wine in a bottle labeled with the name of a famous wine region is what it says it is. Unfortunately, apart from Oregon, which laudably applies a local European-style legislation to its own wines, no such rules exist in the United States.

Beware of cheap American wines labeled "Champagne," "Burgundy," "Chablis," or "Port."

Life on the roller coaster

Two other factors are relevant when looking at California's wine industry. First there is the combination of wealth and marketing dynamism to be found in this state. In Europe, wine estates tend to be passed from parents to children. In California they are often founded by rich lawyers, doctors, show business stars (Francis Ford Coppola has a top-class winery), or multi-million-dollar corporations.

Hollywood and Silicon Valley are not far away, so it is no accident that when new wines are offered to the public they are described as "releases," just like movies, CDs, and computer software, and packaged by highly paid designers who most likely came up with the name of the wine as well as the shape of the bottle and the look of the label.

California hype

California not only invented the varietal wine; it also gave us the superstar wine. But that carries a price, same as in Hollywood. When you pay $40 for a bottle of Cabernet from a "hot" new winery it is no different than a studio having to shell out a few million for the latest teen-idol actor. This system sometimes not only means that the most keenly hyped wine gets to sell at the highest price, but that the most expensive wine gets taken more seriously than it deserves. Some of California's best buys are modestly priced, modestly promoted wines from small wineries. Beware of over-hyped over-priced California wine.

The second factor lies in the way outside circumstances force the California industry periodically to reinvent itself. First, there was Prohibition from 1920 to 1933, which closed all but the few wineries allowed to continue to produce sacramental wine (for which there was a huge demand). Repeal brought opportunities for a new wave of wineries, including companies such as E. & J. Gallo, which grew to become the biggest producer in the world. More recently, in the 1980s and 1990s, the phylloxera louse devastated vines, forcing wineries to replant over 80 percent of the vineyard land in the Napa Valley.

More of the same

These opportunities to review the way vineyards had been planned, coupled with variations of climate and soil and the presence of more than 2,000 wineries, ought to make for a fascinating diversity of styles. Unfortunately, land is expensive – and so are the costs of setting up a winery, crushing and fermenting grapes, and maturing wine in new oak barrels. Add to this the apparent preference of critics, restaurateurs, and consumers for styles they know, so California wine producers perhaps unsurprisingly tend to play it safe.

■ **Maturing wine** *in new oak barrels can be very expensive.*

Most wineries offer Chardonnay, Cabernet Sauvignon, and/or Merlot, with optional extras such as Pinot Noir, Sauvignon Blanc, and Zinfandel. In very recent times, the replanting after phylloxera has allowed a move toward introducing varieties from the Rhône (in particular Syrah and Viognier) and Italy (Sangiovese), and seems to have stopped a previous trend toward uprooting the Riesling. But these remain sidelines compared to what California winemakers call the "Fighting Varietals" and copies of the French classics.

When California producers decided to make wines using the same blends as Bordeaux, they labeled them as Meritage – to differentiate them from wines that were intended to taste of a single variety like, say, Cabernet Sauvignon or Merlot.

Winemaking styles also tend to follow similar patterns. In Burgundy, top-class Chardonnay is produced both with and without maturation in new oak barrels. In California, producers brave enough to buck the buttery oaky trend are very rare.

Comparing apples to apples

But if this tendency by the majority of producers to produce the same types of wine makes for a certain element of predictability, it also makes it very easy to compare the influences of different regions and vineyards – and to focus on the house-styles of particular wineries. We suspect, in any case, that this is a temporary phase and that, over the next decade or so, the picture will change, as more producers express the need to offer more distinctive wines.

The Napa Valley

Inevitably our tour of California begins in the Napa Valley. To understand this region, you might find it worthwhile to take a quick trip back to the Médoc in Bordeaux. Both regions have vineyards as far as the eye can see, punctuated by grand buildings. The Napa Valley vines cover the same amount of land as the communal appellations of Medoc, and the 20-mile length of the Valley is around the same as the distance from Margaux to St. Estephe. But there are differences. In the Médoc there are more areas without vines (places where appellation contrôlée wine cannot legally be produced) and in Napa the soil is more varied. Napa has more significant hills than the Médoc – and a wider range of grape varieties.

INTERNET

www.robertmondavi.com

The home site of this great winery features links to other wineries in the Napa Valley.

A confident product

What both regions have in common is extraordinary self-confidence – the knowledge of the financial value to be gained from printing the words "Napa Valley" or "St. Julien" on a label. The grand chateaux of the Médoc were mostly built and extended over the last 250 years. The ones in Napa – the often beautiful, architect-designed wineries – are around a tenth as old, but they serve the same role. Both help to bolster the image of the wine with which they are associated – and help to justify its price. Which helps to explain why the Robert Mondavi winery is now as recognizable a totem of the wine world as Chateau Margaux.

The name game

While great wine is produced in other parts of California, the Napa Valley boasts an extraordinary list of famous wineries. If you imagine a movie boasting most of the bankable stars, you'll have some idea of what we mean. Among the most glittering names, apart from Mondavi, are Beringer, Caymus, Diamond Creek, Dominus, Duckhorn, Dunn, Etude, Flora Springs, Franciscan, Frog's Leap, Harlan Estate, Heitz, Marcassin, Newton, Niebaum Coppola, Opus One, Joseph Phelps, Screaming Eagle, Shafer, Silver Oak, Spottswoode, Stag's Leap Wine Cellars, Swanson, Turley.

Many of these producers make wines in several places, and wineries based in other parts of California buy grapes or own vineyards here.

When buying wines from Napa, first look for the producer, then the sub-region.

The Napa equivalents of Médoc communal appellations such as Pauillac, St. Julien, and Margaux are Oakville, Rutherford, and Stags Leap in the heart of the valley; the hillsides of Howell Mountain and Spring Mountain to the north and Mount Veeder to the west; and the cooler southern region of Carneros in the southwest, which is shared with the neighboring AVA of Sonoma County.

So what comes from where?

The glorious blackcurranty Cabernet Sauvignons (with which Napa is rightly associated) and some deeply spicy Zinfandels tend to come from Oakville, Stags Leap, Rutherford, and St. Helena on the valley-floor and on the lower slopes of the hills, with the richest ripest-tasting wines coming from the northernmost part of the valley. The higher altitude vineyards of Spring Mountain, Mount Veeder, and Howell Mountain have all produced great reds too, plus whites with greater elegance than most of the efforts from those valley-floor vineyards. The best whites and Pinot Noirs have mostly been produced from hillside vineyards and from grapes grown in Carneros, where the fog from San Francisco Bay has its greatest cooling effect.

Sonoma County

Though long in the shadow of Napa, Sonoma County actually has a longer history of winemaking. Its handicap as a region is that it is much more confusing. There are six main sub-appellation regions spread around the town of Healdsburg, the vineyards are interspersed among other forms of agriculture, and many of the wineries have a family-run scale and charm that is rarer in the glitzier Napa Valley. It is very easy to get lost here. And don't confuse sprawling Sonoma County with the Sonoma Valley, a small area around the town of Sonoma in the southeastern part of the county.

THE GRAPE HANDLING AREA OF GALLO SONOMA'S FREI RANCH IN SONOMA COUNTY

So what's the difference between Sonoma and Napa?

At the risk of dangerous over-simplification, we could say that if the Napa Valley is known for its Cabernet Sauvignon, Sonoma has won a reputation for its Chardonnay – from Clos du Bois, Matanzas Creek, Peter Michael, Sonoma Cutrer, Kistler, and Simi – and for the Zinfandels that have been produced in the Dry Creek AVA.

The best Sonoma Cabernet Sauvignons tend to be from Knight's Valley and Sonoma Valley, though there are good examples from the tiny Sonoma Mountain appellation and the versatile Alexander Valley, where some terrific Merlot is being produced too. Like the Chardonnay, Pinot Noir does well in Carneros, but both varieties also shine in the cool Russian River where great sparkling wines are made by Iron Horse. Another Sonoma specialty is Sauvignon Blanc from Dry Creek, a region that also has some first class old vineyards full of Italian varieties such as the Barbera.

Carneros – the jewel in two crowns

Like the Montrachet vineyard shared between the Burgundy appellations of Puligny-Montrachet and Chassagne-Montrachet, Carneros straddles the line between Sonoma and Napa Counties. The cool micro-climate it owes to the San Francisco Bay fog does not suit the Cabernet Sauvignon, but Merlot can do well. The exciting varieties though, are Pinot Noir and Chardonnay – both as still and as sparkling wines.

North Coast – wild country

To the north of Napa and Sonoma Counties is the North Coast AVS, which includes a number of productive regions that are often overlooked. Mendocino County is wild and woolly country. If the parking lots of the Napa Valley wineries seem to be full of BMWs and Cadillacs, up here you might just as easily happen across aging hippies on Easy Rider motorbikes. But the wines they are tasting can be just as worthwhile – and even more varied. Anderson Valley, for example, is cool enough to allow Roederer U.S. to make California's most stylish sparkling wine. Redwood Valley, by contrast, is warm enough for Fetzer to make rich reds from its organic Bonterra vineyards.

Nearby Lake County is similarly versatile; this is the region where the ultra-dynamic Kendall-Jackson makes its ultra-commercial reds and whites. Green Valley in Solano County is cooler, and Guenoc Valley more versatile. These are all areas of which we will be hearing more.

■ **Pinot Noir is one** *of the most successful varieties grown in Carneros.*

Central Coast

South of San Francisco, heading toward Los Angeles, there are the two regions of the Central Coast and the South Central Coast where some of the most interesting winemaking – and some of the best value – is to be found.

Santa Cruz

The first region here is the coolish Santa Cruz Mountains where the great Ridge winery makes its Monte Bello reds and Mount Eden produces terrific old-vine Cabernet. Santa Clara, where Ridge has its winery and grows some of its Chardonnay grapes, is right next door to Silicon Valley. Livermore in Alameda County is best known as home to the Wente Brothers winery and its commercial but generally unexciting wines.

But Rosenblum Cellars makes glorious Zinfandels around here in the AVA of Contra Costa, and a member of the Wente family produces an excellent red under the Murrieta's Well label. Other producers – including Randall Grahm – are moving in fast.

Mount Harlan is less crowded but its credentials have long been established by the terrific Calera winery, whose long-lived Pinot Noirs are among the best in California.

Monterey County

Monterey County used to have a reputation for making "green" unripe-tasting wines, but different grape varieties in new parts of the region have made this an attractive place to come shopping for both superlative quality and value. For quality, go to Chalone, which has long produced top-class Chardonnay and Pinot Noir (in its very own AVA). For value, try the huge Monterey Vineyards, though some of the wines come from farther afield. This trend is likely to grow in the future as wineries look for the most economic places to buy their grapes.

■ **Monterey County** *now produces good-quality and good-value wine.*

The broader outlook

While most Europeans and many Californians prefer wines to come from small regions because of the individual character this is likely to give them, open-minded people who appreciate value-for-money and interesting flavors will be ready to try wines with broad AVA labels that declare them to be from "California," "North Coast," or "Central Coast." Wines with labels like these include bargains from big wineries and offerings from some of the best producers in California, including Au Bon Climat, Ridge, and Edmunds St. John.

South Central Coast – Zinfandel country

The South Central Coast begins with one of California's oldest and best red wine regions, Paso Robles. This is quintessential Zinfandel country, where specialist producers such as Ridge, Rosenblum, and Peachy Canyon make great intense examples of this variety. Edna Valley is cooler – and better suited to Chardonnay – and Arroyo Grande can be chillier still, and ideal for the sparkling wine made by Deutz. But the great Au Bon Climat makes fine Pinot Noir here – as well as in the Santa Ynez and Santa Barbara AVAs farther south. Santa Maria is another AVA that seems to be perfect for Burgundy-style reds and whites, as examples from Foxen and Byron prove.

Trivia...

Although Burgundy seems to have been the role model for many Central Coast winemakers, there is a growing trend toward introducing both the red and white varieties of the Rhône. Examples of these styles, from wineries such as Ojai, Qupé, Bonny Doon, and Edmunds St. John, are already among California's tastiest wines.

Other regions of California

There are a few vineyards farther south – including a surprisingly serious one called Moraga (planted in Beverly Hills on land previously occupied by a very desirable residence), and some high-altitude white wine vineyards in Temecula to the south of Los Angeles. But the most interesting region we have still to visit is back up north and inland.

The Mother Lode – Zins of the fathers

If California can claim one wine style they make better than anywhere else, it is the Zinfandel.

We have already visited various places where this grape does well – Dry Creek and Paso Robles for example – but its spiritual home is in the Mother Lode gold rush country of Amador County in the Sierra foothills. It's warm enough here for the grapes to develop wonderful spicy brambley flavors, but far enough above sea level to produce some good Rieslings and Sauvignon Blancs.

Other AVAs here include El Dorado, Fiddletown, and Shenandoah Valley. Among the producers to look for, we'd recommend Amador Foothill, Karly, Ironstone, Madrona, Monteviña, and Renaissance.

Central reservations

Finally, there's the Central Valley, the part of California that tends to be left out of most books despite the fact that this is where 75 percent of California's wine is produced. Imagine the pretty rolling hills and tiny family-owned wineries of Burgundy, Tuscany, and Sonoma. Now think of the opposite. This is industrial wine production on a large scale – huge flat irrigated vineyards whose grapes are converted by vast oil-refinery-like factories into branded red and white varietal wines with as much character as a bottle of Schlitz or Coors.

But it's not all like that. Hidden away here are a few jewels. Turley Cellars makes an intensely spicy Zinfandel from century-old vines in Lodi, and Ficklin and Quady both produce delicious fortified wines in Madera County.

RH Philips's Chardonnay from the Dunnigan Hills AVA is less exciting, but it is good easy-going stuff at a fair price, and far better than most of the rest of the wine that is being produced here. Competition from Argentina, Chile, and Australia will improve standards, we hope.

Things to remember about California

✓ The temperature varies quite widely, allowing both cool-climate grapes such as Pinot Noir and warmer ones such as Zinfandel to be grown.

✓ California's key regions are Napa, Sonoma, Mendocino, the Central Coast, the South Central Coast, and the Central Valley, while some of the best wines come from the smaller regions of Carneros, Howell Mountain, and Russian River.

✓ Wines are usually sold by the name of the grape rather than that of the region.

✓ Brands – producers' names – are crucially important.

✓ Many producers make wine in several different regions.

■ **This Carneros vineyard** *is in the important wine-growing region of Napa.*

CALIFORNIA WINE TO BUY — AND WHEN TO DRINK IT

Top producers:

✓ Napa: Acacia, Atlas Peak, Beaulieu, Beringer, Cain 5, Cakebread, Caymus, Chappellet, Chateau Montelena, Chateau Potelle, Chimney Rock, Clos du Val, Crichton Hall, Cuvaison, Diamond Creek, Domaine Chandon, Dominus, Duckhorn, Dunn, Far Niente, Flora Springs, Forman, Franciscan, Frog's Leap, Grgich Hills, Harlan Estate, Heitz, Hess Collection, la Jota, Kent Rasmussen, Lamborne Family Vineyards, Long, Mayacamas, Peter Michael, Robert Mondavi, Monteviña, Mount Veeder, Mumm Domaine Napa, Newton, Niebaum Coppola, Opus One, Joseph Phelps, Saintsbury, Schramsberg, Screaming Eagle, Shafer, Silver Oak, Spottswoode, Stag's Leap Wine Cellars, Sterling (reserve wines), Swanson, Turley, Villa Mount Eden

✓ Sonoma: Adler Fels, Alexander Valley Vineyards, Arrowood, Benziger, Buena Vista, Carmenet, Cecchetti Sebastiani, Chalk Hill, Chateau St. Jean, Clos du Bois, Dry Creek, Duxoup, Gallo Sonoma, Geyser Peak, Gundlach Bundschu, Iron Horse, Jordan, Kenwood, Kistler, Laurel Glen, Mark West, Matanzas Creek, Peter Michael; Nalle, Preston, Quivira, Ravenswood, Ridge; Rochioli, St. Francis; Cecchetti Sebastiani; Seghesio, Simi, Sonoma Cutrer, Joseph Swan, Marrimar Torres, Voss, Williams Selyem

✓ Mendocino, Lake, etc.: Fetzer (top wines), Guenoc, Handley Cellars, Hidden Cellars, Kendall Jackson, Lazy Creek, Parducci, Roederer Estate, Scharffenberger

✓ South, Central Southern, and other regions of California: Au Bon Climat, Bonny Doon, Byron, Calera, Carey, Chalone, Edna Valley, Firestone, Foxen, Jekel, Maison Deutz, Martin Brothers, Meridian, Mount Eden, Ojai, Quady, Qupé, Ranch Sisquoc, Ridge, Sanford, Wild Horse, Zaca Mesa

Lifespans: Very varied. Cheaper wines should be drunk soon after purchase, and all but the very finest Sauvignons within five years and Chardonnays within seven. Pinot Noirs are generally at their best before their tenth birthday. Top Cabernets, Merlots, and Zinfandels can last for 10 to 20 years, but beware of tough wines from the mid 1980s that have never softened.

Good vintages: 1988 (Merlot, Pinot Noir), 1990, 1991, 1992, 1993 (Cabernet), 1994, 1995, 1996, 1997, 1998

The Pacific Northwest

LEAVING THE SUNNY glitz of the Napa Valley far behind us, we head up the coast to the very different ambience of the Willamette Valley in Oregon. Our journey follows in the tracks of a visionary winemaker named David Lett, who headed north from California in 1965 in search of ideal conditions to make Burgundy-style wines from Pinot Noir grapes.

At that time most American experts honestly believed Lett to be mad. Why swap the climatic near-perfection of California for a place that's as cold and damp and unpredictable as, well, Burgundy? And that was the point. Lett and the winemakers who joined him in Oregon understood that the French region's weather contributes to the style and flavor of its wines. Until then, California's Pinot Noir vines had been grown in regions that were too warm. Their wines had none of the wild raspberry fruit of good Burgundy, tasting instead as though they had been made from stewed plums. Oregon's Pinot Noirs, on the other hand, were uncannily similar to the French wine.

■ **Pinot Noir from** *the Willamette Valley can taste remarkably similar to red Burgundy.*

Oh pioneers

In 1979, the pioneering Oregonians were proved right when a 1975 wine from Lett's Eyrie vineyard came second in a Paris tasting – just behind a 1959 Chambolle-Musigny from Joseph Drouhin, one of the most respected producers in Burgundy. Drouhin was sufficiently impressed by this and a subsequent tasting to invest in a vineyard near David Lett's and in a winery now successfully run by his daughter, Veronique.

Drouhin's seal of approval helped to convince the rest of the world that this was a region to be taken seriously. It did not take long before the best examples of Oregon Pinot Noir from wineries such as Eyrie, Domaine Drouhin, Cameron, Adelsheim, Ponzi, and Erath began to appear on restaurant lists. Few people were surprised when the American wine guru Robert Parker revealed that he was going to invest in his brother-in-law's Beaux Freres winery here.

Yes and no

Oregon's best Pinot Noirs are world class, but there are plenty of examples that are actually quite ordinary. Even these are sold at prices that are higher than you would pay for far classier red Burgundies. Beware of over-paying for undistinguished Oregon Pinot.

Though the Pinot Noir did well, at first it seemed that Oregon's Burgundian climate did not suit the Chardonnay – the first examples tasted green and unripe. The explanation was simple. The clones of Chardonnay that had been planted were ones that had been specially selected for the warmer conditions of California.

Now, new clones have been introduced from Burgundy that are producing far better wines. Along with the Riesling, Pinot Gris, Gewürztraminer, and Pinot Blanc, these are Oregon's best whites.

Apart from these cool-climate wines, Oregon produces small quantities of richer reds – including Merlot and Cabernet Sauvignon – in the warmer micro-climate of the Rogue Valley. Foris is a name to watch for.

OREGON WINE TO BUY – AND WHEN TO DRINK IT

Top producers:

Adelsheim, Amity, Argyle, Beaux Frères, Broadley, Cameron, Chehalem, Domaine Drouhin, Duck Pond, Erath, Eyrie, Henry Estate, King Estate, Panther Creek; Ponzi, Rex Hills, Sokol Blosser, WillaKenzie, Willamette Valley, Ken Wright

Lifespans: The best Oregon Pinot Noirs hold up over a decade, but most are at their best before their fifth birthday. Much the same can be said for the whites.

Good vintages: 1991, 1993, 1994, 1995, 1996, 1997, 1998.

Washington State

The western part of Washington State – the area where Seattle residents sip their coffee, write their software, and provide raw material for the writers of the TV show *Frasier* – enjoys cool, often quite rainy weather similar to that of Oregon. Hardly surprisingly, some Oregon-style Pinot Noirs are produced here. But head east, across the mountains, and you move into a very different climate. This is warm dry country where vines need irrigation from the nearby river simply to survive.

■ **It is not only** *the beautiful sunny days that help to produce fantastic wine in Washington State, but also the cool, breezy nights.*

Washington treats

The same grapes are grown here as in California, but there are some different success stories. Riesling, Sauvignon Blanc, Semillon, and Gewürztraminer all do better here as, very often, does the Merlot, which produces wines with lovely soft damsony flavors. The Syrah is another fast-rising star, but it would be a pity to ignore a local specialty, the Lemberger, a berryish wine that is known in Austria as the Blaufränkisch and can produce attractive Beaujolais-like flavors.

INTERNET

www.washingtonwine.org

Here you'll find everything you want to know about the wines of Washington State.

The secret is in the climate

The secret of eastern Washington State's intensely flavorsome wines lies in the contrast between the long, hot, sunny days that ripen the fruit and the cool nights, which provide a fresh acid bite that prevents the flavors from becoming jammy.

While the dusty soil would appear to have little to offer the vines in the way of character, there is no question that Washington State vineyards have very individual characters. Vineyard names Canoe Ridge, Horse Heaven, Ciel du Cheval, Klipsun, and Seven Hills are all worth looking for.

Confusingly, though, as in Burgundy, different wineries produce wines from the same vineyards, and on occasion are even named after those vineyards. So, you can buy a Seven Hills Cabernet from the Seven Hills Winery – or a Seven Hills Cabernet from the Leonetti or L'Ecole No. 41 wineries.

■ **Anything produced** *in the Washington State Vineyard of Horse Heaven, is likely to be worth trying.*

Beware of confusion over the name of the vineyard and producer in Washington State.

Until the mid 1990s, Washington's wines were well-priced. Today, the world has discovered the quality of wineries such as Andrew Will, Leonetti, L'Ecole No. 41, Quilceda Creek, and Woodward Canyon, and bargains are harder to find. Even so, Chateau Ste. Michelle, Columbia, and Columbia Crest all offer good value.

WASHINGTON STATE WINE TO BUY — AND WHEN TO DRINK IT

Top producers:

Chateau Ste. Michelle, Columbia, Columbia Crest, Covey Run, L'Ecole No. 41, Gordon, Hedges, Hogue Cellars, Kiona, Leonetti, Quilceda Creek, Staton Hills, Stewart, Andrew Will, Woodward Canyon

Lifespans: The top Cabernets and Merlots can live to 10 to 15 years. Rieslings, Chardonnays, and Sauvignons (particularly) should be drunk within five years.

Good vintages: 1989, 1990, 1991, 1992, 1993, 1994, 1995, 1996, 1998, 1999

Idaho

The lightly populated state that offers white-water rafting and Clint Eastwood's favorite ski resort also serves as an object lesson in geography and horticulture.

The problem of winemaking in Idaho lies in the extremes of temperature created by the high altitude.

Days are very hot and nights are very old. Grapes prefer to do their growing in more moderate conditions, so they obstinately refuse to ripen.

Idaho is a good place to make sparkling wine — and a generally poor one for rich reds.

New York State

AS RECENTLY AS the 1980s, you could be sure that a restaurant wine list in Manhattan would include bottles from other countries alongside examples from every corner of California, but there would be very little chance to explore wines from New York State. The weather to the north of New York City was thought to be too cold for serious winegrowing, and the notion of making wine among the holiday homes of Long Island smacked too much of weekend hobbyism. Besides, why buy a New York wine when you could get one from California?

INTERNET

www.nywine.com

New York State wines galore are featured at this site.

■ **Wines from** *Long Island vineyards rarely appear on wine lists.*

There was another handicap to be overcome. New York had a long and frankly undistinguished history of producing pretty basic Chablis and Champagne that genuinely didn't stand comparison with bottles from the west coast. Most wine here was traditionally made from labrusca or hybrid grapes, most of which are fundamentally ill-suited for the production of a wine that really tastes good. But, as far as the winemakers of the time were concerned, they had no alternative: Quality vinifera vines would never survive the chilly winters.

The quality revolution

But unbeknown to those Manhattan diners in the 1980s, a quality revolution had quietly been under way since the 1950s when Charles Fournier, former winemaker at Veuve Clicquot in Champagne, asked a Ukrainian immigrant named Konstantin Frank to help him grow vinifera grapes. Frank knew all about winters that were far colder than anything New York had to offer. The answer lay in protecting the vines by piling earth around them. Selecting better, warmer sites, near water, also paid off.

Gradually, despite the skepticism of old-timers, a new generation of winegrowers successfully introduced Riesling, Gewürztraminer, Pinot Blanc, and Chardonnay vines to vineyards in the Finger Lakes and Hudson Valley. Red wine grapes have found it harder to ripen here, but there have been some good examples of light Pinot Noir, Cabernet Franc, and Merlot. Despite their poor reputation elsewhere, two hybrids, Seyval Blanc and Ravat, produce white wines that can be very worthwhile. Benmarl, Clinton, Glenora, Heron Hill, Knapp, Lamoureaux Landing, and Millbrook are all good producers.

Treasure island

While the valiant campaigners were puzzling out how to combat the winter frosts upstate, a young man named Alex Hargrave took a fresh look at the potential of land rather closer to Manhattan, where the cold presented less of a challenge.

Vines had been grown on Long Island as long ago as 1640, taking advantage of a Bordeaux-like micro-climate produced by the Gulf Stream. Unfortunately, the climate here was rather more humid than Bordeaux, and incurable vineyard diseases flourished until new sprays were developed to treat them in the 1970s.

Hargrave took advantage of these sprays to plant vines in a field that had previously been used to grow potatoes. The success of his Merlot and Chardonnay encouraged others to follow him onto the island, where their vineyards are to be found in the North Fork and Hamptons AVAs. Names to look for include Bedell, Bidwell, Bridgehampton, Gristina, Lenz, Palmer, Paumanok, and Pellegrini.

INTERNET

www.liwines.com

You'll find Long Island wines online at this site.

Other Northeastern states

THE CHAMARD, *Crosswood, and Stonington wineries in Connecticut are all worth knowing for Chardonnays and Rieslings. Sakonnet took advantage of a relaxation of Rhode Island's unhelpful laws – until the 1970s, this was a dry state and now offers good Chardonnay.*

William Penn imported vines from France and planted them in what is now Pennsylvania. A state monopoly has hindered more recent progress, but Allegro and Chaddsford are reliable well-established wineries.

The Midwest

Ohio has around 50 wineries – and a winemaking history that stretches back to 1825 and is referred to in a Longfellow poem. Today, the best wines are made by Firelands and Markko.

The South, Southwest, and Hawaii

BYRD AND ELK RUN have made good Cabernet Sauvignons in Maryland. There are some five dozen wineries in Virginia, all following the lead of Thomas Jefferson, who planted vines at Monticello. The most successful wines are white – principally Chardonnay and Riesling – but there are also a few pleasant Cabernet Sauvignons. Barboursville, Horton, Piedmont, and Tarara are all good. The Wiederkehr winery provides people in Arkansas with local bubbles with which to toast their special events.

The Southwest

Under the helpful guidance of the University of Texas, the Lone Star state is showing great enthusiasm and progress with five regional AVAs and over two dozen active wineries. The best reds are the top Cabernets from Cap Rock, Pheasant Ridge, and Ste. Geneviève. Elsewhere, the stars tend to be white. Look for Chardonnays from Fall Creek, Llano Estacado, and Mesina Hof.

New Mexico's potential for sparkling wine is being exploited by two wineries owned by the Gruet and Cheurlin families from Champagne. Spicy reds are produced by Callaghan vineyards in high-altitude – over 4,000 foot – vineyards in Arizona.

Hawaii

Finally, there's Hawaii, where the Tedeschi winery produces a white wine called Maui Blanc. Don't ask about the grape variety, though – this tasty stuff is made from pineapples.

■ **Don't expect to** *find grapes in these Tedeschi vineyards, look out for pineapples instead!*

OTHER U.S. WINE TO BUY – AND WHEN TO DRINK IT

Top producers:

✓ Arizona: R.W. Webb

✓ Arkansas: Widerkehr Wine Cellars

✓ Maryland: Boordy, Catoctin, Elk Run

✓ Michigan: Lakeside Vineyard, Tabor Hill

✓ Mississippi: Almarla Vineyards, Claiborne

✓ Missouri: Hermannhof, Mt. Pleasant, Stone Hill

✓ New Mexico: Anderson Valley Vineyards, la Viña

✓ New York (Hudson/Finger Lakes): Gold Seal, Knapp, Millbrook, Rivandell, Swedish Hill, Treleaven, Wagner, Hermann Wiemer

✓ New York (Long Island): Bedell, Bidwell, Bridgehampton, Glenora, Gristina, Hargrave, Lenz, Palmer, Pindar

✓ Ohio: Debonné, Firelands

✓ Pennsylvania: Allegro, Chaddsford

✓ Texas: Cordier Estates, Fall Creek, Llano Estacado, Pheasant Ridge, Sanchez Creek

Lifespans: Longevity varies from region to region and more particularly from producer to producer. As a general rule, only the rarest whites develop beyond their fifth birthday and reds beyond their tenth.

Good vintages: 1997, 1998, 1999

Canada

TRADITIONALLY EXCLUDED *from the list of the world's leading wine countries, Canada was long famous for producing large quantities of Canadian wine using grape concentrate imported from South America.*

In some parts of the country, the local component is legally as low as 25 percent.

In Quebec, the figure is even rounder, a startling zero percent. This behavior is explained by the fact that most Canadians believed that their intensely cold winters made it more or less impossible to grow anything other than labrusca or hybrid grapes.

■ **The chilly climate** *in Canada makes grape-growing very difficult.*

For those interested in tasting genuine Canadian wine, this country's better producers have joined forces to create the Vintners' Quality Alliance (VQA), which has established appellation regions and a requirement that grapes must be grown locally.

■ **Although** *covered in snow for some of the year, Canadian vineyards are becoming more widely-known for their excellent wines.*

These same producers are also responsible over the last 20 years for revolutionizing the quality of Canada's wines and shifting the focus away from labrusca and hybrid vines. They looked at the globe, reasoned that many of their vineyards are on the same latitude as Provence and northern Italy – and thus have summers that could ripen vinifera grapes – and decided to seek out micro-climates where the vines might survive the winter.

INTERNET

www.winetour.com

This site provides an online tour of Ontario wineries.

Ontario

Their first successes were in Ontario, and perhaps unsurprisingly were whites made from grapes such as Riesling, Auxerrois, Chardonnay, Pinot Gris, Pinot Blanc, and Gewürztraminer. But Pinot Noir, Cabernet Franc (rather than Cabernet Sauvignon), and Merlot can all be good too.

The Niagara Peninsula has a climate similar to Burgundy, Lake Erie North Shore is more like Bordeaux, while the more southerly Pelee Island has a micro-climate that makes for a growing season that can be around four weeks longer than elsewhere.

The top wineries are Cave Springs, Château des Charmes, Henry of Pelham, Hillebrand, Inniskillin, Konzelmann, Magnotta, Pelee Island, Pillitteri Estates, Reif Estate, Stoney Ridge, and Vineland Estates.

Several hybrid grapes are still grown in Ontario, the most important of which is the Vidal. This is ideally suited to ice wine, the style of wine with which Canada is seducing the world.

THE BEAUTIFUL VINEYARDS
OF THE OKANAGAN VALLEY

Until the Canadians began to harvest and crush grapes that had frozen on the vine, Eiswein – as it is known in Europe – was exotic and fiercely expensive stuff that is regularly produced (albeit in tiny quantities) in Germany and Austria. A Canadian Vidal Ice Wine will never match a fine Riesling from a top site in the Rhine or Mosel, and the Canadian Rieslings have some way to go before they are really great. Even so, they offer the chance to experience the extraordinary concentrated ice wine style at a (somewhat) less extravagant price.

British Columbia

Seeing the success of Ontario's wines, British Columbia decided that anything the easterners could do, they could match. The key region here is the Okanagan Valley, but enthusiastic producers are now shifting their attention to Vancouver Island.

The styles of wine are similar to those in Ontario, but the German roots of many of the producers here are apparent in the quality of the Riesling, Gewürztraminer (a particular success), and a Riesling-Sylvaner cross called the Ehrenfelser. Pinot Noirs are showing promise from wineries such as Nichol, Quail's Gate, and Tinhorn Creek. Other producers to look for include Calona, Hainle, Hillside, Inniskillin, Jackson-Triggs, Mission Hill, Peller Estates, and Sumac Ridge.

CANADIAN WINE TO BUY – AND WHEN TO DRINK IT

Top producers:

✔ British Columbia: Calona Wines, Gehringer Bros, Gray Monk, Hainle, Mission Hill, Summerhill, Peller Estates, Jackson-Triggs, Sumac Ridge

✔ Ontario: Brights Wines, Cave Springs, Chateau des Charmes, Henry of Pelham, Hillebrand, Inniskillin, Konzelmann, Pillitteri, Reif Estate, Stoney Ridge, Sumac Ridge, Vineland Estates, Magnotta

Lifespans: Sweet whites can last for 10 to 20 years. Top dry reds are best within a decade and dry whites within five years. Lesser examples should be drunk soon after purchase.

Good vintages: 1996, 1997, 1998

Mexico

THE MEXICANS *have a word – malinchismo – you encounter quite often when talking to them. It refers to an Indian woman named Malinali, who became the mistress and interpreter to the Spanish conqueror Cortés. Malinali's embracing of foreign ways now serves as an emblem of the notion that "foreign" and "better" are often synonymous.*

This national inferiority complex encouraged a belief that, though introduced to winemaking by foreign conquistadores, native Mexicans would never really master the art themselves. Besides, there was little point in trying because wine has never really caught on in this country full of beer and liquor drinkers.

Another reason it may not have caught on was that the Criolla grape introduced by the Spanish produced an inferior wine. This is the same grape that the Franciscan missionaries introduced to California in the 18th century.

New wine, new life

Fortunately, a recent influx of foreigners – in the shape of the Spanish brandy and sherry house Pedro Domecq, the sparkling wine producer Freixenet, and Wente Brothers of California – has helped breathe fresh life into the industry. Two ambitious local producers, L.A. Cetto and Santo Tomás, developed quality vineyards in the Guadalupe Valley in Baja California close to the U.S. border. The success of their efforts and of a more recently launched winery called Monte Xanic helped to push malinchismo into the background. When an LA Cetto Petite Sirah was named Wine of the Year by the U.K. International Wine Challenge, Mexico's winemakers finally began to take themselves seriously.

While most attention has remained on Baja California, other regions are also beginning to show potential. The cool, high-altitude vineyards close to the old colonial town of Zacatecas in the center of the country seem particularly well suited to the usually unimpressive Ruby Cabernet. And Freixenet's still Viña Dolores wines from Querétaro are attracting interest both inside Mexico and north of the border.

Things to remember about Mexico

✔ Mexico has a rapidly improving wine industry, increasingly focused on higher altitude vineyards.

✔ The key regions are Guadalupe Valley in Baja California, Zacatecas, and Querétaro.

✔ The Spanish influence has been stronger than in the countries farther south, but is now losing out to trends from California.

✔ The key grapes include Cabernet Sauvignon, Merlot, Tempranillo, Grenache, Chardonnay, Ruby Cabernet, and Petite Sirah.

■ **The Spanish influence** *is apparent in more than just Mexican wine.*

MEXICAN WINE TO BUY – AND WHEN TO DRINK IT

Top producers:

✔ L.A. Cetto, Domecq, Monte Xanic, Santo Tomás, Viña Dolores

Lifespans: Most white wines should be drunk soon after purchase, and even the very top reds should be consumed within five or ten years of the vintage.

Good vintages: 1998, 1999

■ **Here, in Baja California** *some of the best wines in Mexico are produced.*

A simple summary

✓ North American wines vary hugely from region to region.

✓ In many regions, winemakers have to fight against cold winters that force them to use hybrids and a limited range of vinifera grapes. In cooler regions, vintages tend to be more variable.

✓ Improving skills and technology and a growing understanding of micro-climates are helping winemakers in states a long way from the hyped vineyards of California to make top class, and often very fairly priced wines. New York State, Virginia, and Texas are particularly worth exploring – as are Mexico, which is attracting heavy foreign investment, and Canada, which has aroused international interest with its ice wines.

✓ Most wines are sold under the name of a producer and grape rather than a region, as in Europe.

✓ Producer names are crucially important to anyone looking for good wine. But, some producers are better at some wine styles than others, so be ready to buy Winery A's Chardonnay and the Cabernet from Winery B.

✓ In California, Washington State, and Oregon, prices vary widely – and sometimes reflect marketing effort more than quality.

Chapter 22

Southern Hemisphere

A LL THE WINE COUNTRIES in the Southern Hemisphere– South America, the Antipodes, and South Africa – are New World wine producers, but several of them have a long history of winemaking, and at the beginning of the new millennium, they all now boast some of the most up-to-date vineyards and wineries in the world.

In this chapter...

✓ Chile

✓ Argentina

✓ Uruguay

✓ Brazil

✓ Australia

✓ New Zealand

✓ South Africa

THE SOUTHERN HEMISPHERE PRODUCES SOME OF THE MOST SOPHISTICATED WINES IN THE WORLD

Chile

IN THE 1970S, *some four centuries after Spanish missionaries founded their vineyards, Chile's wines were given a huge boost when overseas wine experts discovered that this entire country had escaped the attentions of the phylloxera louse. Thanks to its isolation and the protective barrier of the Andes mountains, the louse never got here.*

Because the phylloxera louse never reached Chile, while the rest of the world's vines are all grafted onto resistant rootstock, Chile's can be planted directly into the ground, just as you would plant an apple tree in your garden.

■ **These stunning** *mountains saved Chile from the phylloxera louse.*

Pre-phylloxera paradise?

Wine buffs fantasized about the "pre-phylloxera" Claret of the 19th century, licking their lips at the thought of sampling its modern equivalent. In fact, the notion of recreating "pre-phylloxera" Claret in Chile – or anywhere else – is nearly meaningless. 19th-century Bordeaux was made in a different soil and climate, and handled using different methods from the ones common there today. Besides, Chile's phylloxera-free vineyards are far from unique – there are plenty of regions of Australia that have never been touched by the louse, and most of Argentina's vines are ungrafted too.

Climate

But the cachet did Chile no harm, and it helped to foster an image of a country that combined an historic tradition of winemaking with conditions that are almost ideal for vinegrowing. The climate of the 600-mile long Central Valley offers enough sun to ripen grapes reliably and the additional bonus of an almost guaranteed absence of unwelcome rainstorms. In fact, Chile is a country where water doesn't come out of the sky very often in any season. Fortunately for thirsty vines, however, there's usually plenty of liquid available – as melted snow from the Andes Mountains, which spectacularly overlook the vineyards.

Traditionally, irrigation was done fairly crudely by flooding ditches dug between the vines. Often, it was done heavy-handedly, making for dilute wines with uncharacteristically – for Chile – unripe flavors. After a few years when snow-melt was less plentiful than usual, however, most producers began replacing the ditches with drip-irrigation, which can be more effectively controlled.

Catching up

For a time, in the 1970s and 1980s, Chile lived on the image of its climate, its phylloxera-free vines, and the quality of a few wineries' Cabernet Sauvignon, a trickle of which reached wine tasters overseas. But as the Chileans began to export more of their wine and to come up against competition from California and Australia, it became clear that much of its industry was old-fashioned.

The man who deserves credit for modernizing Chile's wines was a winemaker we met back in Europe. In the late 1970s, Miguel Torres arrived in Chile, fresh from rejuvenating the vines and wineries of his native Spain. Torres brought with him such novelties as stainless steel tanks and new oak barrels to replace the large old vats made from the local raule (beech), in which wine had previously been allowed to dry out and lose its flavor.

Over the following years, Torres was followed by a succession of other illustrious foreigners, including Eric de Rothschild of Chateau Lafite (at Los Vascos), Robert Mondavi (in joint ventures with Caliterra and Errazuriz), Mouton Rothschild (at Almaviva), Bruno Prats of Chateau Cos d'Estournel and Paul Pontallier of Chateau Margaux (both at Aquitania/Paul Bruno), and Grand Marnier (at Casa Lapostolle).

Not always what they seem

If outsiders were impressed by Chile's intense, blackcurranty Cabernet Sauvignon, they were confused by the whites that were made here. Sauvignon Blancs tasted weedy and vegetal and decidedly atypical – a characteristic that was subsequently explained by the revelation that the grape used to produce them was in fact a lesser variety called Sauvignonasse. Recently, genuine Sauvignon Blanc vines have been planted and used to make wines that can compete with the best of New Zealand, but some wines still have the tell-tale flavor of the poorer variety.

Semillon can do well – in a Sauvignon-like way – as can Chardonnay, though these often have a melony simplicity that makes them seem like lesser copies of efforts from California.

Trivia...

Some of the keenest investors in South America's vineyards have been Champagne houses, who appreciated the low costs of winemaking here. Unfortunately, unlike the Australian and North American wineries, which employed the same methods and grape varieties as in Champagne, the South American operations took short cuts. The more basic Cuve Close system was used to get the bubbles into the wine that was made from undistinguished varieties. The height of the Champenois' cynicism – not to say hypocrisy – however, lay in labeling their sparkling wine Champaña (in Spanish-speaking Chile and Argentina) and Champanha (in Brazil where Portuguese is spoken). Hardly the most straightforward behavior from representatives of an area whose controlling body, the Comité Interprofessionel de Champagne, has successfully sued chocolate and perfume manufacturers for abuse of a regional "brand" that enjoys legal status in Europe.

It gets confusing

As for red wines, Merlot has recently supplanted Cabernet Sauvignon to become Chile's red success story. Except that many Chilean Merlots are – like Sauvignon Blancs before them – not actually made from that grape at all.

Chile's "Merlot" was in fact another variety, the Carmenère, which used to be grown in Bordeaux but is no longer found there.

Unlike the Sauvignonasse, however, the Carmenère is an interesting spicy grape that can stand alongside the best varieties of Bordeaux and the Rhône.

At the beginning of the 21st century, matters are still confused. Some Chilean Merlots are made from Carmenère; some are genuine Merlot, while others are blends of the two (the two varieties are often mixed in the vineyard and are hard to tell apart). But there is an increasing trend toward bottling Carmenère separately and labeling it as such – or as Grand Vidure, its alternative name in Chile. Other grape varieties that are making good wine in Chile include Pinot Noir, Syrah, Malbec, and Gewürztraminer.

The regions

As Chilean wines developed an international following, producers began to develop a regional appellation system modeled on the European example. Five key regions were defined: Aconcagua, Maipo, Rapel, Maule, and Bío-Bío. Within these, a number of smaller sub-appellations were also recognized, some of which are much more significant than others. As elsewhere in the New World, however, big wine companies tend to make wines in various regions – and to produce multi-regional blends when appropriate for a style or price.

Aconcagua

Aconcagua, the northernmost area, is generally too warm for top-quality wines, but it includes cooler micro-climates. Errazuriz makes top-class reds in Panquehue. In the internationally recognized sub-region of Casablanca, temperatures are moderate enough to be ideal for white varieties such as Chardonnay and Sauvignon Blanc, while still allowing the production of stylish Merlot. Frost can be a problem here, though.

■ **The Maipo Valley** *is at the heart of the Chilean winemaking industry.*

Maipo

Maipo, close to the Chilean capital, Santiago, is the heartland of the wine industry. Vines compete with housing close to the city and thick smog often makes this less a viticultural paradise than it should be. The name probably appears on labels more often than it should – Maipo's wines are not always distinctive enough to warrant the appellation, and historically were often bolstered by wines from nearby Rapel. But there are some great red wine vineyards here, including those of Cousiño Macul and Paul Bruno.

Rapel

Rapel is a generally warm area that includes the exciting sub-region of Colchagua, where some of Chile's top reds are produced by wineries such as Casa Lapostolle. Farther south, Maule and its top sub-region, Curicó, are a little cooler. There is red wine produced here – by Torres, Caliterra, and San Pedro, for example – including some good Pinot Noirs from the Valdivieso winery. But Curicó competes with Casablanca to produce Chile's best whites.

■ **The region of Rapel** *produces some of Chile's top reds.*

Bío-Bío

Bío-Bío, the southernmost region, is cooler still, and is attracting interest from a number of producers as a source of red and white wine.

Things to remember about Chile

✓ A regular climate makes for wines that vary little from one year to the next.

✓ The key regions and sub-regions are Aconcagua, Curicó, Casablanca, Colchagua, Maule, Maipo, Rapel, and Bío Bío.

✓ Wines are usually sold by the name of the grape rather than that of the region.

✓ Merlot, Cabernet Sauvignon, Carmenère, Chardonnay, Pinot Noir, Sauvignon Blanc, and Semillon are the key grapes.

✓ Many producers make wine in several different regions.

CHILEAN WINE TO BUY — AND WHEN TO DRINK IT

Top producers:

Aquitania/Paul Bruno, Caliterra, Canepa, Vina Casablanca, Carmen, Casa Lapostolle, Concha y Toro, Cono Sur, Cousiño Macul, Echeverria, Errazuriz, la Fortuna, De Martino, Montes, la Rosa, Santa Carolina, Santa Emiliana, San Pedro, Santa Rita, Miguel Torres, Unduraga, Veramonte, Villard, Valdivieso, Viña Almaviva, Viña Porta

Lifespans: Most Chilean white wines are best drunk within five years and all but the very top reds should probably be consumed within a decade of the vintage.

Good vintages: 1997, 1998, 1999

Argentina

CHILE'S NEIGHBOR *across the Andes is a country that has been exposed to some very different influences. Where Chile often feels like a former colony of Spain, Argentina can seem to be a cocktail in which three parts of Spanish character have gone into the shaker with one part each of British and German, two parts Italian, and a generous dash of French. You get that impression wandering around the capital, Buenos Aires, or pulling the cork on a few Argentine wines.*

Generous supplies

Even with its wines beginning to appear on shelves and in wine racks around the globe, few people would imagine that Argentina is the fourth largest wine producer in the world. What were the Argentines doing with all this wine before we started to drink it? Well, quite a lot of it – mostly poor-quality stuff made from the local Criolla grape – disappeared between their lips; wine is sold in Argentina in the same kind of carton as milk and drunk just as enthusiastically.

INTERNET

www.argentinewines.com

You'll find lots of links to the burgeoning world of Argentine wines at this site.

Then there were the legal bulk exports to countries such as Japan and Canada, which have historically taken a relaxed view of what precisely should constitute a Japanese or a Canadian wine. And finally there were the rather less legitimate bulk shipments to Europe, which mysteriously took on Italian, Spanish, or French nationality after a bit of deft shuffling of the paperwork.

Spoiled for choice

Argentina's wines may have suited the bulk-wine market better than Chile's because there are some quite different grapes grown here. The most widely planted quality grape is the Malbec, a spicy, berryish variety that used to be part of the recipe for red Bordeaux and is now pretty much restricted to southwest France and the Loire. Given the low opinion of this grape by the Bordelais (who've almost all given up growing it), it is hard to explain why it has proved so successful in Argentina. One simple explanation is that the climate here suits it better; another is that the Malbec vines grown in South America are a different clone than the ones now used in France.

Apart from the Malbec, Argentina can also boast some of the largest plantings of the Sangiovese, Barbera, and Bonarda red wine grapes outside Italy – and just about the only examples of the red Tempranillo and grapey white Torrontes to be found beyond the frontiers of Spain and Portugal.

Understated elegance

The quality of the wines made from these varieties and from the inevitable Cabernet Sauvignon, Sauvignon Blanc, Merlot, Riesling, and Chardonnay depends as much on the skill and ambitions of the winemaker as on the region in which the grapes are grown. There is still a tendency to over-harvest the vines and to make some pretty dilute wine. But the success of Chile's wine industry over the Andes and the arrival of foreign investment (including some hefty helpings of Chilean cash) have helped to raise standards remarkably.

FLOOD IRRIGATION IN A VINEYARD IN MAIPÚ

Today, the understated elegance – some say, more "European-style" – of Argentina's best reds, which comes from a combination of soil and climate, sets them apart from the more forceful character to be found in the wines of most other New World regions, and helps to ease their way onto the lists of some very smart restaurants throughout the world.

If you enjoy both wines made from the Cabernet Sauvignon and Merlot in Bordeaux and the spicy reds of the Rhône, the Malbec could be your kind of grape. At its best, it seems to combine some of the best berryish and peppery qualities of both regions. As for the Torrontes, these white wines made from this other specialty of Argentina smell as though they are going to taste as grapey and sweet as an Italian Moscato – and turn out to be crisp, appley, and dry.

The regions

As in Chile, the Argentines are still sorting out their appellation regions. Most of the best wine, however, is produced in Luján de Cuyo, Maipú, San Rafael, and Tupungato close to the town of Mendoza, where most of the biggest producers are based. At the moment wine labels tend to mention Mendoza rather than the regions, which vary in altitude and soil and are suited to different grape varieties.

■ **Vineyards like this** *one in Maipú are particularly good for red wine.*

San Rafael and Maipú – like the confusingly similarly named Maipo in Chile – are both good for red wine, while Luján de Cuyo and Tupungato are cooler and produce more impressive whites. Other regions for white wines are Salta in the north, where the Torrontes flourishes on hillside vineyards, and Rio Negro way down south on around the same latitude as Bío Bío in Chile.

As in Chile, some of the best wines are made by big companies. Both Trapiche/Penaflor and Catena are producing world-class reds and whites, as is la Agricola. Moët & Chandon's recently-launched Terraza still wines are very impressive.

Things to remember about Argentina

✔ As in Chile, a regular climate makes for wines that vary little from one year to the next.

✔ Wines often have a more European (in particular Italian) style than in Chile.

✔ The key regions are Mendoza, Luján de Cuyo, Maipú, San Rafael, Tupungato, Rio Negro, and Salta.

✔ Wines are usually sold by the name of the grape rather than that of the region.

✔ The key grapes include Malbec, Cabernet Sauvignon, Merlot, Tempranillo, Bonarda, Barbera, Sangiovese, and Chardonnay.

Uruguay

URUGUAY IS NOT *a country that has featured on most people's list of wine regions, but it is beginning to take its wine industry very seriously. Needless to say, there are newly planted Chardonnay and Merlot vineyards, but as in Argentina, the truly distinctive wines are made from grape varieties more usually associated with southwest France. The Tannat of Madiran is used to make reds and rosés. Whites are produced from Petit Manseng, which is usually at home in Jurançon.*

Until recently these wines were not of great quality, but investment and imported expertise are definitely paying off and it will not be long before Uruguay's best wines compete with the cream of Argentina and Chile. As several members of the Uruguayan industry have pointed out, being a little country with a small population, a lot of sheep, and some very successful winemakers for neighbors hasn't done New Zealand any harm.

Wine to watch for

Watch for Domaine Chandon – Moët & Chandon's new operation and a new venture in the historic Los Cerros winery in San Juan between Chateau Pape-Clement of Bordeaux and Juanicó. Also look out for a new winery launched by Castillo Viejo and the Spanish sparkling wine company Freixenet.

Some outside observers believe that Uruguay will some day produce some of the most European-style wines in the whole of South America.

Things to remember about Uruguay

✓ It's an up-and-coming wine-producing country.

✓ Wines often have a "European" style.

✓ Tannat and Petit Manseng are the grape varieties to look for.

Brazil

BRAZIL HAS TWO main vineyard regions. Frontera in the south, close to the Uruguayan border, has irrigated vineyards where the Almaden winery in Palomas makes pleasant commercial wines. But, as they say in school reports, it could almost certainly do better.

Farther north, the hilly Gaucho Sierra region in Rio Grande do Sul, close to Pôrto Alegre, is home to most of Brazil's biggest producers, including Moët & Chandon, Mumm, and Martini & Rossi. Also found here is the huge Aurora cooperative, which produces wines sold in the United States under the Marcus James label. The climate here is quite tricky. It rains often, particularly around the time of the harvest. But decent wine is produced by wineries such as Forestier.

OTHER SOUTH AMERICAN WINE TO BUY – AND WHEN TO DRINK IT

Top producers:

✓ Uruguay: Santa Rosa, Domaine Chandon, Juanicó, Juan Carrau/ Castel Pujol, los Cerros San Juan, Castillo Viejo

✓ Brazil: Forestier, Cave de Pedra, Boscato, Casa Valduga, Baron de Lantier

Lifespans: Most white wines should be drunk soon after purchase, and even the very top reds should be consumed within five or ten years of the vintage.

Good vintages: 1998, 1999

Australia

IF THE WINE WORLD *in the 1970s and early 1980s looked to California for inspiration and innovation, in the 1990s it was the turn of Australia (and New Zealand, below). Rich reds and tropically fruity whites thrust their way onto the stage – at prices with which few other countries could begin to compete. But what was it about this country that made its wines so successful?*

Growing up in isolation

The most obvious thing to say about Australia is actually worth saying: This continent is a very long way from everywhere else. And in the days of sailing ships, it seemed a whole lot farther. Unlike South Africa, it wasn't on anyone's way anywhere, and unlike North and South America, it wasn't being squabbled over by colonial powers.

For much of its 200-year history, Australia's wine industry developed in isolation, focusing on styles that suited the local population.

For a country with a modern history of little more than two centuries, vinegrowing has a long history. The first settlers tried planting a vineyard almost as soon as they arrived – on the site now occupied by Sydney's Intercontinental Hotel. The humid climate did not suit the vines and the pioneering winemakers were forced to seek out drier conditions nearby. The region they found a little farther up the coast was what we now know as the Hunter Valley.

Re-drawing the map

Today, the Hunter Valley is an internationally recognized landmark of Australian wine – and the source of some truly great bottles. But it is only one of a number of Australia's wine regions, and far from the best. More than any other nation, Australia has expanded its wine industry geographically, developing wholly new areas. Some, such as Lenswood near Adelaide, are rapidly acknowledged to produce wine of the same quality as regions founded scores of years earlier.

HARVESTING IN THE HUNTER VALLEY

347

The driving force behind this expansion has been the combined efforts of small wineries and giants, all of whom have been looking, in the words of Dr. Andrew Pirie of Pipers Brook in Tasmania, for "the cheapest place to produce really fine wine."

The big boys

The dramatic growth in Australia's wine industry is largely attributable to the efforts of four giant companies, collectively controlling 80 percent of the country's total production.

DEFINITION

Bag-in-box or, as the Australians call them cask *wines, are ones that come, as the name suggests, in an ingenious bag made of special film to which is attached a tap that lets wine out without allowing air in. Wine sold in this form can be stored for weeks once it has been opened. Over half the wine sold in Australia is in this form, much of it is of highly acceptable quality. American bag-in-box wine, however, is generally a far less attractive prospect and often contains water and flavorings.*

These four main companies are Southcorp (whose brands include Penfold, Lindeman, Seaview, Seppelt Great Western, Wynn's, Rouge Homme, Leo Buring, Killawarra, Kaiser Stuhl, Tollana, Queen Adelaide, Coldstream Hills, and Devil's Lair), the French-owned Pernod Ricard (Orlando, Hunter Hill, Richmond Grove, Montrose, Morris, Jacob's Creek, Gramps, Wickham Estate, Black Opal, Carrington, and Wyndham Estate), BRL Hardy (Hardy's, Chateau Reynella, Yarra Burn, Moondah Brook, Houghton, Leasingham, Barossa Valley Estate, and Renmano), and Fosters (Mildara, Andrew Garrett, Knappstein, Krondorf, Tisdall, Maglieri, Balgownie, Eaglehawk, Saltram, St. Huberts, Rothbury, Wolf Blass, Yarra Ridge, and Yellowglen).

■ **Wine tasting in** *the Rothbury winery owned by the internationally famous Fosters.*

Unlike Europe, where there tends to be a clear division between quality and quantity (Champagne is the only exception to this rule), these big companies produce wines at every price and quality level. Southcorp's Penfolds, for example, makes cheap basic *cask* or bag-in-box wines as well as Grange, which has an international cult following among wine collectors and was named Wine of the Year by the influential *Wine Spectator* magazine.

Cross-regional blends

The role played by these big companies, which offer wine from different parts of the country, helps to explain the peculiarly Australian tradition of producing top-quality and commercial wines by blending across different regions.

Even Grange, for example, carries the broad South Australia appellation, which covers wines produced anywhere in this state. Commercial wines such as Jacob's Creek have an even more all-encompassing appellation in the shape of "South-East Australia," which could be used for grapes grown in South Australia, Victoria, or New South Wales – three states that, among them produce over 90 percent of the annual harvest.

While cross-regional wines are successful, there is a growing appreciation here, as elsewhere in the New World, for the produce of specific regions and vineyards.

New South Wales

Our tour Down Under starts, logically enough, at the beginning, in New South Wales' Hunter Valley where those first successful vineyards were planted. This is a climatically tricky place, where drought during the growing season often alternates with torrential storms that arrive just when it's time to harvest. Despite these handicaps, which can make a winemaker's life here very hard, the Hunter Valley has produced some of Australia's best reds and whites in the shape of smoky leathery Shirazes and lemony nutty dry (usually un-oaked) Semillons that can last for two or three decades.

Chardonnay

While these varieties are the Hunter Valley's tradition, its recent fortunes have lain in the Chardonnay pioneered in the Lower Hunter Valley by Tyrell's, who made Australia's first example. International fame came with wine made by Rosemount, whose Upper Hunter vineyards produce the internationally famous oaky Show Reserve and the limited-production, big, buttery Roxburgh. Today, the other style that attracts Sydney residents who like to take weekends in the Hunter Valley is light lemony wine made from a Portuguese grape called the Verdelho.

■ **The Hunter Valley** *wineries benefit from their proximity to Sydney.*

Acknowledging the problems of the climate, another Hunter Valley pioneer, Rothbury, helped to establish the nearby region of Cowra as a place to make good affordable Chardonnay. Reynolds and Rosemount, on the other hand, have both focused their attention on the apple-growing area of Orange, which seems set to develop a reputation for both Chardonnay and Cabernet Sauvignon, a variety that rarely thrives in the Hunter Valley.

Australian reds

An older region enjoying new success – again partly thanks to the efforts of the dynamic Rosemount – is Mudgee, which made history by declaring Australia's first appellation in 1979. The best wines here are rich reds: Cabernet Sauvignons and Shirazes. A higher altitude area, known both as Young and Hilltops, is proving successful with both reds and whites such as the ones sold by McWilliams under its Barwang label, and the Cassegrain winery is making inventive wines in the Hastings Valley, farther up the coast.

The names of all these areas feature on labels. The Murrumbidgee Irrigation Area (MIA) is familiar to Australian schoolchildren from their geography classes, and to big wine companies who use its grapes for inexpensive blends. The de Bortoli winery, however, proved that deliciously luscious late-harvest wines could be produced in this region (which they call Riverina), and Cranswick Estate is now making very respectable dry reds and whites here.

Victoria

The state of Victoria may boast a fiercely intense regional pride (the cities of Melbourne and Sydney are sworn rivals), but it is impossible to find a single style that characterizes its wines. In fact, if there is one word to describe Victoria's wine industry, it is diverse: You name it, and the chances are that you'll find it here somewhere.

The oldest vines in the state are the 140-year-old Shirazes in Goulburn at Chateau Tahbilk, which uses their grapes to produce classy long-lived wines. Like Goulburn's other best-known winery, Mitchelton, Chateau Tahbilk also makes first-class lemony dry Marsanne.

The reds and whites

Another classic Victorian region is the Pyrenees, where French-born Dominique Portet created some of Australia's most beautiful vineyards and some very European-style reds at Taltarni. Dalwhinnie is also very impressive here. The gold rush area of Bendigo, to the northwest of Melbourne, on the other hand, is a great place to find peppery Shiraz and berryish eucalyptusy Cabernet, as well as blends of both varieties from wineries such as Jasper Hill, Mount Ida, Passing Clouds, and Heathcote. Geelong, close to the shores of Port Phillip Bay, has been made famous by Bonnockburn's Pinot Noir. This variety, which crops up all over the place in Victoria, has also been mastered by Bass Phillip in the recently established area of Gippsland on the coast to the east of Melbourne.

Also on the list of coolish newer areas is Drumborg, where Seppelt makes good reds and whites. Other new areas are Ballarat and Macedon, which both produce interesting sparkling wines as well – in the case of the latter region, Virgin Hills, producer of one of Australia's most impressive red Cabernet-Shiraz blends.

Sparkling wines

The best-known region for sparkling wine is Great Western, thanks to the commercial brand produced here by Seppelt. The white examples are good value, but the really interesting style is the classic, slightly off-dry, red Sparkling Shiraz. The Show Reserve examples are among Australia's – and the world's – longest-lived and most distinctive sparkling wines of all.

Yarra Valley

Another area associated with bubbles is the Yarra Valley, thanks to the presence here of Moet & Chandon's Australian winery, whose wines are sold under the Domaine Chandon and Green Point labels. In fact, Domaine Chandon unashamedly uses lots of grapes from vineyards a long way from Yarra, but this is an ideal base for making sparkling wine because of the quality of Yarra Valley Pinot Noirs (from wineries such as Coldstream Hills, Tarrawarra, and de Bortoli) and Chardonnays. While these two styles have captured the limelight, there is also fine Shiraz (Yarra Yering), Cabernet Sauvignon, and Merlot (Coldstream Hills).

■ **The vineyards** *in the Yarra Valley not only look impressive but they produce some good sparkling wines too.*

Yarra's Pinot Noirs face some of their greatest competition from another Victorian region, the Mornington Peninsula, on the coast close to Melbourne. Stoniers, Dromana, and T'Galant are the names to watch for here. Other styles include Chardonnay, Rieslings, and Pinot Gris.

The rare and unusual

As if all these varied regions were not enough, there are a few other places dotted around that are worth knowing about. Unusual varieties planted in Brown Brother's King Valley vineyards have produced some of Australia's most innovative wines, including the Beaujolais-like Tarrango, while the tiny Giaconda winery in the hills near Wangaratta makes one of the country's finest most Burgundian Chardonnays.

Sweet and strong

Finally, there is a region that produces styles of wine found nowhere else, known in Australia as "stickies" for reasons that will be clear to anyone who has ever spilled these intense sweet wonders on their hands. Rutherglen and Glenrowan in the warm, old, gold-mining country of northeast Victoria are home to an extraordinary range of great fortified wines. There are "Tawnys" that compete with examples from the best port producers in Portugal, rich dark fruit cakey Muscats and distinctive, slightly tea-like so-called "Tokays," made from the Muscadelle, a grape otherwise only known as a bit-player in the blend of white Bordeaux. Dry unfortified wines are less successful, but Baileys and Campbells both produce intense Shirazes.

South Australia

Frequently described as the "engine room" of the Australian wine industry, this is the state where many of the biggest companies are based and where huge quantities of wine are produced. If the Australian wine industry has a capital, it would have to be the small country town of Adelaide, where winemakers and buyers gather in bars to discuss Aussie Rules football, cricket, and prospects for the harvest. This is not as varied a region as Victoria, but the range of wines being produced here is broadening by the year.

Barossa Valley

The traditional heartland of South Australia, the Barossa Valley, produces many of Australia's biggest richest reds, some of which are made using Shiraz grapes picked from vines planted over a century ago. The other traditional style here in the hillside vineyards is Riesling, which owes much of its success to the fact that many of the Barossa's winemaking families originally came from Germany. Just look at the names of some of the wineries – Henschke, Gramp, Lehmann, Krondorf – and at the Germanic architecture in small towns such as Hahndorf.

Intense reds

Look for red wines – usually Shiraz – from Barossa with "Old Vines" on their labels. They are among the richest, most intense wines in the world.

Bottles described as being from "Bush Vines" – referring to the way the plants are grown like bushes or small trees rather than trained on wires – are also often worth buying.

■ **Some of the richest** *reds are produced here in the Barossa Valley.*

Lighter whites

As you climb into higher altitudes, you move into the white and lighter red producing area of the Adelaide Hills, subdivided among sub-regions such as the Eden Valley, the excellent Lenshurst (look for wines from Henschke, Shaw & Smith, and Lenshurst Vineyards), and Piccadilly (where Petaluma makes its great Chardonnay).

Petaluma reds

If Petaluma's white is a success, so too is its red from Coonawarra, an oasis of green vines surrounded by a vast ochre mass of nothingness. The magic here lies in the red soil, which has a particular affinity for the Cabernet Sauvignon and the Shiraz. Coonawarra's best Cabernets – such as John Riddoch – are among Australia's and the world's finest reds and can often be identified by an intense minty character. Nearby Padthaway also has red soil and can and does also produce top class red wine, but it is also so good at white (far better than Coonawarra) that its name is more usually associated with Chardonnay than Cabernet. Around 60 miles closer to the coast, Mount Benson is a new region with great promise. Robe is another name to watch for.

DEFINITION

Basket-pressed *wines are made from grapes that have gone through a traditional round press, in which a screw is steadily turned to drive down a plate that squeezes the juice from the fruit. This gentle method extracts desirable flavors without unwanted hard tannins.*

And the blends

Grapes from both Coonawarra and Padthaway often appear in multi-regional blends such as Penfolds Bin 707. Another region whose wines traditionally went into the blending vat was McLaren Vale, a diverse area of rolling hills near the sea a short drive from Adelaide. Wines here range from subtle and lean (Geoff Merrill) to richly ripe (d'Arenberg). The most classic wines are probably the *basket-pressed* reds of Chateau Reynella.

Peaceful coexistence

One of the most fascinating of South Australia's older established regions is Clare Valley/Watervale, where the Riesling coexists with the Shiraz in a way that would be unthinkable to winemakers growing these grapes in their homelands of Germany and the Rhône. Clare Riesling, like its best counterparts from the Rhine, benefits from slatey soil, but the climate here is far warmer, making for wonderfully limey dry, off-dry, and occasionally late-harvest wines. Grosset is the name to look for.

■ **It's the soil** *that makes the wine from South Australia taste so good.*

South Australia has its own irrigated vineyards along the Murray River. Most of the wine they produce goes into "South East Australian" blends, but there are some remarkable exceptions, such as Yalumba's Oxford Landing. The Adelaide Plains region, another exception, is generally focused on fruit growing but is also the place to find such ground-breaking wines at Primo Estate as a Bordeaux blend made in the same way as an Amarone in Italy.

Western Australia

Tucked away from the rest of the country, Western Australia feels like a region that is content in its isolation. The first vines here were planted in the hot dry region of the Swan Valley near Perth, the largest city. As elsewhere, however, in the last quarter of the 20th century a number of quality-conscious producers realized that this climate was far too warm for high quality dry wines.

■ **Wine tasting** *at Houghton's in Western Australia.*

"Mediterranean" Australia

A clever scientist named John Gladstones studied the climate of the state and suggested that the best place to grow vines would be close to the surfing beaches of the Margaret River, a four-hour drive to the south. The first people to take Gladstones' advice were, curiously, almost all doctors, who began to make wine as a sideline. By the mid-1980s, wineries such as Cullens, Cape Mentelle, Chateau Xanadu, Mosswood, and Leeuwin were all proving Gladstones right by producing Bordeaux-style reds and whites and some fine Pinot Noir and Chardonnay. The climate in this beautiful coastal region is best described as "Mediterranean." Its appeal to winemakers, though, lies in its versatility. Australia's only Zinfandel (an intense 15-percent alcohol effort from Cape Mentellie) is produced down the road from Mosswood's Burgundy-style Pinot Noir.

An illustrious investment

One illustrious overseas producer who has invested here is the Champagne House Veuve Clicquot, which simultaneously bought Cape Mentelle in Margaret River, and Cloudy Bay, its famous sister operation in New Zealand.

Trivia...
One person we've already met almost joined these medical winemakers. Robert Mondavi briefly considered investing here and went so far as to choose an area in which to plant his vines. Proof of the Californian's remarkable instincts came when the Leeuwin winery began to produce one of Australia's – and the world's – finest Chardonnays in some of the vineyards that Mondavi had selected.

Margaret River has become a thriving wine region and its success has helped to encourage producers to explore the potential of vineyard land farther south – in Mount Barker (where Plantagenet makes fine Shiraz), Frankland, and Pemberton (source of fine Pinot Noir). Wines from all these regions are sold under regional labels and as multi-regional blends that sometimes include wine from the traditional vineyards of the Swan Valley. One such wine, for a long time known as Houghton's White Burgundy and now as HWB, is among Australia's top-selling whites.

Tasmania and the rest of Australia

The cool, green answer to Europeans who imagine Australia to be an ochre-colored, sun-baked desert, Tasmania was actually cold and windy enough to attract and finally deter Louis Roederer, one of the most illustrious producers in Champagne. Today, Dr. Andrew Pirie, one of the island's pioneering winemakers, produces good sparkling wine under his own name. His Pipers Brook Pinot Noir and Chardonnay are also fine, as are the Freycinet wines.

Vines are grown elsewhere in Australia, including, extraordinarily enough, at Chateau Hornsby in Alice Springs, where the grapes ripen so early that there is a constant risk of having to pick them in the December of the year preceding the one that will appear on the label. More seriously, there are a few high-altitude wineries in Queensland's Granite Belt to the west of Brisbane, and Lark Hill does well with grapes grown just outside Canberra.

DR. ANDREW PIRIE IN HIS WINERY OFFICE

Things to remember about Australia

✓ Australia is a highly dynamic and varied country with a growing number of quite diverse regions.

✓ Vintages can vary greatly between and even within these regions.

✓ Key regions include: Hunter Valley, Cowra, Riverina, Mudgee (New South Wales); Rutherglen, Mornington, Yarra, South Gippsland, Pyrenees, Gouburn, Great Western, Ballarat, Macedon, Geelong, Bendigo (Victoria); Coonawarra, Clare, McLaren Vale, Adelaide Hills, Padthaway, Eden Valley, Robe, Mount Benson, Penshurst, Piccadilly (South Australia); Margaret River, Mount Barker, Pemberton (Western Australia); Tasmania; Canberra; Granite Belt (Queensland).

✓ While these regions are creating their own reputations, many wines are blends from various areas.

✓ Australia has the broadest range of wines of any country in the New World.

✓ Key grape varieties include Chardonnay, Riesling, Semillon, Marsanne, Muscat, Verdelho, Sauvignon Blanc, Shiraz, Grenache, Cabernet Sauvignon, and Pinot Noir.

✓ Four big companies (and their subsidiaries) make most of the wine, but small wineries abound. One new Australian winery opens every 90 hours.

AUSTRALIAN WINE TO BUY — AND WHEN TO DRINK IT

Top producers:

Alkoomi, Jim Barry, Bridgewater Mill, Cape Clairault, Cape Mentelle, Capel Vale, Coldstream Hills, Cullens, Evans & Tate, Devil's Lair, Freycinet, BRL Hardy, Heggies, Henschke, Hill Smith, Houghton, Krondorf, Leeuwin Estate, Peter Lehmann, Lenshurst, Lindeman, Charles Melton, Moss Wood, Penfolds, Penley Estate, Petaluma, Pierro, Piper's Brook, Pirie, Plantagenet, Ravenswood, Rouge Homme, Shaw & Smith, Vasse Felix, Wignalls, Wolf Blass, Wynns, Yalumba

Lifespans: Inexpensive reds and, more particularly, whites are for early drinking, but Clare Valley Rieslings, Goulburn Marsannes, and top Chardonnays from regions like Yarra will last for a decade or longer. The best Hunter Valley Semillons can mature for 20 years or more. Top Shirazes and Cabernet from regions like Coonawarra, Yarra, and Barossa, and multi-regional blends like Grange can be worth keeping for 10 to 20 years or more. Pinot Noirs are still best within a decade.

Good vintages: ✓ Red: 1989, 1990, 1991, 1992, 1993, 1994, 1995, 1996, 1997, 1998, 1999
✓ White: 1989, 1990, 1991, 1992, 1993, 1994, 1995, 1996, 1997, 1998, 1999

New Zealand

NO COUNTRY *in the New World has made a more dramatic entry onto the wine stage than New Zealand. Until the early 1980s, – it was merely a cool-climate country whose perceived vinous destiny was to produce unsuccessful copies of port and sherry and light, white, off-dry wine to compete with bargain-basement offerings from Germany. For a while, the New Zealand wine producers – in many cases the sons and grandsons of Dalmatian immigrants who had come to New Zealand to tap gum and had turned to winemaking instead – accepted this as their lot. They welcomed visiting German experts and their advice about the grape varieties they ought to grow and the way to produce their wines.*

In doing so, they forgot that, until bulk winemaking edged them out during the early years of the 20th century, Chardonnay, Pinot Noir, and Cabernet Sauvignon were all being grown successfully in the Hawke's Bay region of the North Island.

The renaissance of New Zealand's quality wine came, appropriately enough, in that area in 1980 when a stubborn pioneer named John Buck made his first Te Mata Cabernet Sauvignon, an award-winner from old vines planted in the Awatea vineyard. This wine was followed by the even finer Coleraine Cabernet, Ellston Chardonnay, and Castle Hill Sauvignon Blanc.

■ **The wine in** *New Zealand can be as impressive as the scenery.*

A style is born

While John Buck was restoring the reputation of a previously established region on the North Island, the Montana Winery was quite literally breaking new ground on the South Island with its Sauvignon Blanc vineyard in the gravelly region of Marlborough. New Zealand's first-ever commercial example of this grape was the Montana 1980. Five years later, the smaller Cloudy Bay winery released its first effort with this grape. Between them Montana and Cloudy Bay almost instantly created a new internationally recognizable wine style: the grassy, blackcurranty – or as the British would say gooseberryish – Marlborough Sauvignon Blanc.

If New Zealand's Sauvignons struck the right note with British experts and wine drinkers, they often seemed to hit precisely the wrong one in France and the United States. France was entirely unused to what its commentators called the "exotic" fruitiness of these wines, so they hated it. American tasters, by contrast, enjoyed the fruity flavors, but disliked what they found to be the "vegetal" character that went with them. In 1998, however, nature joined the game by giving the New Zealanders warmer weather than they were used to. The result was richer softer wines, which gained more favor in the United States and less in the United Kingdom. Ever since, many wineries have sought to emulate the 1998 effect by harvesting a little later.

A promising Pinot

The successful Sauvignons were followed by tropically fruity Chardonnays, appley Rieslings, and lovely floral Gewürztraminers. A few classy Cabernet Sauvignons and Merlots have been produced, too, by wineries such as Te Mata, Montana, Corbans, Villa Maria, and C.J. Pask. There's even the occasional Shiraz (from Ata Rangi). But the red wine variety that is showing the greatest promise in this coolish country is the Pinot Noir, whose greatest exponents include Martinborough and Gibbston Valley.

It starts with the vine

The need to get the best flavors possible out of grapes grown in what can be a fairly chilly climate drove the New Zealanders to develop a unique expertise in the best ways to grow vines.

New Zealanders came to understand the benefits to be derived from so-called "canopy management" – the training and pruning of the vines and the plucking of leaves when appropriate to make the optimum use of the sunlight.

Led by Dr. Richard Smart, a succession of New Zealanders are now carrying their knowledge overseas as consultants in countries ranging from Spain to South Africa to the United States.

Initially, unlike their Australian neighbors, New Zealanders shied away from blending wines from different regions, but like them they saw the benefit in not restricting themselves to a single part of the country and growing particular varieties where they did best. So a big company like Corbans, Montana, or Villa Maria, would grow grapes in various regions of both the North and South Islands, offering Merlot, for example from Hawke's Bay, Chardonnay from Gisborne, Pinot Noir from Martinborough, and Sauvignon from Marlborough. More recently, blends that combine the best characteristics of two or more areas are beginning to prove popular.

North Island

Once one of New Zealand's main wine regions, the Kumeu, close to Auckland, tends to be overlooked now. That's a pity because the Kumeu River winery is using grapes grown here to make some of the best Chardonnays this country has yet been able to offer.

Among the other wineries based here but also using grapes from other regions are Matua Valley, Cooper's Creek, Nobilo, and Selaks. Henderson, nearby, has lost many of its vineyards to housing, but it is still the home to Corbans, Babich, Collards, and Delegats. South of Auckland you will find Villa Maria. One of the country's biggest and best producers, like Montana (which single-handedly produces around half of New Zealand's wine), it has wineries dotted around both islands.

Chic wines

Before leaving Auckland, it is worth taking a brief ferry ride to Waiheke Island, where Goldwater, Stonyridge, and Te Motu profit from a beneficial micro-climate to make fine red and white wines in vineyards surrounded by expensive holiday and commuter homes. Unsurprisingly, none of these wines find their way into the bargain bins.

Chardonnay

If New Zealand has one region that seems to suit the Chardonnay, it has to be Gisborne. This isolated area is used by several companies based elsewhere as the source of grapes that can produce deliciously tropically fruity wines, but it is also home to the excellent organic Millton winery, which makes one of the New World's few successful dry Chenin Blancs.

Pinot Noir

The Martinborough/Wairapara Valley, by contrast, has been New Zealand's first spiritual home for the Pinot Noir. Martinborough Vineyards, Voss, and Ata Rangi are the stars with some very Burgundian versions of this variety, but their neighbors are doing well with it too. Ata Rangi's other strongest card is its Shiraz, while Dry River produces New Zealand's finest Pinot Gris. The other name to remember here is Palliser Estate.

Trivia...

Gisborne was one of the very first places to welcome in the new millennium as winemakers ceremonially picked some of the first grapes of the 21st century.

Cabernet Sauvignon and Merlot

Hawke's Bay, the first region where vines were planted in New Zealand, is a large area that seems to offer good examples of most varieties, but excels with characteristically blackcurranty Cabernet Sauvignon and plummy Merlot (from Corbans, Esk Valley, Mission, Te Mata, Villa Maria, Vidal, C.J. Pask, Ngatarawa, Sacred Hill, and Montana's Church Road). Elsewhere on the North Island, Morton Estate, de Redcliffe, and Rongopai are all names to look for.

South Island

The best known region here is undoubtedly Marlborough which, in the two decades since that first Montana Sauvignon hit the streets, has become one the New World's most expensive winegrowing areas outside Europe. Its two sub-regions, Wairau River and Awatere Valley, can, on occasion, enjoy quite different climates. If Marlborough's reputation has been built with its intensely flavored berryish Sauvignons, some of which can easily outlive their Loire counterparts, the Chardonnay (Cloudy Bay and Seresin), Riesling, and Gewürztraminer also do well, and sparkling wines made from Chardonnay and Pinot Noir (Montana-Deutz, Hunters, Cellier le Brun, and Pelorus) are very impressive. Reds are generally unreliable, but Pinot Noir and Merlot can occasionally flourish.

■ **Machine harvesting** *in Marlborough, one of the most expensive wine-growing areas in the New World.*

Highly recommended

The long list of recommendable wineries here is growing constantly. All the bigger companies and even some smaller ones elsewhere offer examples of Marlborough wines. Key names are Cloudy Bay, Jackson Estate, Seresin, Grove Mill, Wairau River, Hunters, Vavasour, Allan Scott, Nautilus, Foxes Island, and Cairnbrae.

Two top-class producers – Neudorf with its Pinot Noir and Semillon and Seifried with its late-harvest Riesling – have made the name of Nelson, to the west of Marlborough. Canterbury to the south owes its current fame to Giesen Estate's Rieslings, though an early Pinot Noir from St. Helena was the wine that first proved how well this variety can do in New Zealand. Rosebank and Pegasus Bay (Pinot Noir) are worth remembering.

A rising star

The newest, brightest star on the horizon of the South Island is the region of Central Otago, which has surprised everyone by ripening grapes successfully despite its cool southern climate. Riesling is the predictable variety of choice for most producers, but the Gewürztraminer, Pinot Gris, Pinot Noir, and Chardonnay all shine from producers such as Chard Farm, Felton Road, Rippon, and Gibbston Valley.

Things to remember about New Zealand

✓ New Zealand is a generally cool country divided between two islands, with a number of quite diverse regions that suit different grape varieties.

✓ Vintages can vary between and even within these regions.

✓ Key regions include Auckland, Kumeu, Marlborough, Hawke's Bay, Martinborough, Nelson, Canterbury, and Central Otago.

✓ Blends from various areas are still less frequent than in Australia, but most bigger wineries offer wines from several regions.

✓ Key grape varieties include Sauvignon Blanc, Chardonnay, Riesling, Semillon, Gewürztraminer, Pinot Noir, Merlot, and Cabernet Sauvignon.

✓ Montana produces around half the wine in New Zealand.

✓ Sparkling wines are particularly successful.

NEW ZEALAND WINE TO BUY – AND WHEN TO DRINK IT

Top producers:

Allan Scott, Ata Rangi, Chard Farm, Church Road, Cloudy Bay, Collards, Cooper's Creek, Corbans, Cellier le Brun, Delegats, Deutz Montana, Dry River, Felton Road, Gibbston Valley, Giesen, Goldwater Estate, Grove Mill, Hunters, Kumeu River, Martinborough, Matua Valley, Merlen, Millton, Mision, Montana, Nautilus, Ngatarawa, Palliser Estate, C.J. Pask, de Redcliffe, Rippon, Rongopai, Saviour Hill, Seresin, Stoneleigh, Te Mata, Te Motu, Vavasour, Vidal, Villa Maria, Wairau River

Lifespans: Sauvignons last better than from many other regions, but they lose the freshness of their early appeal. Most people will prefer them within four to five years. Pinot Noirs may last a little longer. The other best reds will mature for up to a decade or so.

Good vintages:

✓ Red: 1989, 1990, 1991, 1992, 1993, 1994, 1995, 1996 1997, 1998, 1999

✓ White: 1989, 1990, 1991, 1992, 1993, 1994, 1995, 1996 1997, 1998, 1999

South Africa

IN THE 18TH CENTURY, the wines being made in the Cape of Good Hope, the southernmost corner of South Africa, were sufficiently impressive for vines to have been experimentally re-imported to France and planted in Burgundy. Apparently the wine they made there failed to match what they had produced in the Southern Hemisphere. Two hundred years later, South Africa was still the leading New World wine-producing country; then, in the third quarter of the 20th century, progress ground to a halt.

■ **By the late 1990s** *South African winemakers rejoiced as they were producing rich wines that competed with the best in the world.*

There were plenty of reasons for this. First, there was the little matter of trade sanctions and boycotts, which not only slowed exports, but just as importantly dried up most contact between South Africa's winemakers and their counterparts, critics, and experts overseas. Second, there was the fact that the vineyards were riddled with a virus called leaf-roll, which prevented grapes from ripening properly. And third, a supposedly independent but actually quasi-government organization called the KWV was founded to handle a surplus of wine in the 1940s, but soon degenerated into a convenient means of subsidizing uncommercial efforts of grapegrowers' cooperatives – thereby encouraging their members to support the status quo in general elections. Attempts to develop new regions and new varieties of vine were prevented, while around half the annual wine harvest was so unsaleable that it was routinely sent directly to the distillery, mostly to be converted into industrial alcohol.

The unripe

So, while other countries were planting Chardonnay and Cabernet Sauvignon, South Africa (which incidentally refers to grape varieties as "Cultivars") persisted with the undistinguished Welschriesling and the potentially better but still often uncommercial Pinotage and Chenin Blanc.

DEFINITION

The Pinotage is a grape variety almost restricted to South Africa and created by crossing the Cinsault (of the Rhône) with the Pinot Noir. Its wines can be attractively plummy and spicy – or less likeably rubbery in style.

An attempt to import Chardonnay vines into South Africa was made in the 1980s, but it failed when it was discovered that the variety that had been introduced was the less tasty Auxerrois.

Whatever the grapes that were planted – and there were plenty of Cabernet Sauvignon and Shiraz vines – despite the warmth of the weather in the Cape, the wines produced here had a "green" unripe flavor. Leaf-roll virus affected some 90 percent of the vineyards, preventing the fruit from ripening properly. A "clean-up" program was launched to replace the virus-affected vines with healthy clones, but winemakers who were used to the flavor of unripe grapes, and wary of ripe ones, often harvested far too early – thus continuing to produce the same style of wine as they had before.

Their explanation that they were aiming to produce "European-style" wines was countered by visiting Frenchmen such as Paul Pontallier of Château Margaux, who demonstrated as a consultant to Plaisir de Merle that picking a little later produced better flavors.

Richer and riper

Widespread change came in the late 1990s when a new generation of winemakers and exposure to outside influences such as Pontallier led the industry to take advantage of the healthy vines to make richer, riper tasting wines that stood comparison with the best in the world.

The legalities

South Africa developed one of the first and strictest appellation systems in the New World.

The so-called "winelands" are broken down into regions, districts, and wards. To complicate matters for outsiders, while most wineries are adopting the English language on their labels, the terms are often still in Afrikaans. Wyn van Oorsprong indicates "Wine of (regional) Origin," which, as elsewhere outside Europe, means that at least 75 percent comes from the region named. However, Landgoedwyn ("estate") wines must be 100 percent from the estate whose name appears on the label. Unlike most other countries, even some of South Africa's best estate wines are still bottled by merchants (gebottel op) rather than the producer. Their wines will be labeled Gekweek en Gemaak op (grown and made by). A wine whose label states Gekweek, Gemaak, en Begottel op will have been grown, made, and bottled by its producer.

Sweet wines will probably be labeled Stein or Semi-Soet (semi-sweet), Laat-Oes (late harvest), Spesiale Laat-Oes (special late harvest), or Edel Laat-oes (noble late harvest).

Stellenbosch

South Africa's equivalent of the Napa Valley is Stellenbosch. Indeed, to judge by the bottles seen overseas, one might be forgiven for imagining that this was the only part of the Cape that produced wine. In fact, as in California, while the big-name region is the source of some terrific bottles, it has no monopoly at all when it comes to quality – and does indeed produce some fairly disappointing stuff.

The best and the worst

To continue the parallel with the Napa Valley, the trouble is that Stellenbosch is quite varied. There are 50 different soils and different altitudes. The often intensely hot Stellenbosch valley floor, like the flat land in Napa, can make good rich reds – and lots of disappointingly jammy wine. And, just as some of the best Napa wines come from the cooler hillside vineyards of Howell Mountain and Mount Veeder, the top Stellenbosch efforts are often from wards such as Simonsberg (where the excellent Thelema estate grows its grapes) and Helderberg. Remember these names and that of nearby Durbanville (where Bloemendal makes good wine): You will increasingly see them on labels of finer reds and more particularly whites as these sub-appellations develop reputations of their own.

Constantia

The most famous ward in the Cape is Constantia, the area cooled by the sea on two sides, where the game of winemaking was first played in South Africa. The place to visit is the breathtakingly lovely Cape Dutch Groot Constantia estate, where you can get a taste of how things were for the early settlers. Unfortunately the taste of the wine made at this government-owned winery, though improving, is less memorable. Fortunately, the winemakers at Steenberg, Buitenverwachtung, and Klein Constantia do the historic vineyards greater justice. The latter estate

HARVEST TIME IN THE VINEYARDS OF KLEIN CONSTANIA IN CONSTANIA

has also made a wine called Vin de Constance, which revives the tradition of producing late-harvest wines in this area, once as famous as Tokaji in Hungary and Sauternes.

Paarl

The more inland region of Paarl is generally warmer than Stellenbosch, but it has lots of micro-climates that have great potential for quality wine of various styles, including some rich-flavored whites. Wellington has some good estates but the best ward here is probably Franschoek, which owes its name to the French Huguenots who came here in the 17th century. Finer whites – generally Burgundian-style Chardonnays – made by producers such as Danie de Wet on the chalky soil of Robertson to the east are worth watching for, but Worcester's hot-region wines tend to be jammy and dull. Warm weather has not, however, prevented Swartland and Tulbagh from making rich intense Shirazes and Pinotages that age brilliantly.

Other regions

If these areas enjoy long-established histories and international fame, there are other newer regions that are already producing wines of similar and often higher quality.

Overberg, the large area covering the southern tip of the Cape, is attracting interest with the Pinot Noirs (from Hamilton Russell and Bouchard Finlayson in Walker Bay) produced close to Hermanus on the coast. Also in Overberg, but a little farther west, the apple trees in the cool region of Elgin have recently been challenged by the arrival of vines that are producing Neil Ellis's classy Sauvignon Blanc.

There seems to be a close relationship in the conditions favored by apples and grapes. Like Elgin, the Russian River in California and Walla Walla in Washington State are both regions where vineyards flourish among orchards.

South Africa's most promising other region is Olifants River, where Vredendal and flying winemakers have made good commercial wines. The warm dry areas of Klein Karoo and Orange River could probably do likewise, but have yet to prove it.

Things to remember about South Africa

✔ South Africa's generally warm climate is mitigated by winemaking styles that often produce lean European-style wines.

✓ Late-harvest and fortified wines are particularly successful.

✓ Key regions include Stellenbosch, Paarl, Franschoek, Robertson, Overberg, Swartland, Tulbagh, Elgin, and Walker Bay.

✓ Blends from various areas are increasingly sold as "Coastal Region."

✓ Key grape varieties include Pinotage, Cabernet Sauvignon, Merlot, Shiraz, Pinot Noir, Sauvignon Blanc, Chardonnay, Muscat, Semillon, Riesling, and Chenin Blanc (known as Steen).

✓ Bulk-oriented cooperatives still control much (too much) of South Africa's wine production, but individual estates are leading the way toward higher quality.

SOUTH AFRICA WINE TO BUY — AND WHEN TO DRINK IT

Top producers:

Avontuur, Backsberg, Graham Beck, Bellingham, Blauwklippen, Buitenverwachtung, Cabrière, Camberley Clos Malverne, Neil Ellis, Fairview, Blaauwklippen, Bouchard Finlayson, Delheim, Fairview/Charles Back, Glen Carlou, Grangehurst, Hamilton Russell, Hartenberg, Jordan, Kaapzicht Cape View, Kanonkop, Klein Constantia, Lievland, Meerlust, la Motte, l'Ormarins, Nederburg, Neethlingshof, Plaisir de Merle, Platter, Rustenberg, Saxenburg, Simonsig, Stellenzicht, Thelema, Vergelegen, Vriesenhof, Villiera, Warwick Estate, Waterford, de Wetshof, Yonder Hill

Lifespans: Most dry whites should be drunk within five years of the harvest; but late harvest examples last a lot longer. Reds vary greatly. Many wines from the 1970s and 1980s aged poorly; but good wines from the late 1990s should be worth keeping for a decade or more. Top Pinotage can last for 20 or 30 years.

Good vintages:: 1989, 1991, 1992, 1994, 1995 (reds), 1998 (reds), 1999

HARVESTING IN LA PROVENCE
VINEYARDS IN FRANSCHHOEK

A simple summary

✓ Grapes are picked in the Northern Hemisphere spring – so a 1999 Australian wine is six months older than a 1999 from California.

✓ Styles vary enormously from one country and region to the next, depending on climate, soil, grape varieties, and local tradition.

✓ The general youth of the industry and the inflow of outside investment give most Southern Hemisphere countries more modern technology and a more highly trained young workforce than in most parts of tradition-bound Europe.

✓ Most vineyards have historically been planted in warm regions, but there are now increasing moves to cooler, often higher-altitude areas where finer flavors can be achieved.

✓ Throughout the region, the key "international" grape varieties are grown, but there are local specialties (Malbec in Argentina, Carmenere in Chile, Shiraz in Australia, Pinotage in South Africa, etc.) and a trend toward introducing new grape varieties that makes for greater variety of styles than in, say, the United States.

✓ Irrigation is often used to make up for a shortage of rain and this, plus the legal right to blend limited amounts from other vintages, makes for less variation between years than in Europe.

✓ Brands are more important than regional appellations. Indeed, in many countries, wine producers make wine from different areas, blending between them when appropriate.

Chapter 23

The Future

Having traveled the world, visiting the major regions where wine is being produced today, it's time to take a look at the places that will be producing our wine in the future. We'll also be looking at the way styles of wine are likely to change as the 21st century unfolds.

In this chapter...

THE NEW VINES OF THE FUTURE ARE GROWING NOW, AND IN PLACES THAT YOU MIGHT NOT EXPECT!

Heading east

A REGION NOT *mentioned so far will almost certainly be crucially important over the next few decades – Asia. Wine has been produced in various parts of this region over the centuries, but in many cases it went out of fashion until the late 20th century.*

Wine and Levi's

There are various explanations for its renaissance. First, and simplest, there's the fact that bottles of Chardonnay and Merlot share with Levi jeans, Big Mac burgers, and BMW cars the appeal of being aspects of life associated with the West. Wealthy businessmen throughout the region like to use famous bottles of wine and cigars as visible symbols of their sophistication and success. Finally, and in some cases most importantly, there has been the association of wine with health.

Countries with traditions of associating particular kinds of food and drink with physical well-being were especially receptive to news that red wine can reduce the risk of heart attack.

The first beneficiaries of the wine boom were, naturally, producers in the West. But local regional pride, the scent of financial profit, and the availability of foreign expertise and investment has encouraged the planting of vineyards in various parts of the region, ranging from Thailand and India to China and Japan.

> ### Trivia...
> *When the King of Thailand's doctor advised him to drink a glass of red wine daily for his health, sales of imported Bordeaux, Cabernet Sauvignon, and Merlot apparently jumped by over 800 percent almost overnight.*

■ **Japan's best wine** *receives very little praise from the rest of the wine world.*

Japan

JAPAN'S WINE *industry is confusing for outsiders. Land is not plentiful in this highly populated country, and where it can be found, the humidity is far from ideal for wine grapes. Most of the vines that are planted grow less fussy table grapes and Koshu, a variety that is technically classified as vinifera but rarely produces fine wine.*

The imports

Japan also has a long tradition of importing large quantities of grape concentrate from South America, adding yeast and water, and converting it into wine legally labeled as Japanese.

In theory, imported wine should be described as yunyu san, while local produce is called kokunai san. But even assuming that your linguistic skills extend to deciphering Japanese characters, don't place too much trust in these terms.

Their use is voluntary and, in any case, the local element of kokunai san actually refers to where the fermentation took place. In other words, grapes grown in Argentina can legally be used for a kokunai san provided their juice arrives in Japan in an unfermented state.

The best regions

It is easy to understand why quality wine production is unlikely in Japan. But, the negative factors have to be set alongside the famous can-do attitude of the Japanese, fierce national pride, and a recent explosion of interest in wine. Sincere efforts have been made to produce wines of a quality to match the best of Europe.

The best regions are Nagano Yamagata and, more particularly, Katsunama (which has its own label-integrity scheme), while producers and brands that are most likely to be recommendable are Mercian (a trophy-winning Chardonnay), Sapporo (the Polaire label), Chateau Lumière, l'Orient, and Rubaiyat.

■ **In line with** *Japanese thinking, where there is a will, there is a way!*

China

WAY BACK IN 128 B.C. while the Romans were introducing vines to France, the Chinese general Chang Chien visited a country to the east of Samarkand called Fergana, where he discovered large quantities of wine that were being stored for decades. Chang Chien imported vines from Persia. Winegrowing evidently proved popular with the emperor, because vines were subsequently reported to be flourishing near the palace.

In the 13th century, Marco Polo described wine from Tai-Yuan in the Shansi province being shipped around the empire, and 400 years later, the emperor K'an-hi tried planting vines farther afield to see how they performed. Apparently they fared far better in the north of the country.

The first winery

During the early years of the 20th century, a French priest established what is now the Beijing Friendship Winery (now known for its Dragon Seal brand produced with help from the French company Pernod Ricard). Other long-established similar joint ventures include Tsingtao, which is produced with the assistance of the multinational Allied Domecq Dynasty, which was launched by the Cognac firm Remy Martin and Summer Palace, a venture involving Seagrams.

As China has opened its doors to foreign trade, a number of other high-profile overseas investors have arrived, including Miguel Torres from Spain. While these firms have all focused their attention on producing wine from Chinese grapes, it is an open secret that much so-called Chinese wine is in fact produced elsewhere and imported in bulk.

GRAPE PICKING IN QINGDAO, CHINA

■ **Making and drinking** *wine is becoming popular all over China.*

Winemaking in China today

The grapes grown in China range from the local Dragon's Eye, Ju Feng Noir, and Beichun –
none of which is known for its quality – to the better but unspectacular Welschriesling and
Rkastiteli, and the more recently planted Chardonnay, Merlot, and Cabernet Sauvignon.

The best regions for winegrowing so far seem to be Shandong, Heibei, and Tianjin,
all of which are on the same latitude as California and Tuscany and ripen grapes well.
Cold winters, typhoons, monsoons, and general humidity can be a problem, however.
Given China's size, it is likely that, as in Australia, optimum regions will be discovered
over the next few years.

Western partners

Winemaking in the joint venture wineries tends to be of a decent commercial standard
(thanks to Australian and French techniques) but is rarely ambitious. The best of the
Chinese state-owned alcohol-manufacturing factories can compete with the joint
ventures, but most fall far short of international standards. Matters are made much
worse by the way wine is transported and stored – with high temperatures often
removing any freshness it may once have had.

China's wine industry is likely to grow quickly, however, thanks partly to the growing
taste for wine in China, and partly to the input of investment from rich, Hong-Kong-
based wine lovers. The Beijing authorities are also enthusiastic about wine, preferring
alcohol made from grapes (which are not a staple food) rather than the grains used for
beer or spirits.

India

IN THE 16TH *century, the Sultan Babur, founder of the Mogul Empire, apparently relished wine made from grapes grown in the Houzma Valley in modern Afghanistan and in the Hindu Kush. Records such as this, however, are suprisingly rare, considering that India has a history of two millennia of wine production.*

A growing market

The quality of wine making – and storage – in recent times was almost universally poor until the decision by a Mumbai millionaire businessman to launch a winery making sparkling wine.

With the help of visiting consultants from Piper Heidsieck to India, a decent rather than great pair of wines called Omar Khayam and Marquise de Pompadour were produced from a blend of Chardonnay, Pinot Noir, and basic Thompson Seedless (eating) grapes that were grown at an altitude of 2,500 feet in the Sahyadri Mountains near Poona.

Other producers are following in Omar Khayam's wake. None of their wines are yet of a quality to impress many palates overseas, but it is expected that the fast-growing young Indian middle class will soon offer a receptive market for quality wines.

Other regions in Asia

WINE IS ALSO *produced in the east Asian countries of Korea, Thailand, Vietnam, and Taiwan, and the central Asian countries of Tajikistan, Uzbekistan, Kazakhstan, and Kyrgyzstan. For the moment, the only likelihood you have of tasting these would be to travel to these countries.*

Techno-change

ALONGSIDE THE DEVELOPMENT *of new vineyards and vineyard regions, the kind of wine we drink will be affected by two other man-made factors.*

One problem for winemakers is global warming, already having an impact on the climate of vineyards in northern Europe. By some accounts, a rise in temperature will simply make it easier for winegrowers in the less-well-situated vineyards in regions such as Bordeaux and Burgundy to ripen their grapes — and enable their counterparts farther north in Britain to grow sun-loving grapes like the Chardonnay and Merlot.

Life, however, is unlikely to be that simple. One possible consequence of burning up the ozone layer is that the Gulf Stream may change direction, in which case places such as Long Island and Britain may actually find temperatures falling rather than rising.

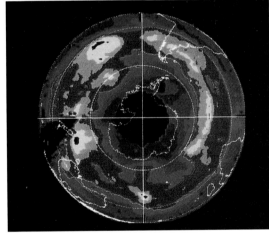

■ **It is foolish to** *think of advantages that may come from the hole in the ozone layer — when it comes to wine, nothing is certain.*

Genetic engineering

The other unpredictable factor is genetic engineering. While most winegrowers share the ecologists' fears of the possible dangers of inserting genes from one species of plant into another, open-minded researchers are aware that there would be undeniable benefits to be derived from exploring the genetic differences between different kinds of vine. What is it about *Vitis labrusca* vines that phylloxera lice don't like? Why do *Vitis amurensis* vines survive bitterly cold winters that would kill *Vitis vinifera*? Discover the answers to these questions, and you could do away with the need to graft vines onto phylloxera-resistant rootstock (thus reducing the cost of planting and reducing the time taken to establish a vineyard). And, even more attractively, you might be able to develop whole new wine regions in places previously thought inappropriate.

More controversially, but still within the limits of research into vines, might it be possible to define the genes that are susceptible to particular types of disease and pest? Might the genetic engineers, as they claim, help organic winegrowers by producing hardier vines that need little or no protection from chemical sprays? The organic producers, for the moment at least, reply "no thanks," believing for their part that tinkering with the vines' genetic makeup could both affect the way they develop in the long-term and jeopardize the environment in which the vines are grown.

Organic answers

Whatever the answer to these questions, it seems pretty certain that the wines of the first quarter of the 21st century will be increasingly organic in their production.

As many as a third of the vines in the huge recently planted vineyards of California, are already being — or soon will be — grown according to internationally recognized rules governing organic farming.

■ **Amongst the vast** *array of vineyards in California, an increasing number are becoming organic.*

Blends: an end to varietals?

HOWEVER AND WHEREVER *the grapes are grown, we'd also predict that the styles of wine and the way they are labeled will change too. After a long era when the most important thing about a wine was the place where it was produced, we have entered a time when the key word is the grape variety.*

But, with scores of thousands of acres of the same varieties planted – principally grapes such as Chardonnay and Merlot – producers are going to have to look for new

ways to make their wines stand apart from the herd. We'd predict that this will often take the form of inventive marriages, often of grape varieties that are currently grown in different regions. These could well be sold as "proprietary blends" in much the same way as perfumes are today. Such thoughts will strike many European traditionalists as heresy, but never forget that, as recently as the 1980s, these same Europeans were convinced that the world would never take to the notion of buying varietal Chardonnay or Merlot.

■ **Today, the grape** *variety is more important than the place of origin.*

A simple summary

✔ Asian wines tend to be produced for local consumption.

✔ In Japan and China, much of the wine is actually made from grapes grown elsewhere.

✔ China and India are likely to produce large quantities of higher quality wine when investment and ambition allow.

✔ Japan is too small and land is too dear for wine ever to be a major industry.

✔ Genetic engineering and global warming will affect the style of the wine we drink – and a growing proportion will be produced organically.

✔ Branded blended wines may grow in importance, compared with wines whose identity is based more on a region or a grape variety.

More resources

Good wine books

Aspler, Tony, *Vintage Canada: The Complete Reference to Canadian Wines*. 2nd ed. McGraw-Hill Ryerson, 1999.

Belfrage, Nicolas, *Barolo to Valpolicella: The Wines of Northern Italy*. Faber & Faber, 1999.

Broadbent, Michael, *Michael Broadbent's Wine Vintages*. Mitchell Beazley, 1998.

Brook, Stephen, *The Wines of California*. Faber & Faber, 1999.

Clarke, Oz, *Oz Clarke's Wine Atlas: Wines & Wine Regions of the World*. Little Brown & Company, 1995.

Coates, Clive, *Grands Vins: The Finest Chateaux of Bordeaux and Their Wines*. University of California Press, 1995.

Cooper, Michael, *Wines of New Zealand*. Mitchell Beazley, 1998.

Halliday, James, *Wine Atlas of Australia & New Zealand*. HarperCollins, 1999.

Johnson, Hugh, *The Story of Wine*. Mitchell Beazley, 1997.

Joseph, Robert, *French Wines: The Essential Guide to the Wines and Wine Growing Regions of France*. Dorling Kindersley, 1999.

Norman, Remington, and Hugh Johnson, *Rhone Renaissance: The Finest Rhone and Rhone Style Wines from France and the New World*. Wine Appreciation Guild, 1996.

Remington, Norman, *The Great Domaines of Burgundy: A Guide to the Finest Wine Producers of the Cote d'Or*. Henry Holt & Company, 1996.

Parker, Robert, *Parker's Wine Buyer's Guide*. 5th ed. Fireside, 1999.

Robinson, Jancis, *Jancis Robinson's Guide to Wine Grapes*. Oxford University Press, 1996.

Robinson, Jancis, *The Oxford Companion to Wine*. Oxford University Press, 1999.

Stevenson, Tom, *Champagne and Sparkling Wine Guide 2000*. Dorling Kindersley, 1999.

Stevenson, Tom, *The New Sotheby's Wine Encyclopedia*. Dorling Kindersley, 1997.

Magazines and newsletters

The Wine Spectator
387 Park Ave.
New York, NY 10016
(800) 395-3364
www.winespectator.com

The Wine Enthusiast
399 Executive Blvd.
Elmsford, NY 10523
(800) 829-5901
www.wineenthusiastmag.com

The Wine Advocate
P.O. Box 311
Monkton, MD 21111
(410) 329-6477
www.wineadvocate.com

Food and Wine
1120 Sixth Ave.
New York, NY 10036
(212) 382-5618
www.pathfinder.com/FoodWine

Wine Access
162 John St., 3rd Floor
Toronto, Ontario M5V 2E5
Canada
(416) 596-1555
www.wineaccessmag.com

Decanter
583 Fulham Road
London SW6 5UA, UK
+44 (207) 610-3929
www.decantermagazine.com

Wine Magazine
www.wine-magazine.co.uk
6-14 Underwood Street
London N1 7JQ, UK
+44 (207) 549-2567

Professional Friends of Wine
www.winepros.org

The Wine Magazine
lifestyle.ninemsn.com.au/winemagazine/
(An Australian publication)

Winestate: Australia and New Zealand's Wine Magazine
81 King William Rd.
Unley, South Australia
5061, Australia
+61(8) 8357-9277
www.winestate.com.au

Cuisine
P.O. Box 37-349
Parnell, Aukland
New Zealand
+64 (09) 307-0702
www.cuisine-mag.co.nz

Wine Magazine
P.O. Box 596
Howard Place 7405
South Africa
+27 21 531 7303
www.winetoday.co.za

Wine on the web

Online retailers

www.a-bestfixture.com
Wine accessories, supplies, and gifts.

www.auswine.com.au
Australian wine specialists delivering worldwide.

www.avalonwine.com
Wines from the Pacific Northwest.

www.bbr.co.uk
This traditional U.K. merchant, Berry Bros & Rudd, offers wines worldwide.

www.clarets.com
Purveyor of vintage Bordeaux, Burgundy, Sauterne, port, and the best Californian wines. Ships throughout the world.

www.connseries.com
An online wine club that claims to be your only convenient source to the world's highest rated limited edition wines.

www.esquin.com
The Internet Wine Superstore also has a wine club.

www.evineyard.com
Good selection, shipping to most U.S. states, and online customer interaction.

www.finestwine.com
Fine, rare, and expensive collectable wines with worldwide shipping.

www.libation.com
Premier wine and beer delivered worldwide.

www.madaboutwine.com
Wines delivered worldwide.

www.thewinebroker.com
Worldwide delivery and online wine club.

www.tinamou.com
Premium French wines and vintage port.

www.wine.com
International shipping, gifts and accessories, and lots of wine links.

www.winebroker.com
Another source to fine wine on the Internet.

www.wineplanet.com
Pioneering Australian-based, now global site.

www.winepros.com
International site launched in Australia by wine authorities James Halliday and Len Evans, and including contributions from Robert Joseph.

www.winetech.com
The place to buy CD-ROMS, including wine guru Robert Parker's ratings.

www.winex.com
A good general catalog of wine

Online auctioneers

www.auctionvine.com
A central online auction site.

www.brentwoodwine.com
An online auction site with fixed price sales as well.

www.internetauctionlist.com
This network of auction company websites offers a list of live and electronic wine auctions.

www.magnumwines.com
The online wine auction house for speciality wines.

www.vines.netauctions.net.au/
Five annual auctions are offered for users seeking to purchase rare and vintage wines.

www.wine-auctiongazette.com
Wine Auction Gazette offers a quarterly calendar of wine auctions in the U.S. and abroad.

www.winebid.com
Fine wines and spirit auctions in the U.S., the U.K., and Australia.

www.winesonauction.com
This wine auction broker provides wine estates with an opportunity to market their vintages to a global market.

www.winetoday.com
An updated archive of articles on wine auctions and events.

News and reviews

www.connectingdrinks.com
The site on which you will find WINE Magazine and the International Wine Challenge.

www.decanter.com
The U.K.-based magazine online.

www.food-and-drink.com
Lots of links to food and drink sites.

www.foodandwine.com
Food and Wine magazine online.

www.goodwineguide.com
The online edition of Robert Joseph's annual Good Wine Guide.

www.grapevineweekly.com
An online magazine with lots of links to the world of wine.

www.interaxus.com/pages/wine.html
Wine reviews of Burgundy, Rhône, Bordeaux, Cabernet Sauvignon, and other wines.

www.intlwinechallenge.com/
www.winechallenge.com
The results of the world's biggest wine competitions in London and Asia. (Robert Joseph, one of the authors of this book, is chairman of the competition.)

www.medalwinningwines.com
Prize winners from around the world.

www.smartwine.com
A web site with market news for the investor.

www.wineadvocate.com
The online link to wine guru Robert Parker's Wine Advocate newsletter.

www.winedine.co.uk
A chatty U.K.-based wine enthusiasts' site.

www.wineenthusiastmag.com
Articles and the latest news on wine. Features a wine-buying guide, vintage chart, chat page, calendar and an online catalog.

www.wineontheweb.com
The talking online wine magazine.

www.winepros.com
Australian-based, now international site, with top experts' opinions.

www.wineratings.com
A site of wine reviews and advice to help find the right wine for you.

www.winespectator.com
The Wine Spectator's online magazine with chat room.

www.winetitles.com.au
Everything you want to know about wine in Australia and New Zealand. Lots of winery links.

www.winetoday.com
Wine news and reviews from the *New York Times*.

www.thewinenews.com
The web site of the print publication, offers commentary, feature stories, reviews, and recommendations.

General web sites

www.ambrosiawine.com
This site has a search engine to find almost any wine, a listing of various clubs, and a live online chat feature.

www.anythingbutchardonnay.com
The site for those who like to stray from the vinous highway.

www.drinkwine.com
All about wine.

www.food-and-drink.com
Lots of food and wine links.

www.4wine.com
Link to worldwide wines.

www.frenchwinesfood.com
Includes information on wine growing regions, grapes, the four French wine classifications, serving suggestions, and a pronunciation guide with sound clips.

www.gangofpour.com
Loads of general information about wine. Reviews and tasting notes.

www.hotwine.com
A link to wine sites, scattered with poetic quotes.

www.intowine.com
From how to make wine, to wine in the Bible.

www.late-harvest.com
For wine lovers with a sweet tooth.

www.nothingbutchampagne.com
Bubbles galore.

www.oenotec.com
The site for wine professionals.

www.purplepages.com
A comprehensive directory of wine-related web sites.

www.r-for-riesling.com
Home for lovers of the Riesling grape.

www.stratsplace.com
Wine labels, tasting notes, wine stores, and interactive bulletin boards.

www.syrah.com
News and views about the Syrah/Shiraz grape.

www.vine2wine.com
A comprehensive web site with links to over 2,000 wine sites and an inexhaustible list of wineries.

www.wine-asia
News and views of wine in the newest wine-drinking countries of Asia.

www.wineart.com
Winemaking supplies and equipment, chat lines, links, online catalog, and wine news.

www.wine-and-health.com,
The good – and bad – that wine can do for you.

www.winebrats.org
The online uncensored voice of the Wine Brats.

www.winecellar.com
A complete source of wine links.

www.wineculture.com
A hip guide to wine on the web.

www.wineinfonet.com
A multilingual portal to the wine industry.

www.wineinstitute.com
A website of California wineries with lots of links into wine cyberspace.

www.wine-lovers-page.com
Robin Garr's wine lover's page, complete with wine forums and chats.

www.wineplace.com
All about making wine, with do-it-yourself wine kits.

www.wine-searcher.com
Search the Internet for all aspects of wine.

www.winesense.com
WineSense promotes the appreciation of wine and the success and professional development of women in wine.

www.wino.net
Learn about laws governing wine, investing in wine, and the health benefits.

www.worldsgreatestwines.com
Nothing but the best.

www.worldwine.com
A website dedicated to wine links.

www.zinfans.com
Zinfandels galore.

Wineries

www.cawinemall.com
Comprehensive directory of California wineries by region or grape variety.

www.edgamesandart.com/wine.html
A database of wine and wineries.

www.haut-brion.com
A brilliant site from this top Bordeaux chateau.

www.hiddenwineries.com
A site exploring the lesser known U.S. wineries.

www.kj.com
Kendall-Jackson's chat area and an online store.

www.penfolds.com
A great site from this Australian wine company.

www.robertmondavi.com
A great U.S. wine site.

www.vinosearch.com
Database of wines and wineries from all over the world.

www.winecollection.com
An online collection of France's wineries.

www.wines.com
An award-winning guide to wine and wineries.

www.winetoday.com
A comprehensive list of wineries from around the world.

www.wineweb.com
Wines and wineries from all around the world.

www.worldwine.com
Lots of worldwide
wine links.

Online wine education

www.lecoleduvin.com
A complete wine course
online.

www.wineeducation.com
Learn about wine from
Certified Wine Educator
Stephen Reiss, Ph.D.

www.wine.gurus.com
The Society of Wine
Educators official home page.

www.wine-school.com
An online diploma wine
course produced by the
authors of this book.

www.wineprofessor.com
Food and wine pairing,
decoding wine labels, and
regional wine characteristics
are included in this site.

Regional sites

www.argentinewines.com
The exciting New World
wines of Argentina.

www.bordeaux.com
A virtual tour of Bordeaux.

www.champagnes.com
An introduction to the
world of Champagne.

www.coonawarra.com
A site dedicated to Australia's
best-known wine region.

www.germanwines.de.com
A multilingual official site
of Germany's wines.

www.indagegroup.com
This promotes India's wine.

www.ivp.pt.com
Port Wine Institute's web site.

www.liwines.com
The official virtual guide
through Long Island
wine country.

www.madeirawine.com
All about Madeira's wines
and history.

www.mrwines.com
The Margaret River area's
web site.

www.napawine.com
Visit Napa wineries and
wine sites.

www.nywine.com
New York uncorked.

www.nzwine.com
The official web site of
New Zealand's wine and
grape industry.

www.sonomawine.com
Sonoma County Wineries
Association.

www.washingtonwine.org
All about wine in
Washington.

www.wine.co.za.com
A guide to South African
wines.

www.winecountry.com
The comprehensive
gateway to wines of
California.

www.winesofchile.com
Ever-expanding guide to
Chilean wines.

www.wine.it
The first Italian
commercial web site for
wine enthusiasts.

www.wines-france.com
A user-friendly guide to
French wines.

www.winetitles.com.au
A complete guide to wine
down under.

www.winetour.com
A guide to Ontario's
wineries.

Online wine chat rooms and clubs

www.auswine.com.au/cgi-bin/auswine/browse
The Australian Wine
Centre's virtual shop – a
search feature, a forum, and
a chat room.

www.bath.ac.uk/~su3ws/
A site set up by wine
enthusiasts at Bath
University in the U.K.

www.cawineclub.com
Join the California wine
club and receive a
newsletter and two bottles
of wine each month.

www.cellardoor.com.au
Australian wine suppliers
answer wine questions
and run a wine lovers'
chat room.

www.chowbaby.com
A food, drink, and cigar
chat room.

www.drinkwine.com
Bulletin board and listing
of associations.

www.evineyard.com
Live talk and wine club.

www.4wine.com
Lists a multitude of chat
rooms.

www.iglou.com/wine/chat
Join a crowd of other wine
lovers and compare notes.

www.nobilevineyards.com
An international wine club
with a chat room.

www.secretcellars.com
A virtual wine club that
brings California's small
family vineyards right to
your door.

www.vineswinger.com
Chat rooms and forums.

www.westcoastwine.net
Forums and wine chat from
the West Coast's wineries.

www.winebrats.org
Access to wine chat rooms.

www.wineculture.com
A resource of chat rooms.

www.wineinstitute.org
Discussion groups or
chat rooms.

www.wine-lovers-page.com/wine.shtml
A wine chat room.

wine.miningco.com/food/wine/
This is a meeting place for
discussing wine and wineries,
from *About.Com Guide*.

www.winerave.com
Website with its own wine
chat room.

www.wines.com
Bulletin board where
questions can be posed to
wine experts.

www.winesite.com
An extensive list of links to
international wine clubs.

Other sites

www.artofwine.co.uk
Sommelier wine cabinets
and loads of storing units.

chat.yahoo.com/c/events/info/092
199kiesel.html
Wine and food pairings
from A–Z.

www.kov.org
The quirky official site of
the Brotherhood of the
Knights of the Vine.

www.ziplink.net/users/mak/
winelabels/
An online collection of
artistic wine labels.

Food and wine

ALMOND Liqueur Muscats or Beaumes de Venise
Trout with Almonds Bianco di Custoza, Pinot Blanc
ANCHOVIES
Salted Anchovies Rioja red or white, Manzanilla or Fino sherry
Fresh Anchovy (Boquerones) Albariño, Vinho Verde, Aligoté
Salade Niçoise Muscadet, Vinho Verde, or Beaujolais
Tapenade Dry sherry or Madeira
ANISEED Dry white
APPLE
Apple Pie or Strudel Austrian off-dry white
Applesauce Riesling (dry or off-dry)
Blackberry and Apple Pie Late harvest Riesling, Vouvray demi-sec
Roast Pork with Apple Sauce Off-dry Vouvray or Riesling
Waldorf Salad Dry Madeira
APRICOT Late harvest Sémillon or Riesling, Jurançon Moelleux
ARTICHOKE White Rhône
Artichoke Frittata Dry Loire whites, Pinot Gris
Artichoke Soup Dry Loire whites, Pinot Gris
ARROZ CON POLLO Côtes du Rhône, young Zinfandel, Navarra or Rioja "Joven"
ARUGULA Pinot Grigio, young Viognier
ASPARAGUS
Asparagus Crêpes au Gratin Muscadet, Vinho Verde, Cider
Asparagus Soup Fresh dry whites, Sauvignon Blanc
AVOCADO
Avocado Mayonnaise Unoaked Chardonnay, Chablis
Avocado Stuffed with Crab Champagne, Riesling Kabinett, Sauvignon Blanc, Pinot Gris, Australian Chardonnay
Guacamole Fumé Blanc or unoaked Sauvignon Blanc

BACON Rich Pinot Gris or Alsace Riesling
Bacon with Marinated Scallops Fino sherry or mature Riesling, Shiraz-based Australians, Zinfandel from the States, or a heavy Cape red
Warm Bacon Salad New World Sauvignon Blanc, California Fumé Blanc or a good Pouilly Fumé
BANANA
Flambéed Banana with Rum Jurançon, Tokaji, Pedro Ximénez sherry, rum
BARBECUE SAUCE Inexpensive off-dry white or a simple, fruity Cabernet
Spare Ribs with Barbecue Sauce Fruity Australian Shiraz, Grenache or Zinfandel, spicy

Côtes du Rhône from a ripe vintage, or an off-dry white
BASIL Slightly sweet Chardonnay (ie California, commercial Australian)
Pasta in Pesto Sauce New Zealand Sauvignon Blanc, Valpolicella
BEANS
Boston Baked Beans Light Zinfandel, Beaujolais, dry rosé, or beer
Bean Salad Spanish reds such as Rioja Reserva and Rueda, or New Zealand Sauvignon Blanc
Cassoulet Serious white Rhône, Marsanne or Roussanne, or reds including Grenache and Syrah from the Rhône, crunchy Italian reds, or Zinfandel
Mexican Beans Côtes du Rhône, Beaujolais, dry Grenache rosé
White Bean Stew (Estouffat) Young Corbières, light Merlot
BEEF
Beef with Green Peppers in Black Bean Sauce Off-dry German Riesling or characterful dry white, like white Rhône or Marsanne
Beef with Scallions and Ginger Off-dry German Riesling or one of the more serious Beaujolais Crus
Beef Stew Pomerol or St. Emilion, good Northern Rhône like Crozes-Hermitage, Shiraz, or Pinot Noir from the New World
Beef Stroganoff Tough, beefy reds like Amarone, Brunello di Montalcino, Barolo, Côte Rôtie, or really ripe Zinfandel
Beef Wellington Top Burgundy, Châteauneuf-du-Pape
Boeuf Bourguignon Australian Bordeaux-style, Barolo, or other robust reds with sweet fruit
Boiled Beef and Carrots Bordeaux Rouge, Valpolicella Classico, Australian Shiraz
Bresaola (Air-Dried Beef) Beaujolais, Barbera, and tasty reds from the Languedoc
Carpaccio of Beef Chardonnay, Champagne, Cabernet Franc, and other Loire reds, Pomerol
Chilli Con Carne Robust fruity reds, Beaujolais Crus, Barbera or Valpolicella, spicy reds like Zinfandel or Pinotage
Corned Beef Loire reds from Gamay or Cabernet Franc
Corned Beef Hash Characterful spicy reds from the Rhône or Southern France
Creole-Style Beef Cheap Southern Rhône reds or Côtes du Rhône, Zinfandel
Hamburger Zinfandel or country reds, from Italy or France e.g. Corbières

Hungarian Goulash East European reds, Bulgarian Cabernet, or Mavrud and Hungarian Kadarka, or Australian Shiraz
Meatballs Spicy rich reds from the Rhône, Zinfandel, Pinotage, and Portuguese reds
Panang Neuk (Beef in Peanut Curry) New World Chardonnay, New Zealand Sauvignon Blanc, or a spicy, aromatic white Rhône
Pastrami Zinfandel, good Bardolino, light Côtes du Rhône
Rare Chargrilled Beef Something sweetly ripe and flavorsome, but not too tannic; try Chilean Merlot
Roast Beef Côte Rôtie, good Burgundy
Steak Pinot Noir and Merlot from the New World, Australian Shiraz, Châteauneuf-du-Pape, good, ripe Burgundy
Steak with Dijon Mustard Bordeaux, Cabernet Sauvignon from the New World, or Australian Shiraz
Steak and Kidney Pie Bordeaux, Australian Cabernet Sauvignon, Southern Rhône reds, or Rioja
Steak au Poivre Cabernet Sauvignon, Chianti, Rhône reds, Shiraz or Rioja
Steak Tartare Bourgogne Blanc, fruity reds, light on tannin; Beaujolais, Bardolino, etc., or, traditionally, vodka
Thai Beef Salad New Zealand or South African Sauvignon Blanc, Gewürztraminer, Pinot Blanc
BEER (in a sauce)
Carbonnade à la Flamande Cheap Southern Rhône or Valpolicella
BEETS
Borscht Rich, dry Alsace Pinot Gris, Pinot Blanc, or Italian Pinot Grigio
BLACK BEAN SAUCE
Beef with Green Peppers in Black Bean Sauce German Riesling or characterful, dry white like white Rhône or Marsanne
BLACKBERRY
Blackberry and Apple Pie Late harvest Riesling, Vouvray demi-sec
BLACK CHERRY
Black Forest Cake Fortified Muscat, Schnapps, or Kirsch
BLACKCURRANT
Blackcurrant Cheesecake Sweet, grapey dessert wines
Blackcurrant Mousse Sweet sparkling wines
BLINIS Vodka or good Champagne
BLOOD PUDDING Chablis, New Zealand Chardonnay, Zinfandel, or Barolo
BLUEBERRIES
Blueberry Pie Tokaji (6 Puttonyos), late harvest Semillon or Sauvignon

BRANDY
Christmas Fruitcake Australian Liqueur Muscat, tawny port, rich (sweet) Champagne, Tokaji
Crêpe Suzette Asti Spumante, Orange Muscat, Champagne cocktails
BRIE Sancerre or New Zealand Sauvignon
BROCCOLI
Broccoli and Cheese Soup Slightly sweet sherry – Amontillado or Oloroso
BUTTER
Béarnaise Sauce Good dry Riesling
Beurre Blanc Champagne Blanc de Blancs, dry Vinho Verde
BUTTERNUT SQUASH
Butternut Soup Aromatic Alsace Gewurztraminer

CABBAGE
Stuffed Cabbage East European Cabernet
CAJUN SPICES Beaujolais Crus
Gumbo Zinfandel or maybe beer
CAMEMBERT Dry Sauvignon Blanc or unoaked Chablis
CAPERS Sauvignon Blanc
Skate with Black Butter Crisply acidic whites like Muscadet or Chablis
Tartare Sauce Crisply fresh whites like Sauvignon
CARAMEL
Caramelized Oranges, Asti Spumante, Sauternes
Crème Caramel Aromatic, sweet white – Muscat or Gewürztraminer , Vendange Tardive
CARP Franken Sylvaner, dry Jurançon, Hungarian Furmint
CARROT
Carrot and Orange Soup Madeira or perhaps an Amontillado sherry
Carrot and Coriander Soup Aromatic, dry Muscat, Argentinian Torrontes
CASHEW NUTS Pinot Blanc
Chicken with Cashew Nuts Rich aromatic white, Pinot Gris, or Muscat
CAULIFLOWER
Cauliflower Cheese Fresh crisp Côtes de Gascogne white, Pinot Grigio, softly plummy Chilean Merlot or young, unoaked Rioja
CAVIAR Champagne or chilled vodka
CELERY
Celery Soup Off-dry Riesling
CHEDDAR (MATURE) Good Bordeaux, South African Cabernet, port
CHEESE (see also individual entries)
Cheeseburger Sweetly fruity oaky reds – Australian Shiraz, Rioja

Cheese Fondue Swiss white or Vin de Savoie

Cheese Platter Match wines to cheeses, taking care not to put too tannic a red with too creamy a cheese, and possibly even to offer white wines – which go well with all but the hardest cheese. Strong creamy cheeses demand fine Burgundy, blue cheese is made for late harvest wines, goat cheese is ideal with Sancerre, Pouilly Fumé or other dry, unoaked Sauvignons. Munster is best paired with Alsace Gewürztraminer

Cheese Sauce (Mornay) Oaky Chardonnay

Cream Cheese, Crème Fraîche, Mozzarella, Mascarpone Fresh light, dry whites – Frascati, Pinot Grigio

Raclette Swiss white or Vin de Savoie

CHEESECAKE Australian botrytized Semillon

CHERRY Valpolicella, Recioto della Valpolicella, Dolcetto

Roast Duck with Cherry Sauce Barbera, Dolcetto, or Barolo

CHESTNUT

Roast Turkey with Chestnut Stuffing Côtes du Rhône, Merlot, or soft and mature Burgundy

CHICKEN

Chicken with Bamboo Shoots and Water Chestnuts Dry German, New World Riesling

Barbecued Chicken Rich and tasty white, Chardonnay

Chicken Casserole Mid-weight Rhône such as Crozes-Hermitage or Lirac

Chicken Chasseur Off-dry Riesling

Chicken Kiev Chablis, Aligoté, or Italian dry white

Chicken Pie White Bordeaux, simple Chardonnay, or light Italian white

Chicken Soup Soave, Orvieto, or Pinot Blanc

Chicken Vol-au-Vents White Bordeaux

Coq au Vin Shiraz-based New World reds, red Burgundy

Cream of Chicken Soup Big dry unoaked white (Chablis, Pinot Blanc)

Curry Chicken Gewürztraminer, dry white Loire, fresh Chinon

Devilled Chicken Australian Shiraz

Fricassée Unoaked Chardonnay

Lemon Chicken Muscadet, Chablis, or basic Bourgogne Blanc

Poached Chicken Beaujolais, Valpolicella

Roast/Grilled Chicken Reds or whites, though nothing too heavy – Burgundy is good, as is Barbera, though Soave will do just as well

Roast/Grilled Chicken with Bread Sauce Côtes du Rhône or herby Provençal reds

Roast/Grilled Chicken with Sage and Onion Stuffing Italian reds,

especially Chianti, soft, plummy Merlots, and sweetly fruity Rioja

Roast/Grilled Chicken with Tarragon Dry Chenin (Vouvray or perhaps a good South African)

Saltimbocca (Cutlet with Mozzarella and Ham) Flavorsome, dry Italian whites, Lugana, Bianco di Custoza, Orvieto

Smoked Chicken Oaky Chardonnay, Australian Marsanne, or Fumé Blanc

Southern Fried Chicken White Bordeaux, Muscadet, Barbera, light Zinfandel

Tandoori Chicken White Bordeaux, New Zealand Sauvignon Blanc

CHICKEN LIVER (Sauté) Softly fruity, fairly light reds including Beaujolais, Italian Cabernet, or Merlot, or perhaps an Oregon Pinot Noir

Chicken Liver Paté Most of the above reds plus Vouvray Moelleux, Monbazillac, or Amontillado sherry

CHILI PEPPER Cheap wine or cold beer

Chili Con Carne Robust fruity reds, Beaujolais Crus, Barbera or Valpolicella, spicy reds like Zinfandel or Pinotage

Hot and Sour Soup Crisply aromatic English white, Baden Dry

Szechuan-Style Dry, aromatic whites, Alsace Pinot Gris, Riesling, Grenache rosé, beer

Thai Beef Salad New Zealand or South African Sauvignon Blanc, Gewürztraminer, Pinot Blanc

CHINESE FOOD (in general) Aromatic white, such as Gewürztraminer, Pinot Gris, English

CHIVES Sauvignon Blanc

CHOCOLATE Orange Muscat, Moscatel de Valencia

Black Forest (Chocolate and Cherry) Cake Fortified Muscat or Kirsch

Chocolate Cake Beaumes de Venise, Bual or Malmsey Madeira, Orange Muscat, sweet German, or fine Champagne

Chocolate Profiteroles with Cream Muscat de Rivesaltes

Chocolate Roulade Canadian ice wine or German or Austrian Eiswein

Dark Chocolate Mousse Sweet Black Muscat or other Muscat-based wines

Milk Chocolate Mousse Moscato d'Asti

CHORIZO (Pork Sausage) Red or white Rioja, Navarra, Manzanilla sherry, Beaujolais, or Zinfandel

CINNAMON Riesling Spätlese, Muscat

CLAMS Chablis or Sauvignon Blanc

Clam Chowder Dry white such as Côtes de Gascogne, Amontillado sherry, or Madeira

Spaghetti with Clam Sauce Pinot Bianco or Lugana

COCKLES Muscadet, Gros Plant, Aligoté, dry Vinho Verde

COCONUT MILK California Chardonnay

Green Curry Big-flavored New World whites or Pinot Blanc from Alsace

COD Unoaked Chardonnay, good, white Burgundy, dry Loire Chenin

Cod and French Fries Any light, crisp, dry white, such as a Sauvignon from Bordeaux or Touraine. Alternatively, try dry rosé or Champagne. Remember, though, that English-style heavy-handedness with the vinegar will do no favors for the wine; for vinegary fries, stick to beer.

Lisbon-Style Cod Vinho Verde Muscadet, light, dry Riesling

Salt Cod (Bacalhão de Gomes) Classically Portuguese red or white – Vinho Verde or Bairrada reds

Smoked Cod Vinho Verde

Cod Roe (smoked) Well-oaked New World Chardonnay

COFFEE

Coffeecake Asti Spumante

Coffee Mousse Asti Spumante, Liqueur Muscat

Tiramisu Sweet fortified Muscat, Vin Santo, Torcolato

CORIANDER

Carrot and Coriander Soup Aromatic, dry Muscat

Coriander Leaf Dry or off-dry English white

Coriander Seed Dry, herby Northern Italian whites

CORN Rich and ripe whites – California Chardonnay

Corn on the Cob Light, fruity whites – German Riesling

Corn Soup with Chicken Chilean Sauvignon, Southern French whites, Soave, Chilean Merlot

Corn Soup with Crab Sancerre, other Sauvignon Blanc

COUSCOUS Spicy Shiraz, North African reds, or earthy Southern French Minervois

CRAB Chablis, Sauvignon Blanc, or New World Chardonnay

Crab Cakes (Maryland-style) Rias Baixas Albariño

Crab Cioppino Sauvignon Blanc, Pinot Grigio

Crab Mousse Crisp dry whites – Baden Dry or Soave

Deviled Crab (spicy) New World Sauvignon, Albariño

CRANBERRY

Roast Turkey with Cranberry and Orange Stuffing Richly fruity reds like Shiraz from Australia, Zinfandel, or modern Rioja

CRAYFISH

Freshwater Crayfish South African Sauvignon, Meursault

Salad of Crayfish Tails with Dill Rich South African Chenin blends or crisp Sauvignon, white Rhône

CREAM When dominant, not good with wine, particularly tannic reds

CURRY

Beef in Peanut Curry New World Chardonnay, spicy, aromatic white Rhône

Coronation Chicken Gewürztraminer, dry, aromatic English wine, or a fresh Chinon

Curried Turkey New World Chardonnay

Curried Beef Beefy, spicy reds; Barolo, Châteauneuf-du-Pape and Shiraz/Cabernet or off-dry aromatic whites – Gewürztraminer, Pinot Gris or try some Indian sparkling wine or cold Indian beer

Tandoori Chicken White Bordeaux, New Zealand Sauvignon Blanc

Thai Green Chicken Curry Big New World whites or dry, tasty Pinot Blanc from Alsace

DILL Sauvignon Blanc

Gravlax Ice-cold vodka, Pinot Gris, or Akvavit

DRIED FRUIT Sweet sherry, tawny port

Bread and Butter Pudding Barsac or Sauternes, Monbazillac, Jurançon Muscat de Beaumes de Venise, or Australian Orange Muscat

Mincemeat Pie Rich, late harvest wine or botrytis-affected Sémillon

DUCK Pinot Noir from Burgundy, California or Oregon, or perhaps an off-dry German Riesling

Cassoulet Serious white Rhônes, Marsanne or Roussanne, or try reds including Grenache and Syrah from the Rhône, berryish Italian reds, or Zinfandel

Confit de Canard Alsace Pinot Gris or a crisp red like Barbera

Duck Paté Chianti or other juicy herby red, Amontillado sherry

Duck Paté with Orange Riesling or Rioja

Peking Duck Rice wine, Alsace Riesling, Pinot Gris

Roast Duck Big, fruity reds like Australian Cabernet, a ripe Nebbiolo, or Zinfandel

Roast Duck with Cherry Sauce Barbera, Dolcetto, or Barolo

Roast Duck with Orange Sauce Loire red or, surprisingly, a sweet white like Vouvray demi-sec

Smoked Duck California Chardonnay or Fumé Blanc

DUCK LIVER

Foie Gras de Canard Champagne, late harvest Gewürztraminer or Riesling, Sauternes

EEL

Jellied Eels A pint of stout

Smoked Eel Pale, dry sherry, or simple, fresh white Burgundy

EGG

Baked Eggs Bordeaux Blanc, Côtes de Gascogne or other simple white, young, fruity red

Crème Brulée Jurançon Moelleux, Tokaji

Eggs Benedict Unoaked Chardonnay, Blanc de Blancs fizz, Bucks Fizz, or Bloody Mary

Eggs Florentine Unoaked Chardonnay, Pinot Blanc, Aligoté, Sémillon

Omelettes Cheap Beaujolais, Bardolino

Tortilla Young, juicy Spanish reds and fresher whites from La Mancha or Rueda

FENNEL Sauvignon Blanc

FIG Liqueur Muscat

FRANKFURTER Côtes du Rhône or lager

FISH (see also individual entries)
Bouillabaisse Red or white Côtes du Rhône, dry rosé from Provence, California Fumé Blanc, Marsanne, or Verdicchio

Fish and Chips Most fairly simple, crisply acidic dry whites (white Bordeaux, Sauvignon Blanc) or maybe a rosé (see Cod)

Fish Cakes White Bordeaux, Chilean Chardonnay

Fish Soup Manzanilla, Chablis, Muscadet

Mediterranean Fish Soup Provençal reds and rosés, Tavel, Côtes du Rhône, Vin de Pays d'Oc

Seafood Salad Soave, Pinot Grigio, Muscadet, or a lightly oaked Chardonnay

Sushi Saké

FOIE GRAS (see Duck and Goose Liver)

FRUIT (see also individual entries)
Berry Pudding Late harvest Riesling, German or Alsace

Fresh Fruit Salad Moscato d'Asti, Riesling Beerenauslese, or Vouvray Moelleux

Fruit Flan Vouvray Moelleux, Alsace Riesling Vendange Tardive

GAME (see also individual entries)
Aged Game Old Barolo or Barbaresco, mature Hermitage, Côte Rôtie or Châteauneuf-du-Pape, fine Burgundy

Cold Game Fruity Northern Italian reds – Barbera or Dolcetto – good Beaujolais or light Burgundy

Roast Game Big reds, such as Brunello di Montalcino, old Barolo, good Burgundy

Game Pie Beefy reds, Southern French, Rhône, Australian Shiraz, or South African Pinotage

GARLIC
Aioli A wide range of wines go well including white Rioja, Provence rosé, California Pinot Noir

Garlic Sausage Red Rioja, Bandol, Côtes du Rhône

Gazpacho Fino sherry, white Rioja

Raw Garlic Rosé

Roast/Grilled Chicken with Garlic Oaky Chardonnay or red Rioja

Roast Lamb with Garlic and Rosemary Earthy soft reds like California Petite Sirah, Rioja, or Zinfandel

SNAILS WITH GARLIC BUTTER Aligoté and light white Burgundy or perhaps a red Gamay de Touraine

GINGER Gewürztraminer or Riesling

Beef with Onions and Ginger Off-dry German Riesling, one of the more serious Beaujolais Crus

Chicken with Ginger White Rhône, Gewürztraminer

Ginger Ice Cream Asti Spumante or late harvest Sémillon

GOAT CHEESE Sancerre, New World Sauvignon, Pinot Blanc

Grilled Goat Cheese Loire reds

GOOSE A good Rhône red like Hermitage, Côte Rôtie, or a crisp Barbera, Pinot Noir from Burgundy, California, or Oregon, or perhaps an off-dry German Riesling

Confit d'Oie Best Sauternes, Monbazillac

GOOSE LIVER
Foie Gras Best Sauternes, Monbazillac

GOOSEBERRY
Gooseberry Fool Quarts de Chaume

Gooseberry Pie Sweet Madeira, Austrian Trockenbeerenauslese

GRAPEFRUIT Sweet Madeira or sherry

GROUSE
Roast Grouse Hermitage, Côte Rôtie, robust Burgundy, or good mature red Bordeaux

GUINEA FOWL Old Burgundy, Cornas, Gamay de Touraine, St Emilion

HADDOCK White Bordeaux, Chardonnay, Pinot Blanc

Mousse of Smoked Haddock Top white Burgundy

Smoked Haddock Fino sherry or oaky Chardonnay

HAKE Soave, Sauvignon Blanc

HALIBUT White Bordeaux, Muscadet

Smoked Halibut Oaky Spanish white/Australian Chardonnay, white Bordeaux

HAM
Boiled/Roasted/Grilled/Fried Ham Beaujolais-Villages, Gamay de Touraine, slightly sweet German white, lightish red, lightish Cabernet (e.g. Chilean), Alsace Pinot Gris, or Muscat

Braised Ham with Lentils Light, fruity Beaujolais, other Gamay, Côtes du Rhône

Honey-Roast Ham Riesling

Oak-Smoked Ham Oaky Spanish reds

Parma Ham Try a dry Lambrusco, Tempranillo Joven, or Gamay de Touraine

Pea and Ham Soup Beaujolais

HARE
Hare Casserole Good Beaujolais Crus or, for a stronger flavor, try an Australian red

Jugged Hare Argentinian reds, tough Italians like Amarone, Barolo and Barbaresco, inky reds from Bandol or the Rhône

HAZELNUT Vin Santo, Liqueur Muscat

Warm Bacon, Hazelnut, and Sorrel Salad New World Sauvignon Blanc, California Fumé Blanc, or a good Pouilly Fumé

HERBS (see individual entries)

HERRING
Fresh Herring Sauvignon Blanc, Muscadet, Frascati, or cider

Pickled Herring Savoie, Vinho Verde, Akvavit, cold lager

Salt Herring White Portuguese

Sprats Muscadet, Vinho Verde

HONEY Tokaji

Baklava Moscatel de Setúbal

HORSERADISH
Roast Beef with Horseradish California Pinot Noir or mature Burgundy

HOUMOUS French dry whites, Retsina, Vinho Verde

ICE CREAM Try Marsala or Pedro Ximénez sherry

INDIAN FOOD (in general) Gewürztraminer (spicy dishes); New World Chardonnay (creamy/yogurt dishes); New Zealand Sauvignon Blanc (Tandoori)

JAPANESE BARBECUE SAUCE
Teriyaki Spicy reds like Zinfandel or Portuguese reds

KIDNEY
Lambs' Kidneys Rich, spicy reds; Barolo, Cabernet Sauvignon, Rioja

Steak and Kidney Pie/Pudding Bordeaux, Australian Cabernet Sauvignon, Southern Rhône reds or Rioja

KIPPERED HERRINGS New World Chardonnay or a good Fino sherry. Or, if you are having it for breakfast, Champagne, a cup of tea, or Dutch gin

LAMB
Cassoulet Serious white Rhône, Marsanne or Roussanne, or reds including Grenache and Syrah from the Rhône, berryish Italian reds or, Zinfandel

Casserole Rich and warm Cabernet-based reds from France or California Zinfandel

Cutlets or Chops Cru Bourgeois Bordeaux, Chilean Cabernet

Haggis Beaujolais, Côtes du Rhône, Côtes du Roussillon, Spanish reds, malt whisky

Irish Stew A good simple South American or Eastern European Cabernet works best

Kebabs Modern (fruity) Greek reds or sweetly ripe Australian Cabernet/Shiraz

Kleftiko (Lamb Shanks Baked with Thyme) Greek red from Nemea, Beaujolais, light Cabernet Sauvignon

Lancashire Hotpot Robust country red – Cahors, Fitou

Moussaka Brambly Northern Italian reds (Barbera, Dolcetto, etc), Beaujolais, Pinotage, Zinfandel, or try some good Greek wine from a modern producer

Roast Lamb Bordeaux, New Zealand Cabernet Sauvignon, Cahors, Rioja reserva, reds from Chile

Roast Lamb with Garlic and Rosemary Earthy soft reds like California Petite Sirah, Rioja, or Zinfandel

Roast Lamb with Thyme Try a New Zealand Cabernet Sauvignon or Bourgeuil

Shepherd's Pie Barbera Cabernet Sauvignon, Minervois, Zinfandel, Beaujolais, Southern French red

LANGOUSTINE Muscadet, Soave, South African Sauvignon

LEEK
Cock-a-Leekie Dry New World white, simple red Rhône

Leek and Potato Soup Dry whites, Côtes de Gascogne

Leek in Cheese Sauce Dry white Bordeaux, Sancerre, or Australian Semillon

Vichyssoise Dry whites, Chablis, Bordeaux Blanc

LEMON
Lemon Cheesecake Moscato d'Asti

Lemon Meringue Pie Malmsey Madeira

Lemon Sorbet Late harvest Sémillon or sweet Tokaji

Lemon Tart Sweet Austrian and German wines

Lemon Zest Sweet fortified Muscats

Lemon Grass New Zealand Sauvignon, Sancerre, Viognier

Lemon Sole Chardonnay

LENTILS Earthy country wines, Côtes du Rhône

Chicken Dhansak Sémillon or New Zealand Sauvignon

Dhal Soup Try Soave or Pinot Bianco

LIME Australian Verdelho, Grüner Veltliner, Furmint

Kaffir Lime Leaves (in Thai Green Curry, etc) Big-flavored New World whites or Pinot Blanc from Alsace

Thai Beef Salad New Zealand or South African Sauvignon Blanc, Gewürztraminer, Pinot Blanc

LIVER
Calves' Liver Good Italian Cabernet, Merlot, or mature Chianti

Fegato alla Veneziana Nebbiolo, Zinfandel, or Petite Sirah

Lambs' Liver Chianti, Australian Shiraz, or Merlot

Liver and Bacon Côtes du Rhône, Zinfandel, Pinotage

LOBSTER Good white Burgundy
Lobster Bisque Grenache rosé, fresh German white, Chassagne-Montrachet, dry Amontillado sherry
Lobster in a Rich Sauce Champagne, Chablis, fine white Burgundy, good white Bordeaux
Lobster Salad Champagne, Chablis, German or Alsace Riesling
Lobster Thermidor Rich beefy Côtes du Rhône, oaky Chardonnay, or a good deep-colored rosé from Southern France

MACKEREL Best with Vinho Verde, Albariño, Sancerre, and New Zealand Sauvignon
Smoked Mackerel Bourgogne Aligoté, Alsace Pinot Gris
Smoked Mackerel Paté Sparkling Vouvray, Muscadet
MALLARD Côte Rôtie, Ribera del Duero, or Zinfandel
MANGO Best eaten in the bath with a friend and a bottle of Champagne. Otherwise, go for Asti Spumante or Moscato
MARJORAM Provençal reds
MARSALA
Chops in Marsala Sauce Australian Marsanne or Verdelho
MASCARPONE
Tiramisu Sweet fortified Muscat, Vin Santo, Torcolato
MEAT (see also individual entries)
Cold Meats Juicy, fruity reds, low in tannin ie Beaujolais, Côtes du Rhône, etc
Consommé Medium/Amontillado sherry
Meat Paté Beaujolais, Fumé Blanc, lesser white Burgundy
Mixed Grill Versatile uncomplicated red – Australian Shiraz, Rioja, Bulgarian Cabernet
MELON Despite its apparently innocent, juicy sweetness, melon can be very unfriendly to most wines. Try tawny port, sweet Madeira or sherry, Quarts de Chaume, late harvest Riesling
MINCEMEAT
Mincemeat Pie Complemented by rich, sweet, late-harvest wine or botrytis-affected Sémillon
MINT Beaujolais, young Pinot Noir, or try a New Zealand or Australian Riesling
MONKFISH A light, fruity red such as Bardolino, Valpolicella, La Mancha Joven, or most Chardonnays
MUSHROOM Merlot-based reds, good Northern Rhône, top Piedmontese reds
Mushroom Soup Bordeaux Blanc, Côtes de Gascogne
Mushrooms à la Greque Sauvignon Blanc or fresh, modern Greek white
Risotto with Fungi Porcini Top-notch Piedmontese reds – mature Barbera, Barbaresco, or earthy Southern French reds

Stuffed Mushrooms Chenin Blanc, Sylvaner
Wild Mushrooms Nebbiolo, red Bordeaux
MUSSELS Sauvignon Blanc, light Chardonnay, Muscadet Sur Lie
Moules Marinières Bordeaux Blanc or Muscadet Sur Lie
New Zealand Green-Lipped Mussels New Zealand Sauvignon Blanc
MUSTARD Surprisingly, can help red Bordeaux and other tannic reds to go with beef which might otherwise accentuate their tough, tannic character
Dijon Mustard Beaujolais
English Wholegrain Mustard Beaujolais, Valpolicella
French Mustard White Bordeaux
Steak with Dijon Mustard Cabernet Sauvignon from the New World or Australian Shiraz

NECTARINE Sweet German Riesling
NUTMEG Rioja, Australian Shiraz or, for sweet dishes, Australian late harvest Semillon
NUTS Amontillado sherry, Vin Santo, and Tokaji

OCTOPUS Rueda white or a fresh, modern Greek white
OLIVES Dry sherry, Muscadet, Retsina
Salade Niçoise Muscadet, Vinho Verde or Beaujolais
Tapenade Dry sherry or Madeira
ONION
Caramelized Onions Shiraz-based Australians, Zinfandel from the States, or a good Pinotage
French Onion Soup Sancerre or dry, unoaked Sauvignon Blanc, Aligoté, white Bordeaux
Onion/Leek Tart Alsace Gewürztraminer, New World Riesling or a good unoaked Chablis
ORANGE
Caramelized Oranges Asti Spumante, Sauternes or Muscat de Beaumes de Venise
Crêpe Suzette Sweet Champagne, Moscato d'Asti
Orange Sorbet Moscato or sweet Tokaji
Orange Zest Dry Muscat, Amontillado sherry
OREGANO Provençal reds, red Lambrusco, more serious Chianti or lightish Zinfandel
OXTAIL Australian Cabernet, good Bordeaux
OYSTER SAUCE
Beef and Snow Peas in Oyster Sauce Crisp, dry whites like Muscadet or a Northern Italian Lugana or Pinot Bianco, white Rhône, Gewürztraminer
OYSTERS Champagne, Chablis, or other crisp, dry white

PAPRIKA
GOULASH Eastern European red like Bulgarian Cabernet or Mavrud, Hungarian Kadarka, or Australian Shiraz

PARMESAN Salice Salentino, Valpolicella
Baked Chicken Parmesan with Basil Chenin Blanc, Riesling
PARSLEY Dry, Italian whites – Bianco di Custoza, Nebbiolo, or Barbera
Parsley Sauce Pinot Grigio, Hungarian Furmint, lightly oaked Chardonnay
PARTRIDGE
Roast Partridge Australian Shiraz, Gevrey-Chambertin, Pomerol, or St. Emilion
PASTA
Lasagne Valpolicella, Barbera, Teroldego, Australian Verdelho or Sauvignon
Pasta with Meat Sauce Chianti, Bordeaux Rouge
Pasta with Pesto Sauce New Zealand Sauvignon Blanc, Valpolicella
Pasta with Seafood Sauce Soave, Sancerre
Ravioli with Spinach and Ricotta Pinot Bianco/Grigio, Cabernet d'Anjou
Spaghetti with Tomato Sauce California Cabernet, Zinfandel, Chianti
Spaghetti Vongole Pinot Bianco, Lugano
Tagliatelle Carbonara Pinot Grigio or a fresh, red Bardolino or Beaujolais
PEACH Sweet German Riesling
Peaches in Wine Riesling Auslese, Riesling Gewürztraminer Vendange Tardive, sweet Vouvray
PEANUTS
Beef in Peanut Curry New World Chardonnay, an aromatic, white Rhône
Satay Gewürztraminer
PEPPERCORNS
Steak au Poivre Cabernet Sauvignon, Chianti, Barbera, Rhône reds, Shiraz, or Rioja
PEPPERS (fresh green or red) New Zealand Cabernet, Loire reds, crisp Sauvignon Blanc, Beaujolais, Tuscan red
PEPPERS (yellow) Fruity, Italian reds, Valpolicella, etc.
Stuffed Peppers Hungarian red – Bull's Blood, Zinfandel, Chianti, or spicy, Rhône reds
PHEASANT Top-class red Burgundy, good American Pinot Noir, mature Hermitage
Pheasant Casserole Top class red Burgundy, mature Hermitage
Pheasant Paté Côtes du Rhône, Alsace Pinot Blanc
PIKE Eastern European white
PINE NUTS
Pesto Sauce New Zealand Sauvignon Blanc, Valpolicella
PIZZA Pinot Grigio, light Zinfandel, dry Grenache rosé
PLAICE White Burgundy, South American Chardonnay, Sauvignon Blanc
PLUM
Plum Pie Trockenbeerenauslese,

Côteaux du Layon
PORK
Cassoulet Serious white Rhône, Marsanne or Roussanne, or reds including Grenache and Syrah from the Rhône, berryish, Italian reds, or Zinfandel
Pork Casserole Mid-weight, earthy reds like Minervois, Navarra, or Montepulciano d'Abruzzo
Pork Pie Spicy reds, Shiraz, Grenache
Pork with Prunes Cahors, mature Chinon, or other Loire red or rich, southern French wine such as Corbières, Minervois, or Faugères
Pork Rillettes Pinot Blanc d'Alsace, Menetou-Salon Rouge
Pork Sausages Spicy Rhône reds, Barbera
Pork and Sage Sausages Barbera, Côtes du Rhône
Pork Spare Ribs Zinfandel, Australian Shiraz
Roast Pork Rioja reserva, New World Pinot Noir, dry Vouvray
Roast Pork with Apple Sauce Off-dry Vouvray or Riesling
Saucisson Sec Barbera, Cabernet Franc, Alsace Pinot Blanc, or Beaujolais (Villages or Crus)
Spare Ribs with Barbecue Sauce Fruity Australian Shiraz, Grenache, or Zinfandel, spicy Côtes du Rhône from a ripe vintage or an off-dry white
Szechuan-Style Pork Dry, aromatic whites, Alsace Pinot Gris, Riesling, Grenache rosé, beer
PRAWNS White Bordeaux, dry, Australian Riesling, Gavi
Prawn Cocktail Light, fruity whites – German Riesling
Prawns in Garlic Vinho Verde, Pinot Bianco
Prawn Vol-au-Vents White Bordeaux, Muscadet
Thai Prawns Gewürztraminer, dry, aromatic Riesling, or New Zealand Sauvignon Blanc
PRUNES Australian, late harvest Semillon
Pork with Prunes and Cream Sweet, Chenin-based wines, or good Mosel Spätlese
Prune Ice Cream Muscat de Beaumes de Venise

QUAIL Light, red Burgundy, full-flavored, white Spanish wines

RABBIT
Rabbit Casserole New World Pinot Noir or mature Châteauneuf-du-Pape
Rabbit in Cider Muscadet, demi-sec Vouvray, cider, or Calvados
Rabbit with Mustard Franken wine or Czech Pilsner beer
Rabbit in Red Wine with Prunes Good, mature Chinon or other Loire red
Roast Rabbit Tasty, simple, young Rhône, red, white

or rosé

RASPBERRIES New World, late harvest Riesling or Champagne, Beaujolais, demi-sec Champagne
Raspberry Fool Vouvray Moelleux

RASPBERRY VINEGAR Full-bodied Pinot Noir
Warm Bacon and Sorrel Salad New World Sauvignon Blanc, California Fumé Blanc, or a good Pouilly Fumé

REDCURRANT
Cumberland Sauce Rioja, Australian Shiraz

RED MULLET Dry rosé, California, Washington or Australian Chardonnay, Sauvignon Blanc

RHUBARB
Rhubarb Pie Moscato d'Asti, Alsace, German or Austrian late-harvest Riesling

RICE
Rice Pudding Monbazillac, sweet Muscat, Asti Spumante, or California Orange Muscat

ROQUEFORT The classic match is Sauternes or Barsac, but almost any full-flavored, botrytized, sweet wine will be a good partner for strong, creamy blue cheese

ROSEMARY Light red Burgundy or Pinot Noir

ROAST LAMB WITH GARLIC AND ROSEMARY Earthy soft reds like California Petite Sirah, Rioja, or Zinfandel

RUM
Flambéed Bananas with Rum Jurançon, Tokaji, Pedro Ximénez sherry, and, naturally, rum

SAFFRON Dry whites especially Chardonnay
Bass in Saffron Sauce Riesling (German, Australian, or Austrian), Viognier
Paella with Seafood White Penedés, unoaked Rioja, Navarra, Provence rosé

SAGE Chianti, or country reds from the Languedoc, otherwise Sauvignon Blancs are great, especially Chilean
Roast Chicken, Goose, or Turkey with Sage and Onion Stuffing Italian reds, especially Chianti, soft, plummy Merlots, sweetly fruity Rioja, and brambly Zinfandel

SALAMI Good, beefy Mediterranean rosé, Sardinian red, Rhône red, Zinfandel, dry aromatic Hungarian white

SALMON
Carpaccio of Salmon Cabernet Franc, Chardonnay, Australian reds, red Loire, Portuguese reds, Puligny-Montrachet
Grilled Salmon White Rhône (especially Viognier)

Poached Salmon Chablis, good, white Burgundy, other Chardonnay, Alsace Muscat, white Bordeaux
Poached Salmon with Hollandaise Muscat, Riesling, good Chardonnay
Salmon Paté Best white Burgundy

SARDINES Fresh Muscadet, Vinho Verde, very light and fruity reds such as Loire, Gamay

SCALLOPS Chablis and other unoaked Chardonnay
Coquilles St Jacques White Burgundy
Marinated Scallops with Bacon Fino sherry or mature Riesling
Scallops Mornay White Burgundy, Riesling Spätlese

SEA BASS Good white Burgundy
Bass in Saffron Sauce Riesling (German, Austrian, or Australian), Viognier

SEAFOOD (see also individual entries)
Paella with Seafood White Penedés, unoaked Rioja, Navarra, Provence rosé
Platter of Seafood Sancerre, Muscadet
Seafood Salad Soave, Pinot Grigio, Muscadet, lightly oaked Chardonnay

SESAME SEEDS Oaked Chardonnay

SHRIMPS Albariño, Sancerre, New World Sauvignon, Arneis
Potted Shrimps New World Chardonnay, Marsanne

SKATE Bordeaux white, Côtes de Gascogne, Pinot Bianco

SMOKED SALMON Chablis, Alsace Pinot Gris, white Bordeaux
Avocado and Smoked Salmon Lightly oaked Chardonnay, Fumé Blanc or Australian Semillon
Smoked Salmon Paté English oaked Fumé Blanc, New Zealand Chardonnay

SMOKED TROUT
Smoked Trout Paté Good, white Burgundy

SNAPPER Australian or South African, dry white

SOLE Sancerre, good Chablis, unoaked Chardonnay

SORBET Like ice cream, can be too cold/sweet for most wines. Try Australian fortified Muscats or see under individual flavors (orange, lemon, etc.)

SORREL Dry Loire Chenin or Sauvignon Blanc

SOY SAUCE Zinfandel or Australian Verdelho

SPINACH Pinot Grigio, Lugana
Eggs Florentine Chablis or unoaked Chardonnay, Pinot Blanc, Aligoté, Sémillon
Spinach/Pasta Casserole Soft, Italian reds (Bardolino, Valpolicella) rich whites

SPRING ROLLS Pinot Gris, Gewürztraminer, or other

aromatic whites

SQUAB Good, red Burgundy, rich Southern Rhône Chianti also goes well
Warm Squab Breasts on Salad Merlot-based Bordeaux or Cabernet Rosé

SQUID Gamay de Touraine, Greek or Spanish white
Calamari Crisp and neutral dry white – Muscadet
Squid in Ink Nebbiolo or Barbera

STILTON Tawny port

STRAWBERRIES Surprisingly, red Rioja, Burgundy (or other young Pinot Noir), especially if the berries are marinaded. More conventionally, sweet Muscats or fizzy Moscato
Strawberries and Cream Vouvray Moelleux, Monbazillac
Strawberry Meringue Late-harvest Riesling
Strawberry Mousse Sweet or fortified Muscat

SWEET AND SOUR DISHES Gewürztraminer, fruity young Sauvignon Blanc (unoaked) or beer

SWEETBREADS Lightly oaked Chardonnay, Chablis, Pouilly-Fuissé, or light, red Bordeaux
Sweetbreads in Mushroom, Butter and Cream sauce Southern French whites, Vin de Pays Chardonnay

TARAMASALATA Oaked Chardonnay or Fumé Blanc

TARRAGON White Menetou-Salon or South African Sauvignon
Blanc Roast/Grilled Chicken with Tarragon Dry Chenin Blanc, Vouvray, South African whites

THYME Ripe and fruity Provençal reds, Rioja, Northern Italian whites
Roast Lamb with Thyme New Zealand Cabernet Sauvignon, Bourgueil

TOFFEE Moscatel de Setúbal, Eiswein
Banana Toffee Pie Sweet Tokaji

TOMATO
Gazpacho Fino sherry, white Rioja
Pasta in a Tomato Sauce California Cabernet, Zinfandel, Chianti
Tomato Soup Sauvignon Blanc

TRIPE Earthy, French country red, Minervois, Cahors, Fitou

TROUT Pinot Blanc, Chablis
Smoked Trout Bourgogne Aligoté, Gewürztraminer, Pinot Gris
Trout with Almonds Bianco di Custoza, Pinot Blanc

TRUFFLES Red Burgundy, old Rioja, Barolo, or Hermitage

TUNA
Canned Tuna New World dry, fruity whites, Côtes de Gascogne

Carpaccio of Tuna Australian Chardonnay, red Loire, Beaujolais
Fresh Tuna Alsace Pinot Gris, Australian Chardonnay, Beaujolais

TURBOT Best white Burgundy, top California or Australian Chardonnay

TURKEY
Roast Turkey Beaujolais, light Burgundy and quite rich or off-dry whites
Roast Turkey with Stuffing Rhône, Merlot, or mature Burgundy

VANILLA Liqueur Muscat
Crème Brulée Jurançon Moelleux, Tokaji
Custard Monbazillac, sweet Vouvray

VEAL
Blanquette de Veau Aromatic, spicy whites from Alsace
Roast Veal Light, Italian whites or fairly light reds – Spanish or Loire
Wienerschnitzel Austrian Grüner Veltliner or Hungarian Pinot Blanc

VEGETABLES
Roasted and Grilled Light, juicy reds, Beaujolais, Sancerre and Sauvignon Blanc Unoaked or lightly oaked Chardonnay
Vegetable Soup Pinot Blanc or rustic reds such as Corbières
Vegetable Terrine Good New World Chardonnay

VENISON Pinotage, rich red Rhône, mature Burgundy, earthy, Italian reds
Venison Casserole Shiraz-based Australians, American Zinfandel, Cape red

VINEGAR
Choucroute Garnie White Alsace, Italian Pinot Grigio or Beaujolais
Sauerkraut Pilsner beer

WALNUT Tawny port, sweet Madeira

WATERCRESS
Watercress Soup Aromatic dry Riesling (Alsace or Australia)

WHITEFISH Fino sherry, Spanish red/white (Garnacha, Tempranillo), Soave

YAMS Depends on the sauce. When subtly prepared, try Pinot Blanc

YOGURT Needs full-flavored wines, such as Sémillon

ZABAGLIONE Marsala, Australian Liqueur Muscat, or a French Muscat such as Muscat de Beaumes de Venise

ZUCCHINI
Zucchini Gratin Good, dry Chenin from Vouvray or South Africa

Vintage chart

This chart only applies to age-worthy wines. Remember that most wines, and in particular nearly all inexpensive wines, should be drunk young. In such cases the most recent vintage is likely to be the best.

> **KEY**
> Each vintage is marked on a scale of 1 to 10, with 10 being the best.
>
> a – keep, b – keep or drink, c – drink now, d – getting past it, r – reds, w – whites

FRANCE	1999	1998	1997	1996	1995	1994	1993
Bordeaux							
Medoc, Graves	6a	7a	7a	7a	8a	6b	5c
St. Emilion, Pomerol	6a	7a	8a	8a	8a	6b	5c
White Graves	7a	7a	8b	7b	6c	7c	7c
Sauternes	6a	7a	8a	9a	7a	5b	3c
Burgundy							
Côte d'Or r	7a	7a	8a	8a	8a	5b	6b
Côte d'Or w	6a	7a	8b	8c	8c	6c	6c
Chablis	6a	7a	9a	8b	9c	7c	6c
Champagne	7a	7a	8a	8a	8a	–	6a
Rhone							
North r	8a	8a	7a	9a	8a	7a	5b
South r	7a	8a	7a	8a	8a	7a	6b
Loire							
Reds	6a	7a	8a	8a	8b	6c	6c
Sweet w	8a	6a	9a	9a	9a	8a	6b
Alsace w	8a	8a	9b	7c	7c	6c	6c
ITALY							
Chianti, Tuscan reds	8a	10a	8a	9a	8b	8c	
Barolo	9a	10a	9a	8a	7b	7b	
GERMANY							
Rhine	7a	8a	8a	8a	7a	7b	8b
Mosel	7a	8a	8a	7a	9a	7a	8a

	1999	1998	1997	1996	1995	1994	1993
SPAIN							
Rioja	6a	7a	8b	8b	8b	6c	
Ribera del Duero	7a	6a	9a	8b	9b	4c	
PORTUGAL							
Vintage port	7a	8a	8a	8a	10a	–	
Austria	7b	8c	6c	7c	7d	8d	
USA							
California							
Cabernet Sauvignon / Merlot	8a	8b	8c	8c	9c	7c	
Chardonnay	7c	7c	6c	9c	8d	7d	
Pacific Northwest							
Pinot Noir	6c	6c	7c	5d	9c	6d	
Cabernet Sauvignon	9c	8c	9c	8d	8d	7d	
AUSTRALIA							
Hunter Valley Chardonnay	7a	8b	7c	8c	7c	7d	7d
Barossa Shiraz	7a	9a	8b	9c	8c	9c	7c
Coonawarra Cabernet Sauvignon	7a	9a	7b	8b	4c	7c	7c
Margaret River Cabernet Sauvignon	8a	7b	8b	8c	7c	8c	7c
NEW ZEALAND							
Sauvignon Blanc	7b	7c	9d	9d	5d	9d	7d
SOUTH AFRICA							
Stellenbosch Cabernet Sauvignon Pinotage	7a	8b	9c	6c	9d	8d	6d

A simple glossary

Abboccato [ah-boh-kah-toh] Italian semi-dry wine.

Abfüller/Abfüllung [ab-few-ler/ ab-few-lerng] German for "bottler" or "bottled by."

Abocado [ah-boh-kah-doh] Spainish semi-dry wine.

Acetic acid [ah-see-tihk] This volatile acid (CH₃COOH) is found in small proportions in all wines. Careless winemaking can result in wine being turned into acetic acid, a substance most people know as vinegar.

Acidity Naturally occuring (tartaric and malic) acids in the grapes are vital to contributing freshness, and also help to preserve the wine while it ages. In reds and many cool region whites, the malic is often converted to lactic by a natural process known as malolactic fermentation, which gives the wines a buttery texture and flavor. In hotter countries (and sometimes cooler ones) the acid level may (not always legally) be adjusted by adding tartaric and citric acid.

Agricola vitivinicola Italian wine estate.

Amabile [am-MAH-bee-lay] Italian semi-sweet wine.

Amarone [ah-mah-ROH-neh] (Veneto, Italy) Literally "bitter;" used particularly to describe Recioto. Best known as Amarone della Valpolicella. Allegrini; Boscaini; Masi; Quintarelli; Tedeschi; Zenato.

Amontillado [am-mon-tee-yah-doh] (Jerez, Spain) Literally "like Montilla." Often pretty basic medium-sweet sherry, but ideally fascinating dry, nutty wine. Gonzalez Byass; Lustau; Sanchez Romate.

Amtliche Prüfungsnummer [am-tlish-eh proof-oong-znoomer] German identification number on all QbA/QmP labels.

Anbaugebiet [ahn-bow-geh-beet] German term for 11 large regions (e.g. Rheingau). QbA and QmP wines must include the name of their anbaugebiet on their labels.

Annata [ahn-nah-tah] Italian vintage.

AOC French. See Appellation Contrôlée.

AP German. See Amtliche Prüfungsnummer.

Appellation Contrôlée (AC/AOC) [AH-pehl-lah-see-on kon troh- lay] French designation guaranteeing origin, grape varieties and method of production and – in theory – quality, though tradition and vested interest combine to allow pretty appalling wines to receive the rubber stamp.

Asciutto [ah-shoo-toh] Italian dry wine.

Assemblage [ah-sehm-blahj] French. The art of blending wine from different grape varieties. Associated with Bordeaux and Champagne.

Astringent Mouth-puckering. Associated with young red wine. See tannin.

Aszu [ah-soo] The sweet syrup made from dried and (about 10–15 percent) "nobly rotten" grapes (see Botrytis) used to sweeten Hungarian Tokaji.

Ausbruch [ows-brook] Austrian term for rich botrytis wine that's sweeter than Beerenauslese but less sweet than Trockenbeerenauslese.

Auslese [ows-lay-zuh] German, mostly sweet wine from selected ripe grapes, usually affected by botrytis. Third rung on the QmP ladder.

Azienda [a-see-en-dah] Italian estate wine.

Balance Harmony of fruitiness, acidity, alcohol and tannin. Balance can develop with age but should be evident (if sometimes hard to discern) in youth.

Beaumes de Venise [bohm duh vuh-neez] Côtes du Rhône, France, village producing spicy dry reds and sweet, grapey, fortified Vin Doux Naturel from the Muscat. Dom. des Bernardins; Chapoutier; Dom de Coyeux.

Beerenauslese [behr-ren-ows-lay-zuh] Austrian and German sweet wines from selected, ripe grapes (Beeren), hopefully affected by botrytis.

Bereich [beh-ri-kh] German vineyard area, subdivision of an anbaugebiet. On its own indicates QbA wine, e.g. Niersteiner. Finer wines are followed by the name of a (smaller) grosslage, better ones by that of an individual vineyard.

Blanc de Blancs [blon dur blon] A white wine, made from white grapes – hardly worth mentioning except in the case of Champagne, where Pinot Noir, a black grape, usually makes up 30–70 percent of the blend. In this case, Blanc de Blancs is pure Chardonnay.

Blanc de Noirs [blon dur nwahrr] A white (or frequently very slightly pink-tinged wine) made from red grapes by taking off the free-run juice before pressing to minimize the uptake of red pigments from the skin. Paul Bara; Duval-Leroy (Fleur de Champagne); Egly-Ouiriet.

Bocksbeutel [box-boy-tuhl] From Franken, Germany, the famous flask-shaped bottle adopted by the makers of Mateus Rosé.

Bodega [bod-day-gah] Spanish winery or wine cellar; producer.

Body Usually used as "full-bodied," meaning a wine with mouth-filling flavors and probably a fairly high alcohol content.

Botrytis [boh-tri-tiss] Botrytis cinerea, a fungal infection that attacks and shrivels grapes, evaporating their water and concentrating their sweetness. Vital to Sauternes and the finer German and Austrian sweet wines. See Sauternes, Trockenbeerenauslese, Tokaji.

Bottle-fermented Commonly found on the labels of U.S. sparkling wines to indicate the Méthode Champenoise, and gaining wider currency. Beware, though – it can indicate inferior "transfer method" wines.

Bouquet Overall smell, often made up of several separate aromas. Used by Anglo-Saxon enthusiasts more often than by professionals.

Bourgogne [boorr-goyñ] French for Burgundy.

Braquet [brah-ket] (Midi, France) Grape variety used in Bellet.

Brut [broot] Dry, particularly of Champagne and sparkling wines. Brut nature/sauvage/ zéro are even drier, while Extra-Sec is perversely applied to (slightly) sweeter sparkling wine.

Buttery Rich, fat smell often found in good Chardonnay (often as a result of malolactic fermentation) or in wine that has been left on its lees.

Cantina (Sociale) [kan-tee-nuh soh-chee-yah-lay] Italian winery (cooperative).

Cap Classique [kap-klas-seek] (South Africa) Now that the term Méthode Champenoise has unreasonably been outlawed, this is the phrase developed by the South Africans to describe their Champagne-method sparkling wine.

Capsule The sheath covering the cork. Once lead, now plastic, or tin. In the case of "flanged" bottles, though, it is noticeable by its transparency or absence.

Carbonic Maceration See Macération Carbonique.

Casa [kah-sah] (Italy, Spain, Portugal) Firm or company.

Cat's pee Describes the tangy smell frequently found in typical Müller-Thurgau and unripe Sauvignon Blanc.

Cava (Greece) Legal term for wood- and bottle-aged wine.

Cave [kahv] French for cellar.

Cépage [say-pahzh] French grape variety.

Chai [shay] French for cellar or winery.

Chaptalization [shap-tal-lih-zay-shuhn] The legal (in some regions) addition of sugar during fermentation to boost a wine's alcohol content.

Chardonnay [shar-don-nay] The great white grape of Burgundy, Champagne, and now just about everywhere else. Capable of fresh simple charm in Bulgaria and buttery hazelnutty richness in Meursault in the Côte d'Or. Given the right chalky soil, in regions like Chablis, it can also make wines with an instantly recognizeable "mineral" character. In the New World, it tends to produce tropical flavors, partly thanks to warmer climates and partly thanks to the use of clones and cultured yeasts. Almost everywhere, its innate flavor is often married to that of new oak. See regions and producers.

Charmat [shar-mat] The inventor of the Cuve Close method of producing cheap sparkling wines. See *Cuve Close*.

Château [sha-toh] (Bordeaux, France) Literally means "castle". Some châteaux are extremely grand, many are merely farmhouses. A building is not required; the term applies to a vineyard or wine estate. Château names cannot be invented, but there are plenty of defunct titles that are used unashamedly by large cooperative wineries to market their members' wines.

Chêne [shehn] French oak, as in Fûts de Chêne (oak barrels).

Chevaliers de Tastevin [shuh-val-yay duh tast-van] From Burgundy, France, a brotherhood – confrérie – based in Clos de Vougeot, famed for grand dinners and fancy robes. Wines approved at an annual tasting may carry a special "tasteviné" label.

Clairet [klehr-ray] The word from which we derived claret – originally a very pale-colored red from Bordeaux, France. Seldom used.

Claret [klar-ret] English term for red Bordeaux.

Clarete [klah-reh-Tay] Spanish term for light red – frowned on by the European Union.

Classed Growth French, the literal translation of Cru Classé, commonly used when referring to the status of Bordeaux châteaux.

Classico [kla-sih-koh] Italian for a defined area within a DOC identifying what are supposed to be the best vineyards, e.g. Chianti Classico, Valpolicella Classico.

Climat [klee-mah] A term from Burgundy, France. An individual named vineyard.

Clone [klohn] Specific strain of a given grape variety. For example, more than 300 clones of Pinot Noir have been identified.

Clos [kloh] French, literally, "a walled vineyard."

Colheita [kol-yay-tah] From Portugal, a harvest or vintage – particularly used to describe tawny port of a specific year.

Colle/colli [kol-lay/kol-lee] Italian for "hill" or "hills."

Commandaria [com-man-dah-ree-yah] Traditional dessert wine from Cyprus with rich, raisiny fruit.

Commune [kom-moon] French, small demarcated plot of land named after its principal town or village. Equivalent to an English parish.

Confréries [kon-fray-ree] French promotional brotherhoods linked to a particular wine or area. Many, however, are nowadays more about pomp and pageantry, kudos and backslapping, than active promotion.

Consejo Regulador [kon-say-hoh ray-goo-lah-dohr] Spanish administrative body responsible for DO wines.

Consorzio [kon-sohr-zee-yoh] Italian Producers' syndicate.

Cookielike Flavor of savory crackers often associated with the Chardonnay grape, particularly in Champagne and top-class mature Burgundy, or with the yeast that fermented the wine.

Corked Unpleasant, musty smell and flavor, caused by (usually invisible) mold in the cork. Affects 3–6 percent of bottles.

Cosecha [coh-seh-chah] Spanish for "harvest" or "vintage."

Côte(s), Coteaux [koht] French for "hillsides."

Coulure [koo-loor] Climate-related wine disorder that causes reduced yields (and possibly higher quality) as grapes shrivel and fall off the vine.

Crémant [kray-mon] French term used in Champagne, denoting a slightly sparkling style due to a lower pressure of gas in the bottle. Elsewhere, a term to indicate sparkling wine, e.g. Crémant de Bourgogne, de Loire and d'Alsace.

Crème de Cassis [kraym duh kas-seess] Fortified fruit essence perfected in Burgundy using blackcurrants from around Dijon. Commonly drunk mixed with sharp local Aligoté as Kir, or sparkling wine, as Kir Royale. Crème de Mûre

(blackberries), Framboise (raspberries), Fraise (strawberries), and Pêche (peaches) are also delicious.

Criado y Embotellado (por) [kree-yah-doh ee em-bot-tay-yah-doh] Spanish for "grown and bottled (by)."

Crianza [kree-yan-thah] Spanish. Literally "con Crianza" means aged in wood – often preferable to the Reservas and Gran Reservas, which are highly prized by Spaniards but can taste dull and dried-out.

Crisp Fresh, with good acidity.

Cru Bourgeois [kroo boor-zhwah] Bordeaux wines beneath the Crus Classés, supposedly satisfying certain requirements, which can be good value for money and, in certain cases, better than more prestigious classed growths. Since around half the wine in the Médoc comes from Crus Bourgeois (and a quarter from Crus Classés), don't expect the words to mean too much.

Cru Classé [kroo klas-say] The best wines of the Médoc in Bordeaux, France, are crus classés, split into five categories from first (top) to fifth growth (or Cru) for the Great Exhibition in 1855. The Graves, St. Emilion, and Sauternes have their own classifications.

Crusted Port An affordable alternative from Douro, Portugal, to vintage port – a blend of different years, bottled young and allowed to throw a deposit.

Cultivar [kul-tee-vahr] South African term for grape variety.

Cuve close [koov klohs] The third-best way of making sparkling wine, in which the wine undergoes secondary fermentation in a tank and is then bottled. Also called the Charmat or Tank method.

Cuvée (de Prestige) [koo-vay] Most frequently a blend put together in a process called assemblage. Prestige Cuvées are (particularly in Champagne) supposed to be the best of a producer's production.

Dégorgée (dégorgement) [day-gor-jay] The removal of the deposit of inert yeasts from Champagne after maturation.

Demi-sec [duh-mee sek] French medium-dry wine.

Deutsches Weinsiegel [doyt-

shur vihn-see-gel] Seals of various colors – usually neck labels – awarded for merit to German wines. Treat with circumspection.

Deutscher Tafelwein [doyt-shur tah-fuhl-vihn] Table wine that is guaranteed German, as opposed to Germanic-style European Tafelwein. Can be good value – and often no worse than Qualitätswein, the supposedly "quality wine" designation that includes every bottle of Liebfraumilch.

Diabetiker Wein [dee-ah-beh-ti-ker vihn] Very dry German wine with most of the sugar fermented out (as in a Diat lager); suitable for diabetics.

DLG (Deutsche Landwirtschaft Gesellschaft) Body awarding medals for excellence to German wines – far too generously.

DO, Denominac/ion/ão de Origen Demarcated quality area in Spain and Portugal, guaranteeing origin, grape varieties, and production standards (everything, in other words, except the quality of the stuff in the bottle).

DOC, Denominación de Origem Controlada Replacing the old RD (Região Demarcada) as Portugal's equivalent of Italy's DOCG.

DOC, Denominacion de Origen Calificada Ludicrously, and confusingly, Spain's recently launched higher quality equivalent to Italy's DOCG shares the same initials as lower's lower quality DOC wines. So far, restricted to Rioja – good, bad and indifferent. In other words, this official designation should be treated – like Italy's DOCs and DOCGs and France's Appellation Contrôlée – with something less than total respect.

DOC(G), Denominazione di Origine Controllata (e Garantia) Italian quality control designation based on grape variety and/or origin. "Garantita" is supposed to imply a higher quality level, but all too often it does no such thing and has more to do with regional politics than with tasty wines. It is worth noting, that while the generally dull wines of Albana di Romagna received the first white DOCG (ahead of all sorts of more worthy candidates), the new efforts to bring Vini da Tavola into the system left such internationally applauded wines as Tignanello out in the cold among the most basic DOCs.

Domaine (Dom.) [doh-mayn] French wine estate.

Dosage [doh-sazh] The addition of sweetening syrup to naturally dry Champagne after dégorgement to replace the wine lost with the yeast, and to set the sugar to the desired level (even Brut Champagne requires up to 4 grams per liter of sugar to make it palatable).

Doux [doo] French sweet wine.

Dumb As in "dumb nose," meaning without smell.

Edelfäule [ay-del-fow-luh] German term for *Botrytis cinerea*, or "noble rot."

Edelzwicker [ay-del-zwik-kur] Generic name used in Alsace, France, for a blend of grapes. The idea of blends is coming back – but not the name (see *Hugel*).

Eiswein [ihs-vihn] Used in Germany, Austria, and Canada. Ultra-concentrated late harvest wine, made from grapes naturally frozen on the vine. Hard to make (and consequently very pricy) in Germany, but more affordable in Austria and Canada.

Elaborado y Anejado por [ay-lah-boh-rah-doh ee anay-hahdo pohr] Spanish for "Made and aged for."

Elevér/éléveur [ay-leh-vay/vay-leh-vuhr] To mature or "nurture" wine, especially in the cellars of the Burgundy négociants, who act as éléveurs after traditionally buying in wine made by small estates.

En primeur [on pree-muh] New wine, usually Bordeaux. Producers and specialist merchants buy and offer wine en primeur before it has been released. In the U.S. and Australia, where producers like Mondavi and Petaluma are selling their wine in this way, the process is known as buying "futures."

English wine Quality has improved in recent years, as winemakers have moved from making semisweet, mock-Germanic to dry mock-Loire and, increasingly, sparkling, aromatic-but-dry and late harvest.

Enoteca [ee-noh-teh-kah]

Italian term, literally "wine library" or, now, wine shop.

Erzeugerabfüllung [ayr-tsoy-guhr-ab-foo-loong] German term for bottled by the grower/estate.

Espum/oso/ante [es-poom-mo-soh/san-tay] Spanish or Portuguese sparkling wine.

Esters Chemical components in wine responsible for all those extraordinary odors of fruits, vegetables, hamster cages, and sneakers.

Estufa [esh-too-fah] Portuguese, the vats in which Madeira is heated, speeding maturity and imparting its familiar "cooked" flavor.

Eszencia [es-sen-tsee-yah] Tokaji, Hungary. Incredibly concentrated syrup made by piling around 100 kg of late-harvested, botrytized grapes into puttonyos and letting as little as three liters of incredibly sticky treacle dribble out of the bottom. This will only ferment up to about 4 percent alcohol, over several weeks, before stopping completely. It is then stored and used to sweeten normal Aszú wines. The Czars of Russia discovered the joys of Eszencia, and it has been prized for its effects on the male libido. It is incredibly hard to find, even by those who can see the point in doing anything with the expensive syrup other than pouring it on ice cream. The easier-to-find Aszú Essencia (one step sweeter than Aszú 6 puttonyos) is far better value.

Fat Has a silky texture that fills the mouth. More fleshy than meaty.

Fattoria [fah-tor-ree-ah] Italian for "estate," particularly in Tuscany.

Fermentazione naturale [fehr-men-tat-zee-oh-nay] Italian for "naturally sparkling," but, in fact, indicates the cuve close method.

Fining Clarifying young wine before bottling to remove impurities, using a number of agents including isinglass and bentonite.

Finish What you can still taste after swallowing.

Flabby Lacking balancing acidity.

Flor [flawr] Yeast that grows naturally on the surface of some maturing sherries,

making them potential finos.

Frizzante [freet-zan-tay] Italian semi-sparkling wine, especially Lambrusco.

Fumé Blanc [fyoo-may blahnk] Name originally adapted from Pouilly Blanc Fumé by Robert Mondavi to describe his California oaked Sauvignon. Now widely used – though not exclusively – in the New World for this style.

Fûts de Chêne (élévé en) [foo duh shayne] French for "oak barrels" (aged in).

Futures See *En Primeur*.

Galestro [gah-less-troh] There is no such thing as Chianti Bianco; the light, grapey stuff that is made in the Chianti region of Tuscany, Italy, is sold as Galestro.

Gamey Smell or taste distinctly, if oddly, reminiscent of aged game. Particularly associated with old Pinot Noirs and Syrahs. Sometimes at least partly attributable to the combination of those grapes' natural characteristics with careless use of sulfur dioxide by winemakers. Modern examples of both styles seem to be distinctly less gamey than in the past. Another explanation can be the presence of a vineyard infection called Brettanomyces which is feared in California but often goes unnoticed in France where gamey wines are (sometimes approvingly) said to "renarder" – to smell of fox.

Garrafeira [gah-rah-fay-rah] Portugal. Indicates a producer's "reserve" wine, which has been selected and given extra time in cask (minimum two years) and bottle (minimum one year).

Generoso [zheh-neh-roh-soh] Spanish fortified or dessert wine.

Giropalette [zhee-roh-pal-let] Large machine which, in méthode champenoise, automatically and highly efficiently replaces the human beings who used to perform the task of remuage. Used by almost all the bigger Champagne houses which, needless to say, prefer to conceal them from visiting tourists.

Gran Reserva [gran rays-sehr-vah] Spanish quality wine aged for a designated

number of years in wood and, in theory, only produced in the best vintages. Can be dried out and less worthwhile than Crianza or Reserva.

Grand Cru [gron kroo] Prepare to be confused. French term referring to the finest vineyards and the – supposedly – equally fine wine made in them. It is an official designation in Bordeaux, Burgundy, Champagne, and Alsace, but its use varies. In Alsace, where there are 50 or so Grand Cru Vineyards, some are more convincingly grand than others. In Burgundy Grand Cru vineyards with their own ACs, e.g., Montrachet, do not need to carry the name of the village (e.g. Chassagne-Montrachet) on their label. Where these regions apply the designation to pieces of soil, in Bordeaux it applies to châteaux whose vineyards can be bought and sold. More confusingly, still St. Emilion can be described as either Grand Cru, Grand Cru Classé – or both – or Premier Grand Cru Classé.

Grand Vin [gron van] The first (quality) wine of a Bordeaux estate – as opposed to its second label.

Grosslage [gross-lah-guh] German wine district, the third subdivision after anbaugebiet (e.g. Rheingau) and bereich (e.g. Nierstein). For example, Michelsberg is a grosslage of the bereich Piesport.

Halbtrocken [hahlb-trok-en] German off-dry wine. Usually a safer buy than Trocken in regions like the Mosel, Rheingau, and Rheinhessen, but still often aggressively acidic. Look for QbA or Auslese versions.

Haut-Médoc [oh-may-dok] (Bordeaux, France) Large appellation which includes nearly all of the well-known crus classés. Basic Haut-Médoc should be better than plain Médoc.

Hochfeinste [hokh-fihn-stuh] German for "very finest."

Hochgewächs QbA [hokh-geh-fex] Recent German official designation for Rieslings that are as ripe as a QmP but can still only call themselves QbA. This from a nation supposedly dedicated to simplifying what are acknowledged to be the most complicated labels in the world.

Hybrid [hih-brid] Cross-bred grape *Vitis vinifera* (European) x *Vitis labrusca* (North American) – an example is Seyval Blanc.

Icewine Increasingly popular Anglicization of the German term Eiswein, used particularly by Canadian producers making luscious, spicily exotic wines from the frozen grapes of varieties like Vidal.

Imbottigliato nel'origine [im-bot-til-yah-toh neh-loh-ree-zhee-nay] Italian estate-bottled wine.

Imperial(e) [am-pay-ray-ahl] From Bordeaux, France. Bottle containing almost six and a half liters of wine (eight and a half regular bottles). Cherished by collectors partly through rarity, partly through the longevity that large bottles give their contents.

Institut National des Appellations d'Origine (INAO) French official body that designates and (half-heartedly) polices quality, and outlaws sensible techniques like irrigation and the blending of vintages, which are permitted elsewhere. Maybe this is why Appellation Contrôlée wines are often inferior to – and sell at lower prices than – the newer Vins de Pays over which this body has no authority.

International Wine Challenge Wine competition, held in London, Tokyo, China, and Singapore. (The author is founder and chairman.)

International Wine & Spirit Competition Wine competition, held in London.

Isinglass [Ih-sing-glahs] Fining agent derived from sturgeon bladders.

Jeroboam [zhe-roh-bohm] Large bottle; in Champagne holding three liters (four bottles); in Bordeaux, four and a half (six bottles). Best to make sure before writing your check.

Jeunes Vignes [zhuhn veen] Denotes vines too young for their crop to be sold as an Appellation Contrôlée wine.

Jug wine American term for quaffable Vin Ordinaire.

Kabinett First step in German quality ladder, for wines that achieve a certain natural sweetness.

Kellerei/kellerabfüllung [kel-luh-rih/kel-luh-rab-foo-loong] German for cellar/producer/estate-bottled.

Kir A mixture of sweet fortified Crème de Cassis (regional specialty of Burgundy) with simple and often rather acidic local white wine (Aligoté, or basic Bourgogne Blanc) to produce a delicious summertime drink. Try it with Crème de Mûre or Crème de Framboise instead.

Kosher Wine made under complex dietary rules. Every seventh vintage is left unharvested, additives are not allowed, and there are other regulations.

Lacryma Christi [la-kree-mah kris-tee] Literally, "tears of Christ," the melancholy name for some amiable, light, rather rustic reds and whites from Campania, Italy. Those from Vesuvio are DOC.

Landwein [land-vihn] The German equivalent of a French Vin De Pays, from one of 11 named regions (anbaugebiet). Often dry.

Late harvest Made from (riper) grapes picked after the main vintage. Should have at least some botrytis.

Late-Bottled Vintage (Port) (LBV) Douro, Portugal. Officially, bottled four or six years after a specific (usually non-declared) vintage. Until the late 1970s, this made for a vintage port-style wine that matured earlier, was a little lighter and easier to drink, but still needed to be decanted. Until recently, the only houses to persevere with this style were Warres and Smith Woodhouse, who labeled their efforts "Traditional" LBV. Almost every other LBV around, however, was of the filtered, "modern" style pioneered by Taylors. These taste pretty much like up-market ruby and vintage character ports, need no decanting, and bear very little resemblance to real vintage or even crusted port. Belatedly, a growing number of producers are now confusingly offering "Traditional" as well as modern LBV. Under their self-imposed laws, the port shippers infuriatingly allow themselves to use the same name for these two very different styles of wine. This

is not very surprizing really: As one very prominent retired port maker admitted, he and his competitors have always done well out of confusing their clients.

Lean Lacking body.

Lees or lie(s) The sediment of dead yeasts that fall in the barrel or vat as a wine develops. Muscadet – like some other white wines – is aged Sur Lie. Producers of modern Chardonnay also leave their wine in its lees, stirring it occasionally to maximize richness – the rich flavor provided by the yeasts.

Length How long the taste lingers in the mouth.

Liebfraumilch [leeb-frow-mihlkh] German seditious exploitation of the QbA system. Good examples are pleasant; most are alcoholic sugar-water bought on price alone.

Limousin [lee-moo-zan] French oak forest that provides barrels high in wood tannin. Better, therefore, for red wine than for white.

Liqueur Muscat A wine style unique to Rutherglen, Australia. Other countries make fortified Muscats, but none achieve the caramelized marmalade and Christmas fruitcake flavors that Rutherglen can achieve.

Liqueur d'Expedition [lee-kuhr dex-pay-dees-see-yon] Champagne, France. Sweetening syrup for dosage.

Liqueur de Tirage [lee-kuhr duh tee-rahzh] Champagne, France. The yeast and sugar added to base wine to induce secondary fermentation (and hence the bubbles) in bottle.

Liquoreux [lee-koh-ruh] French rich and sweet wine.

Liquoroso [lee-koh-roh-soh] Italian rich and sweet wine.

Macération carbonique [ma-say-ra-see-yon kahr-bon-eek] Technique of fermenting uncrushed grapes under pressure of a blanket of carbon dioxide gas to produce fresh, fruity wine. Used in Beaujolais, southern France and, increasingly, the New World.

Maderization [mad-uhr-ih-zay-shon] Deliberate procedure in Madeira, produced by the warming of wine in estufas. Otherwise undesired effect, commonly produced by high temperatures during storage, resulting in a dull flat flavor, tinged with a sherry taste

and color.

Magnum Large bottle containing the equivalent of two bottles of wine (one and a half liters in capacity).

Maître de Chai [may-tr duh chay] French for "cellar master."

Malolactic fermentation [ma-loh-lak-tik] Secondary "fermentation" in which appley malic acid is converted into the "softer," creamier lactic acid by naturally present or added strains of bacteria. Almost all red wines undergo a malolactic fermentation. For whites, it is common practice in Burgundy. It is varyingly used in the New World, where natural acid levels are often low. An excess is recognizable in wine as a buttermilky flavor.

Manzanilla [man-zah-nee-yah] From Jerez, Spain. Dry tangy sherry – a Fino style widely (though possibly mistakenly) thought to take on a salty tang from the coastal bodegas of Sanlucar de Barrameda.

Marc [mahr] French, the residue of seeds, stalks, and skins left after the grapes are pressed – and often distilled into a fiery brandy of the same name, e.g., Marc de Bourgogne.

Master of Wine (MW) One of a small number of people (around 250) internationally who have passed a grueling set of wine exams.

Mercaptans [mehr-kap-ton] See *Hydrogen sulfide.*

Méthode Champenoise [may-tohd shom-puh-nwahz] Term now outlawed by the European Union from wine labels, but still used to describe the way Champagne and all other quality sparkling wines are produced. Labor intensive, because bubbles are made by secondary fermentation in bottle, rather than in a vat or by the introduction of gas. Bottles are individually given the "dégorgémont process," topped up and recorked!

Methuselah Same size bottle as an Imperiale (six liters). Used in Champagne.

Mis en Bouteille au Ch./Dom. [mee zon boo-tay] French estate-bottled wine.

Moelleux [mwah-luh] French sweet wine.

Monopole [mo-noh-pohl] French, literally, for "exclusive" – in Burgundy denotes single ownership of an entire vineyard.

Mousse [mooss] The bubbles in Champagne and sparkling wines.

Mousseux [moo-sur] French sparkling wine – generally cheap and unremarkable.

Must Unfermented grape juice.

MW See *Master of Wine*.

Négociant [nay-goh-see-yon] French for a merchant who buys, matures, and bottles wine. See also *Eléveur*.

Négociant-manipulant (NM) [ma-nih-pyoo-lon] Buyer and blender of wines for Champagne, identifiable by the NM number, which is mandatory on the label.

Nevers [nur-vehr] French term for subtlest oak – from a forest in Burgundy.

Noble rot Popular term for *Botrytis cinerea*.

Nouveau [noo-voh] New wine, most popularly used of Beaujolais.

NV Non-vintage, meaning a blend of wines from different years.

Oaky Flavor imparted by oak casks, which will vary depending on the source of the oak (American is more obviously sweet than French). Woody is usually less complimentary.

Oechsle [urk-slur] German scale indicating the sugar level in grapes or wine.

Oïdium [oh-id-ee-yum] Fungal infection of grapes, shriveling them and turning them gray.

Oloroso [ol-oh-roh-soh] Style of full-bodied sherry from Jerez, Spain, that is either dry or semisweet.

Oxidation The effect (usually detrimental, occasionally – as in sherry – intentional) of oxygen on wine.

Oxidative The opposite of reductive. Certain wines – most reds, and whites like Chardonnay – benefit from limited exposure to oxygen during their fermentation and maturation, such as barrel aging.

Palate Nebulous, not to say ambiguous, term describing the apparatus used for tasting (i.e., the tongue) as well as the skill of the taster ("he has a good palate").

Pasado/Pasada [pa-sah-doh/dah] Spanish term applied to old or fine (fino) and amontillado sherries. Worth seeking out.

Passetoutgrains [pas-stoo-gran] Wine supposedly made from two-thirds Gamay, one third Pinot Noir – though few producers respect these proportions. Once the Burgundians' daily red – until they decided to sell it and drink cheaper wine from other regions.

Passito [pa-see-toh] Italian raisiny wine, usually made from sun-dried Erbaluce grapes in Italy. This technique is now used in Australia by Primo Estate.

Perlé/Perlant [pehr-lay/lon] French lightly sparkling wine.

Perlwein [pehrl-vine] German sparkling wine.

Pétillant [pur-tee-yon] Lightly sparkling wine.

Petrolly A not unpleasant overtone often found in mature Riesling. Arrives faster in Australia than in Germany.

Phylloxera vastatrix [fih-lok-seh-rah] Root-eating louse that wiped out Europe's vines in the 19th century. Foiled by grafting vinifera vines onto resistant American labrusca rootstock. Pockets of pre-phylloxera and/or ungrafted vines still exist in France (in a Bollinger vineyard and on the south coast – the louse hates sand), Portugal (in Quinta do Noval's "Nacional" vineyard), Australia, and Chile. Elsewhere, phylloxera recently devastated Napa Valley vines planted (despite warnings from French experts) on insufficiently resistant rootstock.

Port Fortified wine made in the upper Douro Valley of Portugal. Comes in several styles; see *Tawny, Ruby, LBV, Vintage, Crusted,* and *White port*.

Pourriture noble [poo-ree-toor nohbl] French. See *Botrytis cinerea* or *Noble rot*.

Prädikat [pray-dee-ket] As in Qualitätswein mit Prädikat (QmP), the (supposedly) higher quality level for German and Austrian wines, indicating a greater degree of natural ripeness.

Precipitation The creation of a harmless deposit, usually of tartrate crystals, in white wine, which the Germans romantically call "diamonds."

Premier Cru [prur-mee-yay kroo] In Burgundy, indicates wines that fall between village and Grand Cru quality. Some major communes such as Beaune and Nuits-St.-Georges have no Grand Cru. Wine simply labeled Meursault Premier Cru, for example, is probably a blend from two or more vineyards.

Prestige Cuvée [koo-vay] The top wine of a Champagne house in France. Expensive and elaborately packaged. Some, like Dom. Pérignon, are brilliant; others less so. Other best-known examples include Veuve Clicquot's Grand Dame and Roederer's Cristal.

Primeur [pree-mur] French new wine, e.g., Beaujolais Primeur (the same as Beaujolais Nouveau) or, as in en primeur, wine which is sold while still in barrel. Here in the U.S., known as "futures."

Propriétaire (Récoltant) [pro-pree-yeh-tehr ray-kohl-ton] French term for vineyard owner-manager.

Putto [poot-toh] Italian wine. See *Chianti*.

Puttonyos [poot-toh-nyos] The measure of sweetness (from one to six) of Tokaji, a Hungarian wine. The number indicates the number of puttonyos (baskets) of sweet aszú paste that are added to the base wine.

QbA **Qualitätswein bestimmter Anbaugebiet:** [kvah-lih-tayts-vine behr-shtihmt-tuhr ahn-bow-geh-beet] Basic-quality German wine from one of the 11 anbaugebiet, e.g., Rheinhessen.

QmP **Qualitätswein mit Prädikat:** [pray-dee-kaht] German QbA wine (supposedly) with "special qualities." The QmP blanket designation is broken into five sweetness rungs, from Kabinett to Trockenbeerenauslese plus Eiswein.

Quinta [keen-ta] Portuguese vineyard or estate, particularly in the Douro, where "single Quinta" vintage ports are increasingly being taken as seriously as the big-name blends. See *Crasto, Vesuvio,* and *de la Rosa*.

Racking Drawing off wine from its lees into a clean cask or vat.

Rancio [ran-see-yoh] Term for the peculiar yet prized oxidized flavor of certain fortified wines, particularly in France (e.g., Banyuls) and Spain.

RD (Récemment Dégorgée) A term invented by Bollinger for their delicious vintage Champagne, which has been allowed a longer-than-usual period (as much as 15 years) on its lees.

Recioto [ray-chee-yo-toh] Sweet or dry alcoholic wine from Veneto, Italy, made from semidried, ripe grapes. Usually associated with Valpolicella and Soave.

Récoltant-manipulant (RM) [ray-kohl-ton ma-nih-poo-lon] Individual winegrower and blender in Champagne region of France, identified by mandatory RM number on label.

Récolte [ray-kohlt] French term for vintage, literally "harvest."

Régisseur [rey-jee-sur] In Bordeaux, the cellar-master.

Remuage [reh-moo-wazh] Champagne, France. Part of the méthode champenoise, the gradual turning and tilting of bottles so that the yeast deposit collects in the neck ready for dégorgement.

Reserva [ray-sehr-vah] Spanish wine aged for a period specified by the relevant DO: usually one year for reds and six months for whites and pinks.

Réserve [reh-surv] A French term legally meaningless, as in "Réserve Personelle," but implying a wine selected and given more age.

Residual sugar Term for wines which have retained grape sugar not converted to alcohol by yeasts during fermentation. In France 4 grams per liter is the threshold. In the U.S., the figure is five and many so-called "dry" white wines contain as much as ten and some supposedly dry red Zinfandels definitely have more than a trace of sweetness. New Zealand Sauvignons are rarely bone dry, but their acidity balances and conceals any residual sugar.

Retsina [ret-see-nah] Greek wine made the way the ancient Greeks used to make it – resinating it with pine to keep it from spoiling. Today, it's an acquired taste for non-vacationing, non-Greeks. Pick the freshest examples you can find (though this isn't easy when labels mention no vintage).

Ripasso [ree-pas-soh] Veneto, Italy. Method whereby newly made Valpolicella is partially refermented in vessels recently vacated by Recioto and Amarone. Ripasso wines made in this way are richer, alcoholic, and raisiny. Increases the alcohol and body of the wine.

Riserva [ree-zEHr-vah] Italian DOC wines aged for a specified number of years – often an unwelcome term on labels of wines like Bardolino, which are usually far better drunk young.

Rosato Italian rosé.

Ruby Douro, Portugal. Cheapest, basic port; young, blended, sweetly fruity.

Schaumwein [showm-vine] German low-priced sparkling wine.

Schilfwein [shilf-vine] Austrian luscious vin de paille pioneered by Willi Opitz.

Schloss [shloss] German, literally "castle," vineyard or estate.

Sec/secco/seco [se-koh] French/Italian/Spanish term for dry.

Second label Wine from a producer's (generally a Bordeaux Château) lesser vineyards, younger vines, and/or lesser cuvées of wine. Especially worth buying in good vintages. See *Les Forts de Latour*.

Sekt [zekt] German term for very basic sparkling wine – best won in carnival games. Watch out for anything that does not state that it is made from Riesling – other grape varieties almost invariably make highly unpleasant wines. Only the prefix "Deutscher" guarantees German origin.

Sélection de Grains Nobles (SGN) [say-lek-see-yon day gran nohbl] Alsace, France. Equivalent to German Beerenauslese; rich, sweet, botrytized wine from specially selected grapes.

Servir frais French for "serve chilled."

Silex [see-lex] French term describing flinty soil, used by Didier Dagueneau for his oak-fermented Pouilly-Fumé.

Sin Crianza [sin cree-an-tha] Spanish term meaning "not aged in wood."

Skin contact The longer the skins of black grapes are left in with the juice after the grapes have been crushed, the greater the tannin and the deeper the color. Some non-aromatic white varieties (Chardonnay and Semillon in particular) can also benefit from extended skin contact (usually between six and 24 hours) to increase flavor.

Spätlese [shpayt-lay-zeh] German. The second step in the QmP scale, late harvested grapes making the wine a notch drier than Auslese.

Spritz/ig [shprit-zig] Slight sparkle or sparkling wine. Also pétillance.

Spumante [spoo-man-tay] Italian sparkling wine.

Staatsweingut [staht-svine-goot] A German state-owned wine estate, such as Staatsweinguter Eltville (Rheingau), a major cellar in Eltville.

Stalky or stemmy Flavor of the grape stem rather than of the juice.

Steely Refers to young wine with evident acidity. A compliment when paid to Chablis and dry Sauvignons.

Structure The structural components of a wine include tannin, acidity, and alcohol. They provide the skeleton or backbone that supports the "flesh" of the fruit. A young wine with good structure should age well.

Sulfites U.S. labeling requirement alerting those suffering from an (extremely rare) allergy to the presence of sulfur dioxide. Curiously, no such requirement is made of cans of baked beans and dried apricots, which contain twice as much of the chemical.

Sulfur dioxide/SO2 Antiseptic routinely used by food packagers and winemakers to protect their produce from bacteria and oxidation.

Super Second Bordeaux, France. Médoc second growths: Pichon-Lalande, Pichon-Longueville, Léoville-Las-Cases, Ducru-Beaucaillou, Cos d'Estournel; whose wines are thought to rival – and cost nearly as much as – the first growths. Other over-performers include Rauzan-Ségla and Léoville-Barton, Lynch-Bages, Palmer, La Lagune, Montrose.

Super Tuscan Italian New-Wave Vino da Tavola (usually red) wines, pioneered by producers like Antinori, which stand outside traditional DOC rules. Generally Bordeaux-style blends or Sangiovese or a mixture of both.

Supérieur/Superiore [soo-pay-ree-ur/soo-pay-ree-ohr-ray] French/Italian term, often relatively meaningless in terms of discernible quality. Denotes wine (well or badly) made from riper grapes.

Sur lie [soor-lee] French term for the aging "on its lees" – or dead yeasts – most commonly associated with Muscadet, but now being used to make other fresher, richer, and sometimes slightly sparkling wines in southern France.

Süssreserve [soos-sreh-zurv] German for unfermented grape juice used to bolster sweetness and fruit in German and English wines.

Tafelwein [tah-fel-vine] German table wine. Only the prefix "Deutscher" guarantees German origin.

Tannic See *Tannin*.

Tannin Astringent component of red wine which comes from the skins, seeds, and stalks and helps the wine to age.

Tarry Red wines from hot countries often have an aroma and flavor reminiscent of tar. The Syrah and Nebbiolo exhibit this characteristic.

Tartaric Type of acid found in grapes. Also the form in which acid is added to wine in hot countries whose legislation allows this.

Tartrates [tar-trayts] Harmless white crystals often deposited by white wines in the bottle. In Germany, these are called "diamonds."

Tastevin [tat-van] The silver Burgundy tasting cup used as an insignia by vinous brotherhoods (confréries), as a badge of office by sommeliers, and as an ashtray by the author. The Chevaliers de Tastevin organize annual tastings, awarding a mock-medieval Tastevinage label to the best wines. Chevaliers de Tastevin attend banquets, often wearing similarly mock-medieval clothes.

Tawny Douro, Portugal. In theory, pale, browny-red port that acquires its mature appearance and nutty flavor from long aging in oak casks. Port houses, however, legally produce "tawny" by mixing basic ruby with white port and skipping the tiresome business of barrel-aging altogether. The real stuff comes with an indication of age, such as 10- or 20-year-old, but these figures are approximate. A 10-year-old port only has to "taste as though it is that old." Port shippers, incidentally, get terribly aerated if anyone ever describes an Australian, genuinely wood-aged, tawny as "port-style" or even "port-like." I love real tawny port (and good port-style tawnies, from elsewhere!) – and heartily recommend them to anyone who gets a hangover from vintage port. Colheita ports are tawnies of a specific vintage (also derided by most traditionalist port shippers).

Tenuta [teh-noo-tah] Italian term for estate or vineyard.

Tête de Cuvée [teht dur coo-vay] An old French expression still used by traditionalists to describe their finest wine.

Tokay [in France: to-kay; in Australia: toh-ki] Various regions have used Tokay as a local name for other grape varieties. In Australia it is the name of a fortified wine from Rutherglen made from the Muscadelle; in Alsace, it is Pinot Gris; while the Italian Tocai is quite unrelated. Hungary's Tokay – now helpfully renamed Tokaji – is largely made from the Furmint.

Traditional Generally meaningless term, except in sparkling wines where the "méthode traditionelle" is the new way to say "méthode champenoise" and in Portugal where "Traditional Late Bottled Vintage" refers to port that unlike non-traditional LBV, hasn't been filtered.

Transfer method A way of making sparkling wine involving a second fermentation in the bottle, but unlike the méthode champenoise in that the wine is separated from the lees by pumping it out of the bottle into a pressurized tank for clarification before returning it to another bottle.

Trocken [trok-ken] German dry wine, often aggressively so. Avoid Trocken Kabinett from such northern areas as the Mosel, Rheingau and Rheinhessen. QbA (chaptalized) and Spätlese Trocken wines (made, by definition, from riper grapes) are better. See also *Halbtrocken*.

Trockenbeerenauslese [trok-ken-beh-ren-ows-lay-zeh] Used in Austria and Germany. Fifth rung of the QmP ladder, wine from selected dried grapes that are usually botrytis-affected and full of natural sugar. Only made in the best years, rare and expensive, though less so in Austria than in Germany.

Ullage Space between surface of wine and top of cask or, in a bottle, the cork. The wider the gap, the greater the danger of oxidation. Older wines almost always have some degree of ullage; the less the better.

Unfiltered Filtering a wine can remove flavor – as can fining it with egg white or bentonite. Most winemakers traditionally argue that both practices are necessary if the finished wine is going to be crystal-clear and free from bacteria that could turn it to vinegar. Many quality-conscious New-Wave winemakers, however, are now cutting back on fining and filtering.

Varietal A wine made from and named after one or more grape variety, e.g., California Chardonnay. The French authorities are trying to outlaw such references from the labels of most of their appellation contrôlée wines. "Shiraz" has so far escaped this edict because it is considered a foreign word.

VDP German association of high-quality producers. Look for the eagle.

VDQS (Vin Délimité de Qualité Supérieur) Official French, neither-fish-nor-fowl, designation for wines better than Vin de Pays but not fine enough for an AC. Enjoying a strange half-life (amid constant rumors of its imminent abolition), this includes such oddities as Sauvignon de St. Bris.

Vecchio [veh-kee-yoh] Italian for "old."

Vegetal Often used of Sauvignon Blanc, like "grassy." Can be complimentary – though not in California or Australia, where it is held to mean "unripe."

Velho/velhas [vay-yoh/vay-yas] Portuguese for "old," as of red wine.

Vendange [Von-donzh] French term for harvest or vintage.

Vendange tardive [von-donzh tahr-deev] French Particularly in Alsace, wine from late harvested grapes, usually lusciously sweet.

Vendemmia/Vendimia [ven-deh-mee-yah/ven-dee-mee-yah] Italian/Spanish term for harvest or vintage.

VIDE [vee-day] Italian syndicate supposedly denoting finer estate wines.

Vieilles Vignes [vee-yay veeñ] French wine (supposedly) made from a producer's oldest vines. (In reality, while real vine maturity begins at 25, Vieilles Vignes can mean anything between 15 and 90 years of age.)

Vignoble [veen-yohbl] French for vineyard or vineyard area.

Villages The French suffix "villages" after Côtes du Rhône or Mâcon, for example, generally – like Classico in Italy – indicates a slightly superior wine from a smaller delimited area encompassing certain village vineyards.

Vin de garde [van dur gahrd] French for "wine to keep."

Vin de Paille [van dur piy] Traditional, now quite rare regional specialty of Jura, France; sweet golden wine from grapes dried on straw mats.

Vin de Pays [van dur pay-yee] French lowest/broadest geographical designation. In theory, these are simple country wines with certain regional characteristics. In fact, the producers of some of France's most exciting wines – such as Dom. de Trévallon and Mas de Daumas Gassac – prefer this designation and the freedom it offers from the restrictions imposed on appellation contrôlée wines.

Vin de table [van dur tahbl] French table wine from no particular area.

Vin doux naturel [doo nah-too-rrel] French fortified – so not really "naturel" at all – dessert wines, particularly the sweet, liquorous Muscats of the south, such as Muscat de Beaumes de Venise, Mireval, and Rivesaltes.

Vin Gris [van gree] French, chiefly from Alsace and the Jura, pale rosé from red grapes pressed after crushing or following a few hours of skin contact.

Vin Jaune [van john] Golden-colored Arbois specialty of Jura, France; slightly oxidized – like Fino sherry.

Vin ordinaire A simple local French wine, usually served in carafes.

Vin Santo [vin sahn-toh] Italian, powerful, highly traditional white dessert wine made from bunches of grapes hung to dry in airy barns for up to six years, especially in Tuscany and Trentino. Often very ordinary, but at its best competes head-on with top-quality medium sherry. Best drunk with sweet almond ("Cantuccine") cookies.

Vin vert [van vehrr] Light, refreshing, acidic white wine from Languedoc-Roussillon, France.

Viña de Mesa [vee-nah day may-sah] Spanish for "table wine."

Vinifera [vih-nih-feh-ra] Properly *Vitis vinifera*: Species of all European vines.

Vino da Tavola [vee-noh dah tah-voh-lah] Italian table wine, but the DOC quality designation net is so riddled with holes that producers of many superb – and pricey – wines have contented themselves with this modest appellation. Now being replaced by IGT.

Vino de la Tierra [bee-noh day la tyay rah] Spanish wine designation that can offer interesting, affordable, regional wines.

Vino novello [vee-noh noh-vay-loh] Italian new wine; equivalent to French nouveau.

Vintage Year of production.

Vintage Champagne Champagne from a single "declared" year.

Vintage Character Smartly packaged upmarket ruby port from Portugal made by blending various years' wines.

Vintage Port Produced only in "declared" years, aged in wood then in the bottle for many years. In "off" years, Portuguese port houses release wines from their top estates as single quinta ports. This style of port must be decanted, as

it throws a sediment.

Viticulteur (-Propriétaire) French for vine grower/vineyard owner.

Volatile acidity (VA) Vinegary character evident in wines that have been spoiled by bacteria.

VQA Acronym for Vintners Quality Alliance, a group of Canadian producers with a self-styled quality designation.

Weingut [vine-goot] German term for wine estate.

Weinkellerei [vine-keh-lur-ri] German term for cellar or winery.

White port Semidry aperitif from Douro, Portugal, drunk by its makers with tonic water and ice, which shows what they think of it.

Winzerverein/Winzergenossen schaft [vint-zur-veh-rine/vint-zur-geh-nosh-en-shaft] German cooperative.

WO (Wine of Origin) Official European-style certification system that is taken seriously in South Africa.

Zentralkellerei [tzen-trahl-keh-lur-ri] Massive central cellars for groups of German cooperatives in six of the anbaugebiet – the Mosel-Saar-Ruwer. Zentralkellerei is Europe's largest cooperative.

Index

Picture credits

All pictures courtesy of DK picture library except:

Patrick Eagar Photography: pp. 61, 113, 122, 127, 128, 129, 132–3(all), 135, 158, 222, 224, 225, 229, 232, 234(b), 235, 247(b), 256, 287, 347, 348, 351, 352–3, 354 **Jan Traylen** 72, 130, 162, 182, 184(all), 190, 192, 196, 200, 203(all), 206-7 (all), 208–9, 211, 212(t), 258, 266(t), 267 **Mike Newton** 252, 257 **Karen Spink** 269

Mary Evans: pp. 26(t), 28(b), 32, 35, 38, 40–1, 42(all), 45, 47, 53(b), 160(t)

Christies: pp. 22, 26(b), 39

Topham Picturepoint: pp. 36, 52 ,80 , 105(all), 110, 167(t), 168–9, 170, 172–3, 174, 176, 178, 182(t), 188, 191(all), 195, 198, 204–5, 226, 227(all), 230–1, 242, 247(t), 280, 281, 290, 375

Cephas: pp. **Mick Rock** 50, 66, 68, 74–5(all), 82–3(all), 84–5(all), 86, 88, 93(all), 97, 98(t), 99, 100(t)–1, 102, 104, 120(b), 124, 131(b), 134, 138, 140, 142(b), 151, 155(all),

167(b), 250, 260, 264, 268(all), 270(all), 273(all), 274–5(all), 278, 282, 283, 292, 296–7, 300, 302, 304, 305(t), 310, 318, 324(b), 326, 355, 271 **TOP** 24, 71, 107(b), 118, 119, 121, 123(l), 144–5, 153(t), 157 **Alain Proust** 70, 76, 95, 107(t), 148, 159(t), 367, 377 **Diana Mewes** 77 **Wine Magazine** 78, 96, 120(t), 136, 149, 150(t), 152, 156(b), 295(b) **Steve Elphick** 81, 314, 316, 331 **Kevin Judd** 87, 216, 368 **Stockfood** 89, 108, 142(t), 153(b), 156(t), 246 **Andy Christodolo** 90, 92, 89(b), 336, 338, 340–1, 343, 344 , 362 **Nigel Blythe** 116, 123(r), 371, 370 **John Heinrich** 126 **Ted Stefanski** 131(t), 308, 317, 320, 376 **Diana Mews** 261, 350 **P.A. Broadbent** 277 **David Copeman** 284 **Andrew Jefford** 288 **David Burnett** 293 **Herbert Lehmann** 305(b) **R & K Muschenetz** 322, 324(t) **John Carter** 328 **Kevin Argue** 330 (all) **Angus Taylor** 335, 334 **Juan Espi** 364 **Chris Davies** 372–3

Comstock: pp. 143

Greg Evans: pp. 100(b), 122(t), 146, 150(b), 166, 179, 189, 212(b), 218, 220, 223, 234(t), 238(t), 266(b), 285, 312, 349

Pictorial Press: pp. 111 (all), 112–3 (all)